BEYOND COUNTER-INSURGENCY

'Sanjib Baruah has compiled an exceptionally diverse anthology. Including voices from social science, history, literature, cultural studies, and government, it reveals the region's vibrant public discourse and provides an antidote to security-centric proclamations. *Beyond Counter-insurgency* is a model of creatively engaged and academically astute public intellectual work.'

—David Ludden
Professor of History, New York University

'Baruah and his contributors paint a rich, vital picture of the spatial disorder that has unfolded within Northeast India's multiple "inner lines". This complex and unvarnished story is told without romanticism or cynicism. Between the apparent impossibility of peace through "reconciliation" and victory through repression or terror, the book envisions the possibility of an open, more inclusive future.'

—Siddharth Varadarajan
Strategic Affairs Editor, *The Hindu*

'This rich volume opens up a crucial space for re-imagining this highly complex yet remarkably poorly understood region. Shunning facile remedies, its proposals for a better future include redistributing key resources, restoring public trust in the rule of law, and harnessing the region's exceptional ecological diversity.'

—Willem van Schendel
Professor of Modern Asian History, University of Amsterdam

BEYOND COUNTER-INSURGENCY
Breaking the Impasse in Northeast India

edited by

SANJIB BARUAH

OXFORD
UNIVERSITY PRESS

OXFORD
UNIVERSITY PRESS

Oxford University Press is a department of the University of Oxford.
It furthers the University's objective of excellence in research, scholarship,
and education by publishing worldwide. Oxford is a registered trademark of
Oxford University Press in the UK and in certain other countries

Published in India by
Oxford University Press
22 Workspace, 2nd Floor, 1/22 Asaf Ali Road, New Delhi 110 002

First Edition published in 2009
Oxford India Paperbacks 2011

22nd impression 2025

ISBN-13: 978-0-19-807897-5
ISBN-10: 0-19-807897-8

Typeset in Adobe Caslon Pro 10.5/12.5
by Sai Graphic Design, New Delhi 110 055
Printed in India by Manipal Technologies Limited, Manipal

Contents

acy? A Study of Ethnic Peace
Accords in Northeast India
Samir Kumar Das 232

12. Hills–Valley Divide as a Site of Conflict:
Emerging Dialogic Space in Manipur
H. Kham Khan Suan 263

V. Breaking the Impasse

13. Just Development: A Strategy for Ethnic
Reconciliation in Tripura
Subir Bhaumik 293

14. Grounds for Democratic Hope in Arunachal Pradesh:
Emerging Civic Geographics and the Reinvention of
Gender and Tribal Identities
Betsy Taylor 308

15. Rethinking Delhi's Northeast India Policy:
Why neither Counter-insurgency nor Winning
Hearts and Minds is the Way Forward
Bethany Lacina 329

References 343

Notes on Contributors 370

Index 372

Photographs and Tables

CHAPTER 1

Introduction

SANJIB BARUAH

Indian policy towards its Northeast has seen significant reorientation in recent years. In 2001, a cabinet-level Department for Development of the North Eastern Region (DONER) was launched to put the economic development of the region on a fast track. Northeast India is the only region in the country whose development is the specific mandate of a department of the national government. Enormous public resources are being spent in trying to bridge the region's 'development gap'. There is an industrial policy in place that gives attractive tax incentives for investing in the region. The Northeast Business Summit held periodically since 2002, co-sponsored by DONER and the Indian Chamber of Commerce, showcases potential investment opportunities in the region. The Asian Car Rally and a number of similar events have drawn attention to Northeast India's future as a 'gateway to Asia', in line with the Look East policy—India's efforts to solidify diplomatic and economic ties with Southeast Asia. In 2007, India's External Affairs Minister Pranab Mukherjee visited the cities of Shillong and Guwahati in Northeast India to explain to local audiences the promises of the Look East Policy for the region. Both events were sponsored by the public diplomacy division of the Ministry of External Affairs. Rarely has a country invested so much in 'public diplomacy' at home.

The Look East Policy, in the words of a former External Affairs ministry official, 'envisages the Northeast region not as the periphery of India, but as the centre of a thriving and integrated economic space linking two dynamic regions with a network of highways, railways, pipelines, transmission lines crisscrossing the region' (Sikri 2004). The then Secretary-East of the Ministry of External Affairs, Rajiv Sikri, said that his hope was that one day it would be possible to drive from Kolkata via Dhaka, or from Guwahati to Yangon and Bangkok in three or four days, and trains and buses would carry 'millions of tourists, pilgrims, workers and businessmen in both directions' (ibid.).

Despite such ambitions, when it comes to the festering low-intensity armed conflicts of the region, there are few overt signs of a policy reorientation, or of any awareness that the persistence of armed conflicts and the existing restrictions on travel and on land and labour markets are formidable hurdles to the region becoming a 'gateway'. Yet the exceptional efforts on the part of India's foreign policy establishment to explain the benefits of the Look East Policy probably reflect the expectation that convincing the locals of those benefits would translate into reduced sympathy for the region's rebel groups. The restrictions on land and labour markets are the legacy of the boundaries drawn by British colonial rulers between spaces of law and spaces of custom. Today they serve multiple goals including national security and protective discrimination for scheduled tribes (STs).[1] It is hard to imagine that these restrictions would end without the political resolution of key conflicts. Yet their incompatibility with the vision of a dynamic transnational economic space is rather obvious. The hope in policy circles seems to be that counter-insurgency operations, and negotiations with leaders of insurgent groups, when feasible, would keep armed conflicts within manageable limits, until some day, development, turbo-charged by cross-border economic ties, magically trumps the conflict story. The issue of gradually removing these restrictions, it is assumed, can be safely postponed until that day.

Phrases like 'ethnic insurgencies', 'cross-border terrorism', and 'proxy wars' are the staple of Indian official talk about the Northeast, though there is no evidence that policies spelt out by this vocabulary have successfully grappled with the sources of the region's multilayered conflicts. This vocabulary also underscores tensions between the preferences of national security managers for the close monitoring of borders, and the openness of borders envisaged by a transnational

---

[1] The category 'tribe' despite all its conceptual problems is part of Indian political and policy discourse primarily because of a system of protective discrimination that exists in favour of groups listed as tribes. The term 'scheduled tribe' refers to groups that are included in the official schedule of 'tribes' as being entitled to protective discrimination. Later in this chapter I shall discuss the difficulties that the Indian political system faces for leaving open the question of which groups are entitled to protective discrimination, constitutionally and politically.

economic space. The national security-centric discourse about the Northeast—shaped mostly by former bureaucrats and retired army, police, and intelligence officials—is 'heavily pro-state and insensitive to the vulnerabilities of the common man and dismissive of the frequent transgression of rights of its own citizens by the state' (Dasgupta 2004: 4469). In the scholarship on armed civil conflicts in the world—and on managing, resolving, or transforming them—there has been a virtual intellectual revolution during the past decade or so. But policy thinking in India has been mostly insulated from these debates and insights. Even the Look East Policy has, in effect, been hijacked by the military and security establishment. Unlike China that has been successful in using closer economies ties with Southeast Asia for developing its border regions, says Sushil Khanna of the Indian Institute of Management, Calcutta, comparable Indian efforts at economic integration have been lukewarm. A policy of 'opening up' has been used to 'strengthen ties with the military regimes in Bangladesh and Myanmar and launch counter-insurgency movements against the groups from North Eastern India'. Thus 'the fruits of rapid growth and closer integration with the global economy' that characterize the Indian economy in general have 'totally by-passed the border region of North East India' (Khanna 2008: 9, 14–15).

Viewed through comparative lenses, Northeast India's conflicts are of 'extraordinary duration' and the sheer number of rebel groups makes Northeast India 'an outlier by world standards' (Lacina in Chapter 15 of this volume).[2] Rebel groups remain active for long periods even though they know that goals like secession have little chance of success. The protracted nature of rebellions, mostly by ragtag bands of militants, makes the region a counterpoint to India's present image as a mature democracy, a dynamic economy, and an emerging global power. But thanks partly to the government's travel restrictions—for instance, research visas to foreign scholars to study Northeast India are almost never granted—the story remains marginal to the popular global image of contemporary India. While New Delhi expects the magic bullet of development to eventually come to its rescue, for the moment, in a region that is peripheral to the national imaginary, the costs of letting low-intensity conflicts proliferate and fester are seen as affordable. The naïve and economically deterministic faith in a development fix is not

---

[2] References to chapters in this book are not cited with page numbers. Only references to other works are cited with full bibliographic information.

likely to find much support among contemporary scholars of conflict and peace studies. To be sure, the notion of a development fix does respond to structural factors cited in many popular explanations of armed civil conflicts. Poverty, underdevelopment, and lack of economic opportunities are, after all, everyone's favourite bogey as causes of armed civil conflicts. However, state weaknesses and state failure—the other structural factor typically cited in the academic literature as the cause of such conflicts—evoke little interest in Indian policy circles. But India is not immune to this phenomenon. State weakness, albeit localized, is endemic in areas like Northeast India (Baruah 2005a; Saha and Mallavarapu 2006: 4259). Yet, except for a rhetorical nod, substantive measures for building and nurturing institutions of good governance scarcely feature in the policy agenda of Indian counter-insurgency experts or believers in a development fix.

A World Bank report finds existing institutional arrangements to be the principal obstacle to the utilization of Northeast India's vast water resources for sustainable development. The relevant institutional structure, it points out, is highly centralized: one that suffers from 'the paternalism of central-level bureaucrats, coercive top-down planning, and little support or feedback from locals'. Local stakeholders mistrust these centralized structures: they do not believe that developmental initiatives really have their best interests in mind. So dysfunctional are the institutional arrangements that even an embankment project designed to help people of an area may be opposed by its intended beneficiaries (World Bank 2006: 13–14). This observation can be extended to the institutions of governance in Northeast India more generally: a centralized approach and a gulf between power holders and stakeholders apply even more to the institutions engaged in counter-insurgency. For contributors to this volume, the quality and health of India's democratic institutions, on which Indian policy talk is relatively silent, is perhaps the most important area of policy intervention.

Perhaps one exception to the relative insulation of Indian policy from the academic literature on armed civil conflicts is the theory mooted by some scholars that zeroes in on rebel finances—which they describe as 'greed'—and discounts 'grievances' as the cause of armed civil conflicts.[3] The theme finds an echo in Indian policy talk. Rebellions, in the greed view of armed civil conflicts, are more like organized crime. Rebels are its prime movers, civilians the victims,

---

[3] For a classic formulation of this argument see Collier (2000).

and the state by definition a friend of the civilian population (Marchal 2001). An implicit assumption in this kind of analysis is that once these rebellions are eliminated—by whatever means necessary—a 'normal' peaceful democratic polity would return. Such assumptions underlie many writings by Indian security experts and members of the counter-insurgency establishment. They seem to believe that extortions, violence, and doing the bidding of foreign intelligence agencies are all that is there to the rebellions of Northeast India.

In the public debates in the region, there is deep scepticism about such simple-minded characterizations and explanations, though these ideas, popular among key officials especially in central government organizations, have a profound influence on Indian policy. Thus Hiren Gohain, a widely respected Assamese intellectual, and known for his consistent opposition to the United Liberation Front of Assam (ULFA), asks rhetorically: why is it that Assamese who condemn ULFA's atrocities still 'demur at the plan to physically exterminate them and insist on a sincere attempt at peace'? The Assamese by and large do not believe that the 'extremists' are all puppets of Pakistani intelligence. Whatever may be their shortcomings, the Assamese see them as being related to 'some legitimate and sound ideas of self-determination'. ULFA as a political movement, says Gohain, cannot be understood except in the context of the history of modern Assam. Yet there are 'very powerful and influential quarters determined to choke off all rational discussion of the issue' (Gohain 2007: 1012). Manipuri newspaper editor Pradip Phanjoubam writes in Chapter 7 of this volume that whether or not the charges of 'criminalization and lumpenization' of rebel groups are true they cannot explain Northeast India's rebellions. Unemployment may indeed be a factor, but 'youth frustration and unemployment' is more likely to find an outlet in 'drugs and other socially deviant behaviours' than in rebellions.

While the notion of a development fix, or the premises of the greed theory may be flawed, it does not mean that particular grievances articulated by insurgent organizations are better guides to understanding Northeast India's conflicts. Despite recurring themes in rebel narratives such as political autonomy, economic justice, and cultural rights, any consideration of rebel groups in Northeast India must come to terms with the multiplicity of voices, and the tensions that often exist between competing rebel agendas. A rebel group with a particular ethnic constituency may be at war with another rebel group, and indeed its primary opposition may not be with the Indian state at all. It might even cooperate with government security agencies in fighting a rival group and when such ties with official security agencies develop, the public commitment of such groups to armed struggle or sovereignty can be a source of embarrassment for those in charge of defending the legal political order.

This volume comes out of a project of the Centre for Policy Research, New Delhi. Most of the essays included here were discussed and debated at two workshops held in Guwahati and New Delhi in 2005 and 2006. Dissatisfaction with conditions on the ground, and with the policy prism through which the conflicts are generally viewed, bring the authors of these essays together. The emphasis of the project, 'Rethinking Northeast India's Conflicts', and of this volume, rests on the term 'rethinking': on new ways of approaching these conflicts, and on ways to resolve them. The volume is not intended to be inclusive: notable writers on the region—including well-known security and counter-insurgency experts—are not represented. However, apart from a critical distance from conventional wisdom, the contributors share neither a common theoretical perspective, nor a single political position. They work for a variety of institutions in India and abroad and they include academics—from the social sciences as well as the humanities—journalists, and an administrator. A majority of them have roots in Northeast India. Incorporating local voices has been one of the goals of the project. However, since there are multiple claims made to territory in this region, and multiple memories, counter-memories, and visions of the future at play, it was not our goal to find representative or 'authentic' local voices: there is no singular local voice on any issue. Instead we have tried to incorporate the local by including contributors whose work embodies the critical rethinking of the conflicts that is going on in the region's rich public intellectual life. The authors all come from diverse intellectual traditions, and their political convictions vary.

STRANGE MULTIPLICITY[4] AND THE LANDSCAPE OF CONFLICTS

What explains this multiplicity of mostly ethnically based low-intensity conflicts? Certain factors specific to postcolonial Northeast India[5] provide the backdrop: (*a*) the region's particular ecology and the history of state formation; (*b*) certain legacies of colonial knowledge;

---

[4] I have borrowed the phrase 'strange multiplicity' from Tully (1995).

[5] Parts of this section reproduce material earlier published in Baruah (2007).

(c) the frontier quality of the region and the massive demographic transformation that it has been going through in modern times; and (d) the effects of certain peculiarities of postcolonial India's constitutional political order. James C. Scott's distinction between state spaces and non-state spaces[6] gives us a comparative handle on the region's well-known linguistic and ethnic diversity. One of the world's 'largest, if not *the* largest remaining non-state space', writes Scott, is:

The vast expanse of uplands ranging from northeastern India and eastern Bangladesh through northern Burma, northern Thailand, three provinces of southwestern China, most of Laos, and much of upland Vietnam all the way to the Central Highlands—more than two million square kilometers. Lying at altitudes from 500 meters above sea level to more than 4,000 meters, it could be thought of as a Southeast Asian Appalachia, were it not for the fact that it sprawls across seven nation states (Scott 2006: 8).

Historically, this vast region's ethnic landscape has had a 'bewildering and intercalated "gradients" of cultural traits' (Scott 2000: 21–2). In the case of the Nagas of Northeast India and Burma, for instance, ethnographers and missionaries engaged in a struggle 'to make sense of the ethnographic chaos they perceived around them: hundreds, if not thousands, of small villages seemed to be somewhat similar to each other but also very different, by no means always sharing the same customs, political system, art or even language' (Jacobs et al. 1990: 23).

Scott suggests that such a confusing ethnoscape[7] has something to do with swidden agriculture—the common mode of livelihood in the hills. Historically, in these parts of the world land was abundant, but manpower was in short supply. The problem confronting the states emerging in the valleys was to have large enough subject populations. Wars were not over territory, but about capturing subjects and slaves. The labour-starved states of the plains could not capture the dispersed and mobile populations in the hills for forced labour or military service; nor were tax collectors able to monitor their numbers or their holdings

[6] The argument is premised on the work of James C. Scott (2000 and 2006). I am grateful to Scott for permitting me to cite his unpublished work.

[7] For an elaboration of the term 'ethnoscape' see Arjun Appadurai (1990). Appadurai coined the term to deal with the flows of people across international borders and the emergence of multiple forms of diasporic identities. For Appadurai the suffix 'scape' serves to draw attention to the fact that these are not objectively given relations but 'deeply perspectival constructs'. Ethnic identities in Northeast India too are perspectival constructs.

and income. Thus non-transparency in relation to the surveillance systems of the lowland states, Scott suggests, was the very rationale of the lifestyles of the hills, and might even explain the ethnic landscape (Scott 2000: 2).

The non-state spaces in the hills and the state spaces in the lowlands were in a symbiotic relationship. But categories like hill tribes and valley peoples—product of the hills–plains binary of colonial knowledge—are 'leaky vessels' in Scott's words. There were back-and-forth movements between the hills and the plains. Wars produced movements in both directions. While the attractions of commerce and what the lowlanders like to call civilization may have generated movements of hill peoples downwards, it was not a one-way flow. Thanks to the extortionist labour demands of the lowland states, and the vulnerability of wet-rice cultivation to crop failures, epidemics, and famines, there were also movements to the hills where more subsistence alternatives were available (Scott 2000: 3–4). It is this symbiotic relationship that is probably reflected in a world where languages, in philosopher Mrinal Miri's words, 'live so close to each other' that 'in many cases, one gets inducted into the life of the community not just through one language but several languages, so people grow up as naturally multilingual beings'. When one switches from one language to another and mixes different languages in a conversation, writes Miri, 'one doesn't move from one vision of the world to another in a kind of schizophrenic frenzy; but one is, as it were, a native citizen of a multi-visionary world' (Miri 2005: 55).

In grand historical terms, the consequences of the transformation of non-state spaces and peoples into state spaces become most vivid in the 'massive reduction of vernaculars of all kinds: of vernacular languages, minority peoples, vernacular cultivation techniques, vernacular land tenure systems, vernacular hunting, gathering and forestry techniques, vernacular religion, etc' (Scott 2006: 7). Contemporary Northeast India's linguistic and cultural diversity reflects the resilience of a historic non-state space despite powerful odds. For pre-colonial states such as the valley states of Assam (the Ahom state), Manipur, and Tripura, the project of transforming non-state spaces into state spaces was, to borrow Scott's phrase, no more than 'a mere glint in the eye'. But the colonial state as well as the postcolonial Indian state is able to mobilize unprecedented amount of resources to realize such a project.

The massive demographic shifts in the region that began in colonial times and continue to this day tell a story of this transformation. Some long-term trends in the agrarian history of South Asia give concrete evidence of this process at work. During the century after 1880, writes historian David Ludden, 'when statistics appear for the first time' permanent cultivation expanded at extremely high rates in Northeast India—'faster than almost anywhere else in South Asia'. Much of this expansion was the result of lowland agriculturalists 'investing in land at higher altitudes'. Indeed 'the physical expansion of cultivated farmland remained the major source of additional increments of agricultural production in South Asia until 1960' (Ludden 2003: 17). The expansion of agriculture has also meant massive immigration into the region from other parts of the subcontinent, and increases in the density of population, and along with it, the minoritization of many indigenous communities, and the fear of other such communities of becoming minorities. In that sense the Northeast Indian story is part of the larger story that Scott outlines: the 'world's last great enclosure movement' taking over the vast Asian transnational non-state space 'albeit clumsily and with setbacks' (Scott 2006: 4–5).

A particular legacy of colonial knowledge gives a territorial frame to the postcolonial politics of ethnicity in the region. British colonial ethnography, to borrow Paul Gilroy's words, had a 'bio-cultural' notion of ethnic traits as 'fixed, solid almost biological' and inheritable (Gilroy 1987: 39)—and 'tribes', these officials and ethnographers believed, all had their supposed natural habitats. The distinction between 'hill tribes' and 'plains tribes', and the assignment of particular hills to particular 'hill tribes', fundamentally at odds with local cultural dynamics and spatial practices, is one of its major legacies. The ethno-territorial frame that colonial officials used to create boundaries between administrative units and to devise various rules of exclusion, continue to shape notions of entitlement and the aspirations of ethnic groups—as articulated by political organizations speaking on their behalf.

Certain characteristics of the postcolonial India's constitutional order fuel the proliferation of ethnic demands. India's protective discrimination practices have made 'scheduled tribe' status a passport to educational and public employment opportunities. India's constitution leaves the question of which groups are entitled to preferences constitutionally and politically open (Weiner 1983: 46). Preferential policies, as Myron Weiner has observed, tend to create a particular political process affecting the ways in which groups are organized, the demands that are made, the issues that constitute policy debates, and the way coalitions are formed. By facilitating group mobilization in support of new preferences or the extension of existing preferences, preferential policies create 'political struggles over how the state should allocate benefits to ethnic groups, generating a backlash on the part of those ethnic groups excluded from benefits, intensifying the militancy of the beneficiaries, and reinforcing the importance of ascription as the principle of choice in allocating social benefits and facilitating mobility' (Weiner 1983: 49).

The Indian constitution empowers the president of India to specify by public notification the 'tribes or tribal communities or parts of or groups within tribes or tribal communities which shall for the purposes of the Constitution be deemed to be Scheduled Tribes'. According to Marc Galanter, a major scholar of Indian law, ethnic communities listed on the schedule were 'defined partly by habitat and geographic isolation, but even more on the basis of social, religious, linguistic and cultural distinctiveness—their "tribal characteristics"'. Just where the line between 'tribals' and 'non-tribals' should be drawn has not always been free from doubt (Galanter 1984: 150.) The phrase 'tribal characteristics', for instance, includes criteria such as 'primitive background' and 'distinctive cultures and traditions'. A remarkable contemporary example of a group trying to meet such standards in support of its demand for ST status is the case of those who call themselves Adivasis (or indigenous people) in Assam. Descendants of indentured labourers, who were brought to the tea plantations of Assam in the nineteenth century, trace their roots to the Munda, Oraon, Santhal, and other people of the Jharkhand region. Adivasi activists argue that since their ethnic kin in their places of origin are recognized as STs, they should have the same status in Assam: they use the bow and arrow as an ethnic symbol—presumably to meet the test of 'primitiveness'. A group that provided the muscle for the nineteenth-century capitalist transformation of Assam surely has as solid a claim as any for full citizenship rights and compensatory justice. That they have to borrow an idiom of remembered tribal-ness to assert their claim underscores the contradictions of the Indian policy discourse that carry with it some problematical traces of colonial knowledge, and its constitutive effects on ethnic militancy in the region.

India's demos-enabling federalism (Stepan 2001: 338–9) puts few constraints on the central government's power to make and break states. To create a new state by changing the political boundaries of an existing state, it has to barely consult the elected legislature of the state concerned. While the more powerful states—those with better representation in the Indian parliament or the central government—may be able to block such changes, less powerful states have less capacity to resist. Today the phenomenon of elected state governments under the control of ST politicians, and the presence of a visible and well-to-do ST elite, has captured the imagination of political activists in Northeast India. There is a perception that the STs in the states with the most comprehensive protective discrimination regimes and rules of exclusion have done well economically, and have been relatively successful in insulating themselves from being swamped by immigrants. In most cases of ethnic mobilization, leaders draw attention to legitimate grievances and matters of injustice. But the political forms and the particular demands have a lot to do with the particular constitutional–legal context. Thus new groups demand ST status and those who have it seek territorial autonomy available under the constitution's Sixth Schedule, originally available only to 'hill tribes'—governed by custom, and not by law in colonial practice—and those with Sixth Schedule status demand full-fledged states. Postcolonial political developments reinforce the idea that such demands might be successful if backed by sufficient evidence of political support, including capacity for violence. This is a factor in the persistence of ethnic militancy in Northeast India. On the other hand, the same constitutional and political openness has also produced anxiety on the part of certain groups that parts of their territory can be bargained away in closed-door negotiations between the central government and leaders of some rebel groups.

A number of chapters in this volume, notably 8 and 12, draw attention to conflicts between competing rebel agendas. While the tactical goals of India's counter-insurgency establishment may sometimes coincide with the interests of one or another rebel group, such cooperation does not depend on a commitment of rebel groups to giving up their violent ways. If the absence of collective alternatives defines legitimate government (Przeworski 1991: 54–5), Northeast India's resilient rebel organizations, and the intermittent complicity of civil society with them, coupled with the reliance on a permanent regime of exception by the Indian state for asserting sovereignty, point to a chronic, albeit localized, crisis of legitimacy. Even though the people of Northeast India elect their state governments and representatives to the national parliament in regularly held democratic elections, it is difficult to interpret that as a sign of the relative strength of India's democratic institutions. Democratic politics and the world of armed rebellions intersect in complex ways in Northeast India. It is often hard to draw a sharp dividing line between mainstream and rebel political actors, or as Bethany Lacina puts it, rebel groups are 'embedded in the workings of Northeastern civilian politics' (Chapter 15, this volume).

Drawing on the comparative literature on armed civil conflicts, it may be useful to think in terms of three levels of explanation. There are structural determinants such as poverty and underdevelopment and some of the factors that are specific to postcolonial Northeast India outlined above. But structural conditions do not necessarily lead to armed civil conflicts. A second level of analysis is the nature and politics of weak states, especially strategies adopted by elites to maintain power. The third level is that of agency. The destruction of 'non-violent discourses', and its replacement with socially constructed 'war discourses', is the most important precipitating factor in armed civil conflicts (Jackson 2004: 63–4) and there are identifiable actors responsible for such discursive shifts. The question of agency draws attention to multiple actors with diverse motives. One has to consider the pleasures of agency: 'the positive effect associated with self-determination, autonomy, self-esteem, efficacy, and pride from the successful assertion of intention' (Wood 2003: 235). There is also what has been called the 'subaltern and "popular" character' of ethnic violence, which academic writings typically 'hesitate to acknowledge, much less explain' (Mamdani 2001: 8). On the other hand, it is not merely societal actors that may be involved in the construction of a discourse of violence; the national security anxiety of state managers can, for instance, shape a discourse that emphasizes military solutions to armed civil conflicts. When such a discourse trumps over one that emphasizes political solutions, it can itself become a factor in the resilience of armed civil conflicts. The essays in this volume do not systematically look at all three levels, but they touch on all of them. The essays are organized under five rubrics that highlight an aspect of each essay. However, this structure is somewhat artificial. The same essay could have been as easily placed under another rubric.

STALEMATED CONFLICTS: WHAT COST?

Vaclav Havel once wrote—expressing the kind of hope that makes activism possible during times of state repression and widespread conformism and despondency—that he was not afraid that life in his country would ever 'come to a halt', or that history could be 'suspended forever'. He worried only about the 'surcharge' that would be imposed 'when the moment next arrives for life and history to demand their due' (Havel 1989: 34–5). The costs of the low-intensity conflicts in Northeast India may seem tolerable to India's national security managers, but to assess the less tangible costs of the kind that Havel alludes to, it is crucial to venture beyond their intellectual horizons.

In July 2004, a remarkable act of protest occurred in Manipur's capital city of Imphal. Amidst strong emotions against Indian security forces following the abduction, suspected rape, and killing of a woman, a dozen Manipuri women stood naked in front of the headquarters of the Assam Rifles with banners that read 'Indian Army Rape Us', and 'Indian Army Take our Flesh'. In Chapter 2, political theorist Ananya Vajpeyi reflects on the meaning of that protest. The nakedness of the women, she argues, brought out emotions that may lie 'concealed in every heart'. The state 'neither wins nor loses' in Northeast India but the people are defeated daily. Reconciliation does not seem likely, and yet fighting back is not an option. Only one political emotion makes sense in this condition, says Vajpeyi: resentment. Resentment, according to her, 'counteracts the process of the social acceptance of historical wrongs and ... militates against the arrow of time'. Through their nakedness and the bland and declarative banners—'a semiotic masterstroke', says Vajpeyi—the Manipuri women announced to the world: 'the raping of us Manipuri women is what the Indian Army does. We stand here to say this out loud and clear: this is the way it is. We embody resentment.'

If for Vajpeyi raw emotions that do not easily express themselves through familiar modes of political protest tell a story of the long-term costs of Northeast India's stalemated conflicts, Bodhisattva Kar's provocative question, 'when was the postcolonial?' provides a historical perspective on the region's contemporary predicament. In Chapter 3, he draws attention to one of the legal institutions that restricts land and labour markets in the Northeast: the colonial-era Inner Line that regulates the access of citizens and foreigners alike to the states of Arunachal Pradesh, Nagaland, and Mizoram. Kar reminds us that the Inner Line was 'not only a territorial exterior of the theatre of capital—it was also a temporal outside of the historical pace of development and progress'. The communities beyond the Line were seen as 'belonging to a different time regime—where the time of the law did not apply; where slavery, headhunting, and nomadism' could exist. What provides continuity between the colonial and the postcolonial, Kar suggests, is that peace is still 'imaginable only within the grids of capital and development'. But the postcolonial political order faces an interesting dilemma: it seeks development and progress in a zone that was once marked off as being on the temporal outside of such a process. Yet it lacks the political capacity to change the colonial spatial order and consider removing the Inner Line that had fenced off that region as being outside the 'theatre of capital'.

NATION AND ITS DISCONTENTS

In the national security mindset, the nation is typically viewed as an irreversible 'done deal' rather than a process (Wee and Jayasuriya 2002: 7–8). But if state nationalism is seen as an identity trying to be 'a sort of trump card in the game of identity'(Calhoun 1997: 46), narratives of state nationalism necessarily coexist with its counter-narratives—albeit with different levels of resonance in society. Nations are formed in the tension between unity and disunity.

In Chapter 4, Dolly Kikon looks at this tension and asks how the Northeast figures in the postcolonial Indian national imagination. She uses the National Museum in Kolkata as a site and starts at the museum gates. In Indian government museums and official heritage sites, foreigners are typically charged a higher entrance fee than Indian citizens. But in a country where there is no mandatory personal identification system, an unintended consequence of this practice is that museum security guards sometimes have to make judgements about a person's citizenship status based on phenotypic features. Thus 'as a Naga stands at the queue meant for Indians,' Kikon recalls, 'there is a request to switch over to the foreigners' line'. An impromptu citizenship test follows and it involves 'speaking in Hindi, a brief lecture on history, geography and the Naga people'. Following the test, 'the Naga/Indian' manages to enter the National Museum. Inside the museum, clay and terracotta models represent ethnic groups from the Northeast and their habitats. They are displayed in glass cages that, says Kikon, resemble prison cells. She reads the display as evidence that in India's national imagination, 'the colonial construct of primitiveness and savagery', continues to shape the image of communities like the Nagas. The models all look alike: 'Mongoloid and slightly yellowish' and put together carelessly; a Naga couple wears Karbi fabric, and a Khasi couple wears the attire of the Assamese peasant. The stereotyping and the confusion, she suggests, tie in with the reality outside: that certain people do not have 'a secure place within the nation state'.

In Chapter 5, Rakhee Kalita attempts to construct what she calls a kind of 'situated knowledge' of 'terrorism' in Assam. She examines three Assamese language texts to explore how Assamese society has engaged with 'terrorists'—a term that the Indian security establishment has begun using to describe Northeast India's rebels. Through this exercise in literary criticism, she gives us an extraordinary and intimate account of the ups and downs in the relationship between Assamese society and ULFA—something that has mystified most Indian commentators. The texts she looks at negotiate the binary oppositions that the term 'terrorist' relies on: between the good and the bad, between the hegemonic–national and the subversive–local, and between legitimate and illegitimate forms of violence. It is perhaps not insignificant that the author of one of her texts—a distinguished Assamese fiction-writer and public intellectual—is a former police chief of the state. While only posterity would be able to make a definitive judgement on ULFA—'as rebels, political terrorists, revolutionaries or as mere opportunists', Kalita shows that in contemporary Assamese writing there is a great deal of unease about 'how to name, or more importantly, define the way of these rebels seen both as necessary and problematic in the shaping of Assam's destiny in the larger national space'.

Nandana Dutta, in Chapter 6, looks at how popular narratives in the region of neglect or persecution 'are constructed, refurbished, elaborated and disseminated', and how narrative shifts occur. In Assam there is a history of antagonism between ethnic Assamese and ethnic Bengalis. However, in 2005–6 a significant narrative shift occurred when popular support was mobilized in support of an ethnic Bengali contestant for the title 'Voice of India' in a musical reality show on television. Viewers from all over the country voted by telephone or text messages to decide the winner in each round. Predictably, there were allegations about discrimination against this singer. Certain student organizations in Assam, traditionally associated with a primarily ethnic Assamese constituency, and not generally expected to enthusiastically back an ethnic Bengali singer—repeated 'the conspiracy leitmotif that is implicit in the narrative of neglect and alienation', and organized a campaign urging supporters to vote for him. Thanks partly to those efforts, the singer won the contest and the narrative of Assamese–Bengali confrontation was quietly jettisoned. Dutta's argument is a warning against privileging fixed ethnic identities in explaining Northeast India's conflicts and assuming that pan-Indianism and assertive regionalism—even in its militant form—are always in tension. The celebration of the recognition of a singer from the Northeast as the 'Voice of India', she points out, was 'a tacit political alternative' to separatism: it expressed a wish to 'be counted as part of the Indian nation'.

DISCOURSES OF INCLUSION AND EXCLUSION

As I have earlier said, an important level of explanation in the study of armed conflicts is the question of 'how conflict discourses arise, what distinguishes them from other non-violent discourses, the ways in which they "defeat" alternative (non-violent) discourses, and how they can be de-constructed and replaced with democratic and inclusive discourses' (Jackson 2004: 63). Three essays in this volume directly engage this theme.

In Chapter 7, Pradip Phanjoubam emphasizes the role of ideas in conflict transformation. In the particular context of Manipur, he writes: the 'script-writers of ideologies and ideological wars' must come to terms with Manipur's 'peculiar history, even the most traumatic chapters'. Rather than adhering to 'inward-looking' constructions of identity, he pleads with conflict entrepreneurs to pay attention to changes in the world and to look afresh at the commonly held assumptions about the 'presumably ancient "imagining" called Manipur'. Given what we know about polities in the pre-colonial world outside of Europe, the specificities of ancient Manipur as a 'nation' and a polity need to be rethought. He also calls upon the intelligentsia to debate issues like what development should entail—and not let a 'grotesquely skewed' conception of development dominate political practice. The responsibility for bringing about conflict transformation does not lie on societal actors alone. State managers too find the management of conflict to be 'simpler than formulating a transition of conflict into a condition of peace'.

Bhagat Oinam, in Chapter 8, reminds us of the multilayered nature of the conflicts: that the voices of dissent in multi-ethnic Northeast India that shape the region's many rebellions reject not only the Indian national narrative, but often also the narratives of ethnic communities living closely with one another. One reason why the conflicts are intractable is that discourses are typically 'reiterative and declarative'. Often the same information or an idea is repeated 'without any reasonable justifying criterion' and such discourses become the foundation for rigid knowledge claims. He makes the case for a dialogic discourse that minimizes stereotyping and overcomes the boundary between the 'insider' and the 'outsider'.

Discourses of exclusion can also emerge and become triumphant quite suddenly as products of particular political conjunctures. In Chapter 9, Makiko Kimura looks at the discursive construction of the enemy at the village level during the Nellie massacre in Assam in 1983. The context in which it occurred was the Assam movement of 1979–85 that saw extraordinary mobilization against illegal immigration and the enfranchisement of non-citizens that, said the campaigners, were turning the 'indigenous' peoples of Assam into a minority. The chapter draws attention to a factor that provides the backdrop to many of Northeast India's conflicts: immigration from the rest of the subcontinent and the resultant fear of minoritization by many of the region's 'indigenous' ethnic groups. British colonial officials viewed Northeast India as one of the subcontinent's last frontiers with plenty of 'wastelands' to be settled by immigrants. The flow from densely populated East Bengal began in the 1920s. The Partition of 1947 intensified the migration pressure since Hindu refugees now joined the flow. A controversial election took place in 1983 at the height of the Assam movement. It was boycotted by the campaigners since the inclusion of the names of thousands of non-citizens in the electoral rolls was at the core of their campaign. They labelled the election Assam's 'last battle for survival'. In Nellie, the battle lines were drawn when rumours circulated in the village about violence in villages a few miles away. Kimura finds that the Assamese and Tiwa villagers, who attacked neighbouring Bengali Muslim villages, knew that their neighbours were not recent immigrants. Yet in a climate of deep anxiety, amidst rumours of 'foreigners' finding shelter in those villages, Bengali Muslim neighbours became transformed into dreaded 'foreigners'. Kimura shows that local actors were not pliant tools of those higher up in the movement's hierarchy: village elders made crucial decisions to attack neighbours, bringing Assam's 'last battle for survival' dangerously close to a civil war.

The Assam movement ended with an accord signed between the Indian government and the leaders of the movement. According to the accord, based on various 'cut-off dates' of entry into India, some foreigners were to be given Indian citizenship, some were to be disenfranchised temporarily, and more recent illegal immigrants were to be deported. But in a context where citizens have no mandatory identification papers, among Assam's large population of East Bengali origin, determining who is a foreigner and who is not proved nearly impossible. The most enduring legacy of the failure of the Assam movement is the ULFA. Its position on the issue of foreigners is more accommodative, but it views the failure of the Assam accord as one more piece of evidence that India's political leadership is uninterested in addressing issues the Assamese public cares deeply about.

MAKING PEACE, MAKING WAR: INDIA'S PEACE POLICY

In the literature on Northeast India's conflicts, the negotiated end of the Mizo insurgency is often portrayed as a success story, though some observers disagree with that assessment.[8] In response to the Mizo rebellion that began in 1966, Mizoram, once a district of Assam, was made into a Union Territory in 1971 and into a full-fledged state in 1987 following the accord between the Mizo National Front (MNF) and the Government of India. The guerrilla organization, the MNF, became a mainstream political party, initially winning an election and later losing another, but choosing never to go back to the path of armed struggle. In Chapter 10, M. Sajjad Hassan takes up this story.

Mizoram's peace, according to Hassan, cannot be explained by the peace accord signed between the government and the Mizo rebels alone, but by a number of favourable historical factors, some going back to the colonial era. Colonial administrators promoted 'institutional uniformity' in what was then called the Lushai Hills district, as well as the power of the administration at the expense of local chieftains. The modernizing role of Christian missionaries helped as well. The Mizo rebellion created an inclusive Mizo identity. Today state–society contests in Mizoram are muted because organizations such as the Church and the Young Mizo Association work in alliance with the political leadership rather than against them. A key lesson of the Mizo story for the region's unresolved conflicts, says Bethany Lacina in her chapter in the next section, is that 'the incorporation of rebels into the lawful political process is not a bad thing—what is detrimental is when active insurgents can distort political life through illegal means, most notably extortion and corruption'.

In Chapter 11, Samir Kumar Das reviews India's 'peace policy': that is the approach towards armed rebels. When faced with them, the Indian government tries to 'establish the superiority of violence at its command'. Indeed, the government enters into a peace dialogue only when it determines that a rebel organization is 'considerably

[8] See, for instance, Baruah (2005a: 13, 70–1), Chandra (2007: 52–3), and Samir Kumar Das in Chapter 11 of this volume.

weakened—if not decimated', so that it would accept peace on the terms laid down by the government. Consequently, peace accords in Northeast India do little more than proclaim 'the state's victory in reestablishing its command over the legitimate instruments of violence'. There are small signs of some changes in this policy. For instance, in recent years, the Indian government has been prepared to negotiate with leaders of Northeast Indian rebel groups even in foreign cities like Bangkok, Chiang Mai, Geneva, or Amsterdam. On the other hand, India's counter-insurgency's establishment has remained unenthusiastic about peace talks with the ULFA despite strong support for negotiations among the Assamese public. Clearly, the quest for a victor's peace—that Das believes defines the Indian state's approach to negotiations with rebel groups—is still alive and well.

In Chapter 12, H. Kham Khan Suan draws attention to an important layer of the conflicts in Manipur that makes the task of state building in this part of the country especially challenging. The postcolonial state, he says, is an inheritor to a 'state–society rupture' between the hills and the Imphal valley. Consequently, state building in Manipur, he argues—including the central, the state, and the local levels in his definition of the state—gets implicated in the 'majoritarian language' and the 'totalizing project' based in the Imphal valley. This is resisted 'by the hill people as "alien" and antithetical to their cherished traditional institutions and world view'. India's state-building project has to be sensitive to this divide: state institutions have to be imaginatively redesigned to accommodate this difference.

BREAKING THE IMPASSE

A problem with the idea of a development fix, with which I began this Introduction, is that it avoids one crucial question: what kind of development? In Chapter 7, Pradip Phanjoubam says that development in Northeast India appears to mean little more than 'externally delivered economic packages which can be translated through various backdoor means and leakages, at the soonest possible into hard cash'. He reminds readers of Amartya Sen's ideas about development as freedom: that development is about overcoming 'unfreedoms' imposed by poverty, famine, and lack of political rights (Sen 2001). To a significant extent the crude notion of development that has dominated political practice in Northeast India at least till recently, is shaped by the perceived imperatives of conflict management.

Land, argues Subir Bhaumik in Chapter 13, is the key to any durable political settlement in the region. It is both 'the major resource and also the major source of conflict'. In Tripura, the primary cause of conflict is the loss of land by the state's indigenous tribal population to Bengali settlers. The loss of land occurred through multiple means, including as the consequence of dams built to produce hydroelectric power. Thus, in one area, as the result of a dam, the 'once prosperous tribal peasantry' became 'pauperized'. The contrast between their situation and the 'huge benefits that Bengali urban dwellers gained by electricity and Bengali fishermen gained by being able to fish in the large reservoir was not lost on a generation of angry tribal youths who took up arms'. He proposes the decommissioning of a dam that, even by conventional economic measures, is of questionable value. In 2007, the subsiding water level of the reservoir of the dam opened up large tracks of fertile land. The decommissioning of the dam and redistribution of that land among Tripura's indigenous tribal population, Bhaumik argues, can be a powerful step in achieving ethnic reconciliation.

In Chapter 14, Betsy Taylor outlines an alternative vision of development for Arunachal Pradesh. She laments that some 'see only infrastructure problems in the fiercely precipitous terrain of the eastern Himalayas'. What gets lost in this way of seeing is the fact that the terrain also 'harbours ecological mega-diversity which could provide a uniquely intact material basis for decentralized, post-industrial "green" economies based on small-scale industries'. Under the right political conditions, 'ecologically embedded and resilient economies' could 'diffuse economic prosperity through dispersed rural populations in ways that nurture cultural and political security, creativity, and equity.' She also finds in Arunachal Pradesh 'fascinating, new experiments in, and possibilities for, democracy'. Unfortunately, given the policy prism through which the region is viewed by New Delhi and the national security-centric and developmentalist mindset that dominates Indian policy thinking, there is little chance that Northeast India would embrace the alternative path that Taylor outlines.

There is neither a development fix nor a military fix for Northeast India's conflicts, says Bethany Lacina in the final chapter of this volume. Those who put forward such easy solutions do not address the embedded nature of rebel groups in the political process. Only concerted efforts to establish the rule of law, a system of accountability, and faith in the formal institutions of governance can break the cycle of violence. Since the popular image of most rebel groups today is rather negative, Lacina believes that a political system less ambivalent towards the rule of law—in theory as well as in practice—can marginalize these groups relatively easily. Rather than the Indian state's current 'persecuted attitude' vis-à-vis human rights groups, she believes that it can turn them into allies. At no cost to the state exchequer they can monitor its agents and their infractions. This can be an important asset in efforts to rebuild the public's faith in the rule of law and the procedures of democratic accountability that is critical for creating a culture of peace in the region.

CONCLUSION

Despite their resilience, the narratives of rebel organizations are often vague and confused, and goals like secession—aptly called a 'state-shattering form of self-determination' (Wohlforth and Felgenhauer 2002: 251)—would seem unrealistic to many. Yet the rebellions are also voices of protest by people facing profound threats to their sense of ontological security—a sense of confidence in 'the continuity of ... self-identity and in the constancy of the surrounding social and material environments of action' (Giddens 1991: 92). Many people appear convinced today that they do 'victims of culture death' a favour by 'breaking them out of the stagnant structures of their lives' (Taylor 2007). In earlier centuries, decisions shaped by this mindset had devastated many societies across continents. Albeit in a less imperious form, this style of thinking has become fashionable once again in our era of globalization—and it is rather pronounced in India, given the current triumphalist national mood. The notion of a development fix for Northeast India that fuels the current spending spree exemplifies this mode of thinking. Despite its democratic institutions, when it comes to Northeast India, where the political centre senses danger, India's political and intellectual culture has little room for reading rebel narratives—even from a historically disadvantaged cultural borderland—'through acts of strong hermeneutical generosity' (Benhabib 2002: 44). As long as a crudely developmentalist and national security-centric mindset continues to shape policy, the goal of achieving peace in Northeast India is likely to remain elusive.

PART I

Stalemated Conflicts: What Cost?

CHAPTER 2

Resenting the Indian State
For a New Political Practice in the Northeast

ANANYA VAJPEYI[1]

THE POLITICS OF RESENTMENT

In post-war Germany, and particularly in German literature, there was a long period of time, as W.G. Sebald has discussed, when neither the Holocaust nor the bombardment of the German cities in Allied air raids was addressed as an issue of national importance (Sebald 2003). The reason for such deafening silence about events that had completely ruined Germany, not to mention decimated European Jewry—a silence that lasted many decades—was not forgetfulness. The devastation wrought by the Third Reich, followed by the catastrophic aerial bombings, which together lasted from 1933 to 1945, could hardly have been forgotten by anyone who survived the war years in Europe. What accounts for the silence was, according to Jean Améry, the idea that 'time heals all wounds'. As Germans struggled to rebuild their cities, resurrect their economy, and reintegrate their now-divided nation into Europe, there was every incentive to move on, without addressing a crime and a punishment that were, separately and together, simply too awful to contemplate.

For Améry, who was a concentration camp survivor, such acquiescence to the pressure of the future—'moving on' from Auschwitz— was 'anti-moral'. The moral reaction would have been to acknowledge the unchangeable: what happened, happened. That it ought not to have happened, and that there was no way either to go back and prevent its happening, or to undo what had happened after the fact—these unalterable realities left Améry with a lifelong resentment. In an essay

[1] Thanks to Pankaj Mishra, Siddhartha Deb, Mahesh Rangarajan, and Paul Kockelman for their comments on this piece.

titled 'Resentments', published in 1966, he spoke of the necessity and propriety of this resentment, understood as a political emotion that could drive what he named the 'historical practice' of the victims of the Nazis (Améry 1980). In 1976, he published a book titled *On Suicide: A Discourse on Voluntary Death* (Améry 1999 [1976]). In 1978, he committed suicide. Both resentment and suicide he claimed as rights: he was free to remember, no matter how much it discomfited others, what had gone on in Hitler's regime, and specifically, what had befallen him; so also he was free to take his own life when his trauma, that he neither forgot nor allowed others to forget, became impossible for him to bear. Like Améry, his camp-mate Primo Levi too, enacted a similar period of writing intensely and movingly about the Holocaust, followed by his suicide in 1987.

In considering most of India's wars from 1947 to the present, we notice two imperatives: first, from those wars that were won or lost, we must move on (thus: Partition, 1962, 1965, 1971), and second, in those wars that are ongoing, we must fight to the finish. But in Northeast India, it seems, the war continues without an end in sight. It is a war both undeclared and permanent (and arguably the same is true of Kashmir). Attack and defence, oppression and resistance, nation building and separatism, national security and self-determination—these wheels turn, only to keep the chariot of war moving perpetually onwards. The Indian state neither wins nor loses in the Northeast and in Kashmir, but the people of these regions are defeated daily. In the face of such objective defeat that pervades the past, defines the present, and extends indefinitely into the future, I want to suggest the political value of Améry's chosen stance: that of resentment.

It may or may not be an option for the ordinary citizens of the Northeast to fight back when multiple assailants terrorize them: the Indian Army, the paramilitaries, the counter-insurgency units, the local police, and the rebel groups, sometimes impossible to even distinguish from each other. Resistance, perhaps the dominant political value in Indian modernity, one that has driven so much of the opposition to first the colonial powers and later the postcolonial Indian state, may not be available any longer as an effective counter to these simultaneous onslaughts from different parties involved in the conflict as well as interested in its perpetuation. Reconciliation is not on the horizon, as the conflict is not yet—and to repeat, may never be—resolved. But perhaps there is a way, as yet unimagined, in which resentment can begin to play the role of a political emotion that allows people in the Northeast to say to Indians, as Améry said to the Germans: 'You don't want to listen? Listen anyhow. You don't want to know where your indifference can again lead you and me at any time? I'll tell you' (Améry 1980: 96).

To bear a grudge against what was done to him or her is the moral duty of every victim, according to Améry. It counteracts the process of the social acceptance of historical wrongs, which mimics the natural process of the healing of wounds over time. Resentment militates against the arrow of time. As trauma ties the victim to his painful past, so the victim's resentment ties the aggressor to the same past, and to the same pain, that he inflicted on the victim. If the victim refuses to be reconciled to what was done to him, he also prevents the aggressor from being reconciled to what he did. The victim must not only withhold forgiveness; he must also impede the convenient self-forgiveness that aggressors will devise for themselves simply by falling in with the directionality of time and the inevitable coming of the heedless future. To remember *and* remind, but further, to resent—this can become the only political practice open to those who have been irreversibly wronged by history.

In what way is such resentment, knowingly maintained, different from revenge? It is distinct because the aggressor is not made to undergo what the victim suffered—an eye for an eye—but only to become conscious of what he did to change forever the victim's life. The cognizance of pain caused to another is not in any way the same as the experiencing of pain by the self. An unequal war is not just unwinnable by the weaker side: it is also the case that defeat, would be both unavoidable and, to coin a word, unavengeable. To cope with this situation, Améry advocates the feeling and the articulation of resentment. Such was the gesture of the women of Manipur in July 2004 who came out naked to protest the abduction, torture, rape, and murder of one of their own, Thangjam Manorama, by members of the Indian security forces.

Manorama was taken from her residence in the early hours of 11 July by three Assam Rifles personnel; a few hours later, in daylight, her body, bearing signs of torture and rape, as well as bullet wounds, was recovered 4 kilometres from her house. This incident was horrible enough, but what really shocked the nation was that a dozen middle-aged to elderly women would come out and stand naked in front of the headquarters of the Assam Rifles in Kangla, Manipur, on 15 July 2004. They wore no clothes, and moreover, carried banners that read 'Indian Army Rape Us', 'Indian Army Take our Flesh'. Their demonstration made headlines in the local, national, and international press. Many newspapers, magazines, and channels did not carry images of the naked women, or blurred the images they did carry in order to hide the uncovered breasts and buttocks of the demonstrators (the banners they were holding hid their stomachs and genitals from anyone standing directly in front of them). M.S. Prabhakara, in an article in the *Hindu*, wrote about their 'initiative to protest in … a frighteningly original manner' (Prabhakara 2004). The originality of this protest, so powerfully conveyed in the nakedness of the participating women, lay, I would argue, in their bringing into the public sphere the emotion that probably lies concealed in every heart in the Northeast: resentment against the Indian state.

Note how demonstrating in this manner did not have the same effect as any one of the following possible and impossible outcomes: (*a*) the retaliatory torture and killing of security men by Manorama's family, associates, or rebel groups acting on her behalf, to avenge her death; (*b*) the arrest, trial, and sentencing of the men who raped and killed Manorama by an Army tribunal; (*c*) the return of the slain Manorama to life, and her physical and psychological recovery from the acts of atrocity that she fell victim to. The naked demonstration achieved what it did by setting itself apart, equally, from the discourses of revenge, justice, or transcendence. The suffering of another, whether brought about within the law or outside it, would neither reverse nor neutralize Manorama's suffering. Her death, in any case, like all death, was final. There was no compensating for what happened to her, and there was no undoing it. Manorama lost her life and there was nothing anyone, friend or foe, could do to alter this fact.

The women who came out and stood bare-bodied in front of the Assam Rifles Headquarters were voicing their grudge that this was the way it was. The banners stated in the present tense, in the declarative mode: 'The taking of the flesh of us Manipuri people is what the Indian Army does. The raping of us Manipuri women is what the Indian Army does. We stand here to say this out loud and clear: this is the way it is. We embody resentment.'

RESENTMENT IS NOT SATYAGRAHA

The Gandhian legacy has dominated contemporary Indian interpretations of the subcontinent's colonial and postcolonial history from at least 1857. All dissenting politics tends to get understood in terms of satyagraha. This began happening from the 1920s, as Ambedkar discovered to his annoyance. When he tried to conceptualize and execute the tank and temple mobilizations in the early phase of his political campaign, he had to fight to get away from satyagraha as the only valid and effective mode of protest and resistance, and build a vocabulary of gestures that was more oppositional and less confessional, and, moreover, that based itself on the idea of rights rather than the idea of moral struggle. But Ambedkar's political methods have been recessive, and those of Gandhi have remained the dominant Indian idiom of dissent for almost a hundred years now. In such a climate of opinion, right from Independence on, leaders from Rammanohar Lohia to Jayaprakash Narayan, Sunderlal Bahuguna to Medha Patkar have all modelled themselves, and been perceived, as satyagrahis of one sort or another.

Thus it comes about that even an extremist like Yasin Malik, one of the founders and commanders of the Jammu Kashmir Liberation Front (JKLF), now publicly declares his adoption of a Gandhian stance, based on non-violence and the steadfast assertion of the moral rectitude of the cause, in his case, the freedom of Kashmir from Indian political control and military occupation.[2] By contrast, the Hindu Right has been anti-Gandhian from its very inception; in fact, its first major intervention in national politics was, as Ashis Nandy has been elaborating for decades now, the assassination of Gandhi in January 1948, by Nathuram Godse under the influence of Vinayak Damodar Savarkar (Nandy 2004b).[3] Thus, because the Sangh Parivar has been the single largest current of opposition to all centrist, socialist, and left parties since the Congress lost power in 1989, the Hindu nationalists by and large have not sought to build legitimacy by relying on Gandhian ideology or tactics. But even among the proponents of Hindutva, who

---

[2] Yasin Malik's Kashmiri progenitor, in this regard, is arguably Sheikh Abdullah, even though Sheikh's own engagement, at the level of the ideas, practices, and emotions of politics, was always with Nehru rather than with Gandhi. Malik has publicly declared himself a Gandhian, for example at the World Social Forum in Karachi, Pakistan (26 March 2006). For a man who was tortured for a long period of time in custody, this is a remarkable turn.

[3] I am thinking also of Nandy's recent lecture on Savarkar delivered at Columbia University: 'The Demonic and the Seductive in Religious Nationalism: Vinayak Damodar Savarkar and the Rites of Exorcism in Secularizing South Asia' (Wednesday, 28 March 2007).

as a whole form an exception to the rule, and embrace violence and communalism as central components of their politics, there has been some difference in the behaviour of the Jan Sangh relative to its later avatar, the Bharatiya Janata Party (BJP), at least in the use and abuse of satyagraha (a point that I do not have space to develop here).

A definitive history of alternative politics in the 1970s has yet to be written, but I suspect it is more or less correct to say that satyagraha today enjoys enormous legitimacy among an entire generation of men and women who were left radicals of various descriptions as students, academics, trade unionists, party workers, and civil society activists during the years between Europe's 1968, the Bangladesh War (1971), the Emergency (1975–7), and Indira Gandhi's return to power (1980).[4] The journey of these former Trotskyites, Maoists, and Naxalites, from armed struggle and disruptive revolution to more pacific, agonistic, and internalized forms of bringing about social transformation, and battling inequality and injustice, is a testament to the resilience of the Gandhian repertoire as the hegemonic idiom of indigenous politics.[5] Amitav Ghosh's moving sketch of the unhappy career of George Fernandes over the past thirty years provides an almost tragic counterpoint, showing us what can happen to dissent when it veers away from the high standard set once and for all by the Mahatma (Ghosh 2003). Arundhati Roy's writings on and travels with the Narmada Bachao Andolan (NBA) provide a recent reinforcement and amplification of the mythology of satyagraha. Roy imagines what non-violent resistance as well as a principled and dogged adherence to the truth could achieve for Indian society. She explores (albeit in a polemical way) the value of these modalities of mass politics in an era when people's rights are continually attenuated by the relentless advance of global capital, and moral leadership is woefully missing.[6]

---

[4] As I write, Ramachandra Guha's new history of independent India (Guha 2007) has come into circulation. This promises a thoroughgoing reading of the decade of the 1970s in Indian politics, in Part IV of the book.

[5] An insight into the moral and ideological turmoil of this time—the Emergency and immediately after—is available in Sudhir Mishra's sensitive film, *Hazaaron Khwaaishein Aisi* (2005), and Dilip Simeon's forthcoming quasi-fictional memoir promises to be a similar sort of window into student radicalism from 1968–75. See also a short story by Simeon (1997).

[6] See Roy 1999. This essay is now anthologized in her *The Cost of Living* (1999; New York: The Modern Library) and in *The Algebra of Infinite Justice* (2002; London: Harper Collins) as well. Perhaps we should understand the

It is not surprising then, given these trends in the Indian heartland, that when a group of Manipuri women came out naked on the street to stand in front of the gates of the Assam Rifles Headquarters, they would immediately be read as the Gandhians of the Northeast, engaged in a sort of feminist satyagraha (Butalia 2004). But I dare say this is a misreading of what the naked protest meant. The banners did not read 'Indian Army leave Manipur!' in an exhortative mode, nor did they plead 'Indian Army stop the Rape!' Instead, they neither urged nor asked for anything. They simply stated what had occurred for Manorama, and what recurs for countless civilians, both men and women, in the military regime of the Northeast that has been in place since the late 1950s: Indian Army rape us; Indian Army take our flesh.[7]

There is no demand for justice implicit in these sentences; they are not slogans, but only statements. What they state is the terrible reality of the dynamic between the Indian Army and Manipuri civilians, especially women: that of aggressor and victim, rapist and raped, killer and killed, powerful and powerless. Urvashi Butalia described the protest in terms of the women using their naked bodies as weapons (Butalia 2004). But the idea of 'the body as weapon' implies revenge, retaliation, hitting back, though in a satyagraha such a counter-attack is effected through moral might, not physical prowess. The weapon of choice—in this case, according to Butalia, the body—embodies and deploys moral force, not violence in any literal way.

However, I don't think the women meant to either resist or retaliate, nor were they seeking to avenge Manorama's killing. What

---

defeat of the NBA movement and the eclipse of Medha Patkar, and the iterative electoral victory of Narendra Modi in the Gujarat elections, as two sides of the same coin.

[7] It may be possible to read these slogans in various ways:

(*a*) If 'Indian Army' is taken as a plural noun, then 'Indian Army rape us' is a descriptive sentence, meaning: 'They [= The Indian Army] rape us [routinely]'.

(*b*) However, if the subject of this sentence were taken to be a singular noun, then a descriptive statement *ought* to have read: 'It [= The Indian Army] rapes us [routinely]'.

(*c*) If 'Indian Army' is indeed a singular subject, then 'Indian Army rape us' becomes an exhortation and an invitation, or even an address followed by a command, meaning: 'Indian Army! [Vocative form] Come and rape us [*implied*: like you always do]!'

I am grateful to Paul Kockelman for parsing this sentence for me to bring out its hidden and possible nuances, and its illocutionary force. The same procedure can be followed for the other sentence 'Indian Army take our flesh'.

was happening in Kangla, Imphal, on 15 July 2004, was not passive resistance but active resentment. It was, to return to Améry, not the straightforwardly moral politics of satyagraha to reverse the Indian Army's occupation of Manipur, but the perversely moral politics of resenting the irreversible acts of the Indian Army in Manipur, including the arrest, torture, rape, and murder of Thangjam Manorama who, as far as anyone has been able to establish, was not an enemy of the state and therefore did not, to put it crudely, have this coming to her. In the section titled 'Bare Act and Bare Life' below I elaborate what the naked body meant in this struggle, because in my reading it was not intended to signify a weapon of the weak, but rather to call to mind the very weakness that makes the citizens of the Northeast vulnerable to such constant and terrible violence.

THE PLACE OF NAKEDNESS IN TRADITIONS OF DISSENT

In a context that is related to the modern movements against Untouchability, led by both Gandhi and Ambedkar through the separate and, as D.R. Nagaraj has argued, mutually opposed *as well as* deeply interdependent figures of the Harijan and the Dalit, U.R. Ananthamurthy has explored the place of nakedness in the dissenting traditions of caste politics in Karnataka (Nagaraj 1993; Ananthamurthy 1988). Nakedness as a metaphor for the relationship between the moral person and political power has, as Ananthamurthy shows, a long history in the Kannada cultural world, and plays an important part in the prominent dissenting—non-Brahmin—theologies of that region. The naked body, male or female, is the site where sexuality, sovereign power, asceticism, and caste all intersect to produce different kinds of meaning that Ananthamurthy is interested to read as non-modern or anti-modern forms of critique and protest directed against the oppressions of the Brahminical, and later the colonial, order.[8] The

[8] Ananthamurthy's purpose, in this piece, is to critically examine the tensions between faith and rationality, tradition and modernity, practice and anthropology, conservatism and reform, from the perspective of someone who, like Ananthamurthy himself, is both a believer and a rationalist, a traditionalist and a Westernized person, an immersed native and a man estranged from his own roots by his modern education. The annual festival in Chandragutti (in southwest Karnataka), where low-caste female worshippers of the goddess Yellamma take a ritual dip in holy water and then walk naked up a hill to the temple of their deity, attracts the attention of a number of political groups, media persons, and intellectuals, including Ananthamurthy, who then debate, in quite a charged and

naked itinerant ascetic man or woman, often a poet, without family, property, or status, has been seen as an embodiment of the challenge to caste-based social and political life posed by what we might call Indic liberation theologies, extant from Kashmir to the far south of peninsular India throughout pre-modernity.

I have no idea what the historical provenance of this genre of 'holy' person—a renunciant, an outsider, an iconoclast, a rebel, a critic, or a saint—has been in any of the myriad cultures of the Northeast, or even just in what is today called Manipur. But somehow I doubt that the gesture of 15 July had reference to these broader and deeper streams of politics, wherein the use of nakedness to symbolize dissent is an established and widely understood tactic, with multiple histories in diverse parts of the subcontinent (at least all those parts that have ever fallen in the catchment area of caste society over the course of the past two-and-a-half millennia). There was nothing liberating in the nakedness of the twelve women who stood at the door of the Assam Rifles' office—liberating to the women themselves, to their community, to their fellow-citizens, or to the soul of the deceased. The Indian armed forces did not, that day, give up their posts and leave Manipur or the Northeast forever, in shame for what they had done to Manorama and to thousands of others like her, nor was such a 'liberation' of Manipur the end that the women could have imagined, even in their most Utopian frame of mind.[9] The women were neither defiant nor insouciant, neither detached nor indifferent, neither triumphant nor free. To me, the only way to decipher their nakedness is to say: they were resentful.

---

antagonistic fashion, it seems, the place of such a ritual in contemporary Indian society. Ananthamurthy uses the naked procession (which he describes as 'worship in the nude') to meditate on who is inside and who outside a living culture that still retains traces of the non-modern, especially in the realm of religion. I am not picking up on this question with regards to Manipuri culture; I am only trying to look at how public and collective nakedness, particularly that of women, is read politically in other parts of India. I do not make any attempt to situate the Manipur episode vis-à-vis naked protests in other parts of the world.

[9] What did happen was that the historic Kangla Fort, occupied by the Assam Rifles since 1947, was 'returned' to the people of Manipur in late November 2004, in a special handover ceremony. The Fort was handed over by the prime minister of India, Dr Manmohan Singh to the chief minister of Manipur, Ibobi Singh. Thangjam Manorama's death brought the Fort, as the headquarters of the Assam Rifles, back into public attention, and it came to stand for the Indian Army's occupation of Manipur. I am grateful to Siddhartha Deb for alerting me to the history of the Kangla Fort and to its role as a symbol of Manipuri sovereignty.

Apunba Lub, the consortium of women's groups that organized the naked gathering after Manorama's gruesome end, originally called for the statewide boycott of the Justice Jeevan Reddy Committee. This Committee was constituted by the Congress-led UPA alliance after it was voted into power in New Delhi in 2004, to consider repealing the Armed Forces (Special Powers) Act, 1958 (AFSPA) prevailing in the Northeast. The Report of the Committee itself records this fact—of the boycott call—at the very beginning (GoI 2005b).

However, at a hearing held in Imphal on 28 December 2004, as noted in Annexure III of the Report, Apunba Lub did come forward to file a memorandum calling for the repeal of the AFSPA, and submitted a list of human rights violations in the state of Manipur, 'under the headings extra judicial killings, rape, sodomy, torture, disappearances and illegal detentions', in the language of the Report (GoI 2005b: 98). In first calling for a boycott of the Committee's efforts, and later handing in a listing of the human rights record of the Indian armed forces in Manipur, it seems to me that Apunba Lub was continuing to register its resentment for what was done, with impunity, to Manorama and many others like her. In addition, the Report notes the deposition of Manorama's brother as follows:

Th. Dolendro Singh, younger brother of deceased Th. Monorama Devi of Bamon Kampu Mayai Leikai, Imphal East District:

Th. Dolendro Singh, who was accompanied by 4/5 persons, in his Memorandum, has given details of the incident in which his sister was arrested, tortured, beaten up and raped by the personnel of Assam Rifles on the night intervening July 10 / 11, 2004 and she was found dead on the Yairipok road, the next day. The State Government appointed a Commission to enquire into this case but so far its findings have not been made public. The delegation demanded complete removal of this Act so as to protect the dignity of human beings. He mentioned in his oral submission that they have no objection for Army operation in Manipur but not at the cost of dignity of citizens. The State Police could control the situation (GoI 2005b: 100).

It is noteworthy that Th. Dolendro Singh and his delegation do not go on the record with any objection they might have to 'Army operation in Manipur', but nevertheless demand, in direct contradiction to this oral submission, the 'complete removal' of the AFSPA. What is really at issue for Dolendro, as far as we can tell from the Committee's version, is the 'dignity of human beings' and the 'dignity of citizens', both of which were completely denied to his violated and murdered sister. Améry is torn about the question of dignity: what it is, what it means, and what constitutes its importance for a victim of extreme violence. He takes two separate positions on it in his essays on torture and on being a Jew, a contradiction he recognizes in his preface to the collection in which both essays appear. But, he argues in this preface, he will not make the attempt to reconcile his own contradictory statements (Améry 1980: Preface of 1966).

Summarizing very roughly from his writings: human dignity is intimately related to bodily integrity, and to the trust that another human being will not violate one's physical and psychological entity with an act of violence; that the man in front of one will not overstep the limit of one's being that is one's skin. 'The boundaries of my body are the also the boundaries of my self', writes he (Améry 1980: 28). Torture destroys this trust forever. Dignity is the right to live and to live without being harmed or injured despite one's radical and uninterrupted vulnerability to pain and to death, and this right is bestowed upon one by other people, the same people who could become the agents of harm or the perpetrators of injury. Dignity is what is preserved on account of 'the certainty that by reason of written or unwritten social contracts the other person will spare me—more precisely stated, that he will respect my physical, and with it also my metaphysical being' (Améry 1980: 28). When others become aggressors and tormentors, when they take away one's right to live and to live unharmed and uninjured, one loses one's dignity.

If we take the word in this sense, Manorama's brother is right to refer repeatedly to dignity in the context of what happened, specifically, to his sister, but also what is happening, more generally, to the entire Northeast under the writ of the AFSPA. The nakedness of the women of Apunba Lub tropes the intolerable, and ultimately fatal indignities to which Manorama was subjected, and to which they and other citizens of the Northeast might also be subjected sooner or later. Resentment seems like the only emotion that might begin to be appropriate in such dire circumstances.

RULE, EXCEPTION, AND PARTITION

The AFSPA has been continuously in place in some or all parts of the Northeast for approximately fifty years, at the time of the writing of this essay. It constitutes what Sanjib Baruah has accurately identified, in many of his writings, as a 'permanent regime of exception' to the law that is supposed to be the default all across the Indian Union (Baruah

2007). This means that the overwhelming majority of the people of the Northeast, who account for almost 4 per cent of India's population (2001 Census figures for the eight states of the Northeast = 38.86 million), have never seen a time when the AFSPA was not in force; that is, most of the region's population has only ever experienced the exception without knowing what it might be like to live in the rule of law, unless they have travelled outside the region to other parts of India (excluding the state of Jammu and Kashmir). Exceptionality is the rubric that I too use to think about the Northeast and Jammu and Kashmir, and strictly speaking this is the correct way to describe the relationship of the AFSPA to normal legality in India.[10]

But perhaps it is desirable now to move towards recognizing what the AFSPA effectively does, which is create an entirely separate space within India, a sort of second and shadow nation, that functions as a military state rather than an electoral democracy, and only remains hidden because it is not, at least so far, officially ruled by a general or dictator who presents any sort of overt challenge to the authority of the elected prime minister or chief ministers of different states, including those of the Northeast. What I am suggesting is that within the boundaries of a democratic nation-state, a zone of exception governed by unelected and unrepresentative armed forces (that moreover enjoy complete impunity) should not be thought of as a mere zone of exception, but as a contradiction so extreme that it undoes the totality in which it is embedded, and breaks it down into distinct and mutually opposed regimes: a democracy and a non-democracy; two nations: India and not-India.

The Reddy Committee acknowledges the exceptional nature of the AFSPA, as well as the problems of such exceptionalism:

It must be recognised … that *the deployment of armed forces or para military forces of the Union to restore public order in any part of the territory of India, or to protect a State from internal disturbance is, and ought to be, an exception and not the rule* [emphasis mine]. The deployment of armed forces for the said purposes should be undertaken with great care and circumspection. Unless

[10] I discuss this in papers presented at the Centre for Political Studies, Conference on 'State and Democracy in India', Jawaharlal Nehru University, New Delhi (March 2006), the Annual South Asian Studies Conference, panel titled 'Exceptions to the Rule of Law: National Security, Policing and Caste in India', Madison WI (October 2007), and the American Anthropological Association Meetings, panel titled 'Emergency, Security and the Identification of Crisis', Washington D.C. (November 2007).

it is absolutely essential for the aforesaid purposes, the armed forces of the Union should not be so deployed, since too frequent a deployment, and that too for long periods of time, carries with it the danger of such forces losing their moorings and becoming, in effect, another police force, a prey to all the temptations and weaknesses such exposures involve. Such exposure for long periods of time may well lead to the brutalisation of such forces—which is a danger to be particularly guarded against. This concern applies no less in the case of other armed forces of the Union as well. All this means that as soon as the public order is restored or the internal disturbance is quelled, the forces have to be withdrawn to their barracks or to their regular duties, as the case may be (GoI 2005b: 71–2).

In a fine analysis of the 'act of terror' that is the AFSPA, Bimol Akoijam outlines the full story of the death of democracy in Manipur, from 1949 to 2005 (Akoijam 2005). Included in his article is a detailed retelling of the atrocities that led to the death of Manorama, and the protests that followed the recovery of her body, between July 2004 and February 2005. From Akoijam's reconstruction, it emerges that Apunba Lub testified before the Justice Upendra (retired) Commission instituted to inquire into Manorama's death by the Manipur state government, and that mass rallies and sit-ins followed the naked protest of 15 July for weeks and months. It was this public outcry that brought the Union Home Minister Shivraj Patil to Imphal in September 2004. In November 2004, the Justice Jeevan Reddy Commission was set up, which in December 2004 again asked for Apunba Lub's testimony. Apunba Lub called for a statewide strike and a shutdown of shops and offices, but despite this, many individuals and organizations, including eventually Manorama's brother and the Manipur Working Committee of the Apunba Lub itself, came forward to testify.

From this chain of events it becomes clear that the naked protest that occurred barely four days after Manorama's body was dumped near her house, led, ultimately, to the creation of the Reddy Committee whose mandate was to review the AFSPA. The earlier Upendra Committee was a Commission of Inquiry into the Manorama case; the Reddy Committee could have recommended that the AFSPA be rendered less draconian, or even that it be repealed altogether. In fact, it did recommend the repeal of the act. However, the AFSPA remained in place.

Sanjib Baruah has examined the Reddy Committee's recommendations, the main one being that the AFSPA be repealed, and that it be replaced by extending the jurisdiction of the Unlawful Activities

Prevention Act (ULP, of 1967, amended in 2004), which is applicable in the rest of India, to the Northeast (Baruah 2007; Baruah 2005c). The Reddy Committee describes the ULP as a 'cognate enactment' relative to the AFSPA, and thus recommends that it be made to do the work of the AFSPA (GoI 2005b: 73–5). However, it should do this work not exclusively in the Northeast, but all over the country. This basically amounts to recommending that the exception be generalized, rather than that the rule be reinstated where it had been suspended, which is Baruah's criticism as well.

The irony is that the AFSPA was first imposed ostensibly to secure territories that were not fully integrated into the Indian Union; to bind the not-India that lay at India's peripheries into the Indian geo-national imaginary. But after being applied for half a century and with an ever-expanding scope, the AFSPA has only confirmed the rupture between what is and is not India. What is so astonishing is not that this state of exception exists or persists, nor even that it is spatialized over close to 10 per cent of India's territory (including both the Northeast and Jammu and Kashmir, i.e., nine of the twenty-eight states, or nearly one-third of all states), but that the rest of the country carries on as though it is possible to gloss over the reality of military rule as a temporary aberration and a mere enclave in what purports to be the world's largest democracy.

It would be far more realistic to grasp that the AFSPA unravels the democratic project and renders India schizophrenic, or fractures the nation in a way that is no less traumatic than what happened in 1947. One Partition got over in 1947; another one occurred in 1971; but the Partition that is the extension of the AFSPA just carries on, not the severance of a limb but a slow sickness of the body politic, drawn out over five bloody and painful decades already in the Northeast, and bleeding Kashmir since 1990.

In his review of Sanjib Baruah's work, Sudhir Chandra writes:

The Armed Forces Special Powers Act ... is an ominous illustration of the pervasive perversion of the democratic ethos, not just the democratic process, in India. In a telling example from Manipur ... women stripped themselves to demonstrate in the nude during an angry outburst ... that followed the killing of a young woman. What does this portend if a society drives its women into such morally charged desperation and remains unmoved by it all?

Protests such as this would shame and shake people and governments in many other societies; but not in India, the world's most multiethnic, multicultural, democratic polity. Not only were the political parties that keep the musical chair [*sic*] of the country's democracy going far from scandalized, even the citizenry in India's heartland seemed complacent... (Chandra 2007: 49).

The naked women of Manipur, who tried to storm the gates of the Assam Rifles headquarters, expressed their extreme, pent-up resentment at having been consigned to not-India by the equally naked exercise of state terror in the form of the uninterrupted imposition of a military regime, in place of the rule of law that is available to the other 90 per cent of India. Chandra notes: 'Distrust cannot beget trust. Force, however cloaked, will breed resentment, more so when the remembrance of the exercise of naked force during two decades of insurgency has not diminished in the two subsequent decades' (Chandra 2007: 53).

BARE ACT AND BARE LIFE

Akoijam goes into the 'bare act' of the AFSPA, as does the Reddy Committee, as have numerous other scholars, activists, litigants, journalists in the Northeast, in India and around the world, as well as local, national, and international organizations (Amnesty 2006; *Seminar* 2002). The Reddy Committee notes 'the impression gathered by it during the course of its work viz., the Act, for whatever reason, has become a symbol of oppression, an object of hate and an instrument of discrimination and highhandedness' (GoI 2005b: 75). And yet the AFSPA seems impossible to dislodge. My reading of the predicament of citizens in the Northeast is that they feel reduced to what the Italian political philosopher Giorgio Agamben has called 'bare life'—human life stripped of its political description (*bios*), and rendered merely biological (*zoé*), so extreme are the operations of 'sovereign power' upon it. Bare life is life placed under a 'ban' in two ways—it is 'abandoned' by the law in the space of exception where it has no value and may be extinguished with impunity; it is also life that has been 'banned' in the sense of being segregated into a zone of exception to the rule of law, spatialized as 'the camp' (Agamben 2000; 1998).

Bare life is life completely exposed to the wilful exercise of sovereign power, which in normal circumstances is 'biopolitical', but in the camp is more often than not the opposite, that is, 'necropolitical'. If the AFSPA is the ban under which the sovereign power of the Indian state has placed all of the Northeast, then the exception to the rule of law that is spatialized in the Northeast should be thought of as a camp, precisely a zone where anything can, and anything does happen to people. The citizens of the Northeast have been reduced to bare life, and the operations of the Indian state in this region are, for the most part, necropolitical, designed, as African theorist Achille Mbembe has outlined, for the 'generalized instrumentalization of human existence' and the 'material destruction of bodies and populations' (Mbembe 2003: 13).

My purpose is not to present, elaborate, or critique the categories proposed by either Agamben or Mbembe here, nor to explore the genealogy of their ideas in the work of Michel Foucault and Hannah Arendt. I have undertaken that project at great length in other pieces of writing (Vajpeyi 2007). My interest, rather, is in pointing out how the protest of the women of Manipur on 15 July picks up on the reality of what it means to be reduced to bare life, and makes the naked body an icon of citizenship that has been stripped of rights and is left exposed to the depredations of sovereign power. Under the ban of the AFSPA, citizens of the Northeast are rendered completely vulnerable, and may be searched, arrested, detained, interrogated, imprisoned, or killed at any time by any member of the armed forces, which includes personnel of the army and the paramilitary organizations. The naked body is the perfect icon of this political condition of rightlessness and exposure. Its physical vulnerability tropes the political vulnerability—which may also take the form of physical vulnerability, ultimately—of those who are banned from the rule of law and abandoned by the law in a space where their life could, at any moment, be extinguished.

Thangjam Manorama was not protected from the brutalities of the Assam Rifles men who entered her house, took her away, raped her, killed her, and then shot at her dead body to conceal the traces of their actions. Neither her clothes, nor the walls of her private residence, nor the presence of her family members, nor her rights as a citizen of India provided any sort of protection from the absolute impunity enjoyed by the Rifles personnel under the AFSPA. Manorama's mother and brothers testified that when she was first taken away to be questioned, she re-entered the house with her shirt unbuttoned and her hair in disarray, indicating that the Rifles men had already misbehaved with her and made sexual advances. After this she was driven away in their vehicle, and never returned home. Her body bore the marks of rape and torture whilst alive, and of mutilation after death. Manorama's powerlessness was stark; her tormentors' display of their might was equally naked.

The women of Apunba Lub came forward naked precisely to show, to display, to make explicit the condition to which they and all citizens of the Northeast are reduced by the imposition of the AFSPA: life stripped naked of the civilities and strengths of democracy; life without the vestments of the rights, entitlements, protections, and freedoms that make it possible for people to lead normatively ordered, legally sanctioned, socially organized and politically empowered lives. It would seem that clothing is real, and rights are abstract. But it is when rights disappear that their reality becomes immediately obvious. The citizens of the Northeast living under the writ of the AFSPA and in the exception to the rule of law have no rights; it was to make this condition visible to the eye and apparent to the mind that the dozen women gathered at Kangla without clothes, bare life parading as bare life, rightless and resentful.

We have already looked at how active resentment is not like passive resistance; how the articulation of resentment ought not be assimilated to the practice of satyagraha; how the two are opposed in their orientation to the moral. But many gestures of Gandhi's politics during the nationalist movement and of Gandhian politics in post-colonial India exhibit the same brilliance of iconicity that I read in the naked protest of Imphal 2004. When the industrialization of cotton production in England was destroying the Indian cloth economy, Gandhi literally sat down to weave khadi on a spinning wheel. When the taxation system of the British colonists was crushing Indian subjects, Gandhi literally set out to make salt from the sea. When Untouchability deprived people of both religious rights and civic amenities, Ambedkar, Periyar, and other leaders of the non-Brahmin and anti-Brahmin movements in Maharashtra and south India literally took thousands to drink from tanks and wells, and physically enter into upper-caste temples. When deforestation was ravaging the Himalayan foothills, activists in the Chipko Andolan literally hugged trees.

The repertoire of such gestures can be extended, but the main point I want to make is that the naked protest belongs in this family of powerful images, constructed and deployed by people all across the subcontinent to create metaphors for their political condition and also, in some of the cases mentioned above, to break entrenched social and cultural taboos that work to undermine their rights. Where the comparison between khadi and salt satyagrahas, on one hand, and protesting naked, on the other, might not hold, is, once again, that the women protestors found nothing liberating about their nakedness. Salt can be made and cloth can be spun, trees can be saved and water can be drunk, a sanctum sanctorum can be entered and an idol touched—but a human being once tortured, as Améry has written, stays tortured for the rest of his life; thus is rape irreversible, and so too death.[11] There is no way to reclaim, re-engage, revivify, and reinvigorate the human life that was Manorama. Without rights citizens are exposed to sovereign power; unless the AFSPA is repealed, the citizens of the Northeast will remain bare life, their existence reduced to the level of zoé (biological life) rather than remaining at the pinnacle of bios (political life).

The brilliance of the naked protest though, goes even further. For all that it signifies resentment and not transcendence, the insistence on the past rather than the forgetfulness of the future, the assertion of what happened rather than the anticipation of what has yet to happen, the naked protest is a semiotic masterstroke. For it uses the actual body of a woman to image the abstract body of the citizen; it uses clothes to stand for rights, and thus their absence to stand for rightlessness, and it uses physical powerlessness to trope political powerlessness. As a person without clothing is naked, so a citizen without rights is bare life. Without the rights of self-determination and representation, citizens are invisible, in as much as their political will remains hidden, does not become apparent. But the naked women, who stand for these invisible citizens, are clearly visible, and moreover make their own rightlessness visible. Their presence on the street, in front of the gates, in the flesh, signifies their absence from politics, and their consignment to a zone outside the threshold of power. By baring themselves, paradoxically the invisible citizens gain visibility; the absent citizens gain presence, and the gates of the army stronghold, while not broken down, are rattled sufficiently so that first a commission of inquiry and later a review committee must be instituted by the Union government.

As a citizen under the ban of the AFSPA has no protections, so a woman (and a citizen) under a banner that reads 'Indian Army Rape Us'/'Indian Army take our Flesh' is an icon of another woman, a dead woman, who was banned from full citizenship, abandoned by the law, and left to die a gruesome death at the hands of those who have been vested with absolute power and are protected from the consequences of their actions by the vestment of absolute impunity. The violation of her bodily integrity and the violation of their political integrity are images of one another, and both the causes and the consequences of one

---

[11] 'Whoever was tortured, stays tortured' (Améry 1980: 34).

another. Manorama's sexual violation follows from but also resembles the violation of rights that citizens in the Northeast have endured now for fifty years.

If we recall Améry's discussion of trust in the world and of dignity as the right to live, both are predicated on human beings respecting one another's physical and metaphysical being of which the most visible marker is the body itself—the body in its nakedness, bounded by its bare skin, a fragile home that houses an even more fragile occupant, both poised precariously on the edge of annihilation. In coming out on the street stark naked, the women of Apunba Lub put their trust in the world, as well as their dignity, on the line. They remind every spectator that Manorama's trust was broken and her dignity snatched from her. In a single gesture of astounding semiotic richness, all of these meanings are unleashed, for the public of the Northeast, of India, and the world to see, and to be shocked by.

THE NATION AND THE CAMP

To return to Agamben's terminology, the space that I was earlier calling 'not-India' is what would be called, in his theoretical framework, 'the camp'. Agamben defines the camp as the spatialization of the state of exception, and this is exactly how we are forced to characterize the Northeast, given the prevalence there of the AFSPA.[12] We could say, then, that the AFSPA creates an India and a not-India. Another way to put that would be to say that the AFSPA splits India into a nation and a camp, with the former under the rule of law and the latter in a zone of exception (Vajpeyi 2004). People, too, become differentiated into two groups, the citizens of India, who have a complete set of rights, entitlements, and protections under the law, and the non-citizens of the Northeast, who lack these very rights, entitlements, and protections, since they are not under the law, but under the regime of the AFSPA. We have examined in detail how a small band of these non-citizens confronted the full might of the sovereign state which is instantiated in and operationalized through the armed forces deployed in the Northeast.

This confrontation, however, was not liberating, but resentful. It did not in itself represent a form of passive resistance, but rather took the shape of active resentment. It shared some of the power of Gandhian

[12] See both Agamben 1998 and 2000 for multiple iterations of his conception of the camp.

dissent, which derives from the use of iconicity as a political tactic, but not its premise, which is moral struggle to build a better future, rather than resentment against the painful past, and against the anti-moral effect of the passage of time with respect to the irreversible and ineradicable effects of such a past. However, owing to the history of dissenting political movements in India, the naked protest of the women of Manipur is liable to be misread as just another instance of satyagraha. Satyagraha is meaningless in the camp, which is the state of exception spatialized. Satyagraha is simply not the appropriate weapon of the weak in what Bruno Bettelheim has called 'extreme situations' (Bettelheim 1960). Principles have next to no place in the camp, as Bettelheim has documented, as has Primo Levi (Bettelheim 1979; Levi 1983, 1989).

This is why the hunger strike of Irom Sharmila, a Manipuri woman in her early thirties who has been fasting since November 2000, makes no sense and has failed to generate the moral leverage expected of the fast-unto-death, another Gandhian method. Rather, Sharmila is placed under arrest, forcibly hospitalized, and fed against her will, her satyagraha unrecognized by citizens and sovereign power alike, her protest as futile in Manipur as it is in Delhi. The camp is precisely a space in which life has no value; to put that life at stake, then, is totally meaningless, and this is what renders the hunger strike, despite its tortuous length of almost seven years already, ineffective as a tactic for Sharmila and her supporters.

In the camp, sovereign power and bare life stand face to face; bare life is ultimately extinguished, or so utterly instrumentalized and brutalized that living people become the living dead, what Primo Levi has called the *Muselmann*, borrowing from the vocabulary of Auschwitz.[13] Agamben has examined both the *Muselmänner* of the concentration camp, and other kinds of living dead, as the most extreme 'necropolitical' effects of the operations of sovereign power in the exceptional space of the camp (Agamben 1999). Instead of being acknowledged as an irritant to the nation's conscience, and therefore a living instigation to moral action on the part of both the state and ordinary citizens, Sharmila has been reduced to a *Muselmann*. She is not granted the morally superior status of someone on a fast-unto-death; rather, she has been cast as someone who is wilfully attempting

[13] See Primo Levi, 'The Drowned and the Saved', in Levi 1989.

to starve herself to death for some obscure reason, and therefore must be stopped, by force if need be.

Satyagrahis and hunger strikers are not supposed to become *Muselmänner*. But then the site of action proper to those engaged in Gandhian politics is not the 'necropolitical' theatre of the camp. Manorama, whose rape and murder occasioned the naked protest, embodied the limits to which 'necropolitics' will take the life (and death) of a human being; having returned alive from the threshold of such a limit, Améry advocates the only possible stance for a camp survivor: resentment.

My purpose in pointing out that the naked protest in Manipur should be read as the public expression of the resentment felt by the people of the Northeast towards the Indian state is to highlight both the propriety and the necessity of resentment as a political emotion. Not only is it entirely understandable that citizens trapped in a zone of exception and deprived of their rights, that is, citizens in the space of the camp, feel resentful; it is in fact necessary that they express their resentment publicly, and moreover, that they, and we, learn to recognize the potency of such expressions as gestures of dissent that are related to, but not included in, the repertoire of satyagraha.

Satyagraha is tied to the truth; so is resentment. But satyagraha is tied to the truth of what is yet to come about; resentment, by contrast, is tied to the truth of what has already taken place. In a space of exception where citizens cannot bring themselves to feel hopeful about the future, they must at least continue to feel resentful about the past. This is what can provide them with a basis for collective action, such as the naked protest of the women of Apunba Lub, which in turn could result in some sort of a response from the sovereign power that does not amount to pushing already vulnerable citizens further into the hell of the *conditio inhumana*. The creation of the Upendra inquiry commission and the Reddy review committee are the responses of a state that has gone very far in the direction of militarism and authoritarianism (too far, indeed, for it to be coherent as a democracy), but has not yet become a totalitarian state outright.

Two sorts of parties are prone to object to the comparison between the Holocaust and mass violence in India: Indian exclusivists, on the one hand, and Zionists on the other. Indian exclusivists like to think of the different forms of violence on the subcontinent or in India—communal violence, principally—as somehow historically unique; Zionists insist we treat the Holocaust in the same way. While it is true that historical specificities in both cases cannot and ought not be disregarded, what I am getting at are the modular aspects of both genocidal violence and the state of exception. Thus it can hardly be denied that there is no equivalent to Auschwitz in the Northeast; but to the extent that the Holocaust presents a limit case of several phenomena—having to do with the nature of state power and the relationship of citizens to this power—that are indeed observed in the Northeast, I am not convinced that its invocation is inappropriate. At the very least I have no investment in treating either the depredations of the Indian state or the excesses of the Nazi state as taboo subjects, not to be compared, contrasted, or in any other way analysed with respect to each other or other similar instances. Sovereign power and bare life in the era of the modern state assume forms that we would do well to identify as they are replicated, albeit on different scales and to varying extents, everywhere in the world.[14]

The Partition of British India is normally understood to have affected three regions of the subcontinent most severely: Kashmir, Punjab and, in a staggered fashion (1947, 1971) Bengal. These three regions straddle the borders between India, Pakistan, and Bangladesh, so that each of the new nations carries the wound of Partition within itself. As territories contiguous with these core areas of impact, and as home to hundreds of millions of Muslims, Sindh, Gujarat, Uttar Pradesh, and Bihar are also counted as adversely affected. But the truth is that the Partition is responsible, in addition, for the predicament of the Northeast as well. It was the 'messy divorce' and the 'botched surgery' of Partition, to borrow Willem van Schendel's apt phrases, that resulted in many if not all of the problems of the states of the Indian Northeast, especially Assam, and of Bangladesh's northeast, the Chittagong Hill Tracts.[15] I cannot elaborate here, but the point is that first, we must include the Northeast into the narrative of the Partition and its aftermath, and see the Northeast as falling squarely within the historical catchment, as it were, of the Partition; and second, given that the Partition was the subcontinent's own Holocaust, we must not shy away from making the appropriate comparisons, even as we take care to historicize each catastrophe to its proper time and place.

[14] I have discussed this thoroughly in Vajpeyi 2007.
[15] I take these phrases from Willem van Schendel, speaking at a conference on 'Northeast India and its Transnational Neighbourhood', Indian Institute of Technology, Guwahati, 17–18 January 2008.

In *The Roots of Terrorism*, Kanti Bajpai attempts a defence of the Indian state, calling it liberal, constitutional, democratic, reasonable, and amenable to rational persuasion (Bajpai 2002).[16] According to Bajpai, not only is the Indian state in principle capable of being checked when it uses excessive means, it has in fact demonstrated its willingness to cease hostilities and make peace with its internal enemies on numerous occasions. Moreover, when it has used force it has done so with restraint, taking precautions to protect non-combatants. 'Secessionist terrorism in the borderlands was not caused by the government's use of ethnic cleansing or genocidal violence, nor have these been used against secessionist terrorism. A government that is completely lawless, incorrigible and violent deserves to lose the right to rule. The Indian government has not been any of these things' (Bajpai 2002: 89–90). Bajpai's noble and righteous 'Indian government', alas, has one law for the Northeast (and Kashmir) and another for the rest of India. Given the violence made possible and legitimate by the maintenance of the AFSPA, the Indian state does not *need* ethnic cleansing or genocide to go about doing as it pleases in dealing with what it conveniently describes as the 'secessionism' and 'terrorism' of these 'borderlands'.

Bajpai, however, uses the rubric of secession and terror as though this was a given, and then proceeds to list the 'resentments' of the various border states (in which he also includes Punjab) to account for the secessionism and terrorism that he, along with the Indian state, finds in these troubled areas. For Bajpai, 'the politics of fear and resentment' is what explains how the people of, say, the Northeast relate to both 'distant others' and 'proximate others'—categories that encompass everyone from rival tribes, to migrant communities, to the rulers in far Delhi (Bajpai 2002: 43–4; 84–5). But this notion of resentment is part of the grammar shared by the Indian administration, the defence establishment, the armed forces, and policy analysts of various persuasions, from liberal to realist. It lines up alongside ideas of 'alienation', 'estrangement', 'grievance', 'wrath' and 'anger', all terms used by Bajpai himself to describe the fractious, implicitly juvenile Kashmiris, Sikhs, Nagas, Assamese, and others who have not attained political maturity yet, and who must eventually embrace the Indian state, if they know what's good for them.

---

[16] In Bajpai 2002 the section beginning on p. 42 is titled 'Fear and Resentment in the Borderlands'. On p. 84 this is parsed as 'fear of the heartland and resentment of ethno-religious competitors closer at hand'.

Needless to say, this is not the meaning of resentment that I have been at pains to outline here. I do not mean resentment in the sense of the emotion proper to a spoilt child, who sulks when wiser, more mature adults deny him or her whatever unreasonable demands he or she may have.[17] Resentment in the Northeast is not merely a security concern for the Indian state, if indeed it is that at all. I intend resentment as the emotion—precisely a *political* emotion—that lends such charge to Améry's words: 'What happened, happened. But *that* it happened cannot be so easily accepted. I rebel: against my past, against history, and against a present that places the incomprehensible in the cold storage of history and thus falsifies it in a revolting way' (Améry 1980: xi).

The biggest argument in favour of resentment is that resentment can be, and is, effective, where even the possibility—leave aside the effectiveness—of resistance might be dubious at best. As long as the AFSPA is in force, it remains next to impossible for the beleaguered citizens of the Northeast to resist the power of the Indian state. But resent it they can, and resent it they must. Resentment, as Améry has argued compellingly, has to be not just the historical practice, but the political duty of every survivor, so that his or her suffering at the hands of the tyrant will not have been in vain, and his or her life, that the tormentor sought to exterminate, retains the core of its inextinguishable human value, even after extreme and unforgettable pain.

---

[17] Sanjib Baruah has criticized other fixtures in security discourse, including the ideas of 'neglect' and of 'complexity' that infantilize the citizens of the Northeast and turn the whole area into a problem child for the parental Indian state, to be disciplined into submission with the carrot of development funding and the stick of the AFSPA. See, for example, Baruah 2005a.

CHAPTER 3

When was the Postcolonial?

A History of Policing Impossible Lines[1]

BODHISATTVA KAR

It is not difficult to imagine a fuming Harriet Coutts Trotter returning from a late-night ball in London and darting towards the writing desk without even caring to change her fancy dress. Discovering that Richard, her beloved brother who had been serving the Queen in India for the last thirty-two years, was dumped with a terribly 'inferior appointment' in a godforsaken corner of the empire called Assam, Harriet was certainly upset. She did not like the hint of pity with which the appointment was discussed in her social circle. Of course, poor Richard was hiding the truth from her! Surely a medal winner in the mutiny deserved a more decent place! These ungrateful government people...! Harriet promptly poured her metropolitan worries and sisterly sympathies into an affectionate letter.

When Richard—that is Lieutenant-Colonel Richard Harte Keatinge, the first chief commissioner of Assam who assumed his charge on 7 February 1874—received the letter somewhere near Sadiya after a few months, he found it 'most mysterious': 'You know a person

[1] The research for this paper was made possible by a grant from the South-South Exchange Programme for Research on the History of Development (Sephis) of the International Institute of Social History, Amsterdam. While a substantial part of the paper was presented at the Centre for Policy Research workshop on 'Rethinking Northeast India's Conflicts and the Roads to Peace' in Guwahati, some of its concerns were also tested in the Sephis workshop on 'Contested Nationalisms and New Statism' in Penang, Malaysia (September 2004). It is difficult to name everybody who did me the honour of publicly responding to the presentations. But I am particularly thankful to Sanjib Baruah, Neeladri Bhattacharya, Indrani Chatterjee, Shamil Jeppie, and Tanika Sarkar for their insightful comments on different sections of this paper.

... who was told by another ... to whom it was mentioned ... that I must have been done in a row to get here. Seriously your little bird is I believe wrong.'

'I do not think I have been put down,' Keatinge insisted. 'Assam is the most junior and in some ways least important of the four Chief Commissionerships but it is I think more important than any of the political charges.' Keatinge explained to sister Hal, 'I had told [the] Government so often that I thought their treatment of the chiefs unsatisfactory'; now that the government had asked him to spearhead the new policy of containing the troublesome tribal chiefs, he could not step back.[2] We have no means to verify whether this put Harriet at ease, but it is clear that Keatinge was not overstating his responsibilities. After all, as an official was to put it a decade later,

There is no part of our vast Indian frontier about which we have so little military or geographical information as the north-east; there is no portion of it so difficult to reinforce in case of certain emergencies arising, and there is no like extent of it bordering upon savage tribes, so sparsely garrisoned; yet, in this remote corner of our empire, there is more English capital invested in land than in any like extent of our Indian dominions (Mitchell 1883: iv).

The broken script of this little family drama around an alleged 'hardship assignment' in Northeast India—re-enacted to this day in countless IAS families (Baruah 2005a: 24)—leads us to a wider dramaturgical space: the theatre of everyday control in an unmanageable frontier.

AN IMPOSSIBLE LINE

In the standard histories of Assam, Richard Keatinge is usually described as an enthusiastic advocate of the so-called 'forward policy' (Barpujari 1992: 224–6). Determined expansion of the state space, resolute interventions in intercommunity feuds, and increased formalization of the administrative apparatus marked his four-year term. His daring proposal of opening the Naga and the Abor fronts at the same time, though not sanctioned by the supreme government, reflected his acute intention to be over and done with the border problem once and for all (Mitchell 1883: 63).

[2] Letter from Richard (Harte Keatinge) to Hal (Harriet Coutts Trotter), 'Camp near Sadiya, the top of the Assam Valley', dated 18 March (year not mentioned). European Manuscripts, Oriental and India Office Collections, British Library (henceforth OIOC), No. IOR/ Mss Eur C292/4.

The minimum prerequisite for solving a border problem is a border. Much to his chagrin, the first chief commissioner discovered that in most places this minimum prerequisite did not exist in a readily identifiable shape. 'The Naga Hills District had been constituted in 1867, but its boundaries had not been formally settled' (Robb 1997: 257). Apart from a few miles in the west, the boundaries of Lakhimpur, theoretically the largest district in British India, were 'wholly undefined and unknown'.[3] '[T]he boundaries of the Sibsagar district have never been defined.'[4] While Bivar and Williamson had just laid down the Khasi–Garo boundary in 1873, the Khasi–Kamrup boundary was not yet defined.[5] Even after the successful war in 1864, border disputes with the Deb Raja did not stop.[6] Kelso's 1849–50 demarcation between Goalpara and Kamrup was found to be faulty, and this was a source of tension with the estate of Bijni. In 1872, Beckett had defined the boundaries between Goalpara and the Garo Hills, but Goalpara's boundary with Rangpur was still left undecided.[7] To further complicate the situation, a year before Keatinge was given charge, the Inner Line Regulation was notified and now he had to fix this line of demarcation between the wider territorial possessions of the British state and its constricted jurisdictional limits.

The Inner Line was given the difficult task of providing a territorial frame to capital. It prohibited the British subjects in general from going

[3] Letter No. 6343, dated 20 November 1872, from the secretary to the Government of Bengal, in 'Lakhimpur Inner Line', Foreign Department, Political A, September 1875, Nos 269–72; National Archives of India, New Delhi (henceforth, NAI).

[4] 'Note by L.W. Reynolds, dated 10 February 1909', in 'Inclusion of certain coal bearing lands within the Sibsagar and Naga Hill Districts', Foreign Department, External-A, January 1910, Nos 6–8, NAI.

[5] Secretary to the chief commissioner of Assam to the secretary to the Government of India, Department of Revenue, Agriculture and Commerce, No. 274, Shillong, 20 July 1874, in '"Inner Line" of the Sibsagar District', Foreign Department, Revenue-A Branch, September 1874, Nos 14–21, NAI.

[6] A. Mackenzie, junior secretary to the Government of Bengal, to the secretary to the Government of India, Foreign Department, No. 1418, dated 6 April 1872, in 'Demarcation of British Frontier between Assam and Bhootan', Foreign Department, Political-A Branch, June 1872, Nos 633–4, NAI.

[7] Secretary to the chief commissioner of Assam to the secretary to the Government of India, Department of Revenue, Agriculture and Commerce, No. 274, Shillong, 20 July 1874, in '"Inner Line" of the Sibsagar District', Foreign Department, Revenue-A Branch, September 1874, Nos 14–21, NAI.

without a license and the tea planters in particular from acquiring lands beyond a demarcated line. Enforcing 'more stringent control [over] the commercial relations of our own subjects with the frontier tribes living on the borders of our jurisdiction', stopping 'the operations of speculators in caoutchouc', and restraining 'the spread of tea gardens outside our fiscal limits' were its three explicit objectives (Mackenzie 1884: 56). More deeply, it was also supposed to demarcate 'the Hills' from 'the plains', the nomadic from the sedentary, the jungle from the arable—in short, 'the tribal areas' from 'the Assam proper'. It is beyond the scope of this essay to detail how, through a continual reordering of landscapes, the play between the proper and the proprietorial came to define the scope of colonial governmentality in the area. Suffice it to say here that what lay unenclosed by the Inner Line was not only a territorial exterior of the theatre of capital—it was also a temporal outside of the historical pace of development and progress. Though encountered on the numerous plateaus of everyday life, the communities forced to stay beyond the Line were seen as belonging to a different time regime—where the time of the law did not apply; where slavery, headhunting, and nomadism could be allowed to exist. The Inner Line was expected to enact a sharp split between what were understood as the contending worlds of capital and pre-capital, of the modern and the primitive. Without such a line, 'states of fact', according to Henry Hopkinson, who was in charge of the Assam affairs immediately before Keatinge, 'are so vague, shifty, fluid, and uncertain, that any interpretation may be put upon them, and consequently any judgment either way passed on the course pursued in respect to them.' A deputy commissioner at Lakhimpur, said Hopkinson:

cannot tell what his district is, and what it is not; he cannot define his jurisdiction as to extent, nor say over whom it extends. Some of his people are fully under the laws of the country, some he is told to regard as only partially so, upon some he is to try moral suasion, while in practice it is not always easy to discriminate which class is which. He has to deal with English planters at one end of the scale, have chapter and verse for everything he does, and be driven by them, their attorneys, pleaders, and the High Court, to have regard to all the technicalities which His Honor so much abhors; and at the other end, he has Nagas for whom he has to throw overboard all law; while to make confusion worse confounded, he is called upon ... to administer at one and the same time 'law' and 'no law' to Nagas and planters in mutual conflict.[8]

[8] From the agent to the Governor General in the north-eastern frontier to the secretary to the Government of India in the Revenue Department, in

The line instituted to define the worlds of 'law' and 'no law' was however an impossible line, given the routine insistence of the British Indian state on the informalization of legal agreements in its north-eastern frontier. Captivated by the capital's self-portrait, the historians usually sidestep its large and wide paralegal career. The fascinating web of contraband rubber trade in nineteenth- and early twentieth-century Assam involving the Marwari traders in the plains, the community chiefs in the hills, and the British Indian firms in Calcutta still awaits its historian. The same network was also remarkably active in working timber and ivory beyond the revenue line (Kar 2007: Chapter 2). Exciting histories of cross-border traffic in firearms, particularly after the conclusion of the second Anglo-Burma War, has gone surprisingly unnoticed.[9] Nor do we have a comprehensive account of the numerous localized land use contracts between the European planters and the community chiefs. 'The tea planters had long since in many places, both in Luckhimpore and Seebsagor, taken up lands south of the revenue line, in some instances paying revenue to us, and in others to the Naga chiefs', Mackenzie (1884) explained the situation with some unease: 'The earlier settlers found it to their interest to conciliate the Nagas, and troubled themselves little about government protection. But now the fashion of claiming police assistance in every little difficulty came into vogue, and the government had to consider what course it should adopt' (p. 98).

Over and over again, the government criticized the planters in Assam for their 'bold assertion of legal rights'.[10] The British love for law was undeniably proportional to its fear of extravagance. If tacit understandings, informal arrangements, and verbal promises could save money and energy, the British Indian state—at least for the first fifty

---

'Mr. Minto's Claims to the Garo Hills Gardens', *Proceedings of the Hon'ble the Lieutenant-Governor of Bengal*, Political Department, April 1873, File 29, Assam State Archives (Henceforth, ASA).

[9] See the letter from Captain Hannay to Captain Vetch, dated Saikwahs, 1 February 1840, in Foreign Department, Political Branch, 16 March 1840, Pros. No. 112, NAI, for interesting references. Major C.R. Macgregor, *Military Report on the Kampti-Singpho Countries* (Calcutta: Superintendent of Government Printing, India, 1887) mentions manufacture of gunpowder by the Singphos and the Khamtis.

[10] *Proceedings of the Hon'ble the Lieutenant-Governor of Bengal*, Judicial Department, September 1871, No. 90, ASA.

years in its north-eastern frontier—was not extraordinarily interested in coalescing diverse legal geographies into one uniform whole.

And yet, as we all know, the Inner Line did happen. It happened because the government increasingly realized that because of its lack of control over the communication between the non-rent-paying populations and the speculators the government was losing out on a substantial amount of revenue and, worse still, getting entangled in several legal disputes (which, by the way, gradually became more numerous than before). The planters, on the other hand, came to acknowledge the value of violence that accompanies every introduction of law. Using the increased military strength of the state infantries seemed more attractive than raising costly private militias. Moreover, while old gardens like Mugroo and Koodoo, 'in the very heart of the Singphoo country', or Hookunjooree and Teepum, in the Naga Hills, were helplessly dependent on the labour of local communities,[11] the arrival of a workforce whose legal ability to choose alternative employment was pathetically constrained by the indenture system made the planters more confident in their power to do away with the undisciplined Naga, Singpho, or Cachari labour who could and did walk out on several previous occasions. But could capital ever function within the law that it set for itself? Its phenomenal propensity to spill over and consume the boundaries that it in the first place had helped to bring about necessarily entailed a vast paralegal structure. I want to point to two major modes through which the cursive movement of capital through various terrains of difference was energized. One is the simple expansion of the legal theatre of capital—what Hopkinson called 'the inner side of our fence, ... the fruit side of the garden wall'[12]—by extending the Inner Line. Too much attention to the rhetoric

---

[11] Statement of A.T. Campbell (assistant commissioner, Assam) 14 December 1867, in Appendix A, *Report of the Commissioners Appointed to Enquire into the State and Prospects of Tea Cultivation in Assam, Cachar, and Sylhet* (Calcutta: Calcutta Central Press Company, 1868), p. xviii. See also Assam Company, *Report of the Directors and Auditors made to the Shareholders at the General Annual Meeting, held at the London Tavern, Bishopgate Street, on the 5th May, 1843, with an Appendix* (London: Smith, Elder and Co., 1843), p. 59, and 'Report of the Superintendent [George Williamson]', 16 February 1854, in Assam Company, *Report of the Directors and Auditors for the Annual General Meeting, to be held on Friday 5th May, 1854*, pp. 23–5.

[12] From the agent to the Governor General in the north-eastern frontier and commissioner of Assam to the secretary to the Government of Bengal in the

of fixity has blinded us to the plain fact that contrary to its claim to the givenness of the distinction between the hills and the plains, the Inner Line was in fact a revisable, mobile, and pliant boundary on the ground (cf. Baruah 1999: chapter 2). Well until the second decade of the twentieth century, the Line was repeatedly redrawn in order to variously accommodate the expansive compulsions of plantation capital, the recognition of imperfection in survey maps, the security anxiety of the state, and the adaptive practices of internally differentiated local communities. If new tea or coal tracts were found or valuable forest areas were reported to exist beyond the Line, small insertions in the Government Gazette casually declared unblushing extensions of the Inner Line to include those areas.

A large number of documents are extant to point towards this fact.[13] I shall pick up only a characteristic sample to indicate how, from the

---

Political Department, No. 114, dated 17 April 1872, in 'Demarcation of British Frontier between Assam and Bhootan', Foreign Department, Political-A Branch, June 1872, Nos 633–64, NAI.

[13] Foreign Department, Political-A Branch, December 1876, Nos 148–74; Foreign Department, Political-A Branch, August 1877, Nos 120–232; Foreign Department, Political-A Branch, August 1877, Nos 133–77; Foreign Department, Political-A Branch, August 1877, Nos 310–18A; Foreign Department, Political-A Branch, September 1877, Nos 100–2; Foreign Department, Political-A Branch, November 1877, Nos 55–7; Foreign Department, Political-A Branch, December 1877, No. 109; Foreign Department, Political-A Branch, February 1878, Nos 7–78; Foreign Department, Political-A Branch, October 1878, Nos 7–51; Foreign Department, Political-A Branch, June 1881, Nos 423–33; Foreign Department, Political-E Branch, August 1884, Nos 184–7; Foreign Department, Political-E Branch, June 1884, Nos 113–17; Foreign Department, Political-E Branch, April 1884, Nos 110–12; Foreign Department, External-A Branch, October 1884, Nos 376–82; Foreign Department, External-A Branch, October 1884, Nos 252–9; Foreign Department, External-A Branch, September 1884, No. 163; Foreign Department, External-A Branch, March 1907, Nos 103–05; Foreign Department, External-A Branch, February 1901, Nos 4–5; Foreign Department, External-A Branch, May 1896, Nos 55–6; Foreign Department, External-A Branch, January 1895, Nos 79–80; Foreign Department, External-A Branch, October 1894, Nos 96–151; Foreign Department, External-A Branch, October 1894, Nos 389–94; Foreign Department, External-A Branch, October 1894, Nos 116–18; Foreign Department, External-A Branch, December 1881, Nos 127–47; Foreign Department, External-A Branch, September 1875, Nos 269–72; Foreign Department, External-A Branch, September 1908, No. 123; Foreign Department, External-A Branch, September 1908, Nos 5–16; Foreign Department, External-A Branch, December 1908, Nos 4–17; Foreign Department, External-A Branch,

very beginning, the question of resources had dominated the movement of the Line. Luttman-Johnson, Keatinge's secretary, explained to the higher authorities that the sole object of twisting the Line in south of Jaipur, to enclose 'a tract of country which has not hitherto been subject to the formal and plenary authority of the Deputy Commissioner' was to ensure 'that the three tea gardens of Namsang, Taurack, and Hukanjuri may not be excluded from ordinary jurisdiction.'[14] In the same breath, he also explained that 'all the best coal-bearing tracts [in Lakhimpur] remain outside the proposed "Inner Line"' because '[t]here is no immediate prospect of coal being worked in this locality'.

The extent of the coal tracts is very indefinite as yet, and, even if we knew how far they extended, no well marked line is to be found beyond them. When we want to work them, we can do so under a system of passes, or we can extend the 'Inner Line' so as to include them.[15]

Divisions could be altered and borders could be redrawn if the movement of capital required such displacements. Apart from this principle of resource-sensitive flexibility, the widespread confusion among the frontier officials regarding the function and extent of the Line further complicated the issue. Some interpreted the Inner Line as revenue survey limits, and some others held that it should coincide with the extent of direct control. The confusion arose chiefly from the fact that in the Lower Assam districts, these different stripes did not

---

January 1909, Nos 30–9; Foreign Department, External-A Branch, May 1913, Nos 32–5; Foreign Department, External-A Branch, September 1915, No. 27 (all in NAI).

[14] Similarly, the Lakhimpur Inner Line, which generally followed the course of the Rajghur Alli from the eastern boundary of Darrang to the Subansiri river was made to 'deviate from the Rajghur Alli, so as to follow the western, northern, and eastern boundaries of the Harmati No. 95 and Joyhing No. 65 waste land grants.' Notification by Government of India, Foreign Department, No. 2427 P, Simla, 3 September 1875, in 'Lakhimpur Inner Line', Foreign Department, Political A, September 1875, Nos 269–72, NAI. Again, the proposed Inner Line in Cachar had to accommodate the tea grants of Barooncherra, Bara Jalinga, and Monierkhall. Notification by Government of India, Foreign Department, No. 2299 P, Simla, 20 August 1875, in 'Cachar "Inner Line"', Foreign Department, Political A, August 1875, Nos 393–4, NAI.

[15] H. Luttman-Johnson, secretary to the chief commissioner of Assam to C.U. Aitchinson, secretary to the Government of India, Foreign Department, No. 2600, Shillong, 27 July 1875, in 'Lakhimpur Inner Line', Foreign Department, Political A, September 1875, Nos 269–72, NAI.

widely differ. The hill and plain principle—'taking the best natural line'—worked well in settling the northern boundary of Kamrup and Darrang, and the viceroy, Northbrook, wished this to be the general principle for laying down the Inner Line throughout Assam.[16] Things were very different in the Upper Assam districts of Sibsagar and Lakhimpur, about which—as Keatinge said with a chuckle—the viceroy's informants did not have much idea.[17] Although tea grants were far more numerous in these districts than in any of their three Lower Assam counterparts,[18] the large areas of 'impenetrable' jungle and the emphatic presence of the 'uncontrolled' communities effectively minimized the scope of the revenue surveys. The 'limits of regular cultivation' and the extent of the surveys did not match in many places. The 'line of police outposts' often represented a third line, and with the additional institution of the Inner Line, the legal landscape became as confusing as the ethnic scene.[19] An exasperated Keatinge

[16] Vide Letters of the Secretary to the Government of India, Foreign Department, to the secretary to the chief commissioner of Assam, No. 1661, 24 July 1873 and No. 2487 P, 17 October 1873.

[17] 'The Chief Commissioner can hardly suppose that the difficulty of exercising ordinary civil jurisdiction in a tract of country, into which the Court's officer could only enter axe in hand, by cutting his own path, can have been laid before His Excellency the Viceroy', secretary to the chief commissioner of Assam to the secretary to the Government of India, Foreign Department, No. 142, Shillong, 20 May 1874, in '"Inner Line" of the Sibsagar District', Foreign Department, Revenue-A Branch, September 1874, Nos 14–21, NAI.

[18] According to an estimate made in 1863, the Sibsagar district alone contained 143 tea gardens whereas the combined total of Kamrup, Darrang, and Nagaon was 131. Lakhimpur had 57 tea gardens. Calculated from the list attached to the *Map of the Tea Districts of Assam* (Compiled in the Office of Colonel Henry Hopkinson, Commissioner & Governor General's Agent, North Eastern Frontier, Scale 4 Miles = 1 Inch, 1863)

[19] 'The degrees by which the [Lakhimpur] Deputy Commissioner's authority decreases eastwards are not strongly marked. Up to the limits within which he collects land revenue, whether he collects it by the head, or by the house, or by the plough, or by the acre, he wields plenary authority, though even some tracts within these limits are still vaguely denominated "Agency country". Beyond these limits his authority extends is distinctly political only, but is exercised with more or less strictness, as circumstances may require, at least as far east as the Brahmakund. Speaking generally, the Chief Commissioner holds that what is now considered to be the boundary up to which the Deputy Commissioner's plenary authority extends fulfills the conditions for the Inner Line, as laid down by the Government of India. The attachment of new legal incidents to a line

admitted during the course of demarcation 'that former orders are being construed locally, and after filtration through other authorities, in a manner never intended by His Excellency the Viceroy'.[20]

The Foreign Department of the Government of India, however, thought that the chief commissioner himself was mistaken about the nature of the jurisdictional limit:

[A]lthough all the country on the British side of the frontier is to be under British jurisdiction, it is not necessary nor is it intended that the plenary jurisdiction of our ordinary Civil Courts should be exercised up to that line. It may or may not according to circumstances. Colonel Keatinge has to some extent lost sight of this, and he seems to think that in all cases our ordinary plenary jurisdiction through the usual machinery of our Courts of Law is to have full play up to the boundary line.

The Line was the limit up to which, explained Aitchinson, the state would nominally accept responsibility for the protection of life and property, but even within that line it might have a 'more rigid administration for parts that are suited to it and a less rigid administration for parts that require more delicate handling'.[21] Consequently, the Inner Line was only an incomplete promise of uniform jurisdiction for the territories inside. The personal discretions of the chief commissioner and his deputies—what Aitchinson called 'the local knowledge of the provincial officers'—could and did have substantial sway over the inhabitants of this non-regulation province.

The early subordinate frontier officials on whom the supreme government depended for the local details by and large shared a general

---

which has always been looked upon as a sort of boundary is received by the people of its neighbourhood without much surprise, and they soon accustom themselves to them. The definition of an altogether new line is long in becoming familiar to their minds, and the process may be accompanied by much heart-burning.' H. Luttman-Johnson, secretary to the chief commissioner of Assam to C.U. Aitchinson, secretary to the Government of India, Foreign Department, No. 2600, Shillong, 27 July 1875, in 'Lakhimpur Inner Line', Foreign Department, Political A, September 1875, Nos 269–72, NAI.

[20] Secretary to the chief commissioner of Assam to the secretary to the Government of India, Foreign Department, No. 142, Shillong, 20 May 1874, in '"Inner Line" of the Sibsagar District', Foreign Department, Revenue-A Branch, September 1874, Nos 14–21, NAI.

[21] Note by C.U. Aitchinson, secretary to the Government of India, Foreign Department, 31 July 1874, in '"Inner Line" of the Sibsagar District', Foreign Department, Revenue-A Branch, September 1874, Nos 14–21, NAI.

distrust of the Inner Line scheme. Many demanded, in vain, an absolute annulment of the regulation on the ground that 'the tribes ... cannot grasp the difference between a jurisdictional and a territorial line of frontier'.[22] If the British government declined to exercise its rights beyond the Inner Line, these officials argued, the communities there would be encouraged to understand themselves as independent. In fact, in 1882, the chief commissioner also acknowledged the force of 'this inevitable tendency' to mix up the two lines:

[O]wing to the incidents of the Inner Line Regulation, which prevents settlers from taking up lands beyond the line, and which limits, though it need not necessarily stifle, the intercourse of our District Officers with the tribes beyond, there is an obvious tendency for such a line in the course of time to be deemed a territorial boundary, beyond which neither party can exercise rights of use or possession without being thought guilty of aggression by the other.[23]

This unusually strong fear of mistranslation—that the 'reluctance of the British authorities to enforce their rights' might be 'construed as weakness'[24]—constantly accompanied the sporadic expansion of the Inner Line, instigating different and contradictory reactions at all levels of the government. While the majority of the top officials maintained that the Line 'is a jurisdictional and not a territorial boundary',[25] some

[22] Mitchell (1883: 9). Colonel A.E. Campbell, the deputy commissioner of Sibsagar, continued to argue for a long time 'that the line acts as a barrier to the taking up of good land for tea cultivation, that it leaves valuable forests to be destroyed by the Nagas, and that it restricts free intercourse with the tribes, which he considers it right to promote'. C.J. Lyall, officiating secretary to the chief commissioner of Assam, to C. Grant, the officiating secretary to the Government of India, Foreign Department, No. 147, 26 January 1882, in 'Sibsagar District "Inner Line"', Foreign Department, Political A, March 1882, Nos 36–46, NAI.

[23] C.J. Lyall, officiating secretary to the chief commissioner of Assam, to C. Grant, the officiating secretary to the Government of India, Foreign Department, No. 147, 26 January 1882, in 'Sibsagar District "Inner Line"', Foreign Department, Political A, March 1882, Nos 36–46, NAI.

[24] J.E. Webster, secretary to the Government of Eastern Bengal and Assam, to the secretary to the Government of India, Foreign Department, No. 3923 J, 9 September 1907, in 'Policy to be pursued in dealing with the Abors and other tribes inhabiting the hills to the north of the Dibrugarh Frontier Tract', Foreign Department, External-A, June 1908, Nos 33–8, NAI.

[25] Note by C.U. Aitchinson, secretary to the Government of India, Foreign Department, in 'Demarcation of the Duffla Frontier', Foreign Department, Political A, April 1874, Nos 268–9, NAI.

of them also argued that this 'purely artificial' line 'is not concerned with the administrative arrangements'.[26] Underlying the confusing contradictions was however a theoretical consensus about the Line's unconditional extensibility, deferred only by the Government of India's decision to minimize administrative expenditure. Substantial extensions of the Inner Line were made in 1882 in Sibsagar; in 1904 and 1906 in the Naga Hills; and in 1884, 1886, 1897, and 1904 in Lakhimpur.[27] Understandably, such extensions frequently cut across and destabilized local networks of circulation, protection, and settlement[28] which the state unvaryingly understood as a necessary precondition of development. The Inner Line, as we have already noted, was not only a line in territory; it was also a line in time. The advance of the Line on map was read as the progress from pre-capital to capital, from the time of 'no law' to the time of 'law'.

However, to borrow a phrase from Mbembe, the comings and goings between two temporalities hardly represented an anomaly for either party (Mbembe 2001: 71). Even after the delineation of the Line, critical and inconstant entanglements between the 'capitalists'

[26] Note by J.M. Macpherson, dated 23 December 1908, in 'Inclusion of certain coal bearing lands within the Sibsagar and Naga Hill Districts', Foreign Department, External-A, January 1910, Nos 6–8, NAI. Macpherson further exclaimed, 'The idea of a district of which a part remains practically unadministered and outside the jurisdiction of the Courts is, so far as my knowledge goes, a novel one, and I do not understand on what principle it is based, as the main object of forming districts is, as I have always understood, to provide for the administration of the territory included in them. . . . Nor can I understand how there can be a district of which one boundary is left undefined, which is the position of this district [Lakhimpur] if its territorial boundary does not coincide with the line which has been adopted as its administrative boundary.'

[27] Foreign Department, Political-A Branch, March 1882, Nos 36–46; Letter No. 291-E.B., dated 26 January 1904. No. 131 in Foreign Department, External-A Branch, March 1904, Nos 130–1; Notification No. 4767-P, dated 31 October 1904. Enclo. 3, No. 39, in Foreign Department, External-A Branch, October 1905, Nos 37–40; Notification No. 12151, dated 13 November 1906. Enclo. 90, No. 39, in Foreign Department, External-A Branch, November 1906, Nos 90–1 (all in NAI).

[28] A typical and touching example is available in L.J. Kershaw, officiating secretary to the chief commissioner of Assam to the secretary to the Government of India in the Foreign Department, No. 1601-J, 11 April 1905, in 'Modification of the eastern boundary of the Naga Hills District so as to include the small village of Mangaki', Foreign Department, External-A Branch, October 1905, Nos 37–40, NAI.

and the 'primitives' continued with dynamism, causing insurgence and retribution at some moments and maintaining off-the-record payments at others—the higher government officials being fully aware and even supportive of such unofficial settlements. A well-documented case is that of the early twentieth-century friction between the Dobangs, the Tadungs, and the Pasi-Minyongs of the trans-Lakhimpur region on the one hand and the Sissi Saw Mills and Trading Company and the Meckla Nuddee Saw Mills Company on the other.

The Dobangs, Tadungs, and Pasi-Minyongs—ethnic categories which emerged out of the older and increasingly obsolete category of Abors by the end of the nineteenth century—claimed their rights over different segments of the forest beyond the Inner Line in Lakhimpur. In the early years of their operations in the area, soon after exhausting the simul timber near the Mekhla and the Sissi rivers, the managers of the European saw mills used to employ local contractors who 'employed Miris to fell trees and used to send elephants to drag the logs, often sending mahuts and servants across the Inner Line without passes'. The Miris had to make a payment (alternatively referred to as 'royalty' and 'blackmail' in the British documents) to the said Abor chiefs for working the forests beyond the Inner Line.[29] In fact, while paying a lip service to the standing proprietorial claim of the British state over these forests,[30] Lieutenant-Governor Bampfylde Fuller actually said, in 1904, that 'as matters stood, there was no reason why managers of saw mills

[29] If the report of Needham, the assistant political officer at Sadiya, is to be believed, this arrangement certainly created some tension between the different 'Abor' settlements too: 'I have recently received the report that Minyongs of Yemsing are at loggerheads with four gams of Ledum, because the [latter] took money from one of the Laimekuri saw-mill contractors for permission to cut timber outside the Inner Line. The Yemsing Minyongs assert that they alone are entitled to collect such fees.' Quoted in *Notes on the North-East Frontier of Assam, in continuation of Captain St. John Michell's Report (Topographical, Political and Military) on the North East Frontier of India* (Shillong: Eastern Bengal and Assam Secretariat Printing Office, 1907), p. 35.

[30] At the turn of the century, forests were emphatically inscribed in the code of the new property regime. As Baden-Powell succinctly put it, a forest ought to be seen as 'a *piece of property*—no matter to whom it may belong.' 'People *will* think,' said Baden-Powell, 'that because trees, grass, and fruits of the wild trees are the produce of nature, therefore it is no theft to take them. It is not felt that gold and gems are just as much the produce of nature, and that the art and skill exercised in polishing and preparing them are not distinct in kind from the care and labour that are extended on tending a forest' (1892: 1–2).

should not pay the hill tribes some commission or royalty on timber extracted from this area if they found it convenient to do so'. Exactly like the tea planters who occupied grants beyond the Inner Line, the saw mill managers were also informed by the deputy commissioner 'that Government does not expect to be troubled with the settlement of disputes which may arise from their dealings with the hillmen'.

As 'the big firms', facing stiff competition from the Norwegian and Japanese box-makers, began 'to work the timber business more directly through their own servants, and [were] tempted owing to want of timber elsewhere to extend their operations near the hills', they placed themselves in direct communication with the Abors, 'to whom they have been compelled to pay blackmail to secure their employés from molestation'. The managers complained to Lancelot Hare, the new lieutenant-governor, that '[t]hese exactions have as a matter of fact increased and must go on increasing. The tribes in question have no central Government, consequently each village who come to know of a timber camp anywhere in their vicinity claims to be paid, and there is no finality to the toll we have to pay'.[31]

It was not only absurd but also illegal, said the managers' memorial, because if the forest beyond the Inner Line was the property of the government, in principle no royalty could be paid to the Dobangs, Tadungs, and Pasi-Minyongs. The government should therefore push forth the police posts and assume direct control of the territory in question. Hare, who was entirely in agreement with the subordinate frontier officials and the mill managers that it was absolutely 'inconsistent with the dignity and responsibilities of the Government that it should permit savages to extort money from British subjects in British territory', admitted that with a little force applied, the Abors would be 'more inclined to shift the responsibility on to another village than to stand upon their rights'. And yet, he conceded in the same breath, 'it is not improbable that some extortion from the Miris will go *sub rosa*'. There is no evidence to suggest that Hare's apprehensions were wrong.[32]

[31] 'Memorial from the Sissi Saw Mills and Trading Company Limited, and the Meckla Nuddee Saw Mills Company, Limited [to the Lieutenant-Governor of Eastern Bengal and Assam]', in 'Policy to be pursued in dealing with the Abors and other tribes inhabiting the hills to the north of the Dibrugarh Frontier Tract', Foreign Department, External-A Branch, June 1908, Nos 33–8, NAI.

[32] J.E. Webster, secretary to the Government of Eastern Bengal and Assam, to the secretary to the Government of India, Foreign Department, No. 3923 J, 9

It is this trace of the illegal operative within the very structure of law that we shall follow in the subsequent pages. Troubling the conventional image of the pristine pre-capitalist primitives, we would pause to ponder whether the worlds of 'law' and 'no law' were not in effect two functional sectors of the same economy of extraction and enframing; whether the time of capital had not always been carrying the time of pre-capital *within* itself. Entrusted to straddle the centre line, the state invested much in the reconfiguration of an older institution—the institution of *posa*, the second major mode of escalating capital's movement in the demarcated sector of pre-capital.

PEACE AND ITS BLACKMAILING

A textbook definition of posa would be an annual payment that the British kept making throughout their regime to a number of the 'neighbouring Hill tribes' in continuation of an Ahom custom. Frequently translated as 'blackmail' in imperialist and nationalist histories alike, posa is usually seen as an instance of colonial concession to primitive savagery which in any way was a peripheral and negligible fact of frontier history.[33] Let it be quickly clarified here that this, like much of what we read in the textbooks, is an awfully oversimplified and even misleading rendition of a very complex and critical strategy of the British Indian state in its north-eastern frontier. Far from being a dying trait of a meaningless medieval practice, posa in the nineteenth and twentieth centuries was a dynamic register of shifting relationships between the contending elements of an unofficial biography of capital. Seizing on the traces of the customary rights of some of the non-state space communities recognized by the Tungkhungia kings, the colonial state over the years built an intriguing network of control and constraint beyond its formal jurisdictional limits.

Nothing less than a whole book will draw out the entire gamut of complexities of the posa question. I shall not even attempt a comprehensive account here. But to summarize the main points, what went by the name of posa in the nineteenth and twentieth centuries was in fact a strategic confusion of several discrete practices. Regrouped,

---

September 1907, in 'Policy to be pursued in dealing with ...', Foreign Dept., Ext-A Branch, June 1908, Nos 33–8, NAI.

[33] In the multi-volume *Comprehensive History of Assam*, edited by H.K. Barpujari (Guwahati: Publication Board, Assam, 1992), 'posa' does not find an entry in the index.

restructured, and partly invented by the British, this cluster of practices had at least three distinct tracks of exchange interlaced. The first track was closely related to the massive British reconstruction of 'the Khelwarree System'[34] during the initial years of their rule. David Scott and his subordinate officials (particularly Major White in Upper Assam and Captain Bogle in Lower Assam) inaugurated a vigorous territorialization of *khels* along with the commutation of their services into money payments.[35] The existing land settlements were reorganized in order to press the far-flung strips together into a consolidated and continuous territorial unit. Communities which were imagined to be together only in the tabular space of revenue records were now relocated as compacted groups in the occupied space of the political territory.[36] The *bohotia* khels in the north Lakhimpur area—khels made over by the Ahom kings to certain Dafla and Miri chiefs near the Gohain Kamla Ali in recognition of their local suzerainty—used to pay a very substantial part, if not the whole, of the state share in their services and produces to the Dafla and Miri chiefs. In fact, even at the height of the third and final wave of the Moamaria uprising, the Ahom king Gaurinath Sing reserved two-thirds of the bohotia revenue for the local suzerains.[37]

It is no wonder that the British chose to understand this payment of revenue as an extortion of 'blackmail' by the 'hill tribes', given their preprogrammed and over-ethnicized understanding of the indivisible sovereignty of the Ahom state, to which they saw themselves as the sole rightful successors. Particularly since the last decades of the eighteenth century, the Tungkhungia regime was increasingly forced

[34] This odd term occurs in Mills (1984: 3).

[35] Commonly understood today as 'localized kin-groups' which 'were severally or jointly in control of adjacent fields, pastures and jungles', the term 'khel' has come to suggest a degree of contiguity, compactness, and consistency which is remarkably missing in the documents of early British encounters with the phenomenon. Historians usually declare that the entire *paik* population of the Ahom state space was divided into several *mel*s or *dagi*s, each of which consisted of some 1,000 to 6,000 paiks and was subdivided into a number of khels. A khel in turn comprised of numerous *got*s, or units of three or four paiks. See Guha (1991: 45–7) for a standard definition. However, early British reports suggest radically different pictures.

[36] For a detailed discussion of this issue, see Kar (2007).

[37] Letter from Captain E.T. Dalton, the officiating political agent, Upper Assam, to the agent to the Governor General, north-eastern Frontier, No. 162, dated 19 March 1852, Foreign Department, NAI.

to enter into a series of negotiations with new powerholders, without necessarily vacating its legitmatory status.[38] Unexposed to the logics of the expansion of state space in the Brahmaputra Valley, which could occur only by encouraging different elites of discrete groups to participate in the polity we are now taught to identify as Ahom,[39] the British were probably thinking in terms of their long experience with the 'freebooters' in the Scotland borders.[40]

The persistent British portrayal of the collection of the bohotia revenue, commonly called posa, or one-fifth, as an unfair and even unlawful exaction by the terrorizing tribes from the honest, poor, and ever-frightened 'ryots' of the plains clearly exposes the anthropological binds of political economy. Communities that habitually moved in and out-of-state spaces in the area, who were not 'agriculturalists' and therefore surely were 'idlers',[41] whose military expertise was no longer needed by the new British state in the region,[42] stayed away from the sacrosanct sphere of 'revenue'. Seen through the new thicket of law, all

[38] For a detailed discussion, see Kar (2007: Chapter 1).

[39] For a helpful, if overzealous, discussion of the dynamics of ethnicization of the term Ahom, see Saikia (1999). A modified version of this argument has also appeared in Saikia (2004).

[40] Historians of legal developments in Britain point out that much before the 1843 Libel Act or the 1861 Larceny Act, which are usually taken as the early reference points of the blackmail issue, the British statutes of 1567, 1587, 1601, 1722, and 1754 relate a different set of conditions of 'blackmail'. As Winder (1941: 24) said, 'Blackmail was originally the tribute exacted by free-booters in the northern border countries to secure lands and goods from despoilment or robbery. In the Elizabethan Statute which deals with the exactions in the northern countries, "commonly there called by the name of blackmail", it is worthy of note that the person who gave "money, corn, cattle, or other consideration, called blackmail" is guilty of felony equally with the robber or despoiler: the policy was to suppress blackmail by punishing the victim for being so timid as to submit to it instead of seeking the protection of the law.' James Lindgren (1984: 675 fn) also mentions that blackmail 'referred to mail, that is, tribute or rents, exacted in crops, work, goods, or a metal baser than silver (such as copper). This distinguished blackmail or black rents from white rents, which were tribute or rents exacted in silver.'

[41] For details, see Kar (2007: Chapter 2).

[42] By 1845, both Hannay's cherished *Doaneah Militia* and the much-valued *Upper Assam Sebundy* had to be disbanded as most of the hill community recruits had withdrawn from the corps. See L.W. Shakespear's, *History of the Assam Rifles* (1929).

such claims were bound to be translated as acts of unsanctioned violence and encroachment; as 'blackmails' or as disruptions of peace.

The word blackmail is of crucial interest to our present discussion, not only because of the several semantic reversals that it contains, but also because it quite candidly brings the question of market back into the discussion of peace: a not-so-legal and not-so-moral market, where the state *buys* peace from the peace breakers. The second and third tracks of posa are distinctly related to this point. When, in 1862, the British were determined to enforce their permanent military occupation of the Meyong Hills, the communities classed as Abors were offered 'small stipends' to enable the chiefs 'to keep up among their own people a police for the express purpose of preventing marauding attacks on villages within British territory'.[43] While explicitly recognizing the complete absence of a pre-colonial tradition in this case, the British still chose to christen this practice posa and earmarked an annual sum of Rs 3,312 for this purpose, almost Rs 150 more than what was allowed for the Daflas and Miris of north Lakhimpur. Similarly, the rights of the Bhutia duars were bought off under the name of posa. The agent to the Governor General in the north-eastern frontier told the deputy commissioner of Lakhimpur, 'the money will indeed be well spent if we can purchase security to the inoffensive people of the plains'.[44] Probably it is not coincidental that such foregrounding of peace as a purchasable condition—a condition both internal to and causative of market relations—ostensibly took place in the annual *haat*s or fairs that the British took special care to establish to encourage trading habits among the 'savages'.[45]

[43] The full text of the agreement can be found as No. XCIII: 'Agreement entered into by the Meyong Abors on 5th November 1862' in Aitchinson (1909: 245–9).

[44] Quoted in '"Posa", or "blackmail", payable to certain hill tribes on the Assam Frontier': From the chief commissioner of Assam, No. 1792, 11 May 1876, in '"Posa" payable to certain Hill Tribes on the North Eastern Frontier', Foreign Department, Political B, July 1877, Nos 83–6, NAI.

[45] Although negligible in terms of the value of total transactions, the annual fairs at Udalgiri, Kerkaria (later Khagrapara), Daimara, Subankhata, Darranga, and most importantly Sadiya were zealously supervised and meticulously reported upon by the British officials from the 1870s. Primarily calculated to bring the sector of 'pre-capital' into a structured conversation with the sector of 'capital', these fairs also functioned as the site where the annual posas of the authorized communities were delivered by the district authorities. The annual (triennial since

It should be clear by now that the British reconstruction of posa implied several important innovations. If quick labels have any power to convey the sense of a host of complexities, I would suggest monetization, regularization, hierarchization, and authenticization as the four major ways in which the British state rearranged the customary practices. The commutation of services and products into cash payments has already been referred to. By progressively converting the claims from kind to cash the British were able to make the transborder communities vulnerable to the forces of inflation and market. The monetary value of the bohotia revenue claims was actually calculated in the mid-1840s, by a certain Brijonath Bhandari Barua, the sadar amin of Lakhimpur, at the insistence of Hamilton Vetch, the district collector.[46] With a little alteration, this determination of the posa sums remained virtually the same for almost the next hundred years. This caused acute hardship to a large number of villages as often the splintering of large settlements owing to population growth entailed a division of the total amount set aside for a community.[47] From the very beginning, corruption of the establishment clerks adversely affected the communities, and absence for one year could lead to a permanent disqualification.[48] Moreover, by the time the World War I started, the inflation made the amount ridiculously inadequate. But as a chief commissioner said in the 1880s, 'In dealing with savage tribes finality is of greatest importance; an unequal distribution definitively settled is better than a more equal distribution which creates a feeling of unsettlement.'[49]

1886–7) *Reports on the Trade between Assam and the Adjoining Foreign Countries* are singularly helpful in this regard.

[46] Letter From the collector of Luckimpore to the agent to the Governor General in the north-eastern Frontier, dated 24 October 1849, Dibrugarh, in Foreign Department (F.C.), 18 January 1850, Nos 73–6, NAI.

[47] For an interesting case, see 'Report on the Abor Villages beyond the British Frontier', *Proceedings of the Chief Commissioner of Assam*, Foreign Department, January 1885, ASA.

[48] 'The Abors of Mankong and Rukang failing to claim their *posa* in 1864, their names were struck out of the list, and their *posa* ceased from that date.' Extract from the Proceedings of the chief commissioner of Assam in the Judicial Department, No. 718, dated 4 May 1885, in '"Posa" payment to the Hill Tribes of the Lakhimpur District', Foreign Department, External B, June 1886, Nos 96–100, NAI.

[49] 'Report on the Abor Villages beyond the British Frontier', *Proceedings of the Chief Commissioner of Assam*, Foreign Department, January 1885, ASA.

The great faith in regularization meant irreversibly fixing both the money amount and the time and place of delivery (it could be collected only from the government officials at particular haats in specified times). Lieutenant Bigge, principal assistant commissioner of Darrang, categorically told the seven rajahs that no 'wandering through the country' would be permitted, and the posa was only to be had from the Collector at Jeypore.[50] That the reconstruction of posa was designed to control and monitor the mobility of targeted communities inside Assam proper is understandable.[51] Nor is it beyond our guess how the static hierarchized pattern of distribution of posa was reflective more of the power relation between the British and particular communities since the mid-nineteenth century than of any ancient Ahom tradition, which had been more revisable and contingent on the shifting power balance between the Ahom kings and their neighbours. The invention of the posa-rolls, and the introduction of signing and fingerprinting receipts during the annual occasions of payment would make another predictable though extremely interesting story. But let us now pause here and ask what made the British state invest so much in posa.

An acute sense of embarrassment runs through the vast colonial archive on posa. Usually defended as a necessary mechanism for procuring 'peace', posa was often criticized as an obstacle to 'improvement'. A number of officials repeatedly argued that nothing corrupted the 'idle, happy-go-lucky people' more than easy money.

They live in a hand-to-mouth fashion and do as little work as they can; the men spend most of their time hunting and fishing; this they vary by making blackmailing excursions to the Mönba villages, then they swagger about as if the country belonged to them, demanding and obtaining from the villagers whatever they fancy. They make the inhabitants of Konia, Büt, and Thembong come over the Bichom Valley and cultivate their fields for them. If these blackmailing raids were put a stop to the Miji would have to exert himself, and might in time become a useful self-supporting person. His country is a

[50] Lt. H.L. Bigge, principal assistant commissioner, Durrung, to F. Jenkins, agent to the Governor General, Jeypore, 27 June 1843, in Foreign Department (F.C. Branch), 12 August 1843, 108, NAI.

[51] '[T]hey would confine themselves to the marketplaces and not deal with the ryots at their private dwellings'. "Posa", or "blackmail", payable to certain hill tribes on the Assam Frontier': From the chief commissioner of Assam, No. 1792, 11 May 1876, in '"Posa" payable to certain Hill Tribes on the North Eastern Frontier', Foreign Department, Political B, July 1877, Nos 83–6, NAI.

rich one, there are quantities of land available and could support a much larger population than there is at present (Nevill 1914: 4).

Complaints about how the communities routinely misread the British compliance with the posa demand as a sign of the state's weakness were recurrent. Many argued that this annual payment actually held back the 'primitives' from becoming full-blooded 'labourers'. The fact that the Mishmis, who were not posa receivers, started to work on the roads, or sought employment in cutting canes and clearing jungles in large numbers since 1890 led many frontier officials to argue that discontinuing posa would teach the Abors and the Daflas to appreciate the superior value of labour and thus enhance development.[52] Posa, like the Inner Line, was a performance of difference between the two imagined worlds—of labour and indolence, of capital and pre-capital. And yet, I would repeat, staging this difference was necessary for and even integral to positing the 'forward march of capital'. The planters' huge pressure on the government to secure peace on the frontier by paying the 'blackmail money' to the hill communities suggested the fascinatingly irresolvable paradox that has seemingly stayed with us till today: what holds development back is important for keeping peace and without peace development cannot begin.

What is this excess, I would like to ask through the instances of posa and the Inner Line, which is always excluded as an irrational outside, as an incommensurable temporality, from the structured domains of economy and law but which is always at work within the very hearts of the systems (cf. Mitchell 2002: 291–2)? Contrary to the dreams and declarations of the do-gooder state, paralegal networks and informal agreements can hardly be wished away as deviations or corruptions of the otherwise fine blueprints. Rather their haunting of the law and the economy is constitutive of these very entities, and the more we try to exorcise these conditions, the more we end up exercising their very warranty and certification. Law requires 'no law'; capital requires 'pre-capital'; development requires 'underdevelopment'—not only for defining their own sense of identity, but also for their everyday operations and occupations.

Posa was indeed a form of blackmail: the posa-receiving communities were made responsible for their own acts as also of the communities

---

[52] *Annual Report upon Native States and Frontier Tribes of Assam*, Shillong; printed at the Assam Secretariat Printing Office, 1891.

staying on farther lands. It was the singular mechanism through which the population outside the limits of the British law could be held by the state in ransom.[53] Along with the temporary blockading of the communities from trading with the valley, withholding the posa payments of the 'offenders' was the most important measure to bring them under submission.[54] The sum of Rs 17,339—the total annual posa allowance sanctioned by the Government of India—was not misspent. Contrary to Captain Mitchell's fears, in the least garrisoned frontier of the empire, the largest investment of British capital remained more or less safe and secure. Law and order requires paralegal networks.

WAS ANYBODY EVER AFRAID OF LOOKING EAST?

Let me conclude by briefly defending the title of this essay. By now, the readers have every reason to be sceptical of its validity. Posa does not exist any more and the Inner Line is bereft of its crucial dynamism. Is not that enough proof that we have finally exited the moment of the colonial? I fear not. Had the point of this paper been simply to indicate the brazen continuity in the state policy of letting loose trigger-happy peacekeepers in the frontier, a straight comparison between the Abor Expedition of 1911 and the Operation Bajrang of 1990 would have sufficed. But let there be spaces in our histories where we can move beyond such little empiricities and crass formalisms, and hold a little longer in the face of the temptations of the obvious. This essay is designed to discuss concerns which, I would claim, are hardly outdated. How is peace tied to the fate of being imaginable only within the grids of capital and development? This question is hardly exhausted. It is scarcely our case that the present-day 'problems' of Assam are merely a continuation of their nineteenth- or early twentieth-century

[53] See the letter from secretary to the chief commissioner of Assam to the deputy commissioner of Lakhimpur, No. 81-For./723P, 27 February 1896, in 'Attitude of the Bor Abors, and proposals to raise the blockade against the Passi Meyongs and Chulikata Mishmis', Foreign Department, External-A, May 1896, No. 65.

[54] See 'Report by Sub-Divisional Officer of Mangaldai of Tibetans having gone from the Khampa country to recruit the Tibetan army in Sikkim. Proposal to stop payment of "posa" to Towang Bhutias in consequence rejected', Foreign Department, External A, February 1889, Nos 75–8, NAI; letter from the comptroller, Assam, to the secretary to the chief commissioner of Assam, No. 3489, Shillong, March 1886, in 'Posa payment to the Hill Tribes of the Lakhimpur District', Foreign Department, External B, June 1886, Nos 96–100, NAI.

antecedents. But it will be too costly to overlook the continuity of the *problematics*. Indeed, in these days of the vigorous lobbying for the Look East policy, it is important, nay, imperative for us to open the founding terms of the current discussion to a critical reinterrogation.

Nobody but the commissioned-to-be-ignorant believes today that the Indian nation-space is an eternal and organic verity. Much has been written to pull apart such spatial metaphysics of nations.[55] However, contrary to another common assumption, nothing additional is to be gained by prioritizing the 'region' over the 'nation'. It will be naïve to think that the regions are somewhat more durable, more historical, and more authentic than the nations, precisely because the seemingly more homogenous space of the region is also an effect, and not the natural theatre, of the same historical practices through which the tempting forms of national internality and territorial coherence are generated, understood, and performed. While I am far from arguing that capital is the sole motor of 'the spatial forms and fantasies through which a culture declares its presence' (Carter 1987: xxii), I do claim that the lost histories of fabrication of regions are partly recoverable within the found narratives of uneven development.[56] A straightforward David Harvey says,

[T]he territorial and regional coherence that is at least partially discernible within capitalism is actively produced rather than passively received as a concession to 'nature' or 'history'. The coherence, such as it is, arises out of the conversion of spatial restraints to accumulation. Surplus value must be produced

[55] For three different approaches, see Carter (1987); Winichakul (1998); Goswami (2004).

[56] I use 'fabrication' in the wake of Timothy Mitchell. Mitchell calls the economy a fabrication, 'but that term should not be misunderstood. It does not mean that the economy is merely a work of imagination, or that the problem with the economy is that it is not real. Such criticisms slide back into the language of real versus imaginary, original versus copy, an object world versus its representation. These distinctions are complicit in the project of making the economy and cannot be used to understand it.... [T]he politics of the late-nineteenth and twentieth centuries attempted to organize a world whose complexities were resolved into the simple dualities of real and representation, objects and ideas, nature and techno-science, land and the abstraction of law, the country and the map. The social sciences emerged in the same period to confirm and reproduce this binary world. The role of economics was to produce the economy, not as a work of imagination but as a practical project. The economy is an artifactual body—a fabrication, yes, but as solid as other fabricated objects, and as incomplete.' See T. Mitchell (2002: 301).

and realized within a certain time span. If time is needed to overcome space, surplus value must also be produced and realized within a certain geographical domain (Harvey 1999: 416).

As the brief history of the Inner Line shows, the legal theatre of capital is not fixed beyond capital's expansive potentials. Revisability of legal jurisdictions, rewritability of political borders, and reducibility of the sovereign outside have always provided the theoretical groundwork for capital's movement. They still do. The recent academic attention to the 'unbundling of territorial sovereignty' in the regime of hyper-mobile financial capital has by and large underplayed the elements of continuity from the earlier and less mobile regimes of capital (cf. Hudson 2000; Ruggie 1993; Sassen 1996: 28–31, *passim*). Indeed, too much has been said about the immobilizing aspects of colonialism, its maps, its objectifications, and its stereotypes. Even without minimizing the intensity and criticality of these forces, it is possible to recognize the corresponding expansive and productionist thrusts. This is certainly not the place to take up the issue at length. But it is important to reiterate here that both globalization and development have longer genealogies than what their autobiographies acknowledge. If the security anxiety and hardening of the borders is a legacy of the colonial state, so is the urge to open the borders to capital and labour flows.

The current policy literature on the Indian Northeast is focused on the much-trumpeted 'Look East' programme of the Indian government. Formulated during the 'liberalization' of the Indian economy in the early 1990s, the programme calls for 'deeper integration of the economies of ASEAN [Association of Southeast Asian Nations] and India in coming years'.[57] '[O]pening up the natural outlet of the Northeast' for this purpose has remained a more or less steady concern of the Government of India. Indeed, even some of the most sophisticated recognitions of the 'artificiality' of the colonial boundaries have dissolved into the argument that the government should actually allow the 'natural economic region' to emerge 'without the constraints of national boundaries' (Baruah 2005a: 221). It is this fantasy of natural economic regions which requires some critical unpacking today.

Focus on the northeastern region of India has been marked as a priority area in the Asian Development Bank's (ADB) 2005–07 Country Strategy and Program. What exactly are on the cards, of course,

[57] See the special issue on the subject in *Seminar*, 550, June 2005.

cannot be known. But in its 2004 statement on 'Technical Assistance to India for Preparing the Northeastern States Trade and Investment Creation Initiative', the ADB clearly observed that the 'northeastern states in India have lagged behind other parts of the country in terms of integration into the world economy and competitiveness'. In order to develop, said the Bank, the 'subregion' must emphasize its 'bridge function': '[T]he private sector will increase its productivity, while the northeast of India can increasingly serve as an important land bridge for trade between South Asia and Southeast Asia and the Greater Mekong Subregion' (Asian Development Bank 2004).

In November 2005, ADB and Confederation of Indian Industry (CII) organized a meeting of the Mekong Development Forum in New Delhi, involving 'high-level representatives from the GMS Governments', 'representatives from the GMS chambers of commerce and industry and private companies', and 'senior executives of about 60–80 large private sector enterprises in India'. There are reasons to believe that the effort at 'fostering regional economic integration in GMS and South Asia' will not stop here.[58] As one vice-president of the ADB categorically said in the meeting, 'Regional integration is a building block, not a substitute, to greater integration with the global community.' 'Harmonization' of the several bilateral trade agreements among the Asian countries 'with the World Trade Organization's guidelines on global trade' remains a declared objective of the ADB (Jin 2005). Explicitly promoting the coherence of the region in this context 'to create economies of scale', the ADB is keen on resolving or mitigating particularly those cross-border problems which 'serve as barriers to trade and investment liberalization' (Guttal 2003).

Such idioms and practices of regional coherence provide the context of the ADB's focus on 'the subregional transport corridors' through Northeast India (Asian Development Bank 2004). Perhaps it will not be out of place to remember that in 2004, the transport and communication sector received the largest portion (38 per cent) of a total of $5.3 billion of ADB lending to South Asia, over three times more than what the agriculture sector received.[59] Plans for upgrading

[58] http://www.adb.org/Documents/Events/2005/MDF-India-Mekong-Cooperation/default.asp

[59] 'Demystifying Asian Development Bank [ADB]: Note prepared by Bank Information Center-South Asia Office as input towards CSO preparations for ADB's 2006 Annual General Meeting', November 2005.

the old Burma Road to provide access between Yunnan and Assam via Myanmar are being prepared. In fact, it is hoped that the renovated Burma Road would be the 'backbone' for all 'ongoing plans for road and access development' between China, Myanmar, and India. Once the transnational transport grid is in place, we are told by the Greater Mekong advocates, it would unfailingly help 'to attract new markets from India and other parts of South Asia to the GMS'.[60] The twenty-first-century developmentalists wish to believe that these are fresh ideas and new beginnings. I am sorry to spoil their joy, but under the surface of the Greater Mekong palimpsest, it is not difficult to find the traces of a worn-out nineteenth-century blueprint. 'Connectivity', 'integration into the world economy', and 'bridge function' are not merely fashionable watchwords; they are the newest relics of the oldest capitalist speculations in the north-eastern frontier. Throughout the nineteenth century, finding a land route to Yunnan through Assam was one of the major concerns of the British Indian state. Want of space does not allow us to detail the series of government and private endeavours to burst open the doors of the Chinese market.[61] But even a casual reader of the frontier history cannot fail to notice the consistency and urgency of the British efforts to use the north-eastern frontier as a corridor to China.

The frequency of the early nineteenth-century attempts by the government officials (Neufville in 1825, Wilcox and Burlton in 1826, Burnett in 1828, Hannay in 1835–6, Griffiths in 1837, to name only the most important ones) to explore an overland commercial route to China either through 'the Khampti country' or via Mogaung (west and north-west of Burma) certainly declined in the middle of the century with the gradual extension of British political control over a significant section of the Irrawaddy. The idea was in fact revived by the tea industry in the early 1860s when it was facing an acute labour shortage. Drawing 'the surplus population of Western China' into Assam by way of an overland route became quite a popular slogan among the planters at that time. The contemporary experiments with Chinese immigrant labour in Cuba, Peru, and in the Pacific seaboard of the United States only encouraged them to put pressure upon the

---

[60] http://www.adb.org/Documents/Reports/Consultant/37626-01-GMS/vol2/annex7.pdf.

[61] For a comprehensive account of the early British endeavours, interested readers might be referred to Thaung 1954.

government for exploring and utilizing the route to Yunnan.[62] Their sympathizers in the government circle held out even greater pictures:

The throwing open of all India to all China, the access of a country containing 200 millions to the produce of a country occupied by 400 millions, and the opposite (to say nothing of Central Asia), would be of its kind a work of such magnitude as that nothing approaching to it has ever yet been seen in the world; and the export of a large portion of the produce of Western China for Europe through our own principal port of Calcutta is an imperial question of the very first importance (Read 1867: 232–3).

Is this argument too unfamiliar to us? (Of course, we have to update the population statistics and substitute 'imperial' with 'global'!) This line of reasoning has been the primary motivation for generations of 'explorers' in Assam.[63] The most notable of the private and public adventures after 1860 in this connection are those of Cooper (1868), Jenkins and Peal (1868–9), Woodthorpe and Macgregor (1884–5), and Needham (1885). In 1873, M'Cosh was already talking in terms of establishing 'an international thoroughfare between Assam, Burmah and China', and under instructions from the secretary of state for India, copies of M'Cosh's pamphlet were printed and distributed from London.[64] The proposal for extending the northeastern railway of Bengal over the hills of Manipur across Burma through Bhamo, Momein, and Talifu to Yunnan was seriously discussed since the 1880s.[65] What the ADB is selling today to the Government of India is neither a novel nor an original vision.

---

[62] For a detailed treatment of the state of the tea industry at this time, see *Report of the Commissioners Appointed to Enquire into the State and Prospects of Tea Cultivation in Assam, Cachar, and Sylhet*, Calcutta, Calcutta Central Press Company, 1868.

[63] There is indeed huge literature on the issue. See, for example, Cooper (1873); Cooper (1867–8); Jenkins (1868–9); MacGregor (1887); Young (1907); Williamson (1909).

[64] Quoted in Thaung (1954: 440). See also M'Cosh (1860–1).

[65] Indian Tea Districts Association, *Sixth Annual Report*, 1886. Private papers of Indian Tea Association. European Manuscripts, OIOC, No. IOR/Mss Eur F174/1. In fact, in 1920, a preliminary survey for a railway line to connect India and Burma *via* Hukong Valley was officially sanctioned. But the plan for a railway connection between Burma and Yunnan was shelved owing to the 'disturbed state' of China. Foreign Department, Sec.-E, February 1920, Proceedings Nos 267–87, NAI.

The history of the nineteenth century further testifies that what appeared as a difficult and inaccessible terrain to the Europeans was almost a form of social capital for the people inhabiting it. It is interesting to see how the people who possessed the knowledge of the routes always appeared as secretive, evasive, and even jealous about this knowledge in the representations of colonial officials and native informants from other communities. Knowledge of inhabited places and frequented routes could be crucial in determining the relation of power between the many communities.[66] It was extremely difficult if not altogether impossible to effectively intervene in the complex of inter-group exchanges and trans-territorial expeditions without this knowledge. The resistance to survey and road building was not simply about defending access to the resources of territory, it was also a struggle over social capital.[67]

Today, endorsing the suspicions of Anil Agarwal, Sanjib Baruah reminds us that apart from the enormous environmental costs which it carries, the project of road building in the Northeast has other sinister implications: 'If industry is slow to take off because of the lack of a local market, roads could become, in Agarwal's words, "excellent corridors to siphon off the existing natural resources of the region, its forests"' (Baruah 2005a: 34). Given the recurring suggestive references to the 'unexploited natural resources' in '[s]ome parts of Assam and the more remote states in the east' in the ADB documents (ADB 2004), Baruah's anxieties are hardly ill-founded. After all, we know a little more about the ADB than what it wishes us to know (Cornford and Simon 2001; Guttal 2003; Withanage et al. 2006).

Nevertheless, the Union Ministry of Development of North Eastern Region and the ADB have already started to collaborate on the North Eastern State Roads Project without attending to the larger infrastructural issues. (Indeed, in the first phase of the programme, '[r]oads from Nagaland could not be included because of the State Government's insistence on proposing only new roads whereas the ADB project was for upgrading existing roads.'[68]) The citizens are

---

[66] For an early and very interesting account of how the Khamptis kept a path secret from the Singphos, see Wilcox (1832: 444–5).

[67] For an elaboration of this argument, see Kar (2007: chapter 1).

[68] Tour note of D.S. Poona, joint secretary to Meghalaya, 17 January 2006, Government of India, Ministry of Development of North Eastern Region, http://mdoner.gov.in/writereaddata/officernotes/Tour%20Report%20%20IFAD (130).PDF.

routinely assured that roads are alleviating poverty as markets are being connected and disparate productive units are being conjoined into a wider network of prosperous interdependence. 'Over the recent years,' admitted the vice-president of ADB, 'it seems that economic and social disparities, among and within countries in the [Asian] region, are widening due in part to unequal or inadequate access to markets, finance, and technology.' But, he went on to claim, 'this phenomenon is not the consequence of economic integration; rather it is the lack of regional integration and cooperation that has left some countries in the lurch, particularly lowest income ones with weak institutional capacity' (Jin 2005).

Clearly, this line of argument has no place for understanding poverty and inequality as issuing from the dominant developmentalist politics.[69] Those who continue to believe that the privatization of resource management and forcing subsistence and semi-subsistence communities into the competitive world of cash economy would not adversely affect the poor also continue to see peace as a purchasable condition. There are indeed, as the title of this volume suggests, a number of roads to peace. But let us also be sensitive to the possibility that there might be, and I hope there are, contending and irreconcilable understandings of peace. Opening tea gardens in the Singpho territories was always seen as the most useful mechanism of turning the Singphos into 'peaceable subjects'.[70] Before rising into an insurrection in 1843, the Singpho chiefs told the British in a letter, 'Now wherever you find tea, you make a tea garden. If it is to be so, there will be no room for the 12 *gaums* to remain and if you do not allow the Singphos to remain, I can say nothing.'[71]

How much more powerful are we?

---

[69] A great deal has been written to demonstrate these connections. For a basic bibliography, see Escobar (1995).

[70] Hamilton Vetch, political agent of Upper Assam, to Francis Jenkins, the agent, Governor General, north-eastern frontier, dated 3 January 1848, in 'Report on Captain Vetch's visit to the Abor tribes', Foreign Department (Political FC Branch), Nos. 199–201, NAI.

[71] 'Translation of Beesa Gaum's letter in Reply', Appendix-G, Foreign Department (F. C.), 12 August 1843, Nos 90–106, NAI.

PART II

Nation and Its Discontents

CHAPTER 4

From Loincloth, Suits, to Battle Greens

Politics of Clothing the 'Naked' Nagas

DOLLY KIKON[1]

INTRODUCTION

There is an old photograph of four Naga national leaders outside a detention centre in England in the 1960s.[2] The four are dressed alike, wearing modest suits and staring awkwardly at the photographer. The accompanying text is a report about how the four Naga tribesmen, with insufficient travel documents, were finally allowed to stay on in London as citizens of the Commonwealth. The four were visiting England to present their case for independence from postcolonial India to the British people. The photograph was published after a time when colonial anthropologists had traversed the course of the Naga Hills in order to study their mores, food habits, fabrics, and so on. The four Naga political leaders in the photograph were, therefore, an odd and unnerving reminder of the colonial encounter between the Nagas and the Occident, between Christianity and animism, and among notions of freedom, justice, and visions of the world. While postcolonial Indian intellectuals and policy makers knew and had studied Christoph von-Fürer-Haimendorf's *Naked Nagas*, once clothed in suits and demanding to enter England to renegotiate terms of engagement between the Nagas and the world, the men in the photograph seemed to be an embarrassing reminder to twentieth-century colonial authority and to postcolonial India, about just how much had gone wrong with the

[1] I thank Professor Liisa Malkki, Xonzoi Barbora, Jonathan Hunt, Georgia Lawrence, and Carol Shabrami for their comments. The usual disclaimers apply.
[2] This photograph appeared in the 12 September 1962 edition of *The Times*.

remapping and reclassified imperial historical and political geography of South/Southeast Asia.

Given the complexities arising out of these political and historical processes, I am motivated by several questions: How does colonial ethnography and visual representation shape the understanding of the *Other* in postcolonial India? Is there a collective postcolonial national imagination that corresponds to these colonial constructs? Finally, how do communities such as the Naga, find their own basis for social and political representation under these representational regimes within the postcolonial nation?

Two frontiers in colonial India significantly shaped the political, historical, and legal histories of several communities inhabiting these regions. The North West Frontier Province and the North Eastern Frontier Province demarcated geographical spaces, constructed identities, and eventually witnessed the break-up of British colonialism and the rise of new modern states, such as India, Pakistan, and Burma. Referring to colonial institutions which transformed the colonized worlds, Benedict Anderson describes how institutions such as the census, map-making, and museums shaped the imagination of the colonial state, its subjects and colonial geography (Anderson 1991: 163). McClintock explains that these technologies of knowledge, such as maps, operated as technologies of possession. As a result, while colonialists mapped out areas and identified groups, cultures, and territories, the unexplored regions usually depicted as 'blank spaces' were inhabited by cannibals and monsters in the colonial imagination (McClintock 1995: 27–8).

The incorporation of 'blank spaces' and frontiers into postcolonial nations goes beyond the issue of purely geographical sovereignty. For Gupta, 'sovereignty does not solely depend on protecting spatial borders but on its ability to control the flow of commodities, cultures and ideas' (Gupta 1997: 190). Mitchell takes the concept of idea further when he highlights that the term 'idea' comes from the Greek verb 'to see', which is associated with the concept of mental imagery (Mitchell 1987: 5). Thus, ideas, like commodities and culture, are not only controlled and protected, they form an integral part of producing or reproducing a national imagination.

However, with respect to the idea of geographical spaces, Malkki argues that territoriality is not only a visual device and a concept on a map, but is felt to be synonymous with people's natural identity with their homeland. For Malkki, the connection between people and their national territory is experienced as generally thought to be metaphysical (Malkki 1992: 26–7). Thus, the imagination of the colonized subjects and regions were informed by the colonialists' influence and association with a system of structures and representations about societies (in the West), which were external to the colonies. Therefore, the nineteenth-century explorer's imagination was a bewildering colonized geography extending from Africa to the north-eastern frontiers of India and beyond. The construction of the *Others* who inhabited such geographies was primarily a racial construction, which not only led to the establishment of disciplines such as anthropology, but eventually became a mechanism for assessing civilization, decency, and culture among other things.

Colonialists frequently referred to the colonized as 'savages' or 'primitives'. Colonial representations and images of 'savages' regularized a system of knowledge and practices in accordance with what Bourdieu would term as the colonial *habitus*. These were durable as an objective collective history of groups and transposable even in the postcolonial nations.[3] As Said argues, *Orientalism* could not represent itself and had to rely on the West and its authoritative domination of power and hegemony over the histories of its colonies; similarly, formerly colonized people can also end up applying the same colonial structures of defining and regulating its own people (Said 1979: 24).

The process of postcolonial citizenship for groups like the Nagas, categorized as perennial troublemakers inhabiting the nation's borderlands or 'anomalous danger zones' (Malkki 1992: 25), resembles Victor Turner's concept of initiation rites and the transition from a liminal stage to a distinct recognized member of society. Power therefore is defined and regulated through a process, or a series of initiation rites which Turner calls the rites of passage where individuals or groups undergo a transition from an ambiguous state to a stage of maturity and social status where he/she is obliged to follow societal rules and regulations (Turner 1967: 93–5). Thus, the rite of passage involves a *transition* from an ambiguous and unclassified world to a phase where

[3] As Bourdieu argues, what appears 'regular' can be attributed to a group's structure and the habitus they inhabit; habitus, for Bourdieu, is a collection of 'durable, transposable' structures which function as 'systems of generation and structuring of practices and representations which can be objectively "regulated" and "regular" without in any way being the product of obedience to rules, objectively adapted to their goals without presupposing a conscious aiming at ends' (Bourdieu 1977: 72–94).

the ambiguous is recognized, defined, and bestowed a status. However, this rite of passage of decolonization does not *transform* the centres of power: peripheral regions and groups in the former colony remain outside the domain of political power and production of knowledge. In a similar vein, Schendel argues that people who produce knowledge of these spaces cannot become part of the power elite: 'In true mandala fashion, these marches are sometimes claimed as part of some regional problematique, but always from the vantage point of the court. These borderlands are rarely worth a real fight—they are often forgotten' (Schendel 2002b: 650–1).

In postcolonial India, distinctions between 'nationals' and 'sub-nationals' or 'local' and 'national' highlight social and political movements relating to identity and homeland. Arguing for locating the 'local' and the 'national' as different categories, Saikia notes:

[I] use the term local to distinguish the identity movements from the national movements to homogenize Indian identity. The national movement, as is generally understood, is linked to capital, the West, and, at present, to the discourse on globalization. Local movements, on the other hand, attempt to override the power of the national. They seek to create a 'different' sense of collectivity based on specific constructs that are emotional, sentimental discourses that give meaning to locality and enable the construction of a 'homeland' as a different space from the homelands of 'others' (Saikia 2004: 38).

Emphasizing the transition of the North East Frontier Province to the 'Northeast region' of India in the postcolonial period, Baruah argues that the region is not only an important cartographic reality in Indian politics but also a space where physical power plays a dominant role in constructing a political discourse of citizenship and people-hood (Baruah 1999: 144–72, 2005a: 183–208). Representations of frontiers and their peoples in postcolonial national imaginations are enforced by a new dominant political discourse—through the lenses of an authoritarian and national objectivity. As Haraway explains, representations and imaginations of the *Other* originate from situated knowledge, defining situated knowledge as an embodied objectivity that accommodates paradoxical and critical doctrines. Much like Baruah and Said, she critiques the world of *objectivity* as a historical and political process honed and produced by a dominant hegemonic discourse (Haraway 1991: 185–90). Where can one locate the Nagas within such existing geographies of representation, institutions, and imaginations?

SITUATING THE PEOPLE

Colonial categorization of Naga people continues to find its way into modern national imaginations in postcolonial India. The Nagas were one of the most widely studied ethnic communities in the north-eastern frontiers of British India in the early twentieth century. They were frequently depicted as a community whose lives were threatened due to contact with dominant cultures, modernity, and developmental policies. However, they attracted a different kind of attention by the middle of the twentieth century. After the transfer of power in 1947, the Nagas along with several frontier groups refused to join India and launched a resistance movement, continuing a broad South Asian tradition of anti-colonial retaliations against the British in the nineteenth century. Such conflicts between the 'natives' and a new postcolonial state resulted in a continuance of the colonial projects: sequestering, pacifying, and subjugating the Nagas. The colonial state saw the Nagas as subjects, and the Indian state was unwilling to see them differently, as its national leaders were engaged in the process of nation building through citizenship and territorializing India's inherited frontiers. With their demands for a sovereign nation, the Nagas therefore appeared as reluctant citizens who were not attuned with the 'great modern desire' to forge a new postcolonial Indian nation.

Pacifying the 'naked Nagas' has, therefore, remained a problematic proposal.[4] The Nagas seem to be an embarrassing reminder to India of just how much went wrong with the grand project of decolonization.[5] Colonial ethnographic writing shaped a particular postcolonial political imagination and therefore an understanding about the Nagas. These writings associated the 'naked' Naga with everything that was uncivilized, barbaric, and primitive, although they also contained extensive sections referring to the Naga people as noble savages and simple warm people. Such discourse of the *Other* became the guiding principles for both colonial and postcolonial policy makers who formulated the developmental, security, and educational policies for the Nagas.

---

[4] Colonial writings described the Naga people as 'naked Nagas' and 'head hunters'. Such representations and writings often found their way in postcolonial publications in India.

[5] Fürer-Haimendorf was an Austrian anthropologist who extensively documented the lives of the Nagas in the early twentieth century.

Just as colonial power emerged from constructing and deducing knowledge and forms of authority, postcolonial nations altered and developed the discourse on existing knowledge stores. With the end of colonialism, memory, constructed identities, and the existing imbalance of power and social structure within colonized natives never vanished. Postcolonialism continues to reproduce collective meanings around groups, places, and representations. Such meanings are framed in constitutional and policy regulations, which result in the construction of citizenship discourses, security issues, and the task of monitoring these institutions. Such a linear knowledge structure from colonialism to postcolonialism exists in modern institutions such as the judiciary and police forces in order to enable them to negotiate 'ambiguous constructions' and 'restless categories' (McClintock 1995: 5–11). For instance, colonial laws and regulations established to control and regulate colonial plantation economy and the exploitation of oil along the Brahmaputra Valley continue to operate in these inherited frontiers.

The colonial process of mapping uncharted space as British territory is explained in a colonial official letter from the British headquarters in Calcutta:

[T]he Lieutenant Governor thinks that a line between civil and political jurisdictions must be drawn in regard to these Nagas, and begs that you will be good...to submit a map showing this part of the Luckimpoor frontier, the situation of all the tea gardens upon it, and the line of jurisdiction you would draw. You should also say in any and what Naga property or privileges is included in what is proposed for our jurisdiction (13 March 1873).[6]

Such practices not only led to the creation of artificial internal borders, but also enabled the colonial administration to further frame its policies along identity and ethno-racial lines. Existing border disputes, changes in land relations, and the politics of land ownership in former colonized areas around the world are not uncommon. One would argue that such disputes are not regional or area specific. On the contrary, the disputes are consequences of British colonial frontier politics of enacting legislation enforcing regulations and the emergence of tools for defining and categorizing communities and peoples as criminals,

---

[6] Foreign Department, Political A. 'From Junior Secretary to the Government of Assam: To Commissioner of Assam dated No. 1317 Calcutta, 3 April 1873', Nos 205–11, National Archives of India, New Delhi.

primitives, and savages, thereby establishing the dominance of the colonial administration as the sovereign authority over these territories. Thus, one could argue, representations of primitives, savages and the existing national imagination in postcolonial societies are the *artefacts* of a colonial historical process.

REVISITING THE NAGA ARCHIVES

Researchers have relied heavily on colonial texts in their analysis of Naga society and politics. Military accounts of British expeditions into the Naga areas in the eighteenth century, monographs of 'barbaric naked' Nagas, and administrative reports from the Naga Hills continue to be privileged documents in examining the Naga people's past (Bower 2002: 1–21; Elwin 1969: 11–46; Hutton 2002: 1–71; Mills 2003: 1–20; Fürer-Haimendorf 2004: 149–55). However, most colonial texts are notorious for their inability to negotiate linguistic and internal socio-political complexities and, thus, ought to be cautiously used to support or refute historical claims (Robinson 1959: 26–8; Thapar 2005:1–6; Woodthorpe 1959: 42–50).

Colonial writers in the Naga Hills often resorted to Western symbols or objects to describe and interpret several Naga customs and rituals. These ethnographies are strong reminders that their research material was designed for a Western audience. For instance, Hutton described the Angami Naga's funeral ritual (of putting up a black and white cloth) as an image that resembles a sail. He commented, 'When any proper man dies, they told me that they put them (the cloths) up so that the dead man might see them, but I could not get any more [information] from them.' Similarly, Woodthorpe noted how the same ritual appeared to him as a large silver chevron turned upside down. Hutton also described how the mithun's (bison) horns adorning the heads of the warriors carved on the gates of houses and villages resembled the wings of a medieval jester's cap. He also compared 'Negros' and Nagas whenever he came across curly haired Nagas (Hutton 1986: 16–23).

Studying the Mru in neighbouring Bangladesh, Schendel says, '...in the mid-nineteenth century, nakedness had been a symbol of wildness.... [but] what the "unclothed native" meanwhile thought of all this remains unrecorded...' (Schendel 2002a: 349). In J.H. Hutton's diary, a British administrator described an encounter between the colonialists and the Nagas during one of his expeditions in the Naga Hills:

To Ukha, a steep climb of about five to six miles after crossing the river. The people here were very shy. They were…obviously afraid of our intentions, no doubt on account of what happened last time, when they tried to ambush Woodthorpe's escort, and succeeded in wounding a sepoy and getting their village burnt…when I turned my camera on a crowded *morung*[7] all the occupants fled, taking it for some sort of deadly weapon, and could not be induced to return. Yet they cannot even have seen or heard of a machine gun. If one looked at them they got up and went away… (Hutton 1986: 18).

For Hutton, such experiences in the wild frontiers of the colonial empire were amusing anecdotes. However, his passing comment about the confusion of mistaking the camera for a gun conceals a deeper story about fierce battles and conflicts between inhabitants and invaders. The consequence for killing a sepoy was severe. Thus, it was a manifestation of received knowledge among the Nagas that modern disciplinarian traditions were to be part of their relationship with the Europeans. This also meant that the Nagas would be viewed within the modernist framework, where their nakedness could also add to their democratic tradition. Thus, a dual policy prevailed wherein the 'savage' could be contained within an area that could be administered tactfully, and the 'primitive' could be protected from the pitfalls of his/her own simplicity. In the meantime, Christian missionaries introduced the Bible and hymns along with mission schools. This led to the introduction of the Roman alphabet which transcribed the Naga spoken words and led to the translation of the Bible and hymnals into various Naga languages in the late nineteenth and early twentieth centuries (Kikon 2003: 235).

Similarly, there were changes among the Nagas who were employed in the colonial administration and those influenced by the missionaries. By the early twentieth century, the Nagas dressed in clothes representing their influences. For instance, those influenced by the Baptist mission wore shorts, khaki shirts, and caps on their tours with the missionaries. Those employed by the administration as the colonial interpreters usually wore red waistcoats to signify their official position (see Photograph 4.1). In the same manner, carrying a red blanket was introduced among the village headmen, which gradually became a protocol for all official meetings.

---

[7] A youth dormitory in Naga villages, usually a centre for social, cultural, and political activities.

Photograph 4.1: Village headmen and *dobashi*s (interpreters) in a meeting
Source: Abraham Lotha, 2005

Fürer-Haimendorf has a colourful description of an Angami Naga interpreter named Thevoni, who wore a bright red waistcoat over his black loincloth. Thevoni is presented as a friendly person eager to share the customs and beliefs of his tribe with the colonialists. His help to the government in mediating village disputes is seen as an important skill. For Fürer-Haimendorf, people like Thevoni were valued by the colonial administration because they were influential among the villages without jeopardizing the social order and customs (Fürer-Haimendorf 2004). Once the clothing and civilization project took off, the Nagas commenced their roles as pastors, teachers, missionaries, and government employees. While very little has been documented from the eyes of the natives, interviews with a Naga volunteer during World War II highlight some of the experiences of Nagas during this period of time.

FAMILY PORTRAIT AND TRANSITION INTO POSTCOLONIALISM

Mr Luke (Photograph 4.2, standing extreme right) was born in Guwahati, Assam, where his father served the American Baptist missionaries. After receiving a mission school education, he went back to the Naga Hills and joined the colonial administration. He served as a medical assistant during World War II, when he and his

Photograph 4.2: Family portrait
Source: Personal archives, circa 1952

young wife (standing, extreme left) helped to set up medical camps for the allied troops. Sharing her experiences of the war, his wife Oreno Kikon says:

I worked along with my husband during the war. There were so many wounded soldiers in the camps. The soldiers were friendly and would share their food with us in the medical camps. I tasted some of the food, but it was particularly exciting to see the parachutes. They were so colourful and interesting. The parachute was made of some very fine soft, silky material. I loved the materials so I requested the soldiers to give it to me. After I finished helping out my husband in the medical camps, I would come back home and cut these fine clothes. I stitched bed covers, some clothes for my children and table covers. I also embroidered flowers on several scarves I had stitched from the parachute material. Once the war was over in the hills, I stood outside the camps and presented a scarf to the soldiers as they waved at us and left the hills singing *...Kohima will shine tonight, Kohima will shine tonight...*[8]

Like many nations and communities around the world, Naga society underwent significant changes in the course of the two world wars. The

[8] Personal interview with Oreno Kikon, age ninety-three, on 1 January 2003 in Wokha, Nagaland.

Nagas were members of the labour corps digging trenches in France during World War I, and fought with the Allied soldiers in World War II along the north-eastern frontiers of India. In the meantime, institutions like the Naga Club, a post–World War I discussion forum, brought together educated Nagas to discuss their future. The Naga Club members were English-educated Naga men in suits. While its initiatives were limited to the administration in the Naga Hills, the club gradually became associated with discussions and debates about the transfer of power in mainland India. Factors such as the Indian national movement and the Simon Commission, a colonial mission that surveyed the Naga Hills collecting feedback on the people's demand for sovereignty, significantly shaped discussions along political and social issues of autonomy, resource management, and administration via indigenous institutions.

Utilizing the logic that India would be granted independence from British rule, the Nagas also demanded that they should be 'left alone' after 1947. By 1951, the Nagas called for a plebiscite around two issues: whether they wanted to remain in India or to establish a separate, independent state; and second, to repudiate the Indian government's view that the call for sovereignty was the work of a few 'misguided' Nagas. The following year, in 1952, the Nagas boycotted the first Indian parliamentary election and continued to demand a Naga sovereign homeland.

Inclusion of and participation in democratic processes are considered to be hallmarks of post-colonial state building in India. However, in postcolonial India, the Nagas, along with several frontier groups, did not figure prominently in the memory and imagery of the new nation. They had to be written in as constituents. What was the manner in which postcolonial India constructed the Nagas within the national imagination? What was the basis of the dialogue or interaction between a hegemonic nation and its reluctant citizens?

WHOSE MEMORY? MUSEUMS AND THE NATIONAL IMAGINATION

James Clifford challenges and questions the status and role of museums as storehouses of memory and culture when he states, 'Whose memory? For what purpose?' (Clifford 1988: 248). National museums are one of the most visible institutions in postcolonial India, signifying the colonial project of representation and producing objectivist knowledge. Museums are hegemonic narratives of national culture and civilization. For instance, the National Museum in Calcutta is one example of an institution representing the *Other*. One begins the negotiation on identity, citizenship, and verification at the ticket counter. As a Naga stands in the queue meant for Indians, there is a request to switch over to the foreigners' line. After speaking in Hindi, a brief lecture on history, geography, and the Naga people, the Naga/Indian is allowed to enter. Inside the grand colonial building, almost every modern state that comprises the Indian union is accorded space to display their contribution to the grandeur of India's great and ancient civilization.

In a musty room, people from the Northeast regions are displayed together, where people of every state are allotted a glass cage resembling a prison cell.[9] Clay and terracotta couples with children smile at all the visitors from carelessly reconstructed villages that they presumably inhabit in their respective homelands. All the models, slightly yellowish in colour, look alike with the epicanthic fold of the eyes but are juxtaposed in a manner that would be typical of a child dressing a doll in a dollhouse. Hence, the Naga couple in the glass cage are adorned in Karbi fabric and prints; the Khasi couple are dressed in the typical attire of the Assamese peasant, and so on. It could well be that the museum is promoting a hybrid Northeast, where, ideally, Nagas, Assamese, Garos, and Apatanis, all wear one another's clothes. But given the immediate memory of being mistaken for a foreigner just outside the precincts of the museum, one is sceptical about the museum's altruistic ersatz of wishing for a politically correct world. Museums, it has been said, often project the memory of a nation.

Symbolically clothed, the Naga couple continues to educate visitors in the National Museum about Indian history at its margins. However, such representations raise serious questions about a national imagination. For instance, the term *chinky*, a derogatory word used in India to refer to people with the epicanthic fold of the eyes, does not identify one's nationality or ethnicity, although it is generally used to refer to people who could be from a wide swathe of land that roughly cuts across the eastern Himalayas, where the Naga territories are situated. Racial stereotyping is so ingrained into the public memory that sexual harassment on the streets of New Delhi, the capital of India, goes something like this: 'Hello chinky baby, honey...*smooch smooch*

[9] The room is referred to as 'Peoples of Northeast India'. This obviously underscores the diversity within the strange administrative region called Northeast India, wherein the region is gridlocked into a political project of nation building where memory and history are deemed dispensable.

[makes kissing sounds]...hot baby, honey, pinky, chinky, ping-pong, ching-chong.'[10] Besides disgusting sounds and derogatory remarks, the perpetrator tries to rhyme it with nonsensical words like ping-pong and ching-chong. Crowds of awkward teenagers seeking out some fun in the streets often shout, 'hey chinky' every time they see people with east Asian features. Such 'innocent fun' that Hindi/Punjabi speaking teenagers in New Delhi engage in reflects a normalization of a visual regime where people like Nagas do not have a secure place within the nation-state.

One would agree that regional stereotyping in India is not uncommon. For instance, people from south India are all supposedly Madrasis[11] or those from the north are all Punjabis. Likewise, inhabitants from the seven states of Northeast India are assumed to be one people. However, for Nagas and several other groups from the region, such stereotyping is linked to a violent historical and unstable political relation with the postcolonial nation. Decades of counter-insurgency operations, anti-democratic laws, and existing armed resistance in several parts of the northeastern region immediately draws a typical instance of regional stereotyping into a matrix of dangerous securitization based on race, culture, and location. Therefore, the transition of colonial representations of 'savages' and 'primitives' has only become more violent and regulatory in postcolonial India. State regulations and security agencies such as police forces are sanctioned to monitor the 'savages' at the margins of the nation. Here, the Constitution of India stands in sharp contradiction with its democratic principles. Even though the Nagas are seen through the lens of citizenship, they are imbued with a collective memory reserved for the other and further located within a specific geographical territory and history.

It is under such conditions that anti-democratic regulations like the Armed Forces Special Powers Act (1958) operate. This legislation

[10] Loosely reconstructed from personal experiences of seven years of living in Delhi (1994–2000).

[11] Southern India has five languages recognized by the Indian constitution. They are Telugu, Tamil, Konkani, Malayali, and Kannada. However, in the national imagination shaped by colonial markers of identity, anyone south of the Vindhya hills is erroneously classified as a 'Madrasi' (a person from Madras; the capital of Tamil Nadu, now called Chennai). According to A.S. Panneerselvam, this is the outcome of several Tamil Brahmins being part of the Indian bureaucracy and power network and also the attempt to domesticate Dravidian politics (Personal communication: 16 August 2007).

imposed in Naga areas (along with several other states in the Northeast) grants the Indian security forces unrestricted powers to conduct military operations including the power to kill on mere suspicion of a violation in order to maintain law and order. Thus, by virtue of the geographical, historical, and political constructions among other issues, the Nagas and several other nationalities from the region are denied access to rights and justice. Considered as perennial troublemakers, the representation of Naga people continues to sway between the naked headhunter and the gun-wielding guerrillas (Photograph 4.3). The image of barbarism remains intact because both representations are mechanically reinforced by uncivilized, violent, and primitive attributes.

Writings in postcolonial India, according to Ranabir Samaddar, represent the frontier and marginalized peoples as headhunters and a land of drug caravans, AIDS, civic strife, military operations, and insurgencies (Samaddar 2001: 286). So strong is this racial/

Photograph 4.3: Naga guerrillas
Source: Akum Longchari, 2005

anthropological regime that the first Indian air force pilots whose plane was brought down by the Naga resistance in the 1960s, were terrified by the possibility of being captured by the headhunting Nagas who they knew were waiting below. As they parachuted down to a fate worse than anything that a 'civilized Indian' security personnel could imagine, they were surrounded by Naga guerrillas the moment they touched ground. The first words uttered by the officer of the Naga resistance army were: 'Your identification numbers, badge and squadron please…you are our prisoners of war.'[12] They cited the Geneva Convention to their prisoners. Those meant to headhunt in loinclothes, had emerged as guerrillas in olive green uniforms by the mid-twentieth century and were armed with international conventions and rights instruments.

PROTESTS AND REFASHIONING NAGA REPRESENTATIONS

Written literature and especially photo documentations of the Nagas still continue to present topless women, naked children, and men in loincloths. There is a disturbing discrepancy between existing representations and lived realities of the people. Such documentation and representation are blind to the radical changes that Naga society has undergone in approximately hundred years, and do not explain the deeper significance. Nagas are no longer naked, but they continue to shed their clothes as symbols of culture and resistance (Photograph 4.4). In many demonstrations and public gatherings, one notices an increasing number of men dressed up as warriors with spears, and women with their sarongs wrapped around their chests. Once a sign of barbarism, these bare bodies have become political tools of protest.

Naga memory and postcolonial imagination reflect contradictory conceptions. Such resistance of the local against the national manifests itself in the realm of representations and images. Symbols and representations have become sites of information where the audience absorbs these meanings selectively. Thus, a journalist for an Indian magazine reporting a state-sponsored cultural event highlighted: 'Naga people by nature are fun lovers, and life in Nagaland is one long festival' (Chaudhuri 2003: 1). Representations of ethnic minorities as fun-loving simpletons are also bolstered through national television and media. They are often featured as sharing their 'way of life'

---

[12] I am grateful to Subir Bhaumik of the BBC for recounting this story. One of the pilots happened to be related to Bhaumik (Personal notes, 7 September 2005, Guwahati).

Photograph 4.4: Naga students in a demonstration, New Delhi
Source: Associated Press, 2008

through dances and songs, which supposedly represent their 'world'. Postcolonial imaginations and representations in India lack the political and historical lens to comprehend how communities like the Nagas have negotiated and engaged with reality. Narrating the political and civil upheavals that Nagas experienced, eighty-five-year-old Matalo Kikon, from Tsungiki village said:

[D]uring 1956–63, villages were burnt down several times. There was constant army operation and the entire village ran away to the jungle. The women and children were the worst sufferers. There was food scarcity since all our granaries were burnt down and we could not go back to the fields to cultivate our farms. Many children died in the jungles because of starvation. The womenfolk from the village started to live in the caves beneath the mountains and in their sorrow and pain cried out if god had forgotten their existence.[13]

[13] The interviewee was a resident of Tsungiki village, Nagaland, on 14 December 2003. This interview was part of a series titled, 'Narratives from a Militarized Society: Experiences Naga Women in Armed Conflict Situation', WISCOMP, New Delhi, 2004.

The stark difference between dancing cultural subjects of postcolonial India as seen on national television and the reality that inhabitants like Matalo Kikon narrate from the Northeast highlights how discourse on culture in India exists within a contentious political history of resistance and violence. Therefore, for many Nagas, bare bodies are sites of culture and resistance. Moreover, in Naga–Indian meetings, besides the political demand for the right to self-determination, the emphasis on culture is significant. From the beginning, the Naga people's demand for a homeland derived from 'being different'. Issues such as culture are contentious subjects which often create a chasm between India and the Naga people during political attempts to resolve the armed conflict. For the Nagas, memories of colonization and postcolonial experiences encompass vivid mental imageries of authoritarian representation, massacres, and destruction. Echoing Belting who points out that 'images contain moments from a narrative....' (1994: 10), Easterine Iralu, a Naga poet weaving mental imageries in her poem 'Kelhoukevira' writes:

Their hearts too grieved to heed the harvest
Maidens ceased song and mourned the brave ones
And blindly followed a broken people
Who turned their backs
And slowly walked away
From a burning village, a burning village
...They trampled her silent hills
And squeezed life out of her
And washed their guilt in her blood,
Washed their guilt in her blood[14]

The Nagas have developed their sense of political and social representation by retrieving and constructing their past. Thus, the representation of their bare bodies in protest demonstrations is in defiance of disciplinary regimes and a provocation to a larger national imagination. As the Nagas and the government compete to define culture, the idea of culture to the state is reduced to the circulation of cultural products through commercial exchanges, thereby living up to the notion of the state as the capitalist exploiter (Kikon 2005: 36–9). However, the peripheral zones of the nation are seldom ascribed a

---

[14] Easterine Iralu is a Naga scholar and a poet. 'Kelhoukevira' is part of a translated piece among other poems by her (Iralu. Kaka. D, 'Nagaland and India: The Blood and the Tears', 2000, Kohima, Nagaland).

neutral space. As Ferguson and Gupta emphasize, 'The fiction of cultures as discrete, object-like phenomena occupying discrete spaces becomes implausible for those who inhabit the borderlands' (Gupta and Ferguson 1992: 7). In 2002, the Government of Nagaland inaugurated the Horn Bill festival as an annual event to boost tourism in the state. While this event has since become an annual event to showcase Naga culture and their way of life, the realities and changes are reflected through the bare back of a Naga youth with the name of an American rock band—Metallica—tattooed on his back (see Photograph 4.5), greeting tourists and audiences in the festival.

For such Naga youth, an annual event such as the Horn Bill festival has become part of a narrative of stories that echo the experiences of their ancestors, guerrillas, and politicians. For an outside audience, Naga savagery and nakedness are reinforced through the display of bare bodies. Yet, the other narrative that alludes to the complex ways in which Naga tradition, culture, and politics are enmeshed with

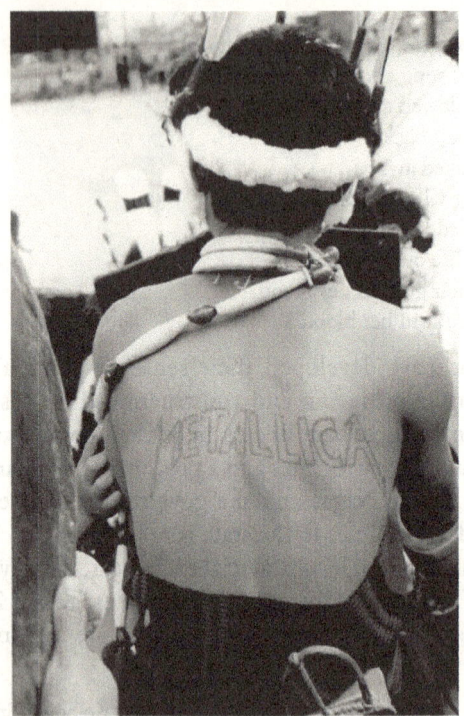

Photograph 4.5: A participant at the Horn Bill festival
Source: Personal archives, 2003

Photograph 4.6: Billboards advertising the milk product 'Komul' and
an Indian Army recruitment campaign
Source: Personal archives, 2005

their historical encounter with modern institutions and modernizing
processes, is somehow subsumed within a reductionist narrative. The
existing world that Nagas inhabit are represented through billboards
outside the Dimapur train station in Nagaland, India: while one
billboard represents a Naga girl advertising milk products as health
food in front of superimposed Swiss landscapes, the second billboard
displays a Naga boy in battle gear beckoning other Naga youths to join
the Indian army and render service to the nation (see Photograph 4.6).
Therefore, it is within contested political, cultural, and historical spaces
that the representations, imagination, and negotiations between the
Nagas and the Indian state operate, and not in staged amphitheatres
of the Horn Bill festival or within discrete national televised cultural
spaces.

CONCLUSION

Literature relating to armed conflicts and anthropological texts continue
to remain prescribed material for an understanding of Naga history and
culture in the postcolonial period in India. Simultaneously, underlying
descriptions of Naga histories enable discourses of development and

progress. Describing the reinvention of the primitivity and nakedness of the Mru people of the Chittagong Hills Tracts after 1947, Schendel points out, 'Primitivity reappeared in …popular literature as a concept to explain the hill people's way of life…nakedness…a century later has become a symbol of underdevelopment' (Schendel 2002a: 348–9).

This essay highlights images of the Nagas, which continue to hold sway in policy-making circles. It emphasizes the need to disaggregate matters beyond simple objectified depictions—representations and imaginations of the 'Naked Nagas'. Images and imaginations of insurgents and missionaries all respectively need to be situated within a context of change and competing constructions, acquiescence, and resistance to historical processes. It also underlines the importance of national imagery in the political representation of groups like the Nagas. Constructed national representations, much like the 'Northeast' sections inside national museums in postcolonial India, are used by counter-insurgency political discourse to dehumanize the *Other*. It is only through an exercise of deconstruction for contextualization that one can engage with the existing political and historical contestations and ambiguities in the postcolonial imagination in India.

CHAPTER 5

Writing Terror
Men of Rebellion and Contemporary Assamese Literature

RAKHEE KALITA[1]

In an essay called 'The Discreet Charms of Indian Terrorism', cultural critic Ashis Nandy looks at the dramatic hijacking of an Indian aircraft by Sikh militants in July 1984 (Nandy 2004a). The incident occurred in the wake of the massive army campaign Operation Bluestar in Punjab.[2] A Delhi-bound plane from Srinagar was hijacked and redirected to Lahore, Pakistan, in a bid to put pressure on the Indian government to release hundreds of Sikhs arrested during the army action at the Golden Temple. Nandy's account of what unfolds inside the aircraft is not a spine-chilling tale of mad violence and gory terror, but a heart-warming account of traditional Indian hospitality and sentimental concern for the well-being of their victims by a group of 'friendly' gun-toting young men. Nandy's essay is a warning against assuming that the phenomenon of terrorism is the same everywhere, lacking in local nuances and specificities—the kind of understanding that has become especially popular since 9/11.[3]

---

[1] The author thanks the participants at the Centre for Policy Research workshop on 'Rethinking Conflicts in Northeast India' in December 2005 for their helpful comments and suggestions on the earlier version of this essay.

[2] Operation Bluestar conducted in June 1984 was one of the largest counter-terrorist army operations in India in which several Sikh militants were taken into army custody at the Harmandir Sahib Temple in Punjab.

[3] Terror, I should think, is not merely the bomb exploding, or the several unsuspecting dying or dead, or even the awareness of who the 'enemy' is. Terror is the sense of being swamped, as it were, by a systemic derangement in which social structures are steeped. It is, perhaps, more significantly, our doubts about who or what is responsible for it. I stress this because there is, in the wake of 9/11, a huge

It has been almost the staple of recent political–bureaucratic policies in Northeast India to 'pluck' out terrorists without weeding away the soil that germinates these rebels. In this essay, drawing on Nandy's insight, I make an effort towards constructing a kind of 'situated knowledge' of terrorism in Assam through contemporary Assamese literature. I examine three Assamese texts: the first, a short story, 'Samiran Borua Aahi Aase' (1993) by journalist Manoj Goswami, written during the heyday of the ULFA; the second, another story, 'Bandiyar' (1996), by Hare Krishna Deka, a senior police official who retired as the director general of police of the Government of Assam and who has been a prominent author and poet widely read in the state; the third and final is a tract titled *Changlot Fenla* (1997) on the guerrilla operations and life of ULFA cadres, by Parag Kumar Das, a journalist often considered one of the organization's leading intellectual sympathisers. Das was gunned down by 'unknown assailants' in the streets of Assam's capital city, Guwahati, about a decade ago.[4] *Changlot Fenla* details the life of ULFA rebels in their training camps and is a serious meditation on the minds of these young rebels. It is arguably the first of its kind in Assamese literature. It is at once a diary and criticism of life of the militants in their hideouts.

THE CONTEXT

ULFA announced its arrival close on the heels of the Assam movement (1979–85) led by the All Assam Students' Union—a resistance fired by the issue of illegal immigration of 'foreigners' into the state. Years of student leadership steering a mass movement, eventually leading to its leader winning the state elections and becoming chief minister of the state, invested the youth in Assam with a rare sense of destiny. During the early years there was little that the Assamese public saw as misplaced and unfounded about many of ULFA's public positions. There was a widespread sense among the local intelligentsia that

---

body of ideological discourse on terrorism that floats in the public realm and is not always adequately equipped to address ideas about conflict and confrontation of other kinds in the rest of the world.

[4] Parag Kumar Das, at once unflinching supporter and trenchant critic of ULFA, was a fiery columnist, human rights activist, and editor of several Assamese publications during this period. Imprisoned in 1992 and 1993 under the National Security Act (NSA) and Terrorist and Disruptive Activities (Prevention) Act (TADA), respectively, his *Swadhinator Prostab*—a manifesto for sovereignty—was proscribed by the state.

Assam had got a raw deal in the postcolonial dispensation. But what started as a statement and expression of grievance shared and vented by the Assamese community at large, snowballed into something much more serious, and on which Assamese society seemed to have quickly lost control.

A discerning political scientist has pointed out that ULFA sought to build a larger and inclusive Assamese nation constituting the smaller communities and little minorities, which posed an alternative idea of nationhood not available under the framework of the Indian state (Das 1994: 98–101). In fact, the extent to which the outfit pervaded the very consciousness of the entire people of Assam can be explained in terms of its appeal to the masses for undertaking a 'horizontal integration' of the various ethnic groups living in Assam. The popular allure of this guerrilla organization rested to a large degree on what came to be seen by the people of the region as an urgent plea for justice, progress, and above all regional autonomy, the prickly but core issue of sovereignty from the Indian nation notwithstanding.

The attention that ULFA drew to Assam's lack of development and the failure to forge ahead while other regions of the country scripted their success stories in the post-Independence era also resonated with the public. That Assam faced poor economic conditions despite possessing, and in great abundance, some of the country's best natural wealth and resources made ULFA's thesis of colonial exploitation seem plausible to many. ULFA's ideologues trace the present predicament to Assam's fateful accession by the British in 1826 (Baruah 2005a: 77–8). ULFA's ideology resonated with the actual experiences of many, a sense of always being on the outside, far away from the centres of power. This sense of alienation and isolation from the mainland is not just a matter of perception: there are frequent instances of people from the rest of the country (especially the metropolises) referring to young people from the region as 'Chinese' or 'Bhutanese', aside from the common manner of alluding to people from the region as 'northeasterners', as if to suggest a distinct, peculiar, and implicitly non-Indian category.

The 1980s and early 1990s saw widespread unemployment, underdevelopment, and gross corruption in the state. Mired in this environment of discontent, the frustrated youth turned easily to rebellion and charted their own course to finding possible justice and retribution. What ostensibly also helped their cause and gave them direction were the familiar if quite different insurgencies in the immediate neighbourhood—primarily Nagaland, Manipur, and Tripura.

ULFA, consequently, like its fellow militias, found itself ensconced in a certain kind of terrain, a rebel country that security and intelligence agencies regard as 'India's militant corridor'.[5] ULFA's influence has, however, declined significantly over time. Yet few in Assam believe that ULFA's present predicament is 'entirely of their own making'. As noted Assamese intellectual Hiren Gohain has recently observed, 'the rest of India must also share the blame' for the current political, economic and cultural crises (Gohain 2007: 1012–18).

Given this context, it is hardly surprising that a significant body of literature has spawned under the rebellion of the last couple of decades which engages the feelings and emotional experiences of the people in their response to the disposition of the rebels. The works I take up for closer analyses, all in their separate ways, carry as baggage a subconscious and sometimes conscious narrative of subversion; for the state in all these fictional accounts is, for most purposes, an enemy of the people. If these writings represent a discourse that is constantly being drowned in the babel of 'official' voices and threatened by the language of power and authority for reflecting the crises we face, they have managed at least to alert an otherwise complacent people to the need for truth, introspection, and justice.

'Terrorists' like anarchists, history maintains, are heroic losers. In the case of ULFA, while this may not be true, at least if recent responses to the outfit's activities are any indication, the somewhat awkward and ambivalent position that the common man on the street takes in any discussion of this rebel group surely beleaguers even the most tolerant of critiques. It is still unclear how posterity will refer to ULFA: as rebels, political terrorists, revolutionaries, or as mere opportunists. Much of the writing, critical and creative, in contemporary Assamese literature reflects the unease that the Assamese have about how to name or more importantly define the way of these rebels, seen as both necessary and problematic, in the shaping of Assam's destiny in the larger national space.

---

[5] In its recently released report, US security think tank Stratfor views the Northeast as such, with Pakistan's ISI working closely with Bangladesh and steadily solidifying insurgency in the region, resulting in ULFA's transformation into a mercenary outfit. See, *The Times of India*, 25 April 2007.

HOMES AND HIDEOUTS

'Samiran Borua Aahi Aase' (Samiran Borua is on His Way) is a narrative based on the crucial moment of return of a dreaded militant after having spent several years as a leader of ULFA. Manoj Goswami reveals the various faces of society—lover, comrade, press, politician, and his own kith and kin—all of whom look upon his homecoming as a moment that will change their lives; the story is thus fraught with implications for each of them. The story is powerful and in the present context of the ongoing if halting peace process significant in that it uncovers the kind of opportunism the return promises to diverse sections of the people. That individual militants whose lives are more deeply implicated by decisions often taken in corridors of power far away from the fields of strife also need sensitive handling is a point Goswami carefully stokes—an aspect mostly missed by the brokers of peace at the political level.

The scenes in the story draw on several significant turns consequent upon the return of the dreaded militant: the police for whom he is a 'prize catch', an excited newsroom waiting for a scoop and a 'first' interview, a former lover caught in the divide between an apparently comfortable marriage and her aching memories of a passionate romance with Samiran, the somewhat jaded bonhomie of his friends whose idea of 'revolution' and struggle have evidently taken a beating, the unease at his own home where an aging father is apprehensive about his militant son and is unsure about his desire to be reunited with him, and finally a frail mother who yearns nevertheless for the return of the prodigal son.

While the peace efforts initiated by civil society groups address crucial issues centring around the question of bringing the militia to the negotiating table, some other less obvious but perhaps more complex realities of dealing with the morally and psychologically impacted youth remain largely unattended. The insidious happenings in newsrooms and the hub of the state police depicted in the story, for instance, reveal the opportunities that such stakeholders expect to reap from what has dissipated into a low-intensity conflict lingering for years. Goswami pits the two faces against one another—the settled ordinary and comfortable lives of individuals in the mainstream against the grim uncertainty of a Samiran Borua living on the edge and years later still on the run. The return, however temporary, is fraught with doubts about his integration, if at all, into the society he has to come back to. Understandably, the transit from his hideout in the deep jungles into civilian life is by no means easy or even welcome. Samiran's homecoming therefore remains only a possibility contingent upon the willingness of a community, and more importantly, the state and the law to handle the situation more sensitively than they are inclined to do.

The attendant problem of what is now referred to as the ubiquitous surrendered cadres of ULFA (SULFA) documents more starkly the complications of a government engineered 'return' of the rebels who roam the streets they once shunned with a certain awkwardness for being 'outlaws', condoned now by police and policy makers in trade-offs that were imagined as mutually beneficial to both the state and the ex-rebels. It is no secret either how many such renegades of the outfit were used by the intelligence and the armed forces for their operations on loyalists and faithfuls of the organization to decimate it. Recently the Indian government has owned up to a number of 'fake encounters' of suspected militants by security forces in Kashmir. Such practices are common in counter-insurgency operations in Assam and Goswami's story makes no bones about it. Moreover, the sudden sanitization of certain former insurgents led to the birth of a new phenomenon of enterprises reliant on unknown sources of money and on muscle power that run with the safe sanction of the government. If that was scant compensation for laying down arms, some militants also got inducted into respectable positions and are now fully integrated into the mainstream. This, if in any way significant, attests to the rare and unique manner in which insurgents in the Northeast are sometimes also political heroes: the former leader of the Mizo National Front, Laldenga, who rose to become chief minister in his state of Mizoram being a case in point. With ULFA, such fortunes seem unlikely at the moment.

Samiran's story, more importantly, elicits the unmistakable feeling of unease and disquiet that is no less than the attribute of terror fixed to its protagonist, the sort of stigma associated with a socially acknowledged outlaw in its most lethal form of the 'terrorist'. What the reader, and by extension society, in this case may necessarily experience is a sense of terror, of being swamped as it were, by a general and systemic derangement. A large portion of what we understand and apprehend as terror, as Geoffrey Harpham argues, is symbolic and 'a feature of the symbolic order, the vast mesh of representations and narratives both official and unofficial, public and private, in which a culture works out its sense of itself' (Harpham 2002: 59). Harpham's question, whether terror itself is fundamental to the contemporary world, finds relevance in Samiran's return, which also brings to surface an order that is apparently hidden beneath layers of social and political hypocrisy and duplicity. The existing social structures are steeped in a terror-producing chain of circumstances, the underbelly of which is up starkly for view in this moment of anticipation of the militant's return and possible capture. While Harpham obviously poses the question in the immediate throes of post-September 11 reflection and introspection, our world has long been witness to a slow and lingering climate of terror, implicit and explicit. The rhetoric emerging out of the social and psychological transactions of these times is intriguing and Goswami's story is informed by the full brunt of such symptoms of terror that confound each member of society into an incapacity to separate the result from the cause and the fear from the confusion over the way we are.

On the other hand, 9/11 was, for a nation besieged suddenly by the threat of destruction, like an ominous flare—alien, fearful, and catastrophic. The terror struck unawares, wiped out innocents and left in its trail death and devastation, while a 'nation challenged' united in shock and sorrow and resolved to set right the wrongs done to them by people they did not recognize; or, as contemporary criticism suggests, wrongs that have unwittingly been perpetrated by themselves.[6] In the Northeast we are plagued by a different set of imbalances—the 'terror' is within us, the players, ostensibly 'our boys'. What we have at hand, as Samiran's situation in the story clearly points to, is an insurgency spawning several such Samirans: ordinary, innocent, albeit disgruntled youth leading nondescript lives who overnight turn their backs to society and take up arms for their 'cause'. Consequently, the people who witness the blowing up of bridges and buses, kidnapping (and at times murder) of individuals, are silent, ambivalent perhaps, and clearly do not voice their antagonisms or their reactions to such acts of terror. At times these people refuse to be terrorized and even rationalize the motivation behind terror. This then brings us to the problematic of identifying the terrorist—who or what then is the terrorist? And where does the real danger lie?

For whether we like it or not, ULFA's plea for sovereignty has been largely 'tolerated' by the Assamese mainstream and even if, as Sanjib Baruah argues, its commitment to the idea of an independent Assam

---

[6] See, for instance, W.J.T. Mitchell (2002: 52).

may have only been to a great extent what he terms 'political rhetoric', this outfit more than any other organization, legal or illegitimate, did attempt to voice its stand on certain central concerns of Assamese life and culture (Baruah 2005a: 150) While one could easily protest that there is very little moral high ground this outfit could take on such issues given the nature of its operation, it may be difficult to ignore the hold of sub-nationalist sentiments and ideas among a large section of the unemployed youth in semi-urban and rural areas. The fact that Assam's modern-day image of backwardness, slow growth, and peripheral status in the country's national indices of progress seems to contrast with its traditionally received history of a people ruled by gloriously wealthy Ahom royalty whose several centuries of monarchy fended off formidable threats—forces like the Mughals and then the British—is much rued in Assamese sentiments.

In the face of such a reality Samiran's story offers a glimpse of the scarred psychology of the youth: Ajit, Dul, Bipul, Bogen, and Rafiul—young men, mostly jobless and frustrated, who seek relief in a night of mindless drinking. Huddled together in a dimly lit room of the small town that is home to Samiran, they are portraits of a failed dream. The bonhomie is superficial, and their noisy banter laden with subtexts of unease, suspicion, and the attendant bitterness of a lost mission. Ajit's poetic announcement, 'it is we who shall usher in the dawn', collides sharply with the grim darkness that insurgency and counter-insurgency exercises have pushed the region into. Also, there is the ironic and unmistakable reminder that the ideologues of ULFA had promised a 'golden Axom' (Deka 1994: 31). While these young men struggle hopelessly to make sense of their lives, insecure and uncertain of their fates and in conflict with their time and society, Samiran, the other face, symbolizes the xenophobic rage of a few gun-toting men choosing to live on the edge. His anger is not unlike that of the maverick group of young Englishmen wanting to join the Irish Republican Army (IRA) in Doris Lessing's *The Good Terrorist* whose naïve radical fantasies turn into a dangerous chaos of destruction well beyond their own revolutionary intentions. His friends who are tired and can no longer renew their mission to 'change the system' must find solace in cursing it. Samiran returning to that society after several years is also no messiah who will lead them 'to heaven' (Goswami 1993: 20). And sadly, the dynamic of a desired change or, even of 'imagining the nation' independent and sovereign, is set off harshly by a social reality still steeped in bewilderment and confusion after more than a quarter century of the region's experience of conflict and insurgent activity.

Thus Goswami's trenchant critique of a widely corrupt media exposes the transformation of an insurgent group by a powerful machinery into little more than 'murderers' and 'terrorists' that are the bane of contemporary Assamese history.[7] One recalls Ashis Nandy's contention that an enterprising media has made terrorism and counter-terrorism into 'consumption items' for the middle class (Nandy 2004b: 20). The resultant narrative created by the authorities is the grave 'threat to national security': a rhetoric used by non-transparent institutional structures to determine and mobilize popular public opinion and thought. This is most evident in Goswami's story in the enthusiastic plans by a local daily to 'set up' an interview with the dreaded criminal revealing the dark underbelly of mass media practices and the real politics of terror behind the structures erected by the state. Consequently, most citizens confront the experience of militancy second hand and often without adequate scope to reflect on its larger implications, political and/or cultural. Yet the story significantly also traces the changing trajectory of popular support for ULFA. Between Samiran's years with the outfit and his return home much water has flowed under the bridge. For every militant killed in action and rebel insurgent still floundering in the jungles and struggling for life amid the killing fields, there are at least a dozen disenchanted young men who have lost their faith, as random inquiries across social groups in urban and rural Assam reveal.

In a careful probe into how terrorist strategies work, Andrew Kydd and Barbara F. Walter (2006) reiterate the importance of the 'domestic audience' for the terrorist. The paper, while making a concerted attempt to reveal the nuanced way in which terrorism works, also indicates that democracies are more likely to be susceptible to and hit by rebel attacks for their easy faith in alternative opinion. Like most other rebel outfits, it has been ULFA's regular modus operandi to provide credible information to their target group. Its easy articulation of its objectives

---

[7] I do not use the term 'terrorist' for ULFA, unlike that of the recent announcements by international security think tanks preferring to allude to them as insurgents, rebels in the main, for it is imperative to arrive at a critical and fair estimation of the nature of this outfit's role and rebellion in the contemporary politics of the Northeast and the intellectual response to it.

to individuals and interest groups on its side ensured their support of the outfit's cause. Indeed, a very large and free domestic audience, to be sure, had rallied support for, and endorsed the claims of, this group seeking to alter the present political dispensation in the Northeast. Official narratives on conflict in the state while maintaining their own truth claims, also concede that it was a combination of vested interests of various political groups and the sense of 'alienation' of a large section of the state's populace from the Indian mainstream, political, economic, and social, that consistently fuelled the increasing influence and expansion of the outfit's activities in the state (Hrishikeshan 2002). However, the changing tactics of the leadership and the obvious shifts of focus have led to internecine developments in this insurgent struggle and to an eventual scepticism about its ideology among the general populace.

'Samiran Borua Aahi Aase' documents not just the contemporary scenario in the wake of militancy in the state but, more importantly, breaks the silence of a community that chooses to remain largely apathetic to the regimes of terror, whether of the state apparatuses or of rebel forces working in tandem or against them. Literature of this kind seems to me to be an honest response to the problem of insurgency plaguing the region and creates in its own way an alternative space for dialogue that we have aborted for too long. One of the common roadblocks to understanding the problem of insurgency and mitigating it is the assumption that dealing in these issues closely or analysing them or perhaps writing a story on them renders one complicit with the phenomenon, or at least makes one liable for abetting or aiding the activity. That very little or significantly small critical work on insurgency and militancy has poured out of the region is indicative of the general hesitation about speaking the truth, or as a critic points out, is an index of the fear of being considered socially irresponsible and of being thus, 'on the other side' (Das 1997: 43)

The story's most remarkable achievement, then, is its ability to boldly bring to surface the several faces of terror—from the state police, the media, and the political stakeholders to even the terror that breeds within the very structures of Samiran's old home town, a tellingly vivid sequence of which is provided in the final vignette of the story. Samiran's return uncovers some of the private hell that his nearest of associates experience. Neela, his former lover, is as it were, a slice of his pre-lapsarian past and his return threatens to destroy the carefully constructed marital peace of her present life. Love in the time of militancy is dramatically transformed into neurotic fear and the dialectic of these emotional aspects assumes significance and interest as a society prepares to deal with these rebel members on its fringes. Neela's fear of Samiran is the most potent form and expression of the social rejection of militants.[8] She is haunted by the possibility of that one phone call from Samiran breaking the lovely loneliness of her afternoons in the vast undisturbed spaces of her husband's affluent home. She reconstructs her lover's image in renewed fashion as an alien savage stalking the boundaries of civil life. In this moment of the story the social divide and the rift in the human situation is perhaps at its widest. Samiran's own unimagined fear of the familiar streets of his home town, once a safe haven, as he now warily treads back to it in the dark of the night ready to take flight, signals the presence of terror of a more severe kind. Even as the reader comes to the end of the story there is no real relief in the fear generated by the idea of contact with what may only be, in the end, a much misjudged person choosing to give up his legitimate claims to his own society, itself both cause and consequence of such turmoil (Gohain 2007: 1012). For Samiran then, the wilderness and its hideouts are the only safe havens: and for many such rebels, confused by the growing unpredictability of their lives, the obscurity of territories outside the state may seem to be the only available option as they retreat deeper seeking refuge beyond the borders, and get sucked into murkier waters.[9]

A Terrorist by Any Other Name

'Bandiyar' (The Captor) articulates more pointedly the terrorizer-terrorized binary in what is another harrowing sequence of events and comes up with a stark revelation of certain other truths. Hare Krishna Deka's narrative picks up the uneasy silence of a long trek through hostile mountainous terrain which the captive state official has to make with his kidnapper to their undisclosed destination, a secret

[8] This and many other such cases of social alienation arising out of insurgency-afflicted families could be subject for a separate discussion involving the inexplicable hardships and trauma of a vast number of unknown women—partners, fiancées, wives, widows, or mothers of the rebels—who dot the dark and blurred landscape of post-militancy Assam and the Northeast. See also, Hussain (2006).

[9] In the wake of renewed military offensives, New Delhi has conveyed its concern over Myanmarese territories used by militant outfits from Northeast India. See, 'Junta Hot On Rebel Trail', *The Telegraph*, 16 February 2007.

hideout where ultimately an encounter between security forces of the state and the militia ends dramatically with the hostage being rescued and the captor meeting a gory death. Ostensibly, the arduous journey made partly on foot and partly by bicycle provides space for a natural bonding to evolve between them, whereby both hostage and captor, in a peculiar turn of emotions and reactions, are strangely bound to each other for their survival.

Deka nuances the idea of fear, central to the whole phenomenon of 'terrorism' or to the credo of rebel groups in operation, in a passage early in the story where the young captor breaks the silent speculations of his older, almost middle-aged hostage as he declares to him:

'Relax! There is no fear here.'

[The word fear elicited a strange reaction in his mind. Behind the apparent simplicity of the meaning of the word lurked several other implications. His eyes strayed towards the bag the young man had carelessly slung off his shoulder... he could fathom (and this despite the captor not revealing it to him) what lay inside. It ought to have symbolized 'fear' to him. Yet how incredible! The boy's words had only brought him reassurance...] (From p. 1, author's translation).

The author's sensitive handling of the relationship between the two people, each wary of the other, uncovers a whole gamut of social and psychological responses and the complexities thereof of dealing with such situations in the terror games played out by men from the rebel outfits. Fear here translates into terror and Deka's story builds on the idea of fear as violence inflicted by members of society upon one another, whether by legitimate or illegitimate forces. Often, a lack of understanding of terrorists and the promotion of 'ineffective hardline strategies' yield more bad results than good, as many recent instances in counter-terrorist moves have demonstrated.[10] Deka's story cautions the reader of the terribly nuanced state of the psychologies of both the rebel and the victim, and that we need to take them into account while making our own observations and judgements on them.

Under scrutiny are the sets of hunter–hunted relationships while the serene landscape of the mountainous deeps they tread is visually evoked: the vast blue skies above, an unbroken silence save the rush of

---

[10] See Silke (2001: 580–81). The media is one such core manipulator of terrorism-related events, Silke contends in his essay, influencing and changing consequences and intentions if media reports run counter to the objectives of the militants.

a hilly rivulet, where the notion of freedom seems encoded in the lone kingfisher darting from the branches of a tree into the swift waters of the gurgling stream in which the captor decides to take a dip, leaving his hostage free to sprawl a while on the patch of green beside it. The dichotomy is clear. Is this freedom or simply an inability to tear oneself away from the newfound trust to which one is beholden? The situation, the hostage thought, resembled the kingfisher's.

Free bird but a strange bond ties it to the waters of the stream. Though free, it is also hostage to the river. Here he is hostage while the boy is free. And yet he is unable to leave. In his captivity the boy too is rendered captive. Until he is freed the boy too cannot be free. And it is the unspoken language of the inanimate gun separating the two that determines the relationship between them (pp. 3–4, author's translation).

Clearly, the situation of conflict has always been more easily summarized than it actually ever purports to be. In his story, Deka delves subtly into the somewhat insidious happenings behind media reported 'terrorist' attacks and activities. What one misses in taking a sweeping security-centric view of such events and incidents, is a larger comprehension of the profile of a rebel outfit and its 'ideology' (if it can have a sustained one), which might greatly help in mitigating further acts of terror and alleviating violence. Perhaps much of the uncertainty over, and fuzzy responses to, ULFA from within the Northeast as also from the centre at New Delhi is itself an index of the lack of a consensus as to how we ought to respond to this rebel group termed variously as extremist, terrorist, separatist, guerrilla insurgents, and ethnic militants. As critiques in recent times point out, though ULFA figures among the 'Other Selected Terrorist Organisations' in the US-published *2004 Country Reports on Terrorism* and despite several failed negotiations with its nominees for a resolution of the conflict in the Northeast, it still manages to inspire sincere attempts at peace building.[11]

[11] As I write the essay, enthusiastic peace initiative efforts, both at the behest of Delhi and civil society groups in Assam, are desperately on at bringing the insurgents to the negotiating table. Prominent among them is the People's Consultative Group (PCG), led by the charismatic litterateur, Mamoni Raisom Goswami, which managed to establish a regular communication with ULFA supremo, Paresh Baruah, before the initiative fell through leading to renewed hostilities between the outfit and the government. See Saikia (2006). Saikia, an independent security analyst of the region, while examining the need for an anti-terrorist doctrine offers an interesting critique of the unique manner in which the

The plot of the story is simple and not unrealistic in that several such kidnappings had taken place during the early years of ULFA militancy with many of them ending in similar fashion or evoking familiar feelings that 'Bandiyar' elicits. While it took one shocking and untypical act like the brutal murder of social worker Sanjoy Ghosh to rattle and shake a watching public in the late 1990s, most other incidents seem, at least in retrospect now, to be more strategies of provocation or intimidation.[12] And though it is hardly justifiable to consign the above incident to an explanatory footnote, the objective here is not to dilate upon the event itself as much as to see the underpinnings of the strategies that the rebel group used to communicate with an audience they saw as potential supporters in what seemed an urgent need to gain social control and redress grievances they nursed against policy makers in New Delhi. Executives of several top public sector oil companies were taken hostage by the group; some of them were kept in custody for several months and returned to their homes with little or no harm, on the face of it. While two rights cannot really undo a serious wrong, and the intention here being clearly not to condone the acts themselves, it may not be quite out of place to examine the kind of 'method' the outfit employed in getting across their message loud and clear, and as to why in the first place these men turned to the path of rebellion.

What has perhaps also not helped is that for a very long time now the press has portrayed terrorists as 'crazy extremists' who commit indiscriminate acts of violence simply with the motive of revenge or the 'desire to produce fear in an enemy population' (Kydd and Walter 2006: 51–2). And while all this is subject for debate and serious analysis at both intellectual and political levels, the fact remains that understanding or even attempting to chart a case study of a militant organization that has existed for more than a quarter century in our present history

---

ULFA has conducted itself and argues for an understanding of the outfit that is sensitive to its particular brand of rebellion, not necessarily subsumed under the general rubric of international terrorism.

[12] 'Sanjoy Ghosh Dead', *The Week*, 14 August 1997. In July 1997, Ghosh was abducted and later killed by ULFA in Majuli where the social activist and NGO worker was based. Probes into this heinous crime revealed that Ghosh was helping local villagers in the developmental work on the island and had, in the course of things, uncovered the ugly corruption of the bureaucrat–contractor alliance that had taken root there. It is suggested that the outfit had a stake in the nexus and decided to do Ghosh in.

demands a careful and comprehensive response which imbricates all the strands of existence and social functions they touch.

By targeting a 'visible' government agent in the hostage-taking incident in 'Bandiyar' the outfit seeks to intimidate the state. But clearly, as the story reveals, just how equipped are these men in the jungles, psychologically or in terms of resource to outdo or outbid the government forces? As the captor reaches the remote village that is the secret outpost where he will keep his hostage under safe cover for the night, the only arms and arsenal the young boys standing sentinel at the village gate seem to possess are sticks and a stray gun or two, more for self-defence than aggression. There is no threat factor here, and the hostage, from whose point of view the story is related for most part, is treated more like a guest of the family of the house he is to stay in and hardly a man at gunpoint, lending substance to the now famous remark on the psychological aspect of the phenomenon: 'Terrorists want a lot of people watching, not a lot of people dead' (Jenkins 1975: 4). Most cases of hostage taking as far as ULFA is concerned have revealed the intention of threat perception by the target rather than real threat. The treatment of these unfortunate victims has thus almost always been soft, as 'Bandiyar' overtly suggests. The old village headman in whose house the kidnapped official is given shelter plays the customary host to the political 'leader' he assumes is visiting them and he is served a simple but freshly cooked meal of steaming rice and chicken curry. Later, as he retires for the night, the hostage takes out his little notebook where he makes entries of the diary he has been keeping since the last three months of his captivity.

In the unintelligible conversation that had flowed around him in the different homes in alien surroundings he had been taken to in these several months he had often caught snatches of familiar phrases, a lexicon made up of 'state', 'revolution', 'colonialism', 'national consciousness', 'government', 'freedom', 'right'. His notion of 'nation' he knew was not theirs for they were governed by their own set of laws. And they had created their own nation. For his nation was in their view simply an imperial force—his kidnapping was to him an act of terror, whereas to them it was clearly 'nationalist responsibility'. And the government he had placed his faith on for social and political security was to them only an illegitimate institution.

As the young captor explains in one of his rare exchanges with him on what they really wanted out of these hostage-taking exercises:

You are not our enemy. But do not misunderstand us. The state seeks legitimacy with the promise of providing security to its citizens. And we need to prove that your government has failed to ensure such protection. My 'organization' or I will not be the cause of your death. Your government will be responsible for your death if and when it happens.

The young man's unfazed justification of killing the hostage seems like strange logic, but the world he inhabits has already legitimized it and there is, as it were, in his scheme of things some rationale for it. If fear of death has stalked the hostage, this conversation has somehow shaken it off him, allowing a quiet resignation to prevail.

The clarity with which the hostage sees the eventuality of his death seems ironic in the turn of events that fateful night as the village and the team of young militants prepare to escape the peril of being raided by an advancing army unit that has found clues of their presence nearby. The captor breaking the news of the impending danger—*we are surrounded by the enemy on all sides*—exhibits a strange calm as he takes his position inside the shack pointing the gun to the hostage with a steady unblinking gaze. The next moment is filled with the bursting staccato sound of gunfire and even as the hostage prepares for his now imminent end he notices, almost surreally, the young boy in front of him violently spewing blood from the mouth and bullets riddling his frail frame as he falls crashing like a chopped tree trunk to the ground. In an instant he finds several army personnel rushing into the shelter, surrounding him while the captain of the group extending a hand introduces himself and expresses his great relief, 'Thank god, you are safe.' The moment is punctuated with dramatic significance as the wireless in his hand suddenly crackles alive and the captain excitedly relays news of his 'successful' operation declaring, '*Target safe, one terrorist killed.*' The hostage, in this case, the author's implied narrator, defeatedly exclaims, 'Oh no!' Deka's take on the semantic shift of the word 'terrorist' through his narrative carries interesting shades of reflection, not to be missed by the reader.[13] For someone who unambiguously encodes the terror and violence associated with the ugly face of militancy here is a fallen young rebel, at once evoking

[13] While there is obviously no easy and consensual definition of the problematical term 'terrorism' available even today, the most acceptable notion remains the use of any violence against civilians by non-state actors to attain political goals. See for the various and differing definitions of terrorism, Schmid and Jongman (1988: 1–38).

overwhelming sympathy and a tragic sense of loss. The captor has ironically turned captive and is slain, and the terrorized is suddenly the terrorist, evoking an unresolved reaction to the polysemous layers of the notion of terrorism. The story ends not in triumph emerging out of the apparent success of a state-directed rescue mission but with almost a gathering sense of elegy for a fellow human being, who has to bite the dust for faults that are not entirely his own. In a recent write-up, freelance journalist Patricia Mukhim suggests that militancy and terrorist crime in the region are euphemistically termed as 'freedom struggle' (Mukhim 2006). While one may agree or disagree with the particular explanation itself, the interesting aspect of the observation lies in the fact that there is, or at least has been, somewhere, in the popular imagination, an attempt to justify the existence of this insurgent group and it is imperative to find out why. Whose terrorists are these anyway?

Speaking from the Far Side of Silence

Parag Kumar Das's 1993 work, *Changlot Fenla*,[14] opens in the hostile fields of Kachin in Myanmar in what is metaphorically called 'Death Valley', in 1989, where guerrilla training is regularly imparted to cadres by the Kachin Independent Army (KIA), an insurgent group that styles itself as an alternative power in the hilly tracts of the Kachin region of the country. As the early morning light whips up a cold breeze, another hard day's work begins at the crack of dawn, for cadres of the 'revolution.' ('Changlot' is revolution, and 'fenla' soldier in Singpho, a dialect of the Tibeto-Burmese language family spoken across the Thai–Myanmarese belt in Southeast Asia.) The scene uncannily evokes stock romantic visions of camp life in the most remote of wildernesses, a situation improbable and most unreal in the imagination of those leading secure and comfortable lives in legitimate societies. And yet, the scene is for real, the players enacting their slow but sure transition from an ideology-based struggle to a desperate stunt for survival and a bizarre show of strength. To be sure, united under a common organization many rebel groups, such as ULFA, NSCN (National Socialist Council

[14] Narratives of this kind, I contend, are always struggling for inclusion and representation. My own nearly failed attempt at procuring a copy of *Changlot Fenla* some time ago stands testimony to its inaccessibility to the general readership of the region and prompts me to believe in the repressive state apparatus that occludes our histories from ourselves.

of Nagalim), UNLF (the United National Liberation Front of Manipur) had emotionally bonded in their quest for liberation along the northeastern borders of India that shared territory with Northwest Burma, now Myanmar.[15]

This facilitated the setting up of guerrilla training camps along the borders, some of which became ideal bases for ULFA from the late 1980s, and Das dispassionately details the activities on ground in this clandestine setting beyond the Indian soil. Even as he weaves a narrative through the peregrinations of his central protagonist Diganta, a senior cadre of ULFA based for the moment in these foreign camps, most of the accounts are validated against dates and locales that bear out the authenticity of the insurgent group's method of armed training and its easy access to Myanmarese territory for shelter. While *Changlot Fenla* is couched in the apparently novelistic plot tracking its hero's fortunes, it does not pretend to be anything other than a rebel's discovery of ground realities in his revolutionary and perhaps utopian search for freedom. Viewed more recently as a 'partisan novel' it however has been regarded as a work based on actual experiences of a former ULFA rebel (Gohain 2007: 102–18). Manorom Gogoi in his recent reminiscences of Parag Das, the author, recounts how the work came into being when the latter was imprisoned in the Tamulpur jail in Assam in 1993 where he came into close contact with several ULFA rebels detained there. The plot of the novel draws heavily on the experiences related by some of the cadres of their perilous mission (Gogoi 2005).

Diganta charts the dramatic destinies of several of his fellow cadres as they succumb to unsuspecting ends, either through virulent diseases, or sudden and violent deaths in the unfamiliar, harsh life of these camps or in their encounters with the army. The author's dedication of his book to one such martyr, Rajen Sarmah alias Uddipta Hazarika of the Nalbari unit of ULFA killed in the late 1980s, clearly signals the intentions with which he wrote it. Reading *Changlot Fenla* one is prompted to recognize the urgent need by an insider to review and scrutinize the activities of the outfit at a time when ULFA was probably required not only to rearticulate but also to revise some of the guiding

[15] Baruah (2005a: 150–2) offers a lucid account of the history of insurgency in the region and the cross-border affiliations thereof between Myanmar, Bangladesh, and the Northeast. The genesis of the ULFA rebels perhaps begins, he explains, in their belief that the 1826 Yandaboo Treaty between British India and Burma ended the independence of Assam; the outfit's main objective, thus, was to retrieve that lost independence.

principles of its operation given the growing perception that popular support to its cause was on the wane. Several upper-rung ULFA cadres, as commentaries on their activities suggest, fell out with hardliners in the camps and the leadership at the top which Parag Das carefully examines in his bold exegesis of the rebel group's original objectives and the subsequent outcome of their implementation.

The early chapters of this tome build the notion of an idealist who equates the organization's foundational strength with a 'people's approach' rather than a citizen-based one and establishes the claim that its identity was sought to be located in peasant agrarian Assam and not in the burgeoning capital of its urban metropolitan societies. The camps envisioned in the uncluttered and idyllic if intractable hill country (in Kachin, Myanmar, for instance) seems insulated from the cunning and capital of the city back home that, according to Diganta, 'festered' the young minds of the cadres who had trekked alien shores with 'dreams of revolution' in their eyes (Das 1997: 16–17). Not surprisingly, the early ideologues of ULFA and its mouthpiece, *Swadhinata*, routinely evoked the mythic land of Doi-Kao-Rong, an unspoilt pastoral where life and liberty seemed, at least on their terms, unthreatened.[16] If all this appears, on the face of it, something like a romantic and unreal escape into a pre-colonial era neither plausible nor pragmatic, some of the unwritten codes by which the cadres conducted their tough and unrelenting camp training belie such an impression. In one of the author's meditations on the changing profile of the cadres on returning to the camps after a spell, he is incredulous at the visibly debased face of the revolution:

(In Assam) several new boys had been inducted. They know nothing of the hardships of running the organization. On their entry they are provided with a Maruti (car). They do not have to stake their lives on some bank heist in order to gather resources. Instead they could by threat and intimidation procure any amount of money for which they are not accountable either. These boys visit the villages in their gypsies … armed with an M-20 they spend a couple of hours overseeing the organizational activity there. And then return to the city to their regular haunts at Janata Bhavan (the State secretariat) where they carry out dozens of favours for well-wishers seeking transfers and permits from the powers that be. In Assam the revolution works that way …. (Das 1997: 14–15).

[16] See, Deka (1994: 84–94). Doi-Kao-Rong, a fabled golden land, figures in the letterhead and almost as a leitmotif in the official pamphlets issued regularly by the outfit's publicity cell.

The leadership's apprehensions about the easy and often corrupt life of cadres in their forays in the city had clearly justified the need for GHQs (general headquarters) in the fringes and along the safer borders from where transactions between camps and cadres moving on the job could be more strictly monitored. Diganta's unhappy observations on the lifestyle of the new ranks of boys stays with him, disturbing his thoughts as he returns to the city where more surprises are in store. Unlike in the past, most shelters provided to the insurgents now are in affluent homes, with unlikely collaborators extending all kinds of help. There is a close-up of a family in the capital city whose opulent house is thrown open to several young men from the outfit: the lady of the house, a glamourous woman, in close alliance with senior policemen and clearly used to the comforts of life and oddly unconnected to their cause evokes something like a scene out of a movie where money, muscle, and material concerns seem to override the primary goals of the men. In sharp contrast Diganta recalls the occasion when, penniless and shelterless, a few years ago he and two other comrades had spent an entire night away from any source of human habitation on plastic bags laid out on dry leaves in the woods, without a drop of water or morsel of food, on a cold wintry night. The vastly different ambience of shelters in the present intrigues and vexes Diganta. The outfit has clearly moved on and it is in Diganta's beleaguered questions that the heart of the critique lies. The scene unfolding in the house of the hostess, Bindu Barua, speaks of the unholy alliance between political powers, men of lucre, forces in the police, and the boys in the outfit (Das 1997: 35).

Disillusion is writ large on Diganta's weary frame as he probes a young and trusted cadre, Ismail, about the decline of the leadership and the faulty ways of the organization. Intended originally to be a guerrilla outfit, the boys of ULFA, the author reveals, has strayed away from its diktat, exchanging the tough life of training in the camps for the comfortable manner of urban kingpins. Besides, they have flouted the basic principle of guerrilla insurgency by not integrating with the common folk, choosing instead the easy road to corruption and extravagance, which further alienates them from the people.[17] Was

[17] Many of these judgements made by Parag Das in the early 1990s, clearly a difficult time for the outfit, seem to be endorsed by later critiques and commentaries that traced the decline and altered image of the militia which had

there something organically wrong with the organization? Had the leadership failed? Where was the flaw, in its concept of revolution, within its structure, or among the cadres? Why has this history not been sufficiently represented in the discourse on insurgency and terrorism in the press? Or more importantly, has there been major exclusions and omissions in writing them? The changed complexion of cadres before and after training, is obviously one major source of weakness. Besides, counter-insurgency operations in the state conducted under the Hiteswar Saikia regime had successfully wiped out a significant part of its core network.[18] In fact, much of the protagonist Diganta's despairing confusion about which way the organization was headed comes from the growing web of extortion, criminalization, and lack of motivation within its ranks and file. In retrospect, *Changlot Fenla's* scathing critique of the ways of the outfit seems to be the first of the honest soul-searching urgently required at that critical moment, and anticipated, as it were, its decline since. As an impassioned Diganta, under incarceration towards the end of the book, reflects, only those who dare to point out the assets and the flaws of the outfit are its true supporters. Earlier, in a candid comment on the social psyche of the Assamese, Gohain Da, his mentor and senior counsel to the outfit sadly remarks that,

. . . the Assamese mindset is typically poised between the two polarities of good and bad whereby an attempt to find a mean is absent. Thus in any given context, if a choice has to be made we either blindly endorse a position or simply rubbish it. And we in the organization too have likewise simplified most matters (Das 1997: 145).

External intellectual guidance for most part was unavailable to the rebels and despite widespread tacit support for ULFA's claim to redeem the 'nation', Assamese society at large failed to address the major question of where it had bungled.[19]

---

earlier garnered valuable support from the Assamese populace at large. See, Sahni (2002: 51–2).

[18] Operation Rhino launched in 1991 under the Saikia government was followed by the announcement of an amnesty to be granted to all militants willing to surrender, culminating in the strange phenomenon of the surrendered ULFA and more ubiquitously SULFA.

[19] The very nature of this organization, calling itself a people's movement, had tacitly invited the Assamese intelligentsia's response into its fold. Yet, when

Very early in the book the author expresses his dismay that the rebels had over a period of time fallen from their moment of glory and had been likened to 'ordinary dacoits' and 'terrorists', suggesting that the core leadership had intended the rebellion to pursue a very different strategy than to engage in terrorism. Taking his readers from the camps in Kachin, through secret hideouts in Cox's Bazaar in Bangladesh, down to the army 'concentration camps' and jails of Upper Assam where Diganta is incarcerated, Das culls these experiences to explore the idea of revolution and freedom that had animated the rebels. If the author is openly critical of the top brass, a leadership now mostly scattered in exile or under detention, he also makes his point about how too many temptations and pressures had weakened the body politic at large. *Changlot Fenla* seemed to be a timely warning of all the perils that lay in the path of the rebels. It was no less a wake-up call to Assamese society that had unwittingly, and for very long, bred in its matrix the seeds of degeneration and decay. And ironically, for its own author, a frightening clairvoyance that rightly judged the rise of anarchic forces which would spin out of control and destroy precious lives.

The harrowing of Diganta in the Dinjan army base in Upper Assam, where he is kept under detention and brutally tortured by security forces, is only one of the instances of the nightmares that these men have endured by taking to arms in their search for a an elusive 'golden Asom'.[20] The question of sovereignty that ULFA repeatedly raised and continued to push as a major agenda in its 'war with India' is perhaps fraught with our peculiar conditions of local political history. Assam, to be sure, has for long struggled to discover its links with its neighbours as a region seeking its regional identity, economically and culturally, which has been felt to have been lost in its incorporation into the 'nation-state', whose centre of gravity is presumably elsewhere. And it is against this canvas that the resistance ULFA had conceptualized, and carried out in its acts, as well as its political tracts must be be understood. And while resistance arguably takes on its most quotidian form in this sort of violence, it is the other less spectacular section of people, the artists and writers, through whom a vision of transformation

---

criticism came, though few and far between, the movement reacted sharply, leaving in its wake a rhetoric of opposition and counter discourse that obviated any capacity for change within its ideology.

[20] Assam, after the intervention of the Asom Sahitya Sabha, is officially called Asom in nearer native manner and ULFA deliberately emphasizes its nativist concerns in evoking a pre-colonial Asom.

of this world of ours can actually take place in their attempt to 'resist' the cultural pressures on their society and meaningfully intervene in it. And although in such an enterprise, questions such as from where, and to whom does the writer write, will invariably be asked, it is the critical exclusivity of the writer as well as his insider knowledge that must remain his vantage. Parag Das, the author in this case, perhaps knew too much. At the end of *Changlot Fenla*, as Diganta the revolutionary is seen walking out of the Guwahati jail, resolving to further his role in the cause for 'independence' with his compatriots, his tryst with that struggle is far from over. Recent events suggest a vastly different trajectory—ULFA is on the run as counter-insurgency intensifies and deaths of cadres and civilians daily make headlines. Diganta too, in the concluding statement of the novel, notes appropriately that it is still a long time before it will be light.

Indeed, the struggle for 'liberty' may continue, but even as these lonely men plunge, for reasons right or wrong, into the killing fields, a world watching them must act: act, to free ourselves, most importantly of all, from fear. And it could begin with the simple act of writing, as these three authors whose works I engage with have. For, all writing is not free, and writers are afraid too: afraid of affiliating, or afraid perhaps of not belonging, and afraid of speaking truth to power (Said 1996b: 97). The words of another writer also engaged in scripting stories of her people in their engagement with resistance pose this important question: 'Do we need a camp, a prison, a war, to free us from our indifference to ourselves and from our fear of others?'[21]

---

[21] Cixous (1993: 44). Cixous, of French-Algerian descent, who grew up as a Jewish girl in France, and is a feminist intellectual today, reveals in this exceptionally lyrical essay her particular anxiety of living in a contested space.

CHAPTER 6

Narrative Agency and Thinking about Conflicts

NANDANA DUTTA

...ethnicity should be viewed as the social and political creation of elites who draw upon, distort and sometimes fabricate materials from the cultures of the groups they wish to represent in order to protect their well being or existence or to gain economic and political advantage for their groups as well as for themselves.[1]

Assam's turmoil in the last three decades has been the result of narratives about it generated by the centre and narratives about itself generated in response. How does one explain such a claim? One could examine public utterances from the nineteenth century onwards about Assam's relationship with the rest of India—a Jyoti Prasad Agarwalla or an Ambikagiri Roychowdhuri, both acknowledging the value of alignment, albeit in different ways, and imagining a great nation of which Assam is a part. Or one might look at the political relationship in the post-Independence era, when the rhetoric about indifference and neglect is fuelled by Nehru's infamous reply to very real fears about invasion by China and immigrant influx from East Pakistan communicated to him by the then chief minister, Gopinath Bordoloi. Or one might study this narrative in its maturity in the last three decades which saw the situation in Assam coming to a boil as a result of the neglect of political, economic, and social issues over the entire post-Independence period. This third option is the one I choose to look at in this essay, noting how the narrative of neglect works, what are the political/ideological investments made in it, and how it is manipulated in different situations. Along with scholarship on the sources and dimensions of the situations in the Northeast, it is also necessary to look at the continuation of the

---

[1] Paul Brass in Phadnis and Ganguly (2001: 26).

situations of conflict, the repetition of the same kinds of problems all over the region—in other words, the 'sustenance' of conflict. One of the possible sources of such sustenance is the way we have represented ourselves, our history and our identity, that is, the role played by narrative, by the story of self, a way of self-projection manifested in the discursive climate of the region—the perpetuation of the problem through attachment to a particular story.

Awareness of how narratives are constructed, refurbished, elaborated, and disseminated, and the significant contributions of mediators— both intellectual and political—in adding or subtracting aspects, is a necessary adjunct to understanding the atmosphere of turmoil and an important step that waits to be taken. In fact, the examination of this 'matured' narrative and the acknowledgment of its constructedness also points to ways in which such manipulation may actually involve the injection of selected elements into the grand narrative, and not only the injection of the politically expedient ones. It is quite possible that the politically expedient element is also the socially, culturally, and economically beneficent one. The following incident is an example of the way in which a silent shift occurs in a narrative in which a whole society has invested in, the actual acknowledgment of the shift sliding under the assertions of the new narrative as if the other older one never was.

On 21 January 2006, the *Assam Tribune* reported a statement made by Samujjal Bhattacharyya, advisor and chairperson, North East Students' Organisation (NESO), and Tapan Gogoi, general secretary, All Assam Students' Union (AASU) on the treatment meted out to a particular singer on ZEE TV's music reality show *Sa Re Ga Ma Pa*.

Last night's episode of *Sa Re Ga Ma Pa* has exposed the plot against Debojit which is only because of the fact that he happens to come from Assam and the North East.

Debojit's case betrays the fact that for a section of mainstream India, particularly for those who matter, there is no India beyond Kolkata. Debojit has established that nothing can suppress talent. Now it is for the people to give a fitting reply to the conspiracy against Debojit and thereby ensure that he scales new heights in the world of music. (pp. 1, 3)

The statement is worth noting for several reasons. First, of course, it emphatically repeats the conspiracy leitmotif that is implicit in the narrative of neglect and alienation that has characterized centre/state, mainstream India/northeastern periphery relations. Second, as subsequent events and further statements revealed, Debojit's victory was ensured; a 'fitting reply' was given. But the third point that emerges from this statement is the most interesting. In taking up the case of this particular young man as a representative of 'Assam and the Northeast' the speakers inducted a new element into their political discourse. Subtly and naturally, without drawing special attention to the fact, they elided over the traditional Barak Valley/Brahmaputra Valley binary. (Debojit hails from the predominantly Bengali-speaking town of Silchar in the Barak Valley.) The manner in which this shift was achieved lends support to the argument that this article seeks to present about the way a discourse may be constructed, changed, and manipulated, and the role that influential figures through their public pronouncements play in such makings.

A dramatic example of the use/deployment of discourse is provided by the Field Day project in Ireland which, among other engagements, publishes pamphlets interpreting the Irish nationalist aspiration against the 'contemporary colonialism' by Britain (Deane 1990: 8). In his Introduction to *Nationalism, Colonialism, and Literature*—the three essays on nationalism and the role of cultural production as a means to understanding colonization—Seamus Deane writes of the need for a 'new discourse' to enable a 'new relationship between our idea of the human subject and our idea of human communities' (ibid.: 3). The Field Day Theatre Company which steers the production of this 'new discourse' is specially engaged in the study of Irish culture as politically produced, and it therefore pays particular attention to 'interpretations' and discursive interventions. As Deane tells us, 'The general trend has been to analyze the various rhetorics of coercion and liberation that are so evident in modern Irish literature (particularly in Yeats and Joyce), in modern Irish political and legal discourse and practice, as well as in the systems of interpretation that have mediated these' (ibid.: 14). The Field Day example points to the existence of such a field of discursivity where various kinds of narratives are afloat. The similarity with the Northeast lies in the perception of the situation of centre–periphery (and not necessarily in the actual political dynamics involved) which is also the perception of a 'contemporary colonialism'.

Conflicts in the Northeast have been the result of a dissatisfaction with the ruling mindset at the centre—with the centre's inadequate understanding of centre–periphery relationships; with limp and shortsighted policies most commonly perceived as 'exploitation' of northeastern states for their rich natural resources of tea, oil, and timber;

and the 'indifference' to its problems with intra-state and international borders. Jairam Ramesh analyses government policies towards the Northeast as structured by four different paradigms succeeding one another from the 1950s onwards:

1. The *culture paradigm*: 'that the Northeast is a phenomenally diverse mosaic of cultures which have to be preserved and enriched'.
2. The *security paradigm*: 'the Northeast ... as a strategically significant region ... in a geopolitical sense of India's role in East Asia and Southeast Asia'.
3. The *politics paradigm*: 'the diverse tribal cultures and diverse sub-nationalities required participation in "mainstream" democratic process ... new states began to be formed'.
4. The *development paradigm*: 'that if we build schools, bridges, internet centres, IITs and refineries, the people will be happy' (Ramesh 2005: 17, 18).

These approaches over the years have merely fed the complex of problems around the issue of border: border transgressions, territorial integrity, and intra-state dissensions.

The historical development of a northeastern narrative about itself, constituted from these elements, is manifested in what is most immediately discernible as the 'narrative of neglect', encapsulating aspirations, dejections, despair, frustrations, and anger. Its circulation and regular attrition from the realm of general and individual articulations has given this narrative a status that puts it virtually beyond the reach of critical scrutiny—a new narreme (or little narrative element) sparked off by a fresh event or political decision unquestioningly added to it and not necessarily calling the narrative into question. Apparent in the functioning of this narrative is the manner in which—like all narrative or discursive representation—it has come to stand in for the 'real', the situation of 'conflict' or the 'problem of the Northeast' subsumed under this influential narrativization (as Hayden White [1981] would nuance it, the telling of the story by an identifiable agent transformed into the story *telling itself*). As one surveys the ground of conflict the question that repeatedly asks itself is: How do we simultaneously achieve integration and difference? This is a question that addresses the peculiar reality of being an integral part of a national formation while being diverse and fractured in ways that demand repeated reorientations of policy.

This narrativization has been both *enabling*—in the articulation of the 'problems of the Northeast' (addressing the perception is as important as addressing the reality of individual problems)—and *obstructive*, because it has frozen into the form and shape of 'knowledge', making it extremely difficult to look beyond its cognitive framework. Therefore, the second aspect of this narrative recognition of the area and its problems is of how it is made or arrived at. This may be a primordialist mode, borrowed from a group's conception of itself; alternatively, it may be the constructivist mode of the scholar, the commentator, or the politician which consciously or deliberately intervenes in the formation of discourses. The latter is probably the only possible mode especially because the constructed nature of the discourse has so often been ignored, sunk as it is into a kind of understructure, somewhat out of the range of scrutiny.

C.A. Bayly, in a study of indigenous nationalisms in South Asia, refers to the way distance or proximity to the imperial centre in India determined the kind of nationalism that emerged; the normative power of the imperial culture felt differently depending on where a people and a region were based (Bayly 2001: 38). This is an insight that one might bring to bear on the relationship of India's border states, in this case the Northeast, to the centre. Harekrishna Deka, writing about the Assamese mindset, notes how Assam became a non-player on the national field because of such 'distance from the centre' and instead became the victim of a political psychology that failed to 'address micro-level inequalities and needs of a people living in a geopolitical unit away from the centre' (Deka 2005: 191).

People in states furthest away from the centre, because of poor communication links, geographical distance, difficult terrain, and therefore emotionally alienated from the discourse of nationalism and identity legitimized by the centre, seek their own ways of expressing sentiments of attachment to a land and to the formation of their identity. This is an explanation that accounts partly for the sense of difference felt and sought to be sustained as empowering and imperative.

Recent narratives about the Northeast are, however, worth a fresh look because the shift I describe in the Debojit incident is in fact making itself felt in other areas as well. What one might call a trans-border exercise is apparent in the organization mentioned earlier called NESO, an organization of student bodies of all the northeastern states which most dramatically made its unity visible to the public eye in the joint felicitation offered to the young man Debojit who virtually transcended his Silchar/Bengali identity to become the iconic representative of all young talented northeasterners who needed to stand tall and make themselves heard on the national scene. The other little noticed and little commented upon aspect of this episode is one which, in the background of the separatist sentiment floated by the ULFA, has its own delicious ironies. By supporting Debojit in a 'national' and nationally televised music show, instead of logically ditching or ignoring him, the NESO and its constituents publicly jettisoned the earlier narrative of Assamese–Bengali confrontation, announced their wish to be counted as part of the Indian nation, and demanded recognition of the talent of these northeasterners who were also Indians (Debojit actually becoming the 'voice of India' that the TV channel had announced was the object of the entire exercise)—an act that not only offered a tacit political alternative but also set up a dialogue with the 'rest of India' represented on the show itself by all those voices in the audience who expressed doubt about the northeastern voice being the truly Indian voice that the programme purported to be seeking. Prior to this episode, the significant inclusion of the Sattriya dance of Assam as a classical Indian dance form like Oddisi, Kathak, and Bharatnatyam by the Sangeet Natak Akademi (a process worth studying for the kind of ideological pressures that led up to its culmination) had similar potential for 'use' as a link by scholarship on the region but perhaps because it did not have the reach of the popular cultural exercise that generally shatters hierarchization, it was largely left alone.[2]

The shift is also apparent in two other large policy changes in the approach to the Northeast, one of which, the so-called Look East policy, is already in the process of a somewhat shaky implementation and is also the subject of serious debate. The second source of a possible shift in the self-construction of the Northeast is the new emphasis on tourism, 'an economic engine in the development of postcolonial societies'(Bruner 2005: 4). Both of these I take up later within the discursive context of this argument as sources of new narrative components that might be usefully and productively added to the narrative. And yet the idea of

---

[2] Harekrishna Deka notes that there is simultaneously a centripetal and a centrifugal force working in Assam's relations with India—protonationalism balanced by cultural bonding (2005: 191–2)—a view that echoes the writings of cultural icons like Ambikagiri Roychowdhuri and Jyoti Prasad Agarwalla, both of whom acknowledge cultural links of the state with the rest of India, and may also be traced in the belief expressed by Prafulladatta Goswami about 'Indian' influence on all communities (quoted later in this essay).

linkages across borders is as old as the migrations of the human race.

In giving myself the onus of rethinking and scrutinizing the way we generally respond to conflicts and the way we respond to conflicts here and now, I take recourse to a narrative consciousness, activating narrative at two levels of understanding—one at the level of critique and the other at the level of experience, that is, the discourse of *conflict assessment* as distinguished from the discourse of *conflict*. My 'object of study' is something pervasive but nebulous and difficult to actually pin down to any single or specific source (obviously it does not appear fully formed in any single utterance or cultural form)—the narrative by which a people and a society live or negotiate their relations with others. I am compelled to find a method of study that will legitimize the object itself but that will inevitably circle round the question: why is such a narrative important; does it really 'exist' or is it in process always, though silent until it is deployed? In addressing these questions of the Northeast narrative one discovers that it is impossible to access it in its overarching form except through its manifestations in small individual narratives that play with some aspects of it. As the Debojit episode—or the narrative representation of it by Samujjal Bhattacharyya and Tapan Gogoi, and the narrative interpretation under which it appears in this essay—shows, we have here an example of a 'narrative of what happened' but the episode itself is inseparable from its narration. From this methodological tangle it is evident that the 'event' is inaccessible except through its narrative existence in the consciousness of a people or an individual who may mediate it in this particular way to a people. And the repetition/reiteration of the narrative is also the process of its change and its taking on fresh components as it adapts and comes closer to the imagination of those who begin to depend on it as an articulation of identity. At the same time, however, I admit that this narrative as 'object of study' is, in a most intriguing way, inaccessible, enjoining the critic/observer to constitute it in the process of studying it and adding to the problem of 'assumption' of the slant already borne by the object or 'transcending' it.

Implicit in this recognition of narrative are three key areas of narrative theory:

1) *The story–discourse debate* that hinges on the difficulty of pinning down that first version or ur-narrative, because the only access we have to it is through its little manifestations, not in neat chronological development.

2) *The relations between narrative and psychoanalysis*, the most useful element of which is the model offered by the talking cure—the retelling of a story with components being added or erased, until the best story coincides with the patient being cured.

3) *The distinction between narrating and narrativizing* is the last key area in the logical sequence to the above two aspects where the story 'telling itself' commonly has a greater weight because it points to the way things 'really are' rather than to an identifiable manipulator of a narrative but where its critique shows how all narratives including the ones that pretend to be telling themselves, all have narratorial agents.

The 'neglect narrative' as I read it shows all three positions in action as it were. There is no single overarching narrative which carries all its components; rather it is an amalgamation of little narratives that feed into it. It has grown in strength and become discernible through reiteration and when I assert that such narrative reiteration is a reason for conflict, I also have in mind the insertion into it of selected elements and the emergence of a new story whose reiteration could also be the beginnings of a solution—another story, a story that is therapeutic, a better story of ourselves to live by.[3] And thirdly, the 'neglect narrative', as we live it, has erased its agents in becoming more convincing for a people and an alternative probably also has to be able to narrativize itself and not merely be narrated in order to be convincing as a story to live by. At the same time, it is as well to point out that recognizing agency in a narrative's fashioning is the necessary first step to deliberately and selectively participating in the fashioning of that 'good' narrative. And Samujjal Bhattacharyya's 'insertions' in the Debojit incident is as much an example of such agency as is Mamoni Raisom Goswami's 'peace curriculum' for the universities of the Northeast.[4]

---

[3] Harekrishna Deka (2005) revealingly uses the term 'mind management' (p. 199) as he also identifies a 'neglect syndrome' that is 'not imaginary' in his analysis of the Assamese mind.

[4] Goswami, well-known Assamese writer and now negotiator between the ULFA and the Government of India, made this suggestion in a paper titled 'North–East India: The Education, Militancy and Peace Linkage' presented at a seminar on 'Road to Peace and Progress in South Asia: Learning from the Neighborhood'.

NARRATIVES OF RESISTANCE

Acknowledging the sensitive nature of national–regional relationships—basic to the situation of conflict and providing the occasion for the emergence of the kind of identity noted in the Northeast is an entry point into the modes of talking and thinking about conflicts. In the larger picture, a historical view of South Asia shows how ethnic plurality contests nation-building processes. A 'unified national identity' or national integration, 'a national identity that coincides with state divisions' but does not reflect ethnic divisions—these general themes find place in several studies of the region and are comprehensively represented by a work like *Ethnicity and Nation-Building in South Asia*.

For a long time, given the ethnic plurality of South Asia, post-colonial nation-building approaches focused almost exclusively on creating a unified 'national identity' based around either common political values and citizenship or a putative majoritarian 'ethnic' identity. The overall aim of both approaches has been to produce a pulverized and uniform sense of national identity to coincide with state boundaries that seldom reflect ethnic divisions on the ground (Phadnis and Ganguly 2001: 13).

And against 'the development of an all-country identity', ethnic diversities though recognized as social givens, were perceived as evoking primordial, sectional loyalties and consequently hampering the developmental processes of the country in general and 'national integration' in particular (Phadnis and Ganguly 2001: 146).

The coming into being of the modern state as also the demands of the globalized economy are antagonistic to the continuation of older, less modernized modes of living represented by ethnic groups and this is evident in the case presented by Adeel Khan (2005) who notes 'the role of the interventionist modern state in creating, hardening and radicalizing national sentiment' among the Baluch, Pakhtun, Sindhi, and the Mohajir. Such polarization and discomfort over homogenization, foundational to the narrative of neglect, are reflected in readings of the Northeast. A collection of essays edited by B.C. Bhuyan (1992) contains essays titled 'Nationalist and Subnationalist', 'Integration in the North East', 'Problems and Prospects of National Integration in the North East', and 'Economic Integration' all registering the dominant obsession in these rather obvious linguistic preferences. Udayon Misra's book on the Naga and Assamese sub-nationalist movements is revealingly titled *The Periphery Strikes Back* (2000)—a title that is virtually repeated in a later essay, 'The Margins Strike Back: Echoes of Sovereignty and the Indian State', that also recalls some of those favourite signposts of the neglect narrative: the exchange of letters between Gopinath Bardoloi and Jawaharlal Nehru over refugee influx, Nehru's 'defence reasons' for not setting up a refinery in Assam, and his virtual abandonment of the entire region to Chinese forces during the 1962 Chinese aggression (Misra 2005: 271).

A similar rhetoric sounds through Sanjib Baruah's book *India Against Itself* (1999) even as it analyses sub-nationalist aspirations that express themselves in conflicts and makes a nuanced and detailed examination of centre–state, national–sub-national configurations, a version of which appeared as Assamese micro-nationalism in a 1994 paper titled '"Ethnic" Conflict as State-Society Struggle'(Baruah 1994).

Patricia Mukhim, Khasi journalist and social activist, writing in the special Northeast issue of *IIC Quarterly*, approaches the problem of the location of the Northeast in a predictable resistance to the much-flogged 'unity in diversity' thesis and makes the following observation:

When India became free, the various tribes of the North-eastern region were made to sign the Instrument of Accession into the Indian Union by coercion. ... It is but natural that freedom from British rule was seen as a mere exchange of masters. The perception remains that India with its sheer might, has co-opted all smaller independent principalities into itself (Mukhim 2005).

This is revealing because it suggests that in identifying the locus of resistance, the target of resistant discourse is as important as the process of resistance itself or what is sought to be put in its place. By once again harking back to the terminology of unity and diversity the door is shut on fresh approaches, on the possibility of asking other questions, and perhaps in accessing other concepts of nationhood. In contrast, by jettisoning these familiar terms the new narrative of transnationalism, in this case represented by the Look East Policy and the Tourism Policy document, does seem to have the potential to chart a new direction.

Mukhim's essay, especially its introductory section, provides another example of the reiteration of the 'neglect narrative':

How can a region within a country be considered a 'difficult region'?... This coterie of bureaucrats/technocrats and politicians from the *Hindi heartland* who have no understanding of the special sensitivities of the North-eastern region actually write the plan documents for the country. Plans that are most unsuitable for the region and therefore not implementable (Mukhim 2005: 178–9).

The problem of inadequate examination of the popularity of the neglect narrative is evident in the subsequent claim that,

in the last two decades . . . people living in central India . . . have suddenly developed a keen interest . . . A ministry (DONER) with the North East suffix was created to ostensibly give the people of this region a feeling that they were being looked after. But this condescension and patronage is resented because the benefits flowing out of that ministry do not reach the people (Mukhim 2005: 179).

The echoes of 'us and them', 'Northeast and rest of India', and accusations of exploitation, ignorance, indifference about faulty implementation of policies, and perhaps most importantly, condescension—all components of the neglect narrative—are heard here.

The perception of neglect is the dominant impression sought to be created by Hiranya Kumar Bhattacharyya (former police officer and sympathetic observer of the 'Assam movement against foreigners') when he quotes Rajmohan Gandhi and Myron Weiner. Rajmohan Gandhi says: 'The rest of India does not see us. If seen we are not recognized. If recognized we are not remembered. And are not heard. This has been the charge of the citizens of the North-east against the Indian majority' (Bhattacharyya 2001: 1). Weiner also articulates a similar observation: 'The Assamese often think of themselves as a "forgotten" and "neglected" state within the Indian Union and as a neglected people in danger of being overwhelmed by migrant peoples and absorbed by neighboring states' (ibid.).

How does one *not* continue to reiterate them, *not* continue to make the same accusations that make the entire approach predictable—a kind of 'boy who cried wolf' syndrome that drowns the voice from its auditors or renders the situation invisible? While the intellectual, as Edward Said suggests, must function as a kind of 'public memory' to recall what is forgotten or ignored (Said 2001: 503) (the circumstances of accession might qualify as such an event), such recollections for the instrumental purpose of ventilating a grievance, is hardly productive for a better centre–state relationship, or for the transcendence of discontent.

In his study of Manipur, P.T. Hitson Jusho (2004: 103) identifies the following as sources of unrest: tribal consciousness, a central administration replacing customary laws, the jostling of several ethnic groups within the same territory and the consequent generation of majority–minority questions, and finally, in an emotive gesture that takes his analysis out of the realm of the critical, 'the indifferent attitude of the state towards the hill people' (p. 103). In marked contrast, the Mizo problem analysed by Phadnis and Ganguly (2001) is traced to the more impersonal and objective 'political and economic policies'. One might, in a similar vein, trace ethnic problems to colonial legacies, the federal structure of the Indian state, etc., none of which carries the same emotion. This hybrid text represents the sentiment that has been predominant in the region. It also ties in with my argument about the native intellectual who is responsible for the discourse and who can therefore be a powerful nodal factor in its 'adulteration' or manipulation.

A collection of essays (written during the decade 1953–63) by Bolairam Senapati (2000), an intellectual of the Tiwa or Lalung tribe of Assam, offers support not only to the persistent fascination for the binary argument, but allows glimpses of the many facets of the relationship that a minority community may have with a majority, showcasing a situation where the narrative spreads internally into the 'dominant community–minority community' site. In an era that precedes the violent turn in present-day conflicts, Senapati contributes to the predominant discourse on the tribal–non-tribal relationship. He too speaks of the 'indifferent attitude' (*abahelito manobhab*) of non-tribals towards tribals. Drawing on the imperialist policy of divide and rule he speaks of political attempts to divide tribals pushing the entire tribal fraternity towards destruction—a point that, he urges, must be appreciated by tribal leaders and immediate interventionist steps taken.[5] The grievance against the majority community is addressed very differently from how it would be today: for example, an essay in the volume, titled 'Asomiya Jati Gathanat, Tiwa Sakaler Abadan' (The Contribution of the Tiwas to the Formation of the Assamese Race), is an invitation to the community to feel good and comfortable about its relationship—a feeling the majority should be able to accommodate as a way out of potential conflict situations. On the other hand, a comment from 'the other side' could very well add fuel to the paranoiac in the discourse. Prafulladatta Goswami adopts the position that 'the Indian way of life has touched communities all over the country'. He speaks of cultural synthesis and admits that 'there are differences but there is a large common ground where the Brahman and the so-called

---

[5] See 'Obstacles in the Relationship of Tribals and Non-Tribals', in Senapati (2000: 39). Translation and paraphrase is mine.

tribal meet' (Goswami 1983: 1). This echoes the integrative nationalist sentiment and is inimical to the desire of the ethnic community for a distinctive identity.

That conflicts can be fuelled and sustained by articulations is evident in the early strains of the narrative of marginalization heard in the pieces by Jnananath Bora—'*Kamrup aru Bharatvarsha*' (Kamrup and India) and '*Asom Desh Bharatborshar Bhitarat thakiba Kiyo*' (Why Should Assam Remain within India): 'The Assamese have always lived in a distinct country with its own distinct administration and never seen Assam as a part of India . . . India's history is not our history. . . . our people consider themselves to be outside India. Like Burma, Afghanistan or Thailand, Assam has always been a neighboring country of India' (quoted in Misra 2001: 33). This is echoed in a statement from *Sadin* (an Assamese daily): 'The government of India policy in this region is to destroy the struggles of the indigenous peoples of the area' and (with regard to military mobilization against militant groups like the ULFA) 'destroy the Assamese nation' (quoted in Baruah 1999: 164).

The elements that characterize conflicts are apparent in these narratives. For example, the fears that precede conflicts are at the following levels: social (demographic change and therefore profile change of communities); political (a minority group's demands going unrepresented); economic (the cornering of limited job opportunities, the exploitation of resources); or cultural (fears of traditional distinctiveness or identity being lost, music, dance, the arts getting adulterated, cuisine tempered, weaving cultures transformed). The threat perception therefore involves one community besieged by another community that by its proximity or its intrusion may engulf the other—a fear manifested most recently in the attacks on people of Bihari origin, but also evident in the hostility expressed towards outsiders or intruders in several northeastern states, or in strict border control achieved by inner line permits. All of this at the psycho-social level has meant a suspicion of the other, the assumption of the rhetoric of neglect, marginality and distance, dissemination and use of narratives of discontent, and the desire for exclusive homelands expressed through calls for autonomy or secession. Each of the above is an issue of border and requires a creative understanding of the concept.

The examples of critique and emotive expression are founded on the assumption of exclusivity—the 'homeland thesis' most recently brought to our attention by the Dimasa–Karbi conflict in Karbi

Anglong. The conception of homeland that is generally assumed is the traditional one of a well-marked territory that coincides with social and cultural boundaries. Surprisingly, even when faced with crises of huge proportions—the taking of life and the torching of homes and property—the crisis situation does not seem to have radicalized thinking which is still trapped in binarism: homeland/loss of homeland without the ability to imagine the in-between.

The questions that arise out of the texts referred to earlier, I believe, demand serious and engaged reflection, not immediate pat answers: What is it that one selects as the target of resistance in a narrative of the self? Which element of the past does one select and how does one therefore read that past? The urgent need is to go back and look at how we came to be the way we are instead of once again offering the same narrative about marginalization as weakness. How does one connect to the theories of marginalization as a position of strength? The necessity of a theoretical or conceptual infusion into thinking about the region really legitimizes itself in these circumstances.

Countering the above discourse which is essentially circumscribed or bounded is one that is open and transgressive, borrowing its terms from an international rhetoric of transnationalism and travel. This is beginning to be evident in government policy for the Northeast (especially in the Look East Policy and the new thrust in tourism) and is matched by a recognition from 'below' that the material conditions of our times have always been liminal; we have always lived without strict and definite borders.

TOWARDS NARRATIVE SHIFTS

In the process of rethinking both the sources of conflicts and their derivatives it would appear that an obsession with issues relating to borders is the defining framework of the neglect narrative—whether it is the relationship with the centre, borders shared with other states or international borders, and communities territorially and culturally bordering on each other—spawning fears of homogenization and its derivative, invisibility, or its opposite, otherization. Ethnic movements for statehood or autonomy have 'a territory orientation with the vision of a "homeland"' (Phadnis and Ganguly 2001: 217); and such orientation is generally exclusivist and therefore dependent on a border. However, this material dimension of the term is only the first step into what I see as a border-consciousness necessary to the understanding and rethinking of conflicts—border as a trope that could be a 'creative space of resistance' (Rosaldo 1989) or the liminal, in-between space (Bhabha 1994) that is the postcolonial's most empowering site, the space where new identities can be forged or disciplines radically challenged.

Against such preoccupations it would appear that the alternative narrative has to speak of a new conception of borders, evince a degree of comfort with multiple identities, and recognize that the agency for transforming the narrative is there to be taken. Recent racial riots in France offer a searing example of the price of keeping a section of the population invisible—France's Muslim minorities, ghettoized in the seedy suburbs of Paris, are also rendered invisible by the state policy of denying Muslim girls the right to wear the hijab or the burqa in schools or in public places, thereby homogenizing them into mainstream French society. In this section my attempt is to find a way of keeping such invisibility or homogenization (the end point feared by most communities in strife) at bay by examining what might constitute an alternative narrative.

Already audible in the narrative shift is a border consciousness that is fertile ground for the introduction of concrete elements that would shape the new narrative and take self-conception in a different and more positive direction. If the Debojit episode is a kind of test case, it is obvious that selected elements can be inserted into the narrative to address the basic grievances. Since the narrative shift addresses (and has to address) the questions of intra-regional relationships, the internal dynamics of the majority and the minority communities (in the case of Assam, the Assamese in their interactions with the Bodo, Karbi, Rabha, Mising, Lalung, and the Dimasa), historical dissensions about the exclusivity of borders, and the influx of outside elements or transgression of these borders, the deployment or access to a conceptual framework is necessary both for the understanding and the 'use' of the narrative. Travel theory developments suggest that tourism, which is a welcome transgression of borders, may well be that area. With the tourism option the exclusivist idea is subtly transgressed and common elements that affect communities, cutting across borders, introduced. Travel theory indeed positions tourism as a 'crucial component in the construction of transnational culture' (Kaplan 1996: 47). And Kaplan cites Donald Horne: 'Tourism as a manifestation of a crisis in reality insists upon proof of the authentic' (ibid.: 60). The compulsion to cater to this desire for the authentic must radicalize the visited culture, compel a re-examination of its status/identity, culture, and enable strong new constructs as well as encourage freedom from old and fixed ones.

James Clifford invites a rethinking of tribal cultures in conjunction with a diaspora discourse of simultaneous 'rootedness and displacement' (Clifford 1997: 254), bypassing the polarity of these concepts. He claims, with examples taken from living museums and tribal cultures that, 'If tribal groups survive it is now frequently in artificially reduced and displaced conditions, with segments of their populations living in cities away from the land'(ibid.). Such a condition is true of tribal groups in the Northeast as well, with substantial numbers existing outside their traditional territories or even outside the region, therefore stressing the importance of understanding how it is possible to live without borders and yet sustain one's sense of rootedness to a culture. The discourses of transnationalism and multiple identity may provide an understructure that a new discourse of the Northeast might build on.

Transnationalism is a version of migration theory that has induced a radical rethinking within the discipline of anthropology. It not only invites unfreezing of borders between states, disciplines, and peoples, but also thereby unsettles the fixity of subject–object positions, of observer and observed, of migrant and host.

Transnationalism is defined as 'a social process whereby migrants operate in social fields that transgress geographic, political and cultural borders', a process facilitated by modern modes of transportation and telecommunications. 'From a transnational perspective, migrants are no longer "uprooted" but rather move freely back and forth across international borders and between different cultures and social systems' (Brettell 2000: 104), something that the Look East policy also purports to do. In the disciplinary site, transnationalism is 'part of an effort to reconfigure anthropological thinking so that it will reflect current transformations in the way in which time and space [are] experienced and represented' (Glick Schiller et al. in Brettell 2000: 104). And it involves a 'general move in anthropology away from bounded units of analysis and localized community studies' and instead looks at social action in a 'multidimensional global space with unbounded, often discontinuous and interpenetrating subspaces' (ibid.). Anthropology's taking on board of a contemporary political reality and its resulting transformation is worth attending to because it points to a way of intellectual engagement that is necessary. But equally significant for this argument is the generation of a new and adventurous rhetoric, the entry of which into our thought horizons must be transformative for the way in which we view our society in crisis and free ourselves from the traps of outmoded thinking.

The second area of radical change comes out of multiculturalist theories of identity, particularly the concept of multiple identity. Multiple identity is a function of border crossing, of transgression and of the breaching of the borders of single identities by difference and *differance*. The 'subjective experience of any social group membership depends fundamentally on relations to memberships in other social groups' (Hames-Garcia 2001: 103). Hames-Garcia takes his examples from race, gender, and sexual identifications which are never singly held but run into one another; but the same enmeshing can also be seen among nation–state–ethnic group identities—a fact that could prove useful in the process we are engaged in. 'What does it mean to be understood exclusively in terms of one's race, gender or sexuality? It means that one is understood in terms of the most dominant construction of that identity' (ibid.: 104). We could very well be back at the same point of misconceptions about the Northeast. Hames-Garcia quotes Maria Lugones ('Purity, Impurity and Separatism') who demonstrates how separating something into pure parts is an act of domination. 'By contrast, she views "impurity" as a way of resisting the social forces of reification. Lugones' paradigmatic example of impurity (curdling) is mestizaje or racial mixing which asserts its impure (undivided) multiplicity and rejects separation into pure, discrete parts' (ibid.: 120).

Behind the process of discovering multiple identities is the acknowledgment of the 'reality of experience and its construction'(ibid.: 109) that has come to be known in literary–theoretical circles as post-positivist realism and that 'self-consciously uses linguistic (and theoretical) mediation to come to a truer, revisable understanding of non-reified multiplicity and its wider social context' (ibid.: 118). The crucial area in this position is that of the acceptance of theoretical and linguistic construction with the help of which one might understand and find oneself as an individual ('consciousness-raising' is an important example)—crucial because with this preliminary recognition which is at the same time a discursive recognition, it is possible to imagine the usability of a discourse or narrative and its deployment for suitable action. The holding of these two theoretical positions, transnationalism and multiculturalism, on one's intellectual horizon is a step towards the insertion of their relevant aspects into thinking about the Northeast since it must be admitted that the isolation or alienation of scholarship about the Northeast from an international discourse that relies so productively on theoretical awareness about these issues has been one of the major reasons for the continuance of the neglect narrative.[6]

NEW NARRATIVES AND THEIR POSSIBILITIES

In the Look East policy and the Tourism Policy document, we have samples of narratives that are empowering because they perform a multidimensional role, echoing but also reshaping and supplementing the existing narrative of self through a tacit dialogue with ideas of transnationalism and travel, involving radical rethinking of the issue of borders and fruitfully engaging with the reality of the multiculturalist situation of the Northeast, lip service to which has been one of the causes for both invisibility and discontent. The underlying caveat about pervasiveness and elusiveness that discomfits this essay still holds because in none of these textual complexes is it actually possible to see the new narrative at work; rather, components of it play about in interpretative positions. However, the narrative of neglect that is predicated on the assumption of the fundamental divide between cultural and political homogeneity and the infinitely heterogeneous is discernibly shifting, taking on elements that are new interpretations of many older ideas relating to borders and closure of boundaries. Jairam Ramesh's dramatic pronouncement that 'we need to really start becoming schizophrenic'—which he explains as 'political integration with the rest of India and economic integration with the rest of Asia' (Ramesh 2005: 19)—is a sharpening of the new narrative that is already heard in the several dimensions of the Debojit incident.

One of the articulations of the Look East policy appears in the special issue of the journal *Seminar*. The rhetoric that is being generated in the new scenario is of particular interest. The establishment line on the policy is announced by Rajiv Sikri, secretary (East) of the Ministry of External Affairs (MEA). He says that it 'envisages the Northeast region not as the periphery of India, but as the centre of a

---

[6] The rationale for such use of a theory is in fact provided by the multiple identities of the Northeast and is available in the earlier narrative of Assameseness in the dual concepts of 'jati' and 'mahajati' used productively by a generation of early twentieth-century Assamese thinkers while referring to Assam and India, with no contradiction perceived in one also being the other. I particularly have in mind the writings of Ambikagiri Roychowdhuri (1986) on these two concepts.

thriving and integrated economic space linking two dynamic regions with a network of highways, railways, pipelines, transmission lines crisscrossing the region' (quoted in Baruah 2005b: 12). Whether it is a question of the Northeast supplying hydroelectric power to its cross-border neighbours, of reviewing water transportation, or of projecting the Northeast as a tourist destination for the Asia-Pacific region, in all of these programmes for the future are heard echoes of that alternative discourse that is slowly taking shape. What may also be of interest is that this policy retrieves and refurbishes one of those attractive components of the old identity narrative—the historical links with East and Southeast Asia.

The Tourism Policy document announces plans to involve stake-holders at the infrastructural levels of hospitality, transport, and maintenance of tourism sites—positive economic interventions that would ensure continuance of the transborder narrative. The two thrust areas are eco-tourism and integrated tourism circuits which might involve a tourist itinerary like the following through several states of the Northeast: Shillong (Meghalaya); Guwahati, Kaziranga, Tezpur, Bhalukpong (all in Assam); Tawang (Arunachal Pradesh); Majuli, Sivasagar (Assam); and Kohima (Nagaland), openly rejecting a state-centred approach and highlighting the positive and quite natural breaching of borders and boundaries, indeed inviting transgression of borders and active economic collaboration across states.

A final element in the document that connects with the question of narrative shifts and agency is the intention to 'plan, and implement a professionally managed integrated communications strategy to be called the "National Tourism Awareness Campaign"' (National Tourism Policy 2002: 13), indicating a mode that would be used to inject a new impetus into the Northeast narrative about itself, through which a more enabling narrative may take shape.[7]

The tourism option offers an emphatic transformation in the area of borders, closure and exclusivity, especially evident in thinking on the ethnographic dimension of travel. The anthropologist/ethnographer Ed

[7] All of these programmes are fluid in that they invite each state to formulate the details of their own particular policies (eschewing the top-down traits of most central policies)—moves that seem to be already under way in several states as evidenced, for example, in the Tourism Policy Document of the Government of Meghalaya which echoes the National Tourism Policy vision of welfare, participation, employment generation, etc., and also mentions schemes for loans to youths to provide several different kinds of tourism support.

Bruner who led a group of tourists to view his own professional site, Bali, speaks of a 'touristic borderzone' which is 'a site for the invention of culture on a massive scale' (Bruner 2005: 193). Such cultural production may also be the route to the preservation of many of the institutions and rituals of a culture that are at risk in the conditions of modern living but that are still perceived as necessary ways for a culture to distinguish itself or keep its separate identity. One of Bruner's examples of such invention is the Balinese frog dance devised for tourists in Batuan in the 1970s which, in the 1980s, was performed at a Balinese wedding: 'What began in tourism entered Balinese ritual' (ibid.: 199). While Bruner speaks only of forms that are invented purely for the sake of tourists, we might borrow his implication of constructedness in understanding how local cultural forms may gain visibility through such a process. Such outright or overt invention is not immediately apparent here, but the demands of tourism and the necessity of providing an 'authentic' experience of the culture of a group among whom the tourist may travel, could very well aid the preservation and consolidation of cultural or social forms. On a visit to the Lalung dominated Morigaon district of Assam, to study its folk literature, a group of us from the English department of Gauhati University had a discussion with local leaders on the institution of the 'boys' dormitory'[8] (common in many tribal societies). We were told that with the new and growing assertion of ethnic identity, the institution which had virtually stopped functioning was being revived and we were actually shown one such dormitory that was in the process of construction—certainly not for regular use but as a mark of cultural distinctiveness that could be displayed. The pressure of presenting such an 'authentic' experience, a corollary of successful tourism, is likely to urge a revival of many dormant forms of cultural practice—dance, music, cuisine, weaving—that in turn should offer economic opportunities and cultural visibility.

Both these new narratives carry the potential to energize the existing narrative out of its apathy. But what they provide is the hope of insidious change in surface and material conditions, addressing and keeping alive

[8] The boys' dormitory is an institution in many tribal communities that is now mostly defunct. Young boys would be taken from their families and brought up together. Here, they would study, eat and sleep, learn the crafts of the tribe, and often when necessary help out a family by bringing in the crops or lend their collective strength in some other sphere of activity. It was an exercise in developing community feeling, leadership qualities, and responsibility. In some tribes there has also been a tradition of girls' dormitories.

difference, embedding into the narrative of the Northeast questions of ethnic visibility, recognition, and admiration, that should be corollaries of difference or distinctiveness. Of special interest therefore is the idea of circuits in the Tourism Policy document which rather than being state- or region-centred highlights borders and boundaries and yet sees them as positively breachable.

The desire, the reality, the investment in one kind of discourse against another, all of these are functions in the evolution of any narrative that seeks to express the Northeast. It would be naïve to suggest that such narrative manipulation can be an exclusive solution to the turmoil of the Northeast. Policy changes, political vision, and timely action are the fundamentals but narrative may be employed as an aide.

Discourses of Inclusion and Exclusion

Part III

Discourses of Inclusion and Exclusion

CHAPTER 7

Northeast Problems as a Subject and Object

PRADIP PHANJOUBAM

Much of the problem in the Northeast has been, among others, the inability to strike a balance between the subjective and the objective visions of the changing world and the inadequacy of the responses to the ever emerging and renewing reality. The two visions, rather than complement each other, have instead been treated and pushed separately, too often at the cost of the neglect of the other. Because the two are treated as mutually exclusive, no serious attempt has been made to build a bridge between them. The broad theme of this essay is to propose that a convergence is needed, for the problem at hand is at the same time subjective and objective. Subjective aspirations give a community the sense of purpose that no worldly incentives can buy, and without this sense of purpose, the basic integrity of the society can fall apart. It may very well be that the high incidence of AIDS, drugs, promiscuity, and general rootlessness amongst the so-called elite section of the youth of the region is directly correlated to this destruction, or at least degeneration, of their subjective worlds. It may be noted that Manipur and Nagaland are amongst the ten states in India to have seen the highest percentage population occurrences of AIDS. Other northeastern states, including Mizoram, are only marginally better off. Modernity can go awry in the event of the inability of the inner and the outer worlds of a community to moderate each other.

The subjective world view, represented by the mushrooming demands for ethnic exclusive rights, hence must negotiate with the viewpoint which sees the problems of the Northeast as fundamentally one of a lack of development and modernity. Unfortunately both have come to occupy the opposite poles of the same issue. The challenge then to a great extent is to evolve structures where the two can be simultaneously addressed and moderated.

THE PROBLEM AS A SUBJECT

A personal experience will illustrate the first proposition, of the vulnerability of the subjective vision as a stand-alone explanation of the problem in the Northeast. In many ways the major onus of correction of this aberration of vision will have to rest on the ethnic communities whose worlds are today on the verge of being shattered by the irreconcilability of their own vision with the world outside.

Towards the end of 2004, I had completed a series of three articles after a trip to Italy. One of them was about how awestruck I was at my first encounter with wireless Internet at the Vienna airport. Barely two years later, in 2006, I reread what I wrote, and to my amazement found it silly. The wi-fi as the technology is known, is practically everywhere today, even in Northeast India. The pace of wireless telephony development has been, to say the least, breakneck. Today, it is not just wi-fi but a lot more. The subject is no longer a matter of mystery, but very much an everyday reality for even those of us in remote Manipur.

If the same article were to be written now, rather than appreciation from readers it would only attract ridicule. In the last two years so much of the contextual background has changed, and the context is what gives meaning to any text. One is also reminded of the classic real-life story of the Japanese soldier who got lost in the jungles of the Philippines during the World War II, and emerged from his hiding thirty years later in the mid-1970s, thinking Japan was still at war with America. The contrast between a subjective world and a changed objective reality could not have been more stark than the dilemma that presented itself to the unfortunate soldier at the time he was found.

The lesson is this: since the context is not a static phenomenon, there is a need for even scriptwriters of ideologies and ideological wars to reassess their thought processes continually against the ever-changing contexts. The inability to do this would, like the wi-fi story, make the ideas themselves redundant, obsolete, and even silly. Such a predicament is today not altogether remote. For far too often, in the Northeast region, today's wars are being fought on yesterday's slogans.

Take, for instance, the issues of 'homeland', 'ethnic identity', 'tradition', or for that matter the struggles for sovereignty from a 'colonizing' nation, etc. They will have to be reassessed against this understanding. Picking up just the last point, the 'colonizing' nation against which the struggles for freedom were launched in the first place, may not be the same nation any longer, so that the struggles themselves stand the risk of becoming caught in a time warp.

The inward-looking definition of identity and ethnicity has other dangers. When a certain identity is made to hang on symbols that have become redundant, the identity itself would sooner than later become redundant too. Perhaps the inadequacy of the answers to these questions is behind the endemic and viciously circuitous nature of many of the conflict situations that have afflicted the region.

THE PROBLEM AS AN OBJECT

In direct contrast to the problem as a subject, the other interpretation is that the problem of the Northeast is one that can be objectively enumerated, and consequently objectified remedies prescribed. The formula is encapsulated in the classic approach to counter-insurgency in a 'carrot and stick' policy frame. Subdue insurgency militarily and at the same time pour in money to accelerate 'development'. Six decades after insurrections first reared their heads in the Northeast, neither the carrot nor the stick has managed to do what they were supposed to do.

The failure of the carrot and stick approach could not have been more pronounced than in Manipur. In September 2006, during a session of the Manipur Assembly, Chief Minister Okram Ibobi Singh made a clarification on the floor of the Assembly that in the sixteen years that the state government had introduced a surrender policy for insurgents, only 377 underground activists from nineteen different organizations had actually bit the bait. This makes for a pathetic story, to say the least. If one were to work out the average it translates into a little less than twenty persons per organization in the sixteen years, or, a little over one person in a year per organization. Considering that a bulk of the surrenders would have been from the numerous vague and seldom heard-of organizations, surrenders from the organizations that really count would practically be nil. So much for a surrender policy. But what is even more surprising is that even the few who have surrendered have not been given what they were promised as part of the policy.

Failing a final settlement of the issues that spawned insurgency in the first place, it is always reasonable to be sceptical about the prospect of success of any surrender policy. This is true even in states where massive surrenders are said to have happened, as was the case in Assam.

In the 1990s, during the height of counter-insurgency operations against the ULFA, code named 'Operation Bajrang', massive well-publicized surrender ceremonies were organized by both the state police as well as the Army. In one such ceremony, more than 1,500 ULFA cadres were said to have laid down arms to the Army. The pictures of those arms, however, raised many eyebrows in the media as well as in other circles.[1]

But even if we give the benefit of the doubt to the authorities responsible for surrenders, the question that cannot escape scrutiny is: have these surrenders made any difference to insurgency in the state as such? For if the surrenders were anything to go by, the ULFA would have been nothing more than a shadow of its former self by now. This is exactly what is not the case and today the exact same authorities are having to court the same underground organization for a negotiated settlement. Is this an undeclared official acknowledgement that all the much-vaunted surrender ceremonies had no more value than the drama they were taken for?

The Manipur case is perhaps the hardest proof that the solution to insurgency is not just about the classic official line of 'carrot and stick' policy. Regardless of the truth in the 'criminalization and lumpenization' of insurgengy in recent times, insurgency is still not a simple matter. The flimsiness of a total equation between insurgency and unemployment was also thoroughly exposed. It may very well be that unemployment is a big factor behind insurgency, but the issue definitely goes much deeper. Youth frustration and unemployment, in this sense, must be finding bigger outlets than insurgency, in drugs and other socially deviant behaviours. Hence a rehabilitation policy would work better with those who have chosen the drugs route, but not the latter, for the latter is also something else besides youth frustration. Exploring that something else is what would provide the magic key to unravel the problem. Unfortunately, not too many who have the power to make the difference have been bothered or resourceful enough to apply their minds to the space where that something else is located.

---

[1] A bulk of the arms were not the usual AK-47, M-16, etc., but shotguns which are usually licensed weapons. Many of these shotguns appeared brand-new too, as if acquired in time for the surrender ceremony. The talk at the time was that many unemployed youth had jumped into the surrenderee wagon, with tacit official consent, to avail the benefits promised.

TRANSFORMING CONFLICT

Transforming conflict to a condition of peace is not simple. The Manipur government's surrender policy has proven this. That there have not been enough surrenders is itself a failure, but equally, the government's inability to find a way to rehabilitate all of the 377 meaningfully is a pointer to the complexity of the issue. In a hypothetical situation where the various insurrections in the region have buried their hostilities with the government, this problem would still remain and quite possibly even compound.

The question would be, what do you do with thousands of young men and women who had given up the best part of their youth pursuing, rightly or wrongly, a nationalistic ideal that involved waging war against the larger nation, into which they would now have to be accommodated? Shouldn't state governments in the Northeast as well as the Union begin thinking in terms of investing some time, energy, and capital into a quest for such answers? After the Manipur surrender policy fiasco, this need should have become at least a little more urgent.

From the Manipur government's surrender policy experience, as well as that of the ongoing 'peace' parleys between the NSCN (both factions) and Government of India, a few other things are clear. The unsaid but universal truth about an insurgency situation is that there is always much more than meets the eye behind its dynamics. The contributory causes are many, including inconsistencies in history, economic structures, development, and identity alienation. It is also closely related to administrative weaknesses and incompetence, but above all, official corruption that continually tramples upon all sense of fair play and justice.

The initial reaction of societies exposed to such conditions is twofold: one of awe and submission amongst the larger masses, and a general cynicism amongst the intelligentsia and elite, both dictated by the sense that if you cannot beat the system, join it. But the social mechanism is not a dead phenomenon, in thought or action. It is organically conditioned to transform itself to respond to any stimulus fittingly. Under a condition of constant and consistent abuse, it mutates and its reaction can become extraordinary, in extremity and cruelty. To a good extent, insurgency is also about such a transformation. Within a matter of a few years, moderate societies have become bloodthirsty. Insurgency in this way is a price that society pays for its neglect and insensitivities of the past.

Managing conflict then, it may turn out, is simpler than formulating a transition of conflict into a condition of peace. While it is true that thoughts of the bridge would become relevant when the river is reached, it is the duty of any government to anticipate future needs. An abject lack of such vision has been far too often the stumbling block of the Manipur leadership; or else the surrender policy it introduced in 1990 (possibly out of a political whim aimed at hogging the limelight rather than producing some result) would not have been such a miserable flop.

POLITICS OF DEVELOPMENT

That insurgency cannot have a solely military solution is widely acknowledged, even though there are still die-hard believers that it can. Without going into this debate let us consider the other proposition that development holds all the keys to a solution to insurgency. The idea of development itself is not so easy to encapsulate. One is never too sure how much of it is subjective and how much of it objective. Can there, for instance, be an empirical method to measure development? Very often, the tendency has been to equate development with growth absolutely, but can this be justified? Many economists believe so, and then there are those who don't. Giving a picture of its complexity and the existence of certain other factors that make development holistic and complete, Amartya Sen in his book *Development as Freedom* calls these factors 'freedoms' and proceeds to calibrate their quality through 'unfreedoms'. The less 'unfreedoms' there are, the more the 'freedoms' (Sen 2001).

In this approach, the popular indices of development such as gross domestic product (GDP) and income are important to the extent that they create the condition for freeing people from 'unfreedoms' to live life as they would by providing the fuel for actualizing their individual aspirations. The example that Sen uses to demonstrate this argument is interesting. It is a known fact that, by and large, African-Americans have lower incomes than white Americans, but their incomes, although lower in comparison to their white countrymen, is significantly higher than people in most developing countries even after taking into account the differences in the costs of living, etc. Yet, statistics say that African-Americans have a much lower life expectancy than the denizens of most countries in the developing world. One thus deduces that quality of life is not always a direct derivative of GDP or income. This is exactly where the 'philosophical economists' see a problem area in conceptualizing the whole notion of development.

It is again precisely because there exists such a problem area that the agenda of development has been prone to politicization. People in the Northeast are all too familiar as to what this means. In fact, the region's understanding of development has been grotesquely skewed to mean only externally delivered economic packages which can be translated through various backdoor means and leakages, at the soonest possible, into hard cash and by expending the least energy. Corruption is the immediate manifestation. The politics of development has also been a very convenient handle for the carrot-and-stick policy makers. This sordid drama is today a part of life for the northeasterners, and true development remains the casualty. The economic bails are necessary but these must actually be 'bails' to kick-start a process that will liberate the people from the binds of poverty, unemployment, and a sense of deprivation resulting from a lack of appropriate skills and education, ill health, malnutrition, etc., and not merely counter-insurgency measures.

This 'philosophical' approach to developmental economic thinking is in many ways an emphasis on the need for the objectification of the subjective visions of the victims. In the end, it is identifying what constitutes quality of life for the people under scrutiny that matters the most. Consequently, it is also the quality and intent, rather than just the size of economic bails that should impress.

DEVELOPMENT PROBLEMS

Obviously, an informed discourse on what 'development' should consist of seems to be what is most essential in Manipur today. Unfortunately, such a discourse precisely is what has been in extremely low decibel for all this while. In its place is impassioned sloganeering from the streets defining 'development' agendas. Quite often the demands are also self-contradictory but the state has been desensitized to the extent that it seldom discovers these contradictory elements in its own visions. This shortfall also results from a peculiar narcissism in the society that makes a major section of its citizenry crave only the fruits of development, without even bothering to think of the cost of having these—an attitude defined by such discordant traditions as demands for more electricity without paying taxes for it, more holidays but fatter salary packets, more employment but less work etc. Too much is taken for granted as the responsibility of the welfare state, even to the ridiculous extent of heaping all ordinary burdens expected to be borne by the individual citizens on the state.

First and foremost though, it is the failure of the intelligentsia in working up an active discourse on what defines 'development'. The continually updated proceeding of such a credible debate should have been omnipresent to inform, moderate, and influence both the ordinary citizens as well as the highbrow policy makers in the state's corridors of power. Therefore, on the current hot issue of the Tipaimukh Multipurpose Dam for instance, one is still not sure what the rational, scientific standpoint should be. It is easy to latch on to the statist vision of magnificent and state-of-the-art multipurpose dams as modern temples, as much as it is easy to simply jump onto the bandwagon of the current mood of political correctness and say no to dams whatever the end result. But neither would constitute what can be defined as a morally and intellectually autonomous decision of the rational self. The earnest plea is for the region's intelligentsia to prepare the grounds on which such rational autonomous decisions, both at the individual as well as at the collective levels, become possible. And this is extremely important indeed, for understanding 'development' is very much also about understanding the future.

It is interesting that the problem is not confined to the underdeveloped regions of the world alone. It is in fact one which has begun to plague the developed West as well, in particular Western Europe. Writing on the violent unrests in France in early 2006 over the government's new labour law that sought to make its workforce more competitive, *Newsweek* columnist Robert J. Samuelson called it a dilemma of advanced democracies: 'Hardly anyone wants to surrender the benefits and protections of today's generous welfare state, but the fierce attachment to these costly and self-defeating programs prevents Europe from preparing for a future that, though it may be deplored, is inevitable. Actually, it's not the future. It's the present.'[2]

He adds later in the column: 'The student protesters in France think that if they march long enough or burn enough cars, they can make the future go away. No such luck.' The French problem may not be an exact parallel as it also has a racial tinge to it, but all the same there would be lessons for our protests-torn region there. While most protests

[2] 'Politics of Make-Believe', *Newsweek*, 3 April 2006. Also available at: http://www.msnbc.msn.com/id/12015271/site/newsweek/

have valid reasons, they must be moderated by informed, intelligent discourses that are clearly able to indicate what the desirable shape of the future might be. After all, as so succinctly said by Samuelson, street politics can alter policies, but they cannot make the future go away.

THINGS FALL APART

So how must the future be tackled? This discussion must necessarily also centre around the notion of modernity. The balance between modernity and tradition is extremely tricky as is demonstrated at practically every issue that confronts a state like Manipur. This is so because the place is arguably only out of the 'pre-modern' era and consequently its experience of the 'colonial modern' is relatively very nascent. Like it or not, the 'colonial modern' is modern. Adding to the problem is also the fact that the rules of the game of 'modernity' were fashioned much before these societies decided, either by fate or volition, to join the league. They were never part of the social processes that forged the terms and understandings of 'modernity' and therefore these societies either show some resistance to 'modernity', or else have a skewed understanding of it. To this day the debate continues within Manipur on whether 'modernity' should be welcomed or the 'traditional' allowed to hold.

The proposition is problematic. Take the instance of land or the notion of homeland. Some of the most gruesome bloodletting, as well as the most vexing conflict situations have resulted out of these. Given a rigid adherence to these notions, there is little choice but to live through these frictions, both between varying and contradictory understandings of these 'traditional' notions, as well as between these 'traditional' notions and the 'modern' land tenureship mechanisms. The case of the Manipur Land Revenue & Land Reforms Act (MLR&LR Act) and its limited applicability because of the resistance to it from many 'traditionalist' quarters, exemplifies this dilemma.

In Manipur, the problem is further compounded because the degree of acceptance of this 'modernity' starkly contrasts between its two distinct geographical regions—the hills and the valley, the former showing much more reluctance to step out into the 'modern'. As to which attitude proves to be more advantageous in the universal struggle for survival, one cannot judge, although one does definitely have an opinion on this. Only time can tell which way the future is inclined, but can any government worth its salt afford to leave things to time? In one's opinion (not judgement), it is 'modernity' which will hold and hence the sooner the communities come to terms with it, the better it will be. In literature, acclaimed African writers like Chinua Achebe have dealt with the subject convincingly and passionately in novels like *Things Fall Apart*.

This is, however, not to suggest a surrender of all traditionally held beliefs blindly and blatantly on the altar of 'modernity'. Instead the entreaty is for an acceptance of an inevitable future, by marrying it with 'tradition'. The offspring would, by the very law of natural selection, be a stronger entity. Take the case of the amalgamated Meitei brand of Hinduism. An amalgamation perhaps catalysed by the enlightened vision of early leaders such as Maharaja Rajashri Bhagyachandra, the monarch to whom the Ras Lila was reportedly revealed in a dream, as so well argued by M.C. Arun in his stage adaptation of the life and times of the eighteenth-century king, *Rajashri Bhagyachandra*.[3] The king evolved a hybrid that does not transgress but instead transcends the 'traditional', incorporating and enriching it with a different world view.

The other question that arises often in discussing modernity is, how free is free choice? Does there exist a meta-narrative which envelops and predetermines all other historical narratives? Many intellectuals in Manipur for instance seem to think there is such a historical predicament forged by what may indeed be the one most important event in the modern era—colonialism. The assumption seems to be that all postcolonial thinking is a product of colonialism, especially in contemplating the issue of modernity. What then can be the alternate modernity?

If it was just a convenient way of classifying historical periods, 'colonial modernity' would not have been so problematic, except it is not so. It is loaded to the core with values and that too of a very derisive nature. It implies a modernity that is a direct derivative of the dehumanizing enslavement that colonialism introduced, in both material and spiritual terms, exhibiting in the process an inability to 're-people' that spiritual landscape, sapped and made barren by colonialism's brutal aggressions—a state of mind where the formerly colonized continue to immortalize the values of their former colonizers, even those that made them less than human. Much of the social stratifications

---

[3] Stage production by Banian Repertory Theatre. Producer: M.C. Thoiba, Director: M.C. Arun.

and dualities that are witnessed in these former colonies today, such as between tribal and non-tribal and forward and backward communities, are supposed to be a result of this. The obvious inference is that in the non-colonized world such stratification would have been very different, or at least not brutal, even if existent.

This is a fallacy, although it must be acknowledged there are strong elements of hangovers of the past era contaminating the present. Thailand is one such case. The country was never colonized, but it treats its peripheral citizenry much worse than many former colonies do. Half of its 'indigenous' populations (a euphemism for 'tribal') lacks citizenship. They are not eligible to vote, nor do they enjoy other rights and entitlements that go with citizenship in a 'modern' nation. In fact, Bhutan or Nepal fare no better in classifying their own populations. In Nepal, which has just joined the league of 'colonial modernity' by ushering in democracy and republicanism, the battle for full citizenship rights has just begun.

The idea of an all pervasive 'colonial modernity' which is supposed to enslave all minds goes against the belief that the human self is fundamentally free, that even in the worst of colonial times this space was never totally lost. The belief, if not a fact of life, is that the creative impulse in a man is always free. A man is able to adapt to the worst circumstances if given the free exercise of this creativity.

CHICKEN NECK SYNDROME

If 'colonial modernity' has a physical manifestation, it is the narrow 22-odd kilometre chicken neck corridor between Bangladesh and Bhutan that connects the Indian subcontinent with the Northeast, often used as an apt image to describe the alienation of the Northeast from the national mainstream. This 22 kilometre border is supposed to constitute only about 2 per cent of the total boundary of the Northeast with the rest of India. The remaining 98 per cent are international borders, with China and Bhutan in the north, Myanmar in the east, and Bangladesh in the south and much of the west. The physical picture is unambiguous. It conveys a stark sense of lack of contact, both physical and spiritual, with subcontinental India. Many have often argued powerfully about how this physical condition portrays an inner psychological distance that is the destiny of the relationship of the Northeast with the soul of India. From its lack of development to the numerous secessionist insurrections it is witnessing, all have been attributed in varying degrees to this distance.

The only shortcoming of this perspective is that it fails to determine how this chicken neck syndrome is not a physical condition but a political one. This is serious because the omission results in the obscuring of a historical fact that the chicken neck is a residual fallout of colonial politics and administration, rather than a natural, physical feature. To be precise, is the Radcliffe Line, the boundary drawn by the British colonial administration before they departed from India in 1947, the culprit behind the 'distance' between the Northeast and rest of India? Did the boundary commission of the then British administration have to have the Northeast connected to India by a chicken neck? If the Radcliff Line did not make this chicken neck a chicken neck, would the alienation of the Northeast have been the same today?

Of course the chicken neck does expose the general mindset of the Indian leadership at the time the Radcliff Line was drawn, and perhaps even today. They allowed the chicken neck to materialize, which it is doubtful they would have done if say Gujarat were to be thus isolated by an international political boundary. No war has been fought over the Radcliff Line's chicken neck, but one was fought over another border demarcating the Northeast—the McMahon Line, again another colonial line that defines the Northeast among others.

These lines did much more to alter the face and psychology of the Northeast. Ever since they came into existence, the sea suddenly became remote, the Barak Valley came to be undermined considerably both politically and commercially, thriving border trades became stiflingly regulated or else condemned to slow strangulation, etc. Without going into the rigmarole of the justness or otherwise of these lines, for indeed they are a reality today not to be undone easily, one simple question begs an answer. What was it like, or what must it have been like, before these lines were drawn, in the case of some of them, not much more than half a century ago? This question is beginning to be asked in so many other situations everywhere in the postcolonial world, and with astounding results. Economic and cultural zones that transcend but do not disturb national boundaries are emerging. The Greater Mekong Sub-region (GMS), the Association of South East Asian Nations (ASEAN), the much heard-of Track-II 'Kunming Initiative' which envisages Bangladesh, China, India, and Myanmar (BCIM) economic cooperation and connectivity, are just a few.

One way of attempting to answer the question as to what it must have been like before the national boundaries came up, would be to have a look at the unofficial relations that still exist despite the boundaries. The popular unofficial trade routes, or smuggling and gun-running channels if you like, is one such area. Would making these routes official make a difference to the scenario and bring what is underground, overground, as much as make what is illegal, legal? The other approach would be to refer to the abiding memories of the time that still linger on. Just as Cox Bazaar and Mandalay are familiar names to unofficial traders, so are Dhaka and Chittagong Universities to many first, second, and even third-generation Western education literate, in places like Manipur. Sylhet too is a fond memory for many in Manipur who still have distant relatives living there. This brings us back to the discussion on development and growth, and how these understandings are also a product of spheres outside mere economic statistics. These are in many ways 'world views'. Interpretations of India's new 'Look East Policy' from the perspective of the Northeast must also have this in mind. It is not just about trade and commerce and economic gain. It is also about ventilating a psychology of claustrophobia by opening up the Northeast to what is its natural surrounding.

HOW UNBROKEN IS PROGRESS

While the postmodern theory of 'deconstruction' cannot be a complete and rounded philosophy as such, there can be little serious doubts about the irrefutability of the cautions it flagged against many presumptions of traditional thinking. This is especially so in the fields of humanities and arts. Take the case of the popular understanding of progress—of history, arts, etc. While history cannot be simply 'one damn thing after another', how far can we be justified in saying it has followed a linear or even a traceable multidirectional locus?

In the world of art, the ridiculous nature of the query was pointed out quite eloquently by someone who is considered to be one of the greatest historians of ideas—Isaiah Berlin. He demolished the unquestioned presumption that art too has always 'progressed' with one era dovetailing the other and, because of the advantage of hindsight, the latest era coming out on top at the end of this continuous progression. Since art has to do with human aspirations and inner urges, it should follow from the progress theory that what a great master like Rembrandt aspired to be would be to a great extent what Picasso represented centuries later, and that his own achievement was lower down on the ladder of that same universal quest. Or Homer's epics *Odyssey* and *Iliad* were incomplete expressions of the writer's aspiration to achieve what John Milton in *Paradise Lost* achieved two thousand years later. This obviously could not have been the case, could it? For all they are worth, a Rembrandt may be a greater work of art than a Picasso, or Homer's artistic talent may be way ahead of Milton's. Or, alternatively, and more plausibly, there are no perfect scales on which these expressions in art can be measured and compared. Epochal achievements in these fields are definitely related and certain elements are most certainly passed down from generation to generation, but it is absurd to even imagine that a progression works in the manner that popular presumptions in social sciences have led most to believe. Human aspirations and creativity are inextricably linked to the contextual backgrounds they developed in, and often they cannot cross the boundaries of these backgrounds. Hence, in all likelihood, epics of the Homerian proportion cannot ever be written again as, in all likelihood, the creativity and imagination that gave birth to them belonged in that epoch only. The proposition, it can be imagined, will have to be true of all other social sciences as well, including history. Even history cannot be characterized as a simple progression of one building block piling atop another in endless succession.

This thought of postmodern 'deconstruction' is often evoked when confronted with the question, sometimes posed provocatively and at other times honestly, as to what the nature of the presumably ancient 'imagining' called Manipur is all about. How could it ever qualify to be a 'nation' or even a polity before the modern times? Where are the proofs that the Kabaw Valley ever belonged to Manipur, etc.? One senses a similar flawed presumption of historical progression in these questions. Who says a nation always has to have hard boundaries with boundary pillars, fenced off by barbed wires, guarded zealously by professional soldiers, etc.? The pre-colonial world outside of Europe did not understand nations and territory this way. Rather than national boundaries, there would have only been frontiers. In the Hindu epic Ramayana (and also Mahabharata) there was a particular ceremony kings performed to demarcate the domain of a kingdom, whereby the king would release a white stallion and let it run free. If anybody stood in the way of the free run of the horse, he would have to face the might of the king and if he managed to stop the king, that would be where the king's kingdom was deemed to end. Such similar alternate understandings would be more applicable in, say, the contested ownership of the uninhabited Kabaw Valley of the time, between the kingdoms of Ava and Manipur. For that matter, the very frontiers of

Ava or Manipur or other Southeast Asian kingdoms, and indeed the rest of the non-European world, would have been determined by such principles. If a king stuck his flag on the bank of a certain river and nobody dared oppose him, that point would become the extent of his kingdom, and so on. These understandings cannot simply be forced into the nineteenth-century European paradigm of nationhood with justice as too many attempt to do naively.

DISCOURSE ON LEGITIMACY

A two-part edit page article in the *Telegraph*, Kolkata, by Pratap Bhanu Mehta after a routine India–China cooperation summit in Beijing in June 2006, had some very absorbing arguments on the sources of legitimacy for different forms of governments. The comparison between India and China, in this regard, is loaded. These lessons could very well be for Manipur too. One of the chief contentions is that the governments of China and India by necessity draw their legitimacy differently and from different sources. Being a democracy, India puts a premium on representation. There is beauty in this but it nevertheless dilutes the question of accountability. It ensures participation of all sections of the people in the governance process but this itself becomes the primary end, leaving the question of performance, the other vital function of any government, as secondary.

Consider this. The official counter against the charge that the Northeast occupies only a peripheral space in the Indian national consciousness and is hence neglected, is that each of the northeastern states is represented in all the institutions of the Indian state, administrative as well as legislative, hence the question of neglect, or injustice, at least at the institutional level, does not arise. The fact that the Northeast still remains backward does not seem to be considered a factor in assessing the legitimacy of the government system. It is as if representation is all.

Likewise, within Manipur, the source of government legitimacy is drawn from similar wells and are invariably beset with the same flaws. Take the case of the hill–valley divide. Here too, as all of us know, the fierce contest for representation is at the crux of politics and is indeed treated as the only legitimate route to systemic as well as social justice. Every community wants as much handle in the government as possible and the equilibrium struck between the numerous pulls and pressures from these demands is what constitutes a stable government. However, after this equilibrium is reached, the other important considerations of accountability and performance are somewhat pushed into the background.

Again, here too, as in the case of the larger canvas of the Indian Union, the counter-argument against discrimination charges by any community or region, most specifically by the hill districts, is the proportion of representation. The hills have been very much a part of the political and administrative processes in proportionate measures and even two Nagas have been chief ministers. These are facts, but must not government legitimacy also take into account performance? Why then have the hill districts lagged behind in development? These questions should be made answerable by state leaders, regardless of whether she or he is from the hills or the valley.

By contrast, the challenges of legitimacy before the government in China are different. Its leaders are nominated and hence the only way they can win this legitimacy is through performance and accountability. As a result, the nature of their motivation and drive are radically different. This onerous expectation has even led China in recent times to treat capitalism and communism not as ideologies, but as instruments of development, to be administered in measured doses as per the developmental needs of the society.

In our situation, this quest for legitimacy would be somewhat similar to that of a President's Rule scenario when a nominated governor runs the civil administration. He too must seek his legitimacy through performance and accountability alone. No state can know this better than Manipur.

PILGRIMAGE TO THE PAST

Every year on 13 August, Manipur officially celebrates Patriots' Day, the day when in 1891 the chief protagonists in the resistance against British aggression into the then kingdom of Manipur were hanged by the victorious aggressors. Among them were Prince Koireng (Bir Tikendrajit), Thangal General, Subedar Niranjan, Kajao, and Cherai Naga. Others, including two princes, were also exiled and imprisoned in the Central Jail at the Andaman and Nicobar Islands (of the Kala Pani notoriety in Indian history). It is indeed a traumatic memory for the people of the state, as any cataclysmic event of such proportion would be. Arguably, after the 1817 invasion by Ava (Burmese), which resulted in the Seven Years of Devastation (Chahi Taret Khuntakpa), and subsequently also the signing of the Treaty of Yandaboo in 1826, this possibly could be the pivotal event that determined the direction of Manipur's history thus far. Although British colonial presence in Manipur dates back way beyond this event, it was on this day that the reign of the kingdom's power became subsumed by the imperial power of the mighty British.

From a layman's understanding of what happened thereafter, Manipur was still not a colony in the classical, economic sense of the term. Politically, however, the same cannot be said. The state administration was free to be itself, but within the limits of acceptability of the British. It was a situation similar to the current dispensation of Manipur as an Indian state where it enjoys the administrative powers of a federal unit of the Indian Union but has no powers beyond the Constitution of India. Hence, perhaps the British interest in Manipur was more strategic than economic.

The more pertinent question, however, is what should constitute Manipur's appropriate attitude to this chapter of its history? There cannot be a shade of doubt on why the heroes who died resisting the aggression should be honoured, as indeed the state has been doing all these years. But respecting heroes who occupy an affectionate space in the hearts of most citizens is not difficulty. The difficulty lies in making an honest assessment of the opponents, and indeed of the heroes themselves. The question, as Cathy Caruth writes in *Unclaimed Experience. Trauma, Narrative and History*, is how does the present generation tell of a traumatic past truthfully without a sense of betrayal. Often the dominant sentiment is one of bitterness, blaming all present failures on the hated other by the vanquished communities of history. Often again, behind the bitterness is also a complex but disguised envy. Habitual West bashers, for instance, often turn out to be the loudest at boasting that their children study or work there. On the smaller canvas, habitual Delhi bashers in Manipur often take pride in sending their children there, and if money is not of consequence, own a flat in the capital as well. It is this dichotomy that needs a credible bridge.

Let us consider an example very close at hand. Once upon a time, India was, by and large, in the habit of blaming Britain for its failures. Today, as the nation grows in confidence and self-esteem, this habit has made a quiet exit and Britain is today more an equal partner than the 'villain'. It is as though India's half a century of de-colonized existence was haunted by a demon of the past and the demon, it seems, has finally been exorcized; suddenly a suffocating weight has fallen off the nation's chest. In the same way, Manipur too must come to terms with its own peculiar history, even the most traumatic chapters. Perhaps the way to move forward is to travel back in time to when the demons haunting the present got introduced and then attempt an exorcism.

Two valiant attempts in the world of arts come to mind. One is *Rajarshri Bhagyachandra* by M.C. Arun in which he tries to demonstrate why the deepening of Hinduism amongst the Meiteis under King Bhagyachandra was predetermined by the reality of the time, and perhaps if history could be rewound and replayed, the best possible outcome would still be what the king chose. The other, much more lyrical and forcefully presented, is *One Valley Nine Hills* by Ratan Thiyam.[4] It was almost a rite of exorcism, in form as well as substance. How would the Meitei *Maichous*, the ancient scholars who wrote the *Puyas*, the books of knowledge and prophesies, interpret the present and the future beyond. He makes the souls of these hoary wise men awake with a start from their eternal resting places and set about writing more books of knowledge after taking into consideration the disturbing developments amongst their descendants. Their objective visions, provided by detachment in space and chronological time, again do not match current demagogic, inflammatory interpretations of history. The therapeutic catharsis is palpable and redeeming.

THE AFSPA: A STAGNATING DEBATE

Do extraordinary situations demand extraordinary measures? This is a relevant question because of the manner in which the Northeast situation is tackled. The ongoing debate on the Armed Forces Special Powers Act, 1958, can illustrate this. If the AFSPA, as it is also known, can be explained within the stimulus–response matrix, we are at a juncture where the very prospect of identifying what should constitute the stimulus and what the response has become blurred and confused. The familiar and frustrating chicken and egg story is being replayed yet again. In this vicious cycle, the state's view is that the AFSPA is a response to the violent challenges to it and its authority. Those on the other side of the fence have been claiming just the opposite—that it is a draconian act and that the excesses committed under it, which have spawned and hardened the violence, are what the AFSPA is supposed to be countering. In all likelihood, the honest answer is somewhere in between. The only problem is, how honest has anybody been in trying to address the matter. And until this honesty shows up in strength, the

[4] Stage production by Chorus Repertory Theatre. Director: Ratan Thiyam.

AFSPA issue cannot possibly progress much beyond the status of a hot debate in which the state and civil activists are pitted against each other, accusing each other of tyranny and treason.

Arguably, the real issue is not just about the repeal of the AFSPA, but of delegitimizing violence. If the stimulus–response matrix were to be taken for granted and if the perceived stimulus were to be removed, the question that remains is: would what is perceived as the response disappear too? If the AFSPA were to be removed today without a replacement, would the violence in the state end? One may not like the question, and even have a different opinion, but from the state's point of view, this is a very legitimate question. The argument in the reverse may not be totally applicable, that is, from the statist viewpoint, if the non-state violence were to be treated as the stimulus and if this stimulus were to be removed, would the state's draconian responses disappear too? It probably would, but this is no argument, for this would amount to accepting unquestioningly the hegemony of the state, which can be crudely translated to mean, 'If you behave you will not be punished' or 'Don't ever dare challenge the authority of the state'. Insurgency, unfortunately, in its cause as well as its manifestation is not as simple, for it is precisely about challenging the structural inconsistencies of the state itself.

But there are much more sublimated ways of posing these challenges and also of accepting these challenges. And because of the sublimation, they often prove to be more effective problem-solving mechanisms. The minute the challengers as well as the challenged begin seeing there are such possibilities to be explored, the conflicts which have generated all the violence will enter a new phase. The Naga peace talks, the ULFA peace overtures, even if it was an aborted one, and the plebiscite offer by the UNLF, can in this way be treated as signs of a thaw in attitude, and that these parties are beginning to see the possibilities of different approaches to reach an honourable solution. Quite obviously there would be the necessity of plenty of give and take from all the parties and not just vis-à-vis the state, but also in resolving differences between themselves. And these routes to a resolution, unlike the tame surrenders that the state has been trying to induce either through force or through statutory incentives, are not in any way 'surrenders' but victories in which nobody is the loser.

The problem is, there are many who disagree and insist on conflict as resolution to disagreements and disputes. They also generally think in terms of what is now popularly referred to as the 'zero sum game'.

From this perspective, in a competitive environment, one competitor's gain has to be the other competitor's loss. The offshoot of this vision is also another rather sinister war game: 'the enemy of my enemy is my friend'. Such players push their 'friends' to be the enemy of their enemies as well. Maybe the 'zero sum game' is unavoidable in a straight equation where there are only two players. But when there are many more players than just two, things get a lot more complicated, and the 'zero sum game', even if it is a legitimate military strategy, often becomes unproductive socially. American mathematician and economics Nobel Prize winning genius, John Nash, said as much in his biography by Sylvia Nasar titled *A Beautiful Mind*, now a major Hollywood movie. Individual players in any multi-players game do not function as isolated, independent units, but conform to a larger pattern or ethics on the acknowledgement and restraint that 'I think that he thinks that I think that he thinks ...' (Nasar 1998). Breaking this unseen bond, even between rivals, whichever player it is that resorts to it, has never proven productive for anybody. This principle of economic rivalry can very well shed some valuable light on why the strategy of 'the enemy of my enemy is my friend', so repulsively rampant in Manipur, is resulting in so much chaos and disillusionment. The strategy is familiar in the rivalry between various ethnic insurgencies where bigger groups patronize and arm smaller groups, and then pit them against their stronger opponents. The strategy in recent times has been notorious in the hands of state forces. Typically, the Army, or the other counter-insurgency police forces would declare a 'suspension of operations' against a militant group, giving its cadres the freedom to bear arms openly. The objective of such strategies is ostensibly to neutralize other insurgent groups deemed as more dangerous to the state. The social fallouts have been tragic. Since ethnic insurgencies have their roots in the communities they spawn in, a deep mistrust between the communities exposed to such sinister war games as well as a mistrust of the state by the communities has often been the result. Allegations of such Machiavellian games are rife in Nagaland in the ongoing feud between various factions of insurgents there. The same allegations are also common in Manipur after the Army's declaration of 'suspension of operations' against Kuki militant groups in 2005, ostensibly to neutralize the United National Liberation Front (UNLF) which had penetrated and ensconced themselves in much of the southern hills of Manipur, the traditional homes of the Kuki tribes.

Set into motion by such policies is a cycle of insecurity, in which different players begin to want to arm themselves as a measure of self-protection. Much like what Günter Grass (1999) says in his book *My Century*, a collection of a hundred interlinked stories celebrating the twentieth century, each summarizing the mood of each year of the century from the German perspective. In the chapter that depicts the mood in 1911, pre–First World War Europe is marked by wide public insecurity introduced by an arms race. A letter between two friends said it all: 'I wish to be a prince of peace—but a well-armed one' (Grass 1999). This seems exactly the mood in Manipur today in the backdrop of multi-pronged hostile rivalries between various insurgent groups, nudged by the state forces' deft Machiavellian game of playing off one group against another. In this milieu, previously unarmed communities now want a militia of their own.

Under the Indian system, not only is the state supposed to have monopoly over legitimate violence, but also monopoly over legitimate possession of arms. The unwritten understanding is that individual citizens are supposed to repose absolute faith in the state that it will take care of their needs for defence against external as well as domestic aggressions. It is this unwritten article of faith which is degenerating because of these policies, causing an exponential rise in the complication of the matrix of ethnic violence and rivalries. What then is to be done if one or the other militant groups calls for a truce? The answer is simple. Have a truce and agree to a ceasefire, but under definite and strict ground rules that would not compromise the security of the ordinary citizenry. In other words, it is obligatory for the state to allow those who agree to negotiate peace to come under its protective umbrella, but without compromising on the initial article of faith that bearing arms or using them by any organization other than an organ of the state security establishment is illegal.

Or else take the American approach and trust arms in the hands of the citizens for their individual defence against aggression, external or domestic. It is interesting that the very second amendment of the American constitution, incorporated into the constitution in 1791 along with nine other amendments which together form what is now famously known as the 'Bill of Rights', is the right to own and bear arms by citizens. Perhaps this outlook had a lot to do with the nation being a settler state, having for most part of its pre-constitutional history to advance its frontiers westward, encountering in the process hostile resistances. Such a policy however is unthinkable in India. For one, in a country of such diverse nationalities, and such diverse religions, there is considerable legitimacy in the state being insecure about an armed citizenry. But then, if this is the case, it becomes all the more the bounden duty of the state to ensure that nobody is illegally armed to become the cat in the pigeon coop. The sense of security that an armed individual supposedly gets from the possession of arms must under the altered circumstance be had from the knowledge and confidence that an armed state is his or her protector.

BEYOND THE FIRE

But the doubt lingers. Has the complex matrix of multi-pronged conflict situations in the state reached a kind of equilibrium to qualify to be what scholar Sanjib Baruah calls 'durable disorder' in his book by the same title? With the objectives of these conflicts having receded on an incremental basis from any realistic vision, it is reasonable to imagine that the conflicts themselves are beginning to be ends in themselves. For it is unimaginable that the challengers to the Indian nation would not have realized that a militarily victory can only happen in the wildest dreams. Hence, a low-intensity conflict that can be sustained for long becomes the only strategic option left. Similarly, with the increasing realization of a similar diminishing of prospects for a comprehensive solution, the establishment too may in fact have, deliberately or otherwise, shifted its focus in meeting the challenge to an equilibrium where the conflicts are managed and maintained at a pitch that can be described again as a 'durable disorder'. There is plenty of evidence of the latter. The manner in which the state now engages with explosive situations that crop up from time to time in the course of these conflict says this loud and clear.

Arguably, and without intention, a number of ingenuous mechanisms that fit this purpose have evolved. Take, for instance, the modus operandi of instituting judicial or magisterial inquiries into outrageous state atrocities. It is interesting to note that with the exception of a very few, none of these inquiries, some of them extended over and over ad nauseam, ever saw the light of day. But they nevertheless always succeeded in deflating the passion that accompanied the situations that prompted their formation in the first place. Take again the numerous accords, memorandums of understanding (MoUs), agreements, etc., that agitators reach with the establishment. Most of them end up unimplemented or else implemented in watered-down versions, but nevertheless the end result is the same—violent passions get deflated or else precious time is bought. The whole objective seems to be once again to maintain the intensity of conflict at a manageable level. In some ways one even suspects that the ongoing peace talks between the Government of India and the NSCN (IM) are being directed towards a similar track. After nine years of negotiations, a resolution remains elusive, though many have been led to believe such a resolution is just round the corner this time. But the interesting thing also is that the non-state players in this game, in what can only be described as knee-jerk responses, have been willing participants, perpetuating this dreary cycle of 'durable disorder'. Perhaps there is little else that can be done. Nobody can afford or sustain full-scale violent agitations for too long, not even wars between nation-states. Intuitively, everybody understands that extended, open, and violent confrontations have only one possible outcome in which both the victor and vanquished end up as losers. But conflicting parties seldom easily intend to end hostilities or resolve conflicting issues, so both settle for a condition of 'durable disorder'.

The curse of this approach is that it limits everybody's vision and prevents people from looking beyond the conflict situation. What may initially have begun as a strategy for managing conflicts, is ultimately transformed into a trap. For indeed the result is a house perpetually kept on fire even if the flame is never allowed to become a raging inferno. And when your house is on fire, can you think of anything else but the fire. It is easier said than done, but the awesome challenge before all of us today is to find a way of looking beyond the fire, even if the fire must carry on, otherwise we will never get out of the fire. The analogy used by the former American President George W. Bush in arguing the need to upgrade the American military, even while it engages in so many missions simultaneously, so as to be always ahead in the competitive power race, is apt. He said that the prospect would be like overhauling the engine of a vehicle running at 90 miles per hour. Similarly, the challenge before us is intimidating but it needs to be met, or else we will have to be satisfied living with our house perpetually on fire and witnessing periodic horrific incidents.

CHAPTER 8

Preparing for a Cohesive Northeast
Problems of Discourse

BHAGAT OINAM

THE ISSUE

Northeast India as a product of colonial discourse and carried forward
by the Indian state has successfully formed a part of the public discourse
both within and outside the region. In spite of the stereotypes and
the contesting claims, the name is in the process of being shaped to
represent a distinct identity of a region and its peoples. The passage,
of course, has not been smooth as the other view that there is nothing
called a 'unified' Northeast but only differences and disjuncture carries
its own basis. But what remains a likely point of agreement among
these contrary views is this: that which seemingly emerged out of
the functional requirement of a colonial administration is today not
only shaping into a typical identity but also fast becoming a hotbed
of multiple crises.

While most of the problems in the region are direct or indirect
consequences of the discourses adopted by those who hold the seat of
power and those who contest for that power, the problems themselves
have, in turn, set conditions for the kind of power equation that
currently prevails. It is a strange blend of praxis creating *exis*, and *exis*
in turn guiding the praxis (Sartre 1982). The challenge, obviously, is
the search for an authentic understanding of the issues faced by the
region in a comprehensive way.

The apparently visible sites of problems are those of ethnic conflict,
cultural resurgence, nationalist insurgency, poor governance, corruption,
etc. Though it may seem more pragmatic and clear-headed to handle
the issues with symptomatic treatment through economic management,
development programmes, peace initiatives, constitutional reforms,

and so on, there is a need for 'prudence' in this exercise. This is easier said than done. Sixty years of *disengaged* problem-solving has only led to compounding of the crises, making the problems more complex. Mushrooming of insurgent groups in the region is a case in point.

The problem seems to be primarily epistemic in nature; the failure to reach proper comprehension. So far, the discourses in the region have operated through reiterative and declarative tendencies. These tendencies are visible in the following areas of knowledge claims. British travelogues and administrative accounts, and also the nationalist Indian narratives, are heavily burdened with a 'civilizational baggage'. Votaries of cultural resurgence are constantly in search of linear historical trajectories. Neo-colonial subalterns attempt to build nation-narratives within the framework of the colonial ethos. In recent times, there are new entrants in the arena who propose to limit the role of the state only to its instrumentality and shed the 'modes' generally associated with the nation-state. Thus, we apparently see bundles of contradictions existing next to one another.

The term 'Northeast' was formalized through the British colonial administration as a frontier region. It was subsequently endorsed and retained by the Indian state under the 'native' vocabulary as '*Purvanchal*'. Today, talk of the Northeast as a unique (more aptly a 'strange') ghettoized entity is cliché. The obvious implication is that anything goes in ascribing the region. The criticism is not intended to deprecate the term 'Northeast India', but rather to make it more meaningful and real than let it remain disjointed. The plea is to neither highlight the uniqueness nor propound unity, but to look out for a comprehensive understanding of the region. This can be done not by opposing the coinage of the term, but in shaping a reasonable meaning to the term.

Though there is need for a comprehensive picturing[1] of the region, it has to be free from the usual attributes of a domineering, unifying, and patronizing disposition. Currently, the region is marked by exclusive narratives with hegemonic tendencies as often found in a conflict

[1] I use hermeneutic-phenomenologist terminology that our knowledge about the world is not gathered through passive receiving of impressions about things outside, but by actively providing meanings to the things we experience. This suggests (i) active engagement of the agent and (ii) being most often subjective. However, I suggest, we can have comprehensive subjectivity where we can draw upon collective active-agency. This hints at a people-centric approach towards understanding the region.

situation. Colonialism has brought contradictions, which people have unquestioningly or quasi-questioningly internalized. Internalizing half-baked identities not only creates a crisis in mapping one's own collective identity, but also antagonism towards other communities. An alternate discourse is what is called for.

THE PROBLEMATIC DISCOURSES

Northeast India has been witnessing two distinctive discourses: reiterative and declarative. The two seem to be characteristic of not only the Indian state and its machineries, but also its counterparts: the protesting voices in the region.

If Amartya Sen's idea of a characteristic Indian tradition is being argumentative, having the ability to question, and in being self-critical, Northeast India characterizes itself with a different discourse. It could be that the region has not yet imbibed the ideals of an 'Indian tradition', or that the Indian state is yet to treat the region as a major constituent of its tradition to facilitate such a discourse. If the latter makes some sense, the protagonists of the thesis claim that the region still remains a frontier (Baruah 2007), not only in the Indian psyche but also in the forms of governance and policy interventions. These doubts and concerns remain partly because the region's association with India as a political entity as well as an avatar of a long cultural tradition is relatively new. Though there are claims in many parts of the region of closer association and ties with a living 'cultural self' of India, which is argumentative and resilient, those are not free from the politics of authenticity.

But the fact remains that Northeast India today exhibits a tradition that isn't remotely close to any 'ideal Indian tradition'. Even if one argues that such a tradition does not exist, I don't buy such an argument for the utopian character of an ideal Indian tradition does not trivialize the 'difference' and 'the crises of being different' which the Northeast faces vis-à-vis India and its cultural self. Many of the problems that the region has faced in the last sixty years, in the course of India's consolidation as a nation-state, show that these are the results of an intense contest—sometimes consciously and perhaps sometimes not so consciously—among different national forces that could complement one another, but who, for all the wrong reasons, have chosen the path of contrasting and exclusive strands. And what remains today is an undesirable state of affairs driven by discourses that are inherently antagonistic and hostile, and above all, that refuse to be self-critical and self-reflective. I am referring to the discourses of 'reiterative' and 'declarative' tendencies, which have been highlighted in the beginning of this section.

Let me begin with the reiterative discourse. The reiterative discourse is one where a knowledge claim of a specific kind is generated through the repetition of the same information or an idea without any reasonable justifying criterion. This discourse without the last condition, that is, absence of a reasonable justifying criterion, resembles more closely 'testimony' as a valid means of knowledge. In the theory of knowledge, 'testimony' is based on the legitimacy drawn from a trusted source, often an authority, which imparts or makes such a knowledge claim. Some of the means of drawing legitimacy in such a claim lie in 'time-testedness', 'authority of the source', 'already proven as valid', etc. For example, look at the Vedas, as *sruti* handed down over the centuries. The sanctity of the Vedas as a narrative lies, more than the arguments it holds, in the 'time-tested' nature of the narrative. The same narrative has been continuously chanted and handed down to subsequent generations. Nonetheless, 'reasonableness' is a necessary content in all such claims. There seem to be problems with drawing validity from information which is merely based on it being time-tested or generally acceptable due to the lack of certain forms of reasonableness. We have several instances from the history of ideas to disprove the validity drawn from such a discourse. Change in the theory of geostationary movement of heavenly bodies is a stark case in point.

However, the validity of knowledge claims has certain levels of open-endedness in the case of social and cultural facts and their relationships. The truth or falsity of Vedic cosmogony is not to be understood in the way as has been understood in the natural sciences. Often there are myths and narratives on morality that have their significance as knowledge of a different kind. These are not descriptive knowledge claims about the certain state of things in the world, but are often aesthetic and moral judgements guided by a sense of desirability. The knowledge claims of such kind should not be projected as identical with knowledge claims of 'objective description' that are engaged in natural sciences and partly in social sciences; but the two should not be mixed up either.

The problem with Northeast India is that many of the narratives, which either represent myths or morality, are often brought out as cases of objective descriptions of a state of affair. One of the most commonly used phrases to explain the peoples and land (by each community) is 'time immemorial'. The phrase is used to depict the significance of a *historical* past of a community in question. There is certainly a dimension of the 'political' associated with the claim of a community to be 'indigenous' vis-à-vis its 'migrants'. Apart from this political concern, the use of the phrase also reflects a desire in these receiving communities (Oinam 2005) to have a 'history' against the 'history-less' as has often been thrust upon by the colonizers on the colonized (or by the 'donors' on the 'receivers'). The inability to objectively earmark and justify a chronology of events leads to this 'phrasing' as a substitute to gain objective status. Thus, the phrase 'time immemorial' reflects a state of confusion generated by the mixing up of different types of knowledge claims under one typology. One may look at the often-claimed two-thousand-year-old history of Manipuri civilization. The validity of such a narrative—more than the historical methods and their verifications—seems to be based on the popularity the narrative has gained through general public discourse over a period of time. It is indeed difficult to say whether public discourses are based on historical methods or whether historians base the validity of their narratives from popular public discourses. Another popular narrative is of an imagery drawn about the majority Meitei community in the narratives of the smaller communities in the state. For instance, the imagery of domineering and exploitative (also 'casteist') Meitei Manipuris has become an important content of the Naga nationalist narrative that is repeated, updated, and spread to make the imagery a true one. This imagery is projected particularly in the Naga narratives in Manipur. These, over time, have become part of the public discourse almost unchallenged primarily because such information serves the interests of the people for or about whom the claims are made. Both the instances are about knowledge claims based on endless repetition of the same narrative with the same content. However, going by the historical account of the region, no communities in the region remain exploiter, exploited, or neutral arbiters for all times. Their identities in the garb of one or the other role have remained variable. The region has remained politically fluid partly because of such reiterative discourses.

The declarative discourse, on the other hand, carries suppressive and authoritative content. Often, the language of violence is used as a response to any form of dissent. The room for self-reflection and self-critical enquiry to one's beliefs and knowledge is missing. It is not only the Indian state and its various parts that indulge in a declarative discourse, but also its counterparts (the non-state organizations) who equally or perhaps much more violently propagate their narratives through the same kind of discourse. What the latter often endorse are self-justified dictates backed by sufficient power to sanction violence. There is no room for dialogue, of questioning the basis of those declaratives. Even the issue of morality is left far behind.

Take the case of Armed Forces (Special Powers) Act, 1958, which has today become a symbol of state repression in the region. This is declared by none other than the Justice Jeevan Reddy Committee, which was instituted by the Government of India (GoI) after mass protests in the aftermath of the rape and the killing of one Manorama Devi by the personnel of Assam Rifles on 11 July 2004.[2] While the killing of Manorama was one among many instances of brutality perpetrated by the state forces (that include the military, the paramilitary and the police) indicative of state repression, there are a few significant issues that need to be raised. One, the rationale behind conceiving of such a draconian act initially for the region. Two, the subsequent mode of military operation that is protected by the act. And three, the longevity of the act—it has been in operation in one or the other part of the region for more than fifty years. These need to be seen within the perspective of the declarative discourse that the state adopts. The response of the Indian state to any form of 'violent' dissent has been by and large through force. It is through intimidation and coercion that the state machinery operates. Instead of addressing the content of the dissent, what has been witnessed is a language of command—a declaration—that forbids any form of violent dissent. A concern to understand the genesis of 'violent dissent' is totally absent. Today, fifty years of militarization driven by this kind of declarative discourses has sown the seeds for a murky and opaque state of affairs. The dissenting non-state (insurgent) forces have also imbibed this kind of discourse, so have the civil society and student bodies. The state of violence today is near total.

[2] The Justice Jeevan Reddy Committee was instituted by the GoI after the women's upsurge protesting against the rape and killing of Th. Manorama Devi by the security personnel of the Assam Rifles in Manipur. On 15 July 2004, after twelve elderly women staged a nude protest at the gate of Kangla Fort, which was then under the control of 17 Assam Rifles, mass agitation geared up for the repeal of the AFSPA. The AFSPA was seen as a draconian law for under this act an army/defence personnel cannot be subjected to any judicial proceedings unless allowed by the central government.

These discourses are conveniently used by both the contesting parties, as well as by the arbiter to strengthen their self-interests. There is little that can transform or subvert the discourses. In fact, the number of stakeholders in the benefits drawn by the results of these discourses is not only getting larger but also becoming more powerful.

THE MYTHS AND BAGGAGES

The aforementioned discourses employ various narratives and phrases that describe the Northeast and its people, which in turn shape the identity of the region in a particular way. Even a generic term such as the 'Northeast' is a product of this trend. In the process, the region is often subjected to several stereotypes: the 'land of flora and fauna', 'land of headhunters', 'land inhabited by indigenous people', 'frontier region', 'Scotland of the East', 'Switzerland of India', and many more. These depictions are both complementing as well as conflicting. They explain, more than the region, the intentions of those who engage in this 'naming game'.

The extended form of the 'naming game' is the 'narratives' that either shape the *identities* of communities or supposedly underscore the *values* of certain community-oriented ways of life. These narratives are often generated by external forces, either accepted and internalized, or modified and reshaped to soothe the local ethos. The influence of the dominant discourses prevailing in the developed world is visible in these receiving communities not only in the form of imprints, but also in the form of the complete shift from the indigenous world view to the external weltanschauung. While the trend is invariably visible in all the major parts of the developing world, Northeast India experiences a blend of two typical discourses, reiterative and declarative, in the new imports of narratives and weltanschauung. In other words, reiterative and declarative characters reshape not only the content but also the patterns of the narratives experienced today.

An understanding of the Northeast requires successful dismantling of the prevailing discourses that will help demystify the region. The foremost challenge is to deconstruct both the imageries cast on the region as well as the intentions and circumstances that have shaped those who have made these imageries. This is to be followed by a reframing of the content and the patterns of the narratives and associated imageries. The reiterative and declarative discourses need to be checked so that these myths and narratives are set in their rightful places, and a desirable discourse looked for. Unfortunately, over time, several narratives and myths have become burdensome baggage.

Civilizational Baggage

Though the Indian nation-state is shown to carry a long and rich civilizational heritage, this is largely a product of a nineteenth-century Indian response to British colonialism. We are aware of India's nationalist historians and philosophers engaged in mapping a long tradition of civilizational heritage of the country. The aspirations of nationalist leaders like V.D. Savarkar to own a history as much as the West sowed the seeds for mapping India's civilizational history. Sri Aurobindo's writings reflected a strong zeal to project the rich cultural heritage of the country vis-à-vis the West. Even nationalist (academic) philosophers like Dr S. Radhakrishnan and S.N. Dasgupta focused their works on projecting parallel Indian accounts to then prevalent themes in Western philosophy and philology. The trend that is still visibly witnessed is of seeing the West as a yardstick.

These civilizational narratives are seen as more representative of a few than all. We have already witnessed violent protests against such narratives in southern parts of the country, particularly on the issues of 'language' and 'cultural pasts'. Several social and political movements (including the insurgent movements) in Northeast India, too, reflect similar dissent, often associated with inventing or discovering alternate narratives. The voices of dissent raise reservations to the grand narratives as propounded by the Indian nationalist projects. Each narrative is seen as attempting to encapsulate within itself other parallel narratives as sub-narratives.

British travelogues and administrative accounts have also had their own mode of filtering information. They were not free from their self-imposed burden of 'civilizing the savages'. This peculiar mindset was rather pronounced in the writings and other general activities of the Christian missionaries. It was a tedious task to first uproot the traditional world views and knowledge systems as something pagan and irrational, and supplant a new knowledge system and a weltanschauung to fill the void. It would have been difficult to install a new weltanschauung without creating that void. Had there been an interface between a native and the new weltanschauung, it would suggest a case of cultural assimilation or exchange. Complete installation of an alien system is a case of complete transformation.

Interface of the receiving communities with the alien knowledge systems and weltanschauung is witnessed at various levels. Different receiving communities experience different forms of interface. It ranges from a strong response of 'having a history' against being 'history-less', to accepting the 'history-lessness' and choosing a 'history' that has been readily shaped for the communities. In the latter case, accepting and internalizing the qualifiers 'barbaric' and 'uncivilized' soothe both the parties. While for the 'uncivilized' it is about entering the doorsteps of 'civilization', for the 'civilized' it is about gaining legitimacy of its responsibility of 'civilizing the savages'.

Interestingly, different receiving communities conveniently change the roles of the 'civilized' and the 'uncivilized'. While each of the communities changes its role, the two opposing *colonial* categories remain. For instance, a 'history-less' India invents/discovers a history that not only empowers itself with a knowledge system and weltanschauung, but also influences the *lesser* receiving communities (say, of Northeast India) to own the newly found knowledge system and the weltanschauung. Within the Northeast, the Bengalis, the Assamese, and the Manipuris engage in the same exercise vis-à-vis the *lesser* communities of the region. Thus, the communities in Northeast India show a complexity of responses both in their inter-regional and intra-regional encounters.

While different communities play varying roles of 'civilized' and 'uncivilized' vis-à-vis their counterparts, their responses to the knowledge systems and weltanschauung of the communities and nations outside of the region are selective and exhibit variance. With regard to Northeast India, I have in mind two distinctive knowledge systems and weltanschauung exhibited by (*a*) the British colonial rule and (*b*) the Indian national narrative(s). While some of the communities internalize the qualifiers given by one of the two external weltanschauungs in shaping their identities, the same communities may in turn summarily reject the other weltanschauung. This is reflective of the hill communities whose encounter with the Western world started much earlier than with the Indian nation. This is in both fields—'political' as well as 'cultural'. However, acceptance or denial cannot be determined by a mere *temporal sequence* of the encounters, but by a deeper politics of choice and identity.

What I mean by 'deeper politics of choice and identity' is this: In the cultural discourse of the Indian state, the 'sacred' and the 'profane' play a major role. In its cultural tradition, the 'profane' is not only limited to the Dalits, but is extended to various ethnic communities who reside in the periphery of the geographical and political boundaries of this nation-state. Thus, the refusal by many of these ethnic communities to be part of the tradition that treats them as profane is but obvious. The 'profane' cannot be on the same plane as the 'sacred'. The 'otherness' inbuilt in the hierarchical structure between the 'sacred' and the 'profane' has been internalized by these communities. This helps them to assert their own distinctive identities. The refusal to be part of such a tradition is meaningfully asserted by accepting another tradition and weltanschauung that is either ideationally superior or parallel in the eyes of the parties involved. The assertions of the Dalits and the tribes of the Northeast and in other parts of India, explain the thesis more clearly.

Another response that is witnessed in the region is not one of an explicit refusal, but of a complex struggle where refusal and acceptance gain partial ground, shaped yet again by the politics of identity. The receiving communities under question aim for respectable identities in the endorsed narratives. This can be witnessed among the Meitei Manipuris and a large section of Assam's varied communities. These communities claim to possess a civilizational heritage and refuse to become part of the Indian narrative's 'profane'. The alternatives obviously are: either struggle to gain a part of the 'sacred' in the grand Indian narrative, or search for a memory that can regain a lost 'civilization' different from the one they are lured with. I can find clearer examples within the history of Manipuri identity formation. Tracing the ancestry of the Meiteis (by a few native scholars) to the Kiratas and other such tribes of the Himalayan foothills are attempts to join the prevalent grand Indian narrative.[3] Further, endorsing the sub-narrative of the Manipuris as descendents of Mahabharata's Arjuna is another desperate attempt to enter the domain of the 'sacred'. There are yet other attempts to relate the traditional narratives with the external narratives to show a common weltanschauung of the traditions in interface. Religious symbols, sites, and practices are often common contents of these intersecting narratives. For instance, it is interesting to see how pre-Hindu Meitei deities like Nongpok Ningthou and Panthoibi are

[3] Take the writings of Atom Bapu Sharma, Wahengbam Yumjao Singh, Asangbam Miniketan Singh, and many others who engaged in the process of discovering a past that was close to Vedic lineage. The migration of the Kiratas was highlighted to make the Meiteis closer to Vedic Bharata.

equated with Shiva and Parvati respectively in the Manipuri Vaisnava narrative. It would also be equally interesting to see the origins of sites such as the Kamakhya temple and the *Namghar* in Assam, which have become part of a grand Indian narrative. It would equally be worth investigating how local religions of smaller/receiving communities have been added to the Vaisnava or Saivite folds by accommodating the local deities in the grand narratives with new additions to the existing narratives. It would be useful to investigate the process of assimilation that has been witnessed in Assam and Manipur and compare it with similar phenomena occurring in parts of Himachal Pradesh (Sharma 2001) and the adjoining foothills. Several similar trends are likely to emerge from such research.

The alternative to the search of the 'sacred' is to trace a memory of a long-drawn civilization parallel to the one in the interface; to search for an 'indigenous' origin of the community identity. The pre-Vaisnava Meitei scholarship[4] in Manipur that traces a civilizational heritage as old and sacred as the Vedic scholarship in the dynasty of Pakhangba (dated AD 33) is a case in point. Interestingly, some Vaisnava Manipuri scholars have attempted to enter the above narrative as sub-narrative of the grand Indian (Aryan) narrative. For example, these scholars have projected the Sanamahi as a sect of a larger Vedic weltanschauung (a view which is now considered faulty). A conflict over constructing a past heritage is still very much alive. Similarly, the Seng Khasi movement in Meghalaya is another instance of constructing a unique cultural heritage that can be claimed as 'indigenous'. Assam also experiences a similar issue in the Tai Ahom narratives about its historical past vis-à-vis other fraternal communities/sub-communities. It, however, remains to be seen whether the validity of such claims can be established; whether these are cases of cultural assimilation or are 'totally indigenous' as is often claimed.

Linear Historical Trajectories

The influence of modernist discourses among the receiving communities is wide and overarching. Often, attempts are made to locate the civilizational baggage that is being carried through the modernist trajectories of 'history'. Certainly, 'history' as an objective, justified discipline is the precondition in the minds of the claimants.

---

[4] Reference may be made to the works of native scholars like Sairem Nilabir, Kangjiya Gopal, etc.

And modernist historical trajectory of linear time is adapted and used to justify the claims of the 'civilizational pasts'. The influence of the modernizing projects in this area is quite obvious. It, however, remains incidental that the projects accompanied colonial rule.

Since the idea of linearity provides a sense of the progress in history, civilizational narratives tend to make a conceptual as well as temporal distinction between the primitive and the modern, the savages and the civilized. As much as the Indian historiography constructs a linear story of civilizational progress through four thousand years of history, the native scholars, too, follow the same pursuit. The projection of a two-thousand-year-old history of Manipur was recovered and heightened in the public discourse during the time of the proposed break-up of Manipur to carve out areas for a 'possible' Nagalim.

All the claimants of a 'historical past' resort to drawing linear historical trajectories—both the endorsers of the grand Indian narrative who are also the 'insiders', and those who oppose the narrative as a form of cultural hegemony. The impact of modern historiography has been so strong that all forms of identity politics and cultural resurgence turn on attempts to construct historical trajectories. The authenticity of a civilization or a culture is presumed to be achieved from the 'maturity' of the peoples to 'record' its past.

Even those who depend on the phrase 'time immemorial' take recourse to constructing such trajectories. Take the case of Naga politics of identity and its historical past. Though the community opts to tread the path of constructing a history of its own in a modernist framework, the shortcomings are *overcome* through the idea of a 'unique history'. The 'unique history' thesis attempts to erase the gap between what has often been termed as 'sovereign village republics from time immemorial' and the ever-expanding idea of Naga nationhood. The gap in the trajectory is filled (or covered) through this 'unique history' thesis. The legitimacy to this claim is drawn not only from the colonial masters who popularized the term and entered them into official records, but to the present Indian state which has accepted the uniqueness thesis.

Nation-State and Territorial Claims

It has become a trend for almost each ethnic community in the Northeast to claim nationhood. Obviously, the next step is the corresponding search for a geographical space where the nation-state would operate. It seems to be a necessity to have a material correlate for a nation—a state to hold not only the nation narrative, but also the corresponding land and people. The idea of a nation without a fixed territory as propounded by scholars like B.K. Roy Burman is yet to find serious takers in the public discourse. As it stands today, it is the struggle for land as territory that each emerging ethnic 'nation' claims to own as a right. For example, the assertion of Naga identity and its nationhood seeks to assert claims to the Naga nation's corresponding territory of Nagalim as the 'extended self'.

In recent times, it is the electoral politics in the region that has spread ethnic conflict among communities. Violent conflict between the Dimasas and the Karbis illustrates this phenomenon. Though electoral politics is the prime mover, the issue of territoriality has been a key factor behind the animosity and violence. This violence is only symptomatic of the far-reaching declarative discourse—communities tell only their side of the story unquestioned and unscrutinized.

Though the entire region may be seen as subaltern in a neo-colonial dispensation, the value of a united common cause is yet to be registered in the collective psyche of these communities. Ethnic politics is one area where neo-colonial powers play their game effectively. The only commonality claimed to be found in all these communities is the 'right to self-determination'. This remains less problematic as long as the issue is handled at an ideational level, but it leads to crises once located in a context. In fact, the territorial claims of most of the communities lead to 'non-negotiable' contestations. Tools of repression and co-option, thus, become the passwords of this kind of politics. The marginal, subaltern communities have not succeeded in working as one group against the neo-colonial power structure. This is reflected in the way inter-ethnic conflict has spread over almost the entire Northeast. The series of conflicts between the Naga and the Kuki, Kuki and Paite, Meitei and Pangal, Meitei and Naga, Mizo and Bru, Hmar and Dimasa, Karbi and Dimasa, Assamese and Bengali, Khasi and Bengali, Khasi and Assamese, Khasi and Nepali, are endless combinations that only show the extent of the division and segregation among the communities, which earlier were largely non-inimical in terms of the quantum and spread of violence. This is not to say that these communities have been very friendly since 'time immemorial'. These communities were/are as friendly or hostile as the Tamils are with the Kannada, or the Punjabi Jats are with the Punjabi Khatris.

The crisis is in making identity assertions and communications using external knowledge systems and weltanschauung that are but partially internalized. This seems to have become one of the major sources of the crises of postcolonial states. The assertion of national claims along smaller tribal and ethnic lines has become a trend. It has become all the more problematic with the inclusion of territorial claims. This is witnessed not only in Northeast India, but all over the developing world—the African states, South Asia, and the Southeast Asian states.

Militarization and the Language of Violence

Closely connected with the assertions just discussed is the language of violence that has become its general medium of expression. Identity claims and counter-claims that are starkly 'political' get associated with violence when met with any form of dissent. Violence is being used not only by the state, but also by the non-state forces, equally and conveniently. Thus an atmosphere of militarization has been generated and the entire Northeast is visibly characterized by this trend.

I would suggest that Northeast India has become the object of the country's militarist agenda. It operates through what I call the 'declarative discourse'. As far as the Indian state is concerned, dissenting groups and communities are viewed with suspicion, largely because of anxieties about national security and a 'foreign hand' conspiring to destabilize the nation, and those that grow out of a centre relating to 'racial' difference on a 'frontier'. The refusal of the Indian state to repeal the act even after the Justice Reddy Committee report shows what a mockery democracy can be, and the influence of the military and a militarist frame of mind.

Another development since the late 1980s that has compounded the crisis is the emergence of several non-state counterparts in the region following the same declarative discourse. Violence as a means of protest and as a means to contain such protest has been the inclination of the insurgents and the Indian state. The contest was once binary—between the Indian state and the insurgents as two opposing camps. But over time, the contests have shifted from a binary to a multi-cornered one. The conflict is no longer between the Indian state on the one side and the insurgents on the other, but also among the different insurgent outfits. This is due to the emerging trend of assertions by numerous ethnically based insurgent outfits, often working for their respective ethnic and community interests, translating community differences and animosity into the language of violence. The loss in human lives as the result of this violence has become immense with each insurgent outfit targeting one another. And thus, insurgency as a form of political struggle has lost its objectives in today's Northeast India. In spite of several setbacks, the Indian state has stood to gain the most. One, it has been able to dilute the objective of insurgency and corrupt the method of violence as a legitimate means of political struggle. Two, it has freed itself from being a collective single target of this entire struggle. How far it will help in bringing long-lasting peace in the region, however, remains a big question. Perhaps, the Indian state is not prepared for such an agenda, nor is the protesting side, for the language of violence helps every group and institution capable of asserting violence of one kind or the other. And it goes back to the classic case witnessed all over the world—the majority or the masses remain the real victims.

SEARCH FOR AN ALTERNATE DISCOURSE

Reiterative and the declarative discourses have several fallouts. Such narratives are marked by stances of 'denial' or 'subjugation'. Take for instance, the grand Indian narrative and the Naga nationalist narrative which mutually negate one another. The present peace talk between the Government of India and the NSCN is part of the mutual effort to understand and connect with one another. The Indian government seems to express its cognizance of Naga identity and history as different from the grand Indian narrative as reflected in the recent proposal of a federal relationship. If endorsed, this would be a major 'shift in discourse'. So far, the Indian national narrative either negates or encompasses other narratives and parallel narratives are yet to be endorsed. A change in the existing mindset can enable a shift in the nature of the discourse.

Theoretically, there appears to be two possible ways of handling the issue. This is presuming that the reiterative and declarative discourses—and through which different forms of narratives and myths are nurtured—are problematic. Either we throw away the baggage or discard what is redundant and lighten the burden. Both these approaches have their own advantages and disadvantages.

The 'Instrumental State'

Nationalism is a heavy baggage for a state to carry. The idea of the nation-state has often created contesting histories among communities living under the same roof. As stated earlier, India has experienced, during the post-Independence period, two vociferous narratives between two sets of historians: the Left-and-Liberal nationalist scholarship on the one hand, and the Right nationalist scholarship on the other. But there are also alternate historical narratives emerging through Dalit historiography, feminist historiography, etc. Each of these groups tells a different history, sometimes complementing and sometimes contesting, about the same nation-state called India. Yet for many (non-historical) liberals telling contesting histories does not solve the problems of a state. An alternative approach is to leave the baggage if it is too heavy. Such an approach identifies the root of the problem in visualizing the state as a 'nation-state'. The only reasonable way out is seen in discarding the tag of 'nationalism' and looking at political life as a meaningful and *useful* endeavour. Such a thesis visualizes 'individual' and 'liberty' as the epitome of human existence. The usefulness of the state is seen in terms of safeguarding the interest of the individuals who are capable of entering into hypothetical contracts to form institutions such as the state (Rawls 1971). It is certainly problematic to include contents of nationhood (such as language, ethnicity, and weltanschauung) in such a liberal paradigm of the state. The state is seen to have only one qualification—the 'instrumentality'—and ceases to carry its own being.

While such an approach is appealing insomuch that it can do away with all these problems at the outset, a more rigorous and meaningful investigation is called for. A twofold question may be raised regarding such an approach. One, how far is the 'instrumentality of the state' self-sufficient to define the nature of the state? Is this the only nature of the state? Two, how far is it feasible in the real sense to exclude the nationality tag from the state? The problems raised by these questions are distinctly different; the first raises a methodological issue and the second a practical one. It would be immature to engage such an approach without satisfactorily handling the questions.

Imagining a Dialogic Discourse

Another alternative is to envisage what I call a 'dialogic discourse'. This discourse involves a dialogue or a possible dialogue not only between two or more than two participants but also self-reflection or self-questioning. The participant could be an individual or a collective. The act, either as a dialogue between (at least) two participants or a self-reflective conversation by a participant, would be seen synchronically/uniformly as 'dialogic'. Another aspect of the 'dialogic' is that dialogues are not engaged in a vacuum or in mere mutual convenience of the participant(s); but on *hard* material grounds (social and political conditions, for instance) upon which the participants are located (facticity). Further, dialogues are 'acted upon' in 'time'—in historicity.

The problem with Northeast India is that instead of a meaningful dialogic engagement between different voices, the opposing voices summarily reject the other. For instance, the dissenting voices in the region not only reject the Indian national narrative, but also that of one another. Anything that falls short of rejection is 'appropriation' or 'subjugation' of the other in one's narrative. So much so that as the Assamese national narrative attempts encompassing other smaller ethnic narratives in the state, the Bodo narratives not only oppose but also counter the *encompassing* Assamese narrative. A similar relationship exists between the Naga narratives and the Manipuri narratives in Manipur.

These opposing narratives are marked by some forms of incompleteness, a 'lack' in capturing the flow of emerging identities. While many of these communities make knowledge claims, they often tend to ignore the historicity upon which these claims are made and this makes the assertions self-limiting. Human beings are indeed located in the 'present', but their 'present' is based on their capturing the 'past' as memory, and visualizing the 'future' as possibility. Comprehending the three temporal sequences is made possible only by acting upon material conditions. Unless we correlate these sequences, our claims and assertions are bound to be inauthentic. One of the major problems in the region is that either the entire Northeast, or some parts of it, has been constructed out of proportion in this 'imaginative flight of the present'. This could be about a Zou nation, a Kuki nation, a Naga nation, or a Bodo nation. Materiality must set the grounds for justly mapping the past and visualizing the future.

Though there are theoretical positions that we know of the 'past' through the 'present' with a goal towards the 'future', but the 'naked past' can never be comprehended (Ricoeur 1994). We are bound to make subjective judgements. Further, the same memory may change its meaning through these judgements. Two conditions ought to be fulfilled in order to arrive at a verifiable objective judgement. One, there is a need for the contending parties to correlate each other's fields of experiences (Ricoeur 1994). The texts and events that are either left behind or recorded (in whatever way) are an entirely different narrative than the ones we are concerned with today. But we can still cross-check each other's experiences of those past. Two, we cannot deny the materiality available before us. The materiality, such as socio-political conditions, must be allowed to 'restrict' us in our imaginative flight.

I do not subscribe to throwing away the historical or the civilizational 'baggage', even that which is too heavy to carry. It would be meaningful to see these burdens as unavoidable contents of human finitude. Existential anguish inherently associated with human freedom is well known (Sartre 1993). We have to invent devices to carry the baggage along, keeping at the same time the benefit of each community and nation in mind.

What is urgently needed today is to construct a cohesive and comprehensive narrative(s) of the Northeast that relate(s) more than exclude(s). Chronicles of the pre-colonial period have their own merits and limitations.[5] We gather immense information about kingdoms from the *Buronjis*, the *Rajmala* and the *Cheitharol Kumbaba*. British colonial writings (Pemberton, Hodson, Brown, etc.) and official records are useful to understand the region and colonial policies. But these only provide partial knowledge about one or other part of the region, or the rulers. The need is to narrow down the gap between one community and the other, to minimize stereotyping and to diminish the boundary of the 'insider' and the 'outsider' as often played through the politics of the indigenous and the migrant. This is possible through a dialogic discourse. It is all about constructing transparent, participatory, and objective narratives, which are construed through 'rational' consensus. Constructing narrative is a political act. And political decisions are largely consensual.

In the state of chronic conflict the region is acutely suffering from (perhaps more than any moment in the past), the role of the Indian state in this discursive struggle—either as contender, arbiter, or otherwise—cannot be ignored. Many of the problems would be solved with sincere involvement of the state in engaging these narratives through a dialogic discourse.

---

[5] I refer here to the first contact with the British administration as a marker of the divide between pre-colonial and postcolonial. If we go by temporal specificity, there are likely to be different years as markers for each state or community because the communities/kingdoms came into contact with the British at different times. The idea of 'pre-colonial' is more to be understood at the conceptual plane.

CHAPTER 9

Agency of Rioters

A Study of Decision-making in the Nellie Massacre, Assam, 1983

MAKIKO KIMURA

INTRODUCTION

There are still a number of unexplained factors in the phenomenon called 'riot'. Prominent among them is: why do ordinary people attack their neighbours or colleagues with whom they have shared long social relationships, and furthermore, how do they go back to their normal lives after the killings.

The last decade has seen a number of studies—in history, political science, sociology—on collective violence, or the so-called 'communal riot' in India. In the area of political science and sociology, it is a common understanding that there is a routinization of violence in urban areas in India, and in order to analyse it we need to study the political and social systems or institutions that produce communal riots. Brass argues that there is an 'institutionalized riot system' in cities and towns where riots repetitively occur (Brass 2003: 30–4). Thanks to these studies, we have overcome a primordialist bias, and rioters are no longer viewed as barbaric mobs. These studies presuppose that the routinization of violence is due to the involvement of politicians and large-scale political organizations. In this model, the participants of riots are described as goondas or mere puppets controlled by larger political forces.

There have also been cases where apart from the culpability of politicians and goondas or criminal elements, 'ordinary people' participate in such attacks. This is usually at the time of political transformation and large-scale breakdown of law and order. The Nellie Massacre which took place in Assam in 1983 was one such incident. The aim of this article is to analyse the perspectives of rioters through their narratives by examining the Nellie Massacre that took place during the anti-foreigners movement in Assam—commonly referred to as the Assam Movement (1979–85). In this incident, right after the state legislative assembly election, more than 1,600 Muslim peasants of East Bengal origin were killed in an attack organized by the Tiwa (a tribal group) and Assamese villagers. It was the largest violent incident during the movement, and one of the largest rural riots in India after Independence.

In a study conducted in the 1980s, Beth Roy tried to examine the issue of the agency of rioters through a study of a rural riot in Bangladesh—one generated by a trifle quarrel over a cow owned by a Muslim which ate some plants of a Hindu neighbour—by solely depending on the villagers' accounts of what happened. By focusing on how the villagers chose to riot, Roy saw that there was an awareness of history understood in terms of lived experience of *ordinary life* among the villagers. She argues,

The experiences of villagers in Bangladesh are foreign to outsiders. We cannot know their history unless we listen to their stories.... To talk across such a gulf we must first understand the language spoken. Couched in terms both abstract and immediate, of crops and rage, the story told in Panipur was clear for the hearing (Roy 1994: 193–4).

Inspired by Roy's work, what I try to do here is to study the decision to attack through the narratives of the participants in the riot. Based on the fieldwork conducted in the Nellie area in 2001–02, I try to grasp how they perceived the movement and the disturbance generated by the election, and subsequently decided to attack their neighbouring villages.

In the Nellie incident, both the attackers and the victims were rural peasants. The victims were Muslims, who trace their roots to East Bengal, and the attackers were mostly Tiwas, a 'plains tribal' group in the area, but also included other Assamese-speaking groups seen as 'backward', such as the Hiras and Kochs, and a few caste Hindus. In earlier writings, it has been discussed that the Tiwas were merely utilized by the movement leaders, or that the long-standing problem of land alienation was the root cause of the attack (Baruah 1999: 132–4; Hussain 1993: 141–2).

My aim is not to specify the root cause or the sole reason for the attack, but to analyse how those participating in the riots understood these factors when they made a decision. There are competing and sometimes contradicting narratives on the incident, and a close look at the complicated and fragmented accounts by the participants will help us comprehend the phenomenon better. It will lead to a new understanding of the rural impact of the anti-foreigners movement in Assam.

NELLIE: HISTORY OF IMMIGRATION AND ALIENATION OF TRIBAL LAND

Before we proceed with the analysis let us look at the socio-historical background of the area. The site of the incident, Nellie, is situated between Guwahati, the political centre of Assam, and Nagaon,[1] a district headquarter in central Assam. At the time of the incident, the area was under the jurisdiction of Nagaon district, but later, in the mid-1980s, the districts in Assam were reorganized and it came under the newly constituted Morigaon district.

Most of the areas of erstwhile Nagaon district are rural. The main crops are jute and rice, and both are mostly cultivated by the Muslims of East Bengal origin. In the district, due to the colonial policy of introducing immigrants from the overpopulated East Bengal region, notably Mymensingh district, there are a large number of the descendants of immigrants from the area. According to the 1971 census, 39.39 per cent of the population of the district is Muslim, and most of them are of East Bengali origin. In 2001, the number of Muslims exceeded half the population in both Morigaon and Nagaon districts.

Prior to the colonization, there existed a Tiwa tribal kingdom called Gobha which was located between Guwahati and the town of Nagaon. The Nellie area is close to the capital of the kingdom and there are a substantial number of Tiwas in the area. In 1905, Tiwas comprised more than 10 per cent of the population of the district. When the immigration started in the 1920s and the 1930s, the Muslim settlers first started to settle down in the areas close to the banks of the Brahmaputra River, which constitutes the northern border of the district. Nellie, located in the southern part of the district, had fewer immigrants in the initial years. However, by the 1940s, the number of immigrants had increased to the extent that land became scarce in the northern part of the district. Political demands were made by the

---

[1] Nagaon district was spelt in its anglicized form, 'Nowgong', till the mid-1980s. In this article, I use 'Nagaon' which is closer to the Assamese pronunciation.

Muslim League, backed by largely Muslim immigrants, to abolish the Line System[2] and open up some of the government land such as the Professional Grazing Reserves (PGR) to accommodate the Muslims. After appointing an officer to study the PGR, the Muslim League government decided to make available some of the PGRs in 1943 for the new settlers in the so-called 'waste land' (Das 1986: 34). The location of the Nellie incident was a PGR called Alichinga Grazing Reserve, and it was opened to immigrants in 1943.[3] Presently, there are nine to ten villages on the location, and all of them became the target of the attack in the Nellie incident.

For the Tiwas, the immigration marked the beginning of the loss of their traditional land. Having their origins in the hill areas[4] they continued shifting cultivation even after they migrated to the plains. The British colonial officers had introduced the private land ownership system in Assam in the late nineteenth century, which worked adversely for the tribes, including the Tiwas. Primarily shifting cultivators, they preferred the annual lease over a periodical lease of their lands, continuing to shift their agricultural land frequently. Meanwhile, immigrants who were keen on taking periodical leases had bought land from them. British colonial administrators called shifting cultivation 'fluctuating cultivation' and saw it as an outdated and ineffective way to utilize land; they planned on abolishing it in due course and encouraged the spread of the intensive cultivation practised by the Muslim immigrants. Such a situation is described in *Report of the Line System Committee* published in 1938.

Since the tribes were the worst sufferers from this migration, some measures to protect their land were proposed. This proposal was included in the resolution by the Line System Committee's report, and finally the Tribal Belts and Blocks were created in 1946 (Das 1986: 35–7). In the Tribal Belts and Blocks, the settlement of non-tribal

[2] The Line System was an administrative measure to divide the areas inhabited by the immigrants and the local populations. It was introduced by the officials of Nagaon district in order to prevent any friction over occupation of land between the immigrants and the local populations.

[3] Maps of the area are available in *Report of the Special Officer Appointed for the Examination of the Professional Grazing Reserves in the Assam Valley* (1944), Assam Government Press, Shillong. For the discussion on the PGR, see Guha (1977: 281, 284–5).

[4] Tiwa people still live in the hill areas in Karbi Anglong district, which is adjacent to present-day Morigaon and Nagaon districts.

or non-backward classes was prohibited.[5] The area just north of the attacked villages where the people participated in the riot was inhabited by Tiwas. The villages were also specified as a tribal block called Tetelia Tribal Block in 1950 (Bordoloi 1999: 14).

On the other hand, immigrants who were subjected to exploitative treatment under the zamindari system in East Bengal, particularly those from Mymensingh district, were hard-working cultivators accustomed to intense cultivation and a cash economy. Here is an account on the immigrants in Laharighat mauza,[6] one of the areas where immigrants became dominant in the 1930s. This illustrates the difference between the immigrant Muslims and the local Assamese, including tribes such as Tiwa.

The Assamese are un-ambitious and are easily satisfied. They do not usually go in for debts; small amounts which they might borrow are quickly repaid after harvest. The immigrants are however habitual borrowers. They spend a lot of money recklessly in litigation, good houses, cattle and dress and for buying more land. In normal years they clear off their debts. When they want money they do not hesitate even to execute bonds for double amount they actually borrow. (Mauza Note: Laharighat 1931: page number not indicated)

Although the colonial bias about 'lazy natives', lacking an understanding of the traditional culture and way of life, is quite apparent in this account, it illustrates a picture of Muslims successfully adapting to changes brought about by colonization, and of Tiwas losing out. It was alleged that Muslim immigrants often harassed local populations to grab land, but the enquiry of the Line System Committee found that although there were such cases, the allegations were largely exaggerated (*Report of the Line System Committee* 1938: 18).

The situation had not changed much even in the 1980s. It has been reported that the Tiwas in the area often sold land due to their indebtedness to moneylenders belonging to the immigrant communities. They often borrowed money for illnesses and ceremonies, but due to the high rate of interest many of them were unable to pay back the same. As a result, they resorted to selling their lands and became agricultural labourers or moved to other areas. Such a situation was prevalent even in the Tribal Blocks where the transaction of land to non-tribals is illegal (Sharma-Thakur 1986: 101–2).

[5] The Assam Land & Revenue Regulation 1886, Chapter X, passed in 1947.
[6] Village unit adopted for administration and survey.

When the anti-foreigners movement started, its leaders raised the issue of land alienation among the tribals in order to back their claims that the influx of foreigners created socio-economic problems in Assam. Considering the history of the area and the problem of land alienation among the tribes, it is not surprising that when the violence broke out many academics and journalists cited land alienation among the tribes as a root cause of the violence. However, there were other reasons behind the violence as well.

MOVEMENT, ELECTION, AND VIOLENCE

The late 1970s and the mid-1980s saw a large-scale movement led by a student organization and some political parties in Assam. It was triggered by the abnormal increase in the number of people on the electoral roll prepared for a by-election to the Mangaldoi parliamentary seat. The leaders of the All Assam Students' Union (AASU) argued that the unusual rise was caused by the influx of illegal immigrants from Bangladesh. They demanded the detection of the names of foreigners on the electoral rolls, the deletion of those names, and the deportation of foreigners.

The movement succeeded in mobilizing the masses, and the AASU managed to have several rounds of talks with the Congress (I) government at the centre, headed by Indira Gandhi at the time. The central government conceded that most of the claims of the movement leaders were right, but they proposed to deport only those foreigners who had entered Assam after 1971, even though the movement leaders demanded that 1951 be the cut-off year. The central government and the leaders of the movement failed to come to an agreement on this point, and the latter continued their activities by calling bandhs, and organizing satyagrahas and oil blockades.

From December 1979 to December 1982, because of the movement, President's Rule was imposed in Assam a number of times, and there were only two short-term Congress (I) governments. In December 1982, as the period for the President's Rule came to an end, the central government decided to hold the state legislative assembly election. The AASU and the All Assam Gana Sangram Parishad (AAGSP) leaders decided to boycott the election because the Election Commission proposed to conduct it without revising the electoral rolls. They called it Assam's 'last struggle for survival' and campaigned in every district in the Brahmaputra valley. Although the leaders conducted their activities in a 'peaceful way', in some parts there were burning of bridges and physical blockades of polling booths to prevent people from casting their votes. On the other hand, descendants of Muslim immigrants, who regarded the movement as targeted against them, saw the election as a good opportunity to elect an 'immigrant-friendly' government (Baruah 1999: 131). As a result, a large-scale confrontation occurred over the issue of whether or not to hold the election in Assam.

A series of group clashes occurred just before and after the election. On 13 February 1983, there was a clash between Bodos, a plains tribe in Assam, and ethnic Assamese in Gohpur, Darrang district. In this area, the Plains Tribal Council of Assam (PTCA), an organization demanding an autonomous state for plains tribes in Assam, decided to contest the election, and the Bodos supported it. As a result, there was a clash between the Bodo election supporters and the AASU and AAGSP workers who tried to block access to the polling booth by burning bridges, etc. Almost at the same time, a series of skirmishes between the immigrant Muslims and the Assamese people in *char* areas (flood-prone areas and river islands) in the Brahmaputra River, south of Mangaldoi, started. It is estimated that more than a hundred people died in the group clashes in this area (Gupta 1984: 15–16).

Thus, the Nellie incident, which took place on 18 February 1983, can be seen as a part of the series of violent incidents triggered by the election. Since number of people killed at Nellie on 18 February far exceeded the deaths in the clashes preceeding it, the media dubbed it a 'massacre' and described it as a 'tribal attack'.

Journalists and academics mention a number of factors responsible for the violence. Prior to the election, there were warnings from various quarters about a possible outbreak of violence. However, the central government insisted on holding the election, ignoring those warnings, even though some of them were issued by the local police. This was reported in *India Today*, after the incident, and the central government was criticized for escalating an already tense situation, particularly by the sections of people who supported the Assam movement (Shourie 1983: 28–35).

Another factor considered responsible for the violence was the land alienation suffered by the tribes at the hands of the Muslims of East Bengali origin. In the writings of academics and journalists in Assam, this has been regarded as at least a major background factor, if not the cause, of the massacre (Baruah 1999: 134; Hazarika 2000: 46). As the movement leaders emphasized the issue of tribal land alienation as a problem caused by the influx of foreigners, when the violence broke out many assumed that land alienation was its main source. In any case there is a tendency among Indian academics to regard economic exploitation as the primary cause in analyses of collective violence. Although there is no doubt that immigration and subsequent loss of land by the Tiwas are important factors in explaining the economic and social condition of this area, too much emphasis on these economic factors leaves little room for human agency.

A third factor emphasized in most commentaries is manipulation by the movement leaders, the AASU and the AAGSP. Academics and journalists in Assam who were against the anti-foreigners movement saw the attack as instigated by the student leaders. There are also those who insist that pan-Indian right-wing Hindu organizations such as the Rashtriya Swayamsevak Sangh (RSS) and Bharatiya Janata Party (BJP) instigated the local people to target the Muslims.

All these factors were, to some extent, relevant to the Nellie incident. It is not the aim of this article to isolate one prominent cause, but rather to see how the riot participants saw these factors as relevant in their decision-making.

NARRATIVES OF THE RIOTERS

Narrating the Incident

I would like to begin with a long interview conducted on the disturbances caused by the election and its relation to the decision to attack Muslim villages. The person who gave me this account was a Koch, a group recognized as economically and socially backward in Assam. His village is located in the middle of the Tetelia Tribal Block, where 70 per cent of the population are Koch and 30 per cent are Tiwa. Being a first-year student of college, this person was an active AASU member of the locality at the time. At the same time, he is a grandson of one of the founders of the village. His account shows the link between the movement and the decision to attack in the village.

According to him, in the villages in the Tetelia Tribal Block, the danger that came with the election was first felt when a disturbance took place in a village 10 kilometres north-west to his village. Prior to the Nellie incident, there was a rumour that Muslim outsiders had come to the area and that they were harassing Tiwa and Assamese peasants and trying to grab their land.

There were a few incidents before the Nellie incident took place. In a village called Gorjan, once upon a time the Tiwas were in a majority. However, the number of Muslim peasants slowly increased and ultimately they made up 80 per cent of the population there. They damaged the crops in the fields of the Tiwa people and tried to grab the land. At the time, there were a few cases of murder, I believe. As a result, a part of Tiwa residents came to our village and they planned to get back their land. They fought and were successful in regaining their land, but fourteen to fifteen people died in the process.[7]

From interviews conducted in a few other villages in the area, there are a number of accounts of troubles and harassment of Tiwa and Assamese villagers at the hands of Muslims. These include cases of kidnapping of girls, Muslims cultivating rice in fields belonging to the Assamese and the Tiwas, and Muslims letting loose cows in their fields. According to the ex-AASU activist, however, it was a more acute danger which led them to decide to attack the village.

After the incident, several Muslims came from Gorjan to Muladhari [one of the attacked villages in the Nellie incident] and they left their wives and children in the village. Several Bihari fishermen who lived on the bank of the river Kopili came to know of their existence. They were warned not to tell others about them. However, since the Muslims harassed the Bihari people they told us [the local villagers] about Muslims from Gorjan being there in Muladhari.

We felt scared to hear that the Muslims of Gorjan village had came to Muladhari. There were also cases where a few cows crossed the river and never returned. We suppose that the Muslims ate those cows. Thus, on 13 February, the village elders held a meeting and discussed how to deal with them.

On the fourteenth, the Muslims came to know about the meeting and they attacked the Bihari houses in retaliation. They burned down their houses at night. On the fifteenth the village elders assembled again and we decided to attack the Muslims.

According to my source, leaders from several villages—Sonuabori, Pachalaghat, Mantabori, Silbeta, Borogaon—came to the meeting. It can be seen that though he was an AASU activist in the region, his narratives refer to the village elders as the key decision-makers in the attack. From his point of view it was not the AASU but the village elders who took the final call. His account continues as follows:

[7] Personal interview with a schoolteacher in a village just north of Nellie area, 24 November 2001. All subsequent narratives in this section are from this interview.

The hill Tiwa people had a good relationship with the plains Tiwa people, so we told them about our plans. They agreed to participate in the attack and came down with hand-made rifles and arrows the night before the attack. First, we went to a village called Borbori across the National Highway and killed 300 people there. After that, we crossed the highway and started attacking villages around Muladhari. That time, the villages were already surrounded from three corners. We started burning the houses at 11 a.m. and the attack continued till 3 p.m.

It has been argued that the tribes were merely utilized by the movement leaders or other miscreants who wanted to create disturbances, but there has not been much analysis on the decision-making process among the Tiwa and Assamese villagers. From my source, it is clear that village elders played a key role in triggering the attacks. Given the social structure of the villages, this is perhaps not surprising. Beth Roy points to the importance of such a process of decision-making in her study of riots that took place in rural areas in erstwhile East Pakistan (Roy 1994: 136).

If the meeting by the village elders was decisive in the initiative to start the riot, what was the turning point for them? In order to answer this question, we have to examine the narrative, or rather the rumours, on the series of incidents which took place before the outbreak of large-scale violence.

Interpreting the Narratives: The Role of Rumour

There is no arguing that rumours on the series of incidents prior to the Nellie incident influenced the villagers in their decision to attack. The story consists of the following incidents: (1) In Gorjan village, Tiwas attacked Muslims in retaliation of loss of land and harassment they suffered. Prior to the incident some Tiwas came to my interviewee's village and planned the attack. (It can be suggested that the villagers in that lent a hand in the attack.) The Tiwas got back some of their land. (2) After the first attack, the Muslims of Gorjan came to Muladhari, a neighbouring Muslim village, and left their wives and children there. They also harassed the Biharis who lived on the border of the Muslim villages and the Assamese and Tiwa villages. (3) The first meeting on how to deal with the Muslims was held in the Tetelia Tribal Block. The Muslims, knowing about the meeting, attacked the Biharis and burned down their houses. (4) The village elders held a meeting and decided to attack the Muslims.

How do we interpret this story? Is it a mere rumour which circulated before the riot, as many scholars suggest? Or is there any truth to it? It is clear from the interviewee's account that he was sure that such incidents really took place. Should we take his account to be 'fact', or as an event which was largely exaggerated in a rumour?

At the time, there were many small-scale incidents which took place all over Assam, especially when the elections came close. Just before the Nellie incident there was a report of the murder of Lalung (an old name for Tiwa) children in the Lahorighat area. The memorandum by Lalung Darbar,[8] submitted to the prime minister, Indira Gandhi, just after the incident, noted several incidents that occurred between 12 and 15 February in the Lahorighat and Mayang circle, which lies north of the Nellie area.

However, we should refrain from a hasty judgement that there was a danger of attack on the Tiwas by the Muslims in the Nellie area. The Nellie area is situated in the southern part of the Nagaon district, and Muslims are in a minority there. Around Muladhari, there is a small pocket of about ten villages inhabited by Muslims but they are surrounded by villages inhabited by Tiwa and the Koch people. When we consider this factor, the possibility of Muslims attacking Tiwa and Assamese villages seems very low.

According to Jonathan Spencer, such rumours circulated at the time of large-scale riots like the ones in Colombo in 1983 and in Delhi in 1984. Rumours circulate all the time. But at the time of large-scale violence, people tend to believe certain representations as real and true, either in the absence of immediate empirical evidence or, in many cases, in direct contradiction to what they see around them (Spencer 2003: 1571–2). In the case of the Nellie incident, too, what I discerned from the interviews with AASU activists and other villagers was that they felt the threat of attacks from the neighbouring Muslim villages as acute and real. The only thing I can say is that at the time of the violence, the area was very tense due to the political uncertainty caused by the forced election and the boycott. The breakdown of law

---

[8] The memorandum was submitted to the prime minister of India on 24 June 1983 by Lalung Darbar, a socio-cultural organization of the Tiwas. The organization first submitted a memorandum on demand for the autonomous district of the Tiwas in 1967. I thank Mr Hemendra Narayan for sending me the document on my request.

and order characterized many areas of Assam at that time and it was
certainly true of Nellie.

Rioters and Morality: Self-defence Rather than Economic Deprivation

In any case, the villagers believed the rumours and took what they saw
as appropriate action in response. They gave importance to the 'fact'
that there was trouble between the Tiwas and the Muslims in a village
10–20 kilometres away from them, and saw it as being highly relevant
to them. It should be noted that it was not land alienation which was
emphasized as the main cause of the attack. People emphasized more
the danger of the attack from the Muslim side and cited it as the main
reason for deciding to attack the Muslims. In the section 'Narrating
the Incident', I have quoted my interviewee's narrative of the sequence
as he remembered it.

The tendency to cite self-defence as the motive for the killings is
not unique to Nellie. Spencer argues that in the case of the killing of
Tamils in 1983 and the anti-Sikh riots in Delhi in 1984, rioters mention
self-defence as a motive for the killings. He states, 'What the crowd
was doing to Sikhs and Tamils was what the crowd believed Sikhs
and Tamils were doing, or going to do, to them' (Spencer 2003: 1571).
Horowitz also argues that rumours form an essential part of the riot
process, and their severity is often an indicator of the severity of the
impending violence (Horowitz 2001: 74–5).

In the narrative of participants in Nellie, the danger of attack is cited
as more important and acute than land alienation, which was seen as the
main cause by scholars and journalists writing on the Assam movement.
This point has been partly discussed in my earlier paper on the Nellie
incident. What the attackers, as well as victims, cite as the cause of the
incidents are 'direct causes'[9] such as revenge for election, the kidnapping
of girls by Muslims, or the proposed attack by the Muslims. On the
other hand, what the scholars and journalists had analysed and specified
as the cause of the violence was land alienation which is embedded in
the history and social structure in the area (Kimura 2003: 233–4). Such
'structural causes' are of course not irrelevant to the killings, but what
the rioters see as a cause is usually a more simple and acute danger felt
in their daily lives. It happens that what the villagers perceive as a cause

[9] I thank Professor Virginius Xaxa for pointing out the difference between
direct causes and structural causes in this analysis.

of the violence, and what scholars and journalists, often based in the urban middle class, analyse as a cause of violence are different.

Role of 'Outsiders' and Construction of Community in Violence

It is again through the rumour that the line between enemy and the ally was created. The Tiwas came to 'our' village. The Muslims went to 'their' village. Through the narration of these incidents, the line was demarcated between 'them' and 'us'—and it led to the important marker of deciding who belonged to which community. In other words, rumour is an important process in the construction of community in collective violence.

In the narrative, the coming of the 'outsiders' in Muladhari became the key factor in deciding the attack. According to the narrative, the Muslims came from a village, Gorjan, where they had trouble with the Tiwas earlier. It is worth noting the relationship between such statements and other statements—'we had a good relationship with our Muslims neighbours before those Muslims came from Gorjan', or 'we did not have any problem with them until the time of the violence'. The latter statement was not only insisted on by the attackers, but also heard even among the Muslims who were attacked. Almost all the respondents said that before the Nellie incident there was no disturbance between the Muslims and the Assamese (and the Tiwas, Kochs, etc.).[10]

Such narratives which attribute violence or the cause of violence to 'outsiders' are not unique to the attackers of the Nellie incident. Gyanendra Pandey points out that this is the way local communities where people can recognize each other by face come to terms with disturbing memories. He argues that nations deal with the moment of violence in their past by the relatively simple stratagem of drawing a neat boundary around themselves, distinguishing sharply between 'us' and 'them', and pronouncing the act of violence an act of the other or an act necessitated by a threat to the self. Local communities, on the other hand, have to live with the memories of the violence more uncertainly, and continuously, than nations and states (Pandey 2001: 177). Thus, they attribute the violence or the cause of the violence to outsiders.[11]

---

[10] On this point, see the arguments in my earlier article (Kimura 2003).
[11] Rural communities where people can recognize each other by face.

VIOLENCE AND IDENTITY

Foreigners, Muslims, or Mymensinghia—Views of the Rioters

In the violence which took place during the election disturbance, the Muslims of East Bengali origin was perceived as the important Other who could be a great threat to the local populations such as the Assamese and Tiwa people. It happened not only in Nellie, but also in other parts of Assam. Here, one question arises: Did the claims of the movement leaders that foreigners were grabbing land play any role in demarcating the community? In other words, were they taken to be 'foreigners', as the movement leaders claimed? Or, were they perceived as 'Muslims' and attacked? Or as outsiders? This point is fundamental when we analyse the character of the violence.

In the first place, let us take a look at the perspectives of the participants of the riot again. If we look closely at the narratives of the Assamese and Tiwa villagers, they do not use the terms 'foreigners' (*bideshi*) or 'Muslims' (*Mussalman*s). Mostly, people in villages use the term *miya*s or *Mymensinghia*s. Miya is a term which refers to a Muslim, and in the Assamese context specifically to those from East Bengal, and not to ethnic Assamese Muslims. Mymensinghia derives from a district, Mymensingh, in erstwhile East Bengal, presently Bangladesh. The term indicates peasants hailing from the district, but as most Bengali immigrant peasants came from the district, the terms miya and Mymensinghia are often used interchangeably.

In my interviews, the term 'foreigners' was often used by the top student leaders to describe the target of the movement. However, the local student leaders tended to use the term 'minority' or 'Muslims'. And in rural areas such as Nellie, people often used the term miyas or Mymensinghias. It is important to see from the transformation of the terms how the local leaders—usually located in the smaller towns—as well as the villagers in the rural areas interpret the movement and the violence. The terms they used are important when we analyse how they perceived the threat and the attacks that took place.

The student leader who gave me the account of the decision-making process in the attack used the term Muslim as most other local leaders did. However, a village elder told me it was an attack against miyas, and explained the incident in this way: 'It was not a clash between Hindus and Muslims, but it was targeted against miyas. Miyas are immigrants who came from Bangladesh. The movement aimed to deport bideshis [foreigners]. Thus it was targeted against miyas, particularly Mymensinghias.'[12]

It is important to note that in the narrative above, the term bideshi is used almost as equal to miya and Mymensinghia. It is not that the Assamese and Tiwa villagers were ignorant of the fact that most Muslims in the attacked villages came to Assam in the colonial period. However, because of their East Bengal origins, they were often perceived or mistaken as Bangladeshis. It can be assumed that with rumours gaining ground that foreigners were hiding among the Muslim villages, people slowly started to suspect those residing in the Muslim locality to be foreigners. In this way, the notion of foreigners was slowly connected to Muslims of East Bengal origins, and 'anti-foreigners' was interpreted as 'anti-Bengali Muslim peasants' in the local context. Such a perception is not unique to rural areas, but it is shared by middle-class caste Hindu Assamese as well. Since most Muslims of immigrant origins are located in rural areas, the actual attacks took place in rural areas.

Muslims as the 'Important Other' in Assam: Citizenship and Religion in India

The Nellie incident had a tremendous impact on Hindu–Muslim relations in Assam. Until then, it has been said, the state was relatively free from communal tension. Except for the disturbance in lower Assam districts in 1950, which occurred in relation to the Partition and the violence which occurred in East Pakistan at the time, the Muslims of East Bengal origins were rarely targeted in collective violence. Indeed, during the 1960s and 1970s when the language movement was prominent in the state, it was always the middle-class Bengalis (mostly Hindus) who were targeted and defined as a 'threat' by the middle-class Assamese. The Muslim peasants who declared their mother tongue to be Assamese were not targeted till the anti-foreigners movement started in the late 1970s.

It should be noted that during the elections that we are currently discussing, numerous violent incidents took place and the targets were not only the Muslims of East Bengal origin. In other incidents, Bengali Hindus, Nepalis, Biharis, etc., were also attacked. In the Gohpur incident, another plains tribe group, the Bodos, attacked

[12] A personal interview with a villager in Tetelia Tribal Block, 15 November 2001.

ethnic Assamese. Thus, there were local variations in the profiles of the victims and the victimizers.

At the same time, it has been said that most of the victims were Muslims of East Bengal descent (Baruah 1999: 132). A few of the largest incidents such as Nellie and Chaolkhowa were against Muslims of immigrant origin. The targeting of Muslims is common in what is referred to as communal violence in India. Whenever anti-Pakistan or anti-Bangladesh sentiments are aroused, Muslims are targeted even when they are genuine citizens of India. The loyalty of Muslims becomes an object of suspicion during such times. This is deeply embedded in the history of the Partition and nation-state formation in India and Pakistan (and Bangladesh). In that sense, although the anti-foreigners movement was not explicitly against Muslims, the issue of citizenship did become connected to the issue of religion, whether or not the leadership of the movement had intended it.

After the Nellie incident, Muslims who were earlier active participants or eager supporters of the movement withdrew their support. Many active workers in the AASU stopped participating in blockades and demonstrations. This was not only among the Muslims of immigrant origin, but also with the Muslims who had settled in the colonial period and were seen as 'indigenous' in Assamese society. One of the top student leaders from the indigenous community resigned from his position after the incident. People reacted differently to the Nellie incident[13] and it left a scar in Assamese society which till then was believed to be relatively free from communal tension.

After the anti-foreigners movement and the violence against Muslims, the Muslims of immigrant origin became the important Other. Whenever the slogan against 'foreigners' arises, they fear deportation. There have been many cases where Muslim immigrants are suspected of being illegal immigrants and have had to produce documents in order to prove their place of birth.[14] In later years, the anti-foreigners movement has been influenced by the rise of pan-Indian Hindu nationalism and the BJP brand of politics. Hindutva did not change the politics of Assam, but it took advantage of the Assamese

[13] On the different responses to the Nellie incident among the Muslims see Saikia (2005: 66–7).

[14] Interview with Muslim residents of East Bengal descent in Lahorighat, February 2007.

fear of the Muslims and was thus partly successful in gaining some organizational basis in Assam.

We thus see that the issue of citizenship was partly turned into violence against Muslims in the Nellie incident in Assam in 1983. Although the movement leaders ostensibly wanted only 'foreigners' to be deported, when the violence happened, the victims were largely Muslims who were long-term residents of the area.

CONCLUSION

The analysis in this article reveals that in the narratives of the riot participants, the threat from Muslims as felt by the villagers was crucial when they decided to attack. From their perspective, it was not ideology or land alienation but the more acute and directly felt threat which made them attack neighbouring villages.

This does not mean that the ideology of the anti-foreigners movement or land alienation was irrelevant. They are undoubtedly important factors in demarcating the border when the violence took place. What should be noted here is that it is misleading to assume that ideology or structural causes controlled the village people as mere puppets. Instead, people interpreted these factors from their own perspectives, and took the decision to protect themselves.

Without argument, it can be said that the degree of such agency of the rioters may vary in each case. In rural areas where the village-level community and its hierarchy are strong, the impact of external factors is limited. The scenario may be different in urban areas where riots most frequently occur in India. In urban areas, anonymity is much higher and collective violence by goondas or manipulation by political parties may be much easier. In order to have a theoretical understanding and a comparative perspective on the difference between riots in urban and rural areas, field study is an essential tool, although it may be quite difficult to do in the case of urban riots.

This study shows how ordinary people resorted to attacking their neighbours at a time of extreme political crisis. The villagers were not totally controlled by the movement leaders or communal forces, but they chose to riot. Although the scale of the incident was large, the village is not extraordinary in any sense. It could have happened in any village in Assam. In order to understand this we need to listen to the complicated and sometimes competing narratives, the fragmented accounts of the villagers carefully.

PART IV

Making Peace, Making War:
India's Peace Policy

CHAPTER 10

The Mizo Exception

State–Society Cohesion and Institutional Capability

M. SAJJAD HASSAN

INTRODUCTION

In the political cauldron that is northeastern India, the one State[1] that stands out for the relative absence of violent politics is Mizoram. This exception needs to be explained. Between 1992 and 2005, in ethnic and separatist violence, 6,023 persons died in Assam, 4,016 died in Manipur, 3,327 in Tripura, and 2,167 in Nagaland. In Mizoram, the comparable figure was thirty (GoI 2006b).[2] Organized violence has largely been absent in the State for the past two decades. This is a definite achievement for a territory that was severely affected by prolonged violence, beginning 1966. Though post-conflict Mizoram has experienced its share of group mobilization and ethnic contestations, at no time has the violence in this State paralleled that in other parts of the Northeast. Mizoram has largely remained, in the words of its incumbent chief minister Zoramthanga, 'an island of peace in a sea of turmoil'.[3]

What explains this puzzle? Commentators have mostly attributed the violence in the Northeast to identity politics. The few accounts of Mizoram that do exist have interpreted its apparent peace as proof

[1] I use state with a capital S, to mean a territorial entity—a province of the Indian Union. That with a small 's' is state in its abstract sense—the organizational and institutional arrangement in society to manage contestations and provide services.

[2] Also tabulated by the author using the datasheet from the Institute of Conflict Management (ICM), available at www.satp.org. Accessed on 5 April 2006.

[3] *The Telegraph*, Guwahati, 22 August 2003.

of the absence of identity politics there (Chandhoke 2006). A closer reading of politics in the State will quickly dispel this notion (Sharma and Baruah 2004). Much of the politics in Mizoram, as in the other States in the region, is centred around the question of identity and nationalism. Political parties and public organizations in Mizoram have, like their counterparts in the rest of the Northeast, used ethnic identity to mobilize support among their constituents. Yet the fallout of these mobilizations has been less violent. Some writers have attributed the restoration of peace in Mizoram to 'the devolution of huge economic largesse from the Central government for socio-economic development' and to the 'deft employment of the inherent integrative capabilities of a national political party' (Jafa 2000). Surely, showering 'economic largesse' has been a staple feature of New Delhi's Northeast policy. As has been demonstrated elsewhere, the strategy may, in some cases, have actually fed conflicts, often changing their character, and giving them further lease of life (Baruah, 2005a: 18; Sahni 2001). Further, 'the integrative capabilities' of the Congress party have not been very successful in States like Manipur that have an equally long 'Congress tradition'. And if military victories of the army against the Mizo National Front (MNF) played a decisive role in restoring peace in Mizoram, as some accounts claim (Jafa 2000; Nag 2002: 262–5), why have similar military advantages not led to successes against separatist rebels in Nagaland or Manipur? And crucially, even if peace was restored in Mizoram, how has it been sustained despite the fact that the State shares with the rest of the Northeast much of the fragility that is said to underpin the disorder and collapse there. Some recent accounts of the politics in the region have attributed its disorder to the policies and strategies employed by the central government and its agencies in response to group contestations (Baruah 2005a). While this focus on the working of the State is a useful advance on explanations of the anomie in the region, it still fails to adequately explain the exception of Mizoram.

Part of the explanation for the restoration of peace in Mizoram has been attributed to the undisputed leadership within MNF ranks, helping it clinch a peace deal (that has eluded many other armed groups in talks with the centre), and the ability of religious and social organizations in the State to demand and work for peace (Baruah 2005a: 71). Journalistic accounts have often credited the supposed cohesiveness of Mizo society for the sustenance of peace there. If these are indeed the drivers of peace in the State, the questions that we need to focus on, and which could help explain our puzzle, are: How was the supposed cohesiveness of Mizo society attained? What accounts for the synergy of political leaders and social organizations there to work for and obtain peace and indeed ensure a semblance of good governance? These questions are germane to the discussion on peace in Mizoram, given the empirical observation that society in places like Manipur or Nagaland is so fragmented and that state leaders there find it hard to connect with society and to stand up to pressures from contending social groups.

STATE CAPABILITY AND POLITICAL ORDER

It is evident that while much of the breakdown in the Northeast is because of organized violence, there is much more at play here than just ethnic conflict or separatist violence. Ongoing comparative research on the politics in the region—particularly exploring issues around power in societies and the ability of the state to provide a legitimate basis of authority—is throwing up evidence that supports the claim that the widespread violence and breakdown in the Northeast are not so much about the inherent differences between its social groups as they are about the absence of an effective (institutional and cultural) medium to regulate relationships and moderate contestations. Conversely, the absence of violence in Mizoram may be mainly because society in that province has arrangements in place to mitigate inter-group contestations and promote accommodation. This account of the breakdown is premised on the assumption that it is institutional arrangements in society—embodied in the concept of the state—that regulate and govern political, social, and economic interactions, providing the basis for social order and cohesion. Seen this way, violence becomes a dimension of state failure, that is of the poor capability of the state to manage contestations and provide order on the basis of some sort of a social contract between the rulers and the ruled. The question that we must grapple with then is, what accounts for the capability of the state?

As the experience of state building in much of the developing world—covered today in the rubric of 'governance reforms'—demonstrates, the capability of the state or its strength is not just a function of establishing bureaucracies, acquiring technical know-how, and enacting rules of behaviour. State capability depends fundamentally on the capacity of those who man the agencies of the state for autonomous choice. The key dynamic here is how society empowers (or constrains) the state to act as the chief regulator of public life vis-à-vis other forces in society that may be attempting to provide alternative means of authority. Seen this way, state capability derives from the historical contests between different forces in society over 'social control'—the ability of leaders to influence how citizens behave—which has involved their building institutions and constructing and mobilizing collective identities to gain that competitive advantage (Migdal 1988: 22). These contests and their outcome form the crux of the process of 'state formation'.[4] Empirical research demonstrates that what is crucial for state capability and for political order is whether state formation involved greater emphasis on building statewide institutions and mobilizing inclusive identities (to enable the state to gain statewide legitimacy) or if the pattern was one of social groups investing in community-specific organizations to mobilize narrow and localized identities.[5] The state–society interactions around state formation is clearly a two-way process involving the construction of a society that state leaders could plug into and the building of a state that could provide the basis of legitimate authority in society.[6]

Using this conceptual frame I hope to demonstrate that Mizoram's uniqueness lies in the process of its state formation involving, to a considerable extent, the internal contests and accommodations between social forces over power and authority to create a state that fits society and a society that fits the state. That the basis of this two-way dynamic is largely inclusive—involving building political organizations that have pan-Mizo constituencies and mobilizing collective identities that again use pan-Mizo appeals—means that the resultant legitimacy of the state is widespread, enabling it to be at once embedded in society and be autonomous from contending social forces. This has shored up the capability of the state, cushioning it from crisis and may well be what is preventing the breakdown that is common to the rest of Northeast India.

The aforementioned causal argument is elaborated ahead using empirical evidence gleaned from ethnographic accounts, archival records, public and private documents, press reports, and from

---

[4] Defined as 'a historical process whose outcome is a largely unconscious and contradictory process of conflicts, negotiations, and compromises between diverse groups whose self-serving actions and trade-offs constitute the vulgarisation of power'; Bruce Berman and John Lonsdale, 'Unhappy Valley' (1992), quoted in Hibou (2004: 343).

[5] For this argument, see Hesselbein et al. (2006).

[6] For this discussion see Migdal (2001).

interviews with a host of informants. I have also used secondary material for analysis and interpretation of data. The rest of the article is organized in the following manner. I begin by looking at the history of state formation in the erstwhile Lushai Hills, to explore historically the genesis of state power during pre-colonial and colonial times and then examine the struggles that took place between the Commoners and the chiefs in order to understand how state power has been grounded. I then explore the genesis of the MNF rebellion, its contribution to transforming Mizo society and its overall impact on power relations in the State. Finally, I test how this trajectory of state formation has impacted on the capability of the Mizo state, particularly on its success with providing political goods. I conclude by trying to tease out some lessons for the research in terms of the overall argument as well as the implications of the research on sustainability of peace in Mizoram.

THE MIZO UNION (MU) AND THE CONSTRUCTION OF A COHESIVE STATE

The seeds of the growth of a statewide inclusive political system that we find in Mizoram today must be traced to its pre-colonial past. Two features of the early history of the state stand out: one is the movement of different clans and tribes into the present state and the other is the rise of the Sailo clan of the Lushai sub-tribe as a political force. Mizoram is made up of a collection of tribes and clans, broadly classified as Kuki-Chin, who migrated in many succeeding waves beginning probably from the eighteenth century.[7] The migratory nature of the Kuki-Chin tribes meant that most villages were heterogeneous. Heterogeneity was also encouraged by the Sailo chiefs who, while presiding over most villages, settled prisoners they had captured in raids on enemy villages. This melange of people (called Hanmchawm, meaning Commoners) belonging to a variety of sub-tribes and clans—Hmars, Thadous, Raltes, Rangkhols, and the like—living together in a village under the tutelage of the despotic chief helped in the growth of a feeling of commonality. That the Sailo chiefs patronized Duhlian helped with the growth of the dialect as the lingua franca, even though each sub-tribe continued to have its particular dialect for day-to-day communication (Davis 1894: 6). These tendencies meant an early realization of some sort of a collective consciousness in what is Mizoram today, although

---

[7] For the history of the movement and the rise of the Sailo rulers, see Shakespeare (1912: 3–7).

this was still nebulous. The advent of colonial rule would contribute to movements towards commonness.

The principal pre-colonial political institution in the Lushai Hills was that of village chieftain. Significantly though, like many pre-modern tribal communities, each village head was autonomous of the other. Yet, the chiefs—all of whom belonged to the Sailo clan—had established a network of loose alliances, with relations among them ordered in a hierarchical fashion (Reid 1978: 4). This arrangement of Sailo suzerainty covered pretty much the entire territory of the Lushai Hills, except for the tract in the extreme south. In hindsight, though this institutional arrangement fell very much short of a territorial state system, it did provide the openings for future interventions consolidating a statewide polity.

The Chin Lushai expedition of 1889–90 led to the conquest and incorporation of the Lushai Hills into British India. This was followed by a slew of state-building interventions designed to help colonial administrators maintain peace and extract revenue. Two features of the colonial state-building strategy in the Lushai Hills stand out in comparison to those elsewhere in the region: promoting institutional uniformity throughout the district and strengthening the hand of colonial administrators at the expense of local chieftains. Taken together and in combination with other features such as the modernizing role of Christian missionaries, these measures led to the drilling in of the state's social control throughout the Lushai Hills district. By 1898, the colonial state had consolidated its control over the entire territory and organized it into a single Lushai Hills district with clearly defined boundaries (Reid 1978: 21–2). Within the clearly demarcated area, peace and order were particularly emphasized. Chiefs were forbidden from raiding each other's territories and were required to maintain security of person and property. In 1927, the customary codes and practices of the various tribes in the district were compiled and brought out in the form of a single code for the administration of the district (Parry 1928). The slew of state-building measures had the added effect of encouraging greater interaction among people in the district and promoting commonness within.

And the colonial state, although it apparently went along with what had existed before, ended up drastically compromising the authority of the traditional centres of power—the chiefs—while strengthening the hands of its own agents. Economic considerations dictated that colonial administrators rule not directly but through the chiefs to be able to penetrate society and acquire the legitimacy they needed to rule. But other strategic considerations (mostly the safety of the lucrative tea gardens proliferating around this time in Assam and Bengal on tracts bordering the Lushai Hills) mixed with the activist role of Christian missionaries and individual administrators led to making this rule more direct than it was elsewhere in Northeast India. Thus, while the authority of the chiefs was upheld—they were made responsible for collection of taxes and for maintaining peace within their jurisdiction—the chiefs were gradually made ultimately accountable to the district superintendent for their actions. With the introduction in 1901 of the Circle System, this trend of the diminution of chiefs' powers was reinforced. Introduction of the Rules for the Administration of the district in 1906 (and in its revised form in 1937) further eroded the authority and the autonomy of the chiefs. Many of the powers they had enjoyed over their subjects were taken away. Gradually, from being rulers, they were reduced to being mere eyes and ears of the colonial administrators (Thanhranga 1994: 5). But the measure that most severely undercut the chiefs' authority was the taking away of the proprietary rights that they had traditionally enjoyed over land. Under the 1901 'land settlement' system, each chief was issued a lease over land under his possession, for life. While 'land settlement' stabilized village boundaries, and contributed to preventing inter-village disputes, it also meant that it was the colonial state and not the chiefs that was now the owner of land in the village. This marked a fundamental change in the landholding system in the Lushai Hills and in the authority structure there. Individual administrators also contributed by their actions to expanding the role of the colonial state in the lives of the people by introducing measures for socio-economic development.[8] Colonial state-building policies, thus, built on the pre-existing state-like tendencies of the Sailo chiefs to consolidate the authority of the state by penetrating society, by incorporating rival social forces within its structures, and by successfully becoming the main provider of rule systems for people.

Contributing to the diminution of the social control of the chiefs was the role of the Christian missionaries who introduced modernity in the district that led, inter alia, to the birth of a competitor social force eager

---

[8] Prominently, John Shakespeare took measures to introduce wet rice cultivation and Anthony McCall promoted the organizing of local industry. Administrators also continued popularizing education among the people.

to contest the hold of past rulers. While the missionaries helped create
the conditions for greater integration of society—through their work to
spread Christianity and to develop and popularize Duhlian throughout
the district—it was their role in contributing to modernity that today
seems more significant. The combined efforts of the missionaries and
colonial administrators had the effect of markedly raising literacy levels
in the district (Table 10.1). But rather than the chiefly Lushais, it was
the non-Lushais who took to education first. The popularization of
education in turn led to the strengthening of this new class in Lushai
society, made up of Hmar, Ralte, and other non-Lushai sub-tribes,
jointly called the Commoners. This section drew sustenance from the
education they had acquired and through which they had gained access
to paid employment in the state administration and in church bodies.
The consequence was that by the end of the colonial rule, the social set-
up in the district was such that though the dominant power remained in
the hands of the Lushai chiefs (supported by colonial administrators),
the district's economy was rapidly being monopolized by the newly
educated and mobilizing Commoners. The convergence of ethnic
and class differences in society (between the dominant Lushai and
the excluded Hmars and Raltes and other sections of the population)
helped create a severe schism. The Commoners were resentful of the
authority and powers traditionally enjoyed by the chiefs and hoped to
gain, in the event of the introduction of democracy in the district. It
would be this section that would stake claim to forming the new state
on the eve of Independence by rallying against the authority of the
chiefs. That the rule of the chiefs was seen as being exploitative of the
people was instrumental in helping the leadership of the Commoners
mobilize popular support for their state-making project. Thus was

TABLE 10.1: Trends in Growth in Literacy and Christianity in Mizoram
(1901–51)

Year	Population	Literate (no.)	Literate (%)	Christian population
1901	82,434	771	0.93	24
1911	91,204	3,635	3.98	1,723
1921	98,406	6,183	6.28	34,893 (1925)
1931	124,404	13,320	10.70	59,556 (1935)
1941	152,786	29,765	19.48	74,987
1951	196,202	61,093	36.23	102,280

Source: Census of India (various years); Nunthara (1996: 59)

set the stage for confrontation between the old and the new in the Lushai Hills.[9]

The history of the Lushai district from the mid-1930s to Independence is one of contests between these two forces over forming the new state, centred on the formal system of distribution of power for a post-British Lushai Hills being devised by colonial administrators. The leaders of the Commoners resented attempts to perpetuate the hold of the chiefs in the proposed Lushai Hills Durbar, especially when it was the non-Lushai sections taken together that enjoyed numerical strength in the district[10] (Goswami 1979: 131). The Commoners demanded greater say in any future administrative arrangement of the district, and called for the removal of the privileges that the chiefs had so far enjoyed. The vehicle they used to mobilize support was the Mizo Commoners' Union (MCU), a political party set up in 1946. The name of the party was itself significant: rather than a Hmar or a Ralte union, the leaders called it the Mizo Commoners' Union. The term 'Mizo' was used to signify the general population of the district, being derived from the expression 'mi-zo', meaning man of the hills, and had little ethnic value. This was against the official designation of people living in the district as Lushai, which was an ethnic category. Hence, effectively, there were a lot more people living in the Lushai Hills district who were officially recognized as Lushais but who were not so ethnically. The use of the title was obviously made with an eye to mobilize non-Lushai public opinion in the MCU's favour. This strategy proved useful as the use of a neutral and apparently non-ethnic appellation was instantly popular among those that did not belong to the Lushai clans.[11] This enabled the MCU leaders to forge a commonness among the non-Lushais and expand their popular base, something that the use of a Hmar or Ralte title would on its own have been unable to achieve. This move of the MCU was significant given the notable differences that existed between the groups that were being put together (Davis 1894: 6).

At the heart of MCU's politics was a clear contradiction. They

[9] For further discussion on this clash, see Nunthara (1996: 62–3).

[10] In November 1946, McDonald, the superintendent, organized a district conference of all Lushai notables and laid a plan for a future constitution. This was seen by the Commoners as being biased in favour of the chiefs (ibid.: 122–3).

[11] According to Goswami, during the 1951 census, many Duhlian-speaking Raltes and Renthlais refused to enter themselves as Lushais (1979: 23).

realized that their claim to being the dominant state-making party would remain unfulfilled if those claims were contested by a powerful section of the society—the chiefs. Yet the nub of the MCU appeal and agenda was bringing fundamental changes in the existing political and economic relationships in the district—an objective that impinged directly on the interest of the chiefs. This put the leadership of the MCU on the horns of a dilemma: standing for institutional change while retaining the support of all sections of the population. To be able to act as the true representative of the people in the district the party had to broaden its base and speak for all sections. And to realize their economic agenda they had to push on with their anti-chiefs stand.

To broaden their base, the MCU leaders renamed the organization as the Mizo Union (MU), thereby dropping the Commoner qualification and thus staking claim to speak for all Mizos, not only the Commoners.[12] Notably, at the core of their Mizo construct was the Duhlian language, a dialect that traditionally belonged to the Lushai sections and was patronized by the chiefs. What probably motivated the leadership to use a Lushai symbol in an attempt to contest Lushai power was the place of Duhlian in the lives of the people. It was Duhlian that had, over time, evolved as the common thread connecting people from different clans and backgrounds inhabiting the Lushai Hills, and even beyond. Re-emphasizing this commonness among its target constituents was central to the MU's attempt to forge a common identity to gain political power. These were moves that proved immensely useful to the MU in its state-making efforts and bid for political power. To claim widespread authority, the party sought to gain universal acceptance not only within the district but also outside.[13] While claiming to act as the representative of the Mizo people, it listed the following among its objectives: 'to unify and integrate all Mizo people', 'to normalize relations between chiefs and the commoners', 'to popularise the Mizo language', and 'to better the standard of all Mizos'.[14] Thus, by consolidating their appeal, the MU leaders sought to create a greater force for their anti-chiefs demands.

[12] This discussion is based on interviews with R. Vanlawma, founder-member of MCU and MU (Aizawl, 11 July 2004).

[13] The constitution of the MU listed forty-one sub-tribes as those belonging to the Mizo family. This included the Lushais. Many of these tribes have their traditional homes outside the Lushai Hills district, in Manipur, Tripura, and even in Burma and Chittagong Hill Tracts of present Bangladesh.

[14] Constitution of the MU as quoted in Bhattacharya (1998: 268–80).

Mobilizing support for institutional change whilst constructing and investing in an inclusive Mizo identity helped the MU to gain popularity and capture political power. The party won seventeen of the eighteen seats in the first elections to the Lushai Hills District Council (LHDC). The party also won elections to most of the 381 Village Councils (VCs) the same year. In the first elections to the Assam State Assembly, the MU won all three seats from the district. It had earlier won all but one of the twenty-four seats to the Advisory Council in elections held in 1948. With political power attained, one of the first tasks that the MU-dominated LHDC undertook was the passing of the Lushai Hills (Abolition of Chiefship) Regulation in 1952, enabling the ending of the rule of the chiefs in the district and the taking away of their proprietary right over land. This institutional change was to have a profound impact on the authority structure in the Lushai Hills, fundamentally changing the basis of power relations there. The authority of the chiefs was taken over by the state and now vested in the popularly elected LHDC and VCs. Alongside, indeed to strengthen its claim to speak for all Mizos, the MU pressed on with its strategy of formalizing its inclusive Mizo mobilization. In 1951, under pressure from the LHDC, the centrally appointed Census Commission had recognized Mizo as one of the tribal categories in the Scheduled Tribe list of Assam state. The official recognition of the 'Mizo' worked to consolidate the gains that the Mizo identity had already made, so that by 1961 the Lushai, Ralte, and Paite categories were recording nil figures and most people were calling themselves Mizos (Table 10.2). Further, the MU-dominated LHDC had already renamed the Lushai Hills as the Mizo Hills district. These measures helped the MU leadership to carry out its economic agenda while mobilizing inclusively to prevent the fallout of those changes on Mizo society. This two-pronged strategy—engender programmatic reforms and build a collective Mizo consciousness—was evidently popular among the masses, enabling the MU to dominate politics in the district for much of the next decade (Tables 10.3 and 10.4).

The MU's contribution to state formation in Mizoram has been far-reaching. Firstly, they achieved considerable success in consolidation of the authority of the state, reinforcing the trend that the colonial administrators had started. The abolition of chieftainship, reforms and consolidation of the administrative and legal framework, and those regarding land ownership and distribution—encompassing written laws, defined rights of tenants, and protection of their property

TABLE 10.2: Community-wise Categorization of Population, Mizoram

Tribe /Year	1901	1951	1961
Hmar	10,411	–	3,119
Lai/Pawi	15,038	10,395	4,587
Lushai	36,322	162,665	–
Mara/Lakher	Na	6,350	8,790
Mizo	–	–	213,261
Paite	2,870	3,368	–
Ralte	13,827	–	–

Source: Census of India 1951, 1961; Lalthangliana 1998

TABLE 10. 3: Results of the Village Council Elections, Mizoram (1952–71)

Parties	1952	1957	1960	1963	1971
MU	Most	Most	280	228	66
UMFO			83	12	–
MNF			–	145	–
Congress			–	16	48
Independents +			18	10	44
Total	381	381	381	411	158

Source: Tabulated by author from Nunthara (1996: 77)[15]

TABLE 10.4: Results of the Mizo District Council Elections, Mizoram (1952–70)

Party	1952	1957	1962	1970
MU	17	13	16	9
UMFO	1	7	–	–
Congress	–	–	–	10
PLTU[1]		2	2	2
Others	–		4	1
Total	18	22	22	22

Source: Tabulated by author from Nunthara (1996: 131–7)
Note: [1] Pawi Lakher Tribal Union

[15] Some VCs were split in 1963 and Village Grouping in 1967 led to a reduction in the number of VCs. After restoration of normality, some original VCs have been revived. No VC elections were held in 1966 due to the outbreak of the MNF rebellion.

through issue of land certificates—helped bring state institutions centre stage in the lives of a majority of the people. The bringing of land tenants directly in contact with the state and the regulations promoting equity in management of land enhanced the downward reach of the state and the consolidation of its authority while resulting in considerable autonomy for state leaders from constraining social pressures. Significantly, administrative and legal rearrangements, land reforms, and electoral ascendance, together, led to a complete shift in the power structure in the Lushai Hills. The Lushais, who had dominated political and social life until 1954, were sidelined. It was the Commoners who now began to dominate state power. As is evident from the previous discussion, much of the ability of the leaders of the MU to dominate the contest with the chiefs and monopolize social control was on account of their success in constructing and mobilizing an inclusive Mizo identity that they could deploy to get broad-based support for their state-building agenda. The MU's remarkable feat of social engineering that helped integrate ethnically diverse groups in the district into the Mizo fold does not find much parallel in the Northeast. In this task, the MU leaders used the pre-colonial seeds of Mizo commonness, but more the integrating thrust of the colonial state-making project in the Lushai Hills (defined boundaries and territory, widespread administrative machinery, common codes, peace and order within, a dominant language, common religion) to their political advantage.

THE MNF AND THE REPOSITIONING OF STATE POWER

So if state consolidation was such a success during the MU movement, how can we explain the MNF rebellion and the resultant violence and collapse? Perhaps, in MU's success itself lay the seeds of the breakdown. The MU had kick-started postcolonial state-making in the Lushai Hills by resorting to institution building and identity mobilization. The party's politics had succeeded in strengthening the state by consolidating its reach in the mass of society, especially the rural areas. But in excluding, indeed sidelining the traditional elites, the MU leaders had perhaps gone too far. Excluded from political power, the section represented by the chiefs saw little scope or involvement for themselves in the structures of the new state. This also meant that the resultant state was precariously balanced.

Most of the resentment of the chiefs was directed at the then leadership of the MU—men like Sabrawnga and Bawichuaka, who stood for dissolution of chieftainship. Some of the anger was also aimed at the Assam state and the central leaders who, most Mizos felt, did not have Mizo interests at heart. A series of developments, beginning in the late 1950s, in the district as well as in Assam generally—where effective political power lay—provided the openings for those excluded from political power to switch public mood drastically away from what had been MU-devised intra-Mizo contestations over power towards concretizing and protecting pan-Mizo interests against the non-Mizos. The increasing ethnicization of politics in Assam, the hardships during the devastating famines of 1959, a common feeling among the people that the Assam state government had done little to ameliorate public sufferings during the crisis; and similar perceptions about the LHDC (now called Mizo District Council or MDC) provided anti-MU leaders the opportunity they were seeking to counter MU attempts to consolidate its hold over state power.

By extensively using a pan-Mizo identity, and leveraging the fears of the subjugation of that identity in a largely non-tribal Assam and India, as a mobilizational tool, the erstwhile chiefs and their followers mobilized support to contest MU's dominance of Mizo politics. The success of these measures, moderated as they were by the failures of the Assam state apparatus, led to the strengthening of the hand of the section represented by the United Mizo Freedom Organization (UMFO), which was gradually drawn to the MNF. Post-famine, the MNF increasingly became the locus of revolt by this section.[16] Ultimately, the MNF threat represented the return of the anti-MU sections in Mizoram politics. Crucially, with chieftainship already abolished in 1954, the electoral capital that the MU had enjoyed in the past and which had helped it monopolize political power for so long, was no longer available to it. Slowly, the MNF, led by its charismatic leader, Laldenga, began to win over support, raise finances, and mobilize people around its separatist ideology. The party also began to register electoral gains.[17] The MU's attempt to retain its political base through the use of confrontational politics against the MNF—such as its 'direct action' in rural areas—resulted in intense charging of the political mood in the district in the years around 1963–5, often leading to violence. A variety of factors, not least of them the fact that the MNF increasingly

[16] For a survey of these developments see Nag (2002: 216–24).

[17] While the MU won 55 of the 110 VCs, the MNF was able to capture an impressive 49.

found itself pushed into a corner by the MU's rising anti-MNF mobilization, led to the MNF striking by declaring an armed rebellion in 1966.[18] In the final analysis then, it was the widespread economic frustration born out of the famine hardships that provided the section excluded from the MU-dominated state structures the opportunity to stake claim to authority once again. The MNF was the vehicle they used for this purpose.

The MNF rebellion raged on for some twenty years until 1986, when Laldenga signed a peace agreement with the central government. In hindsight, Laldenga's (and along with him the section he represented) claim to political power was helped by a variety of external factors, most ironically by the central and provincial state's response to the MNF rebellion. These measures that in the ultimate analysis strengthened the MNF's identity appeal and enhanced its social base severely cut into the MU's constituency. Of particular note here were the instruments used by the army to restore order.[19] The social and psychological costs of these measures, not to mention their economic burden, were to prove telling. They helped alienate large sections of Mizos away from national politics and, equally, encouraged large numbers in the camps of the MNF. Remarkable of course in this Mizo story is the return of peace and its sustenance, something that does not find much parallel in the region, or indeed elsewhere in a conflict situation. The driver here appears to be as much the instruments and attitudes of central leaders as the demand of Mizo society to work for and achieve peace. What explains this exception?

Internal conflicts between the MU and MNF (and later between the MNF and the newly formed People's Conference [PC] party) resulted in much bloodshed in Mizo society, especially in the 1970s. This, along

[18] The hostility between the MNF and the MU was so strong that it was believed many might have joined the MNF not for any romantic notions of independence but to contest the hold of the MU (Letter from Paul Zakhuma, Aizawl Citizens' Committee to chief minister, Assam, dated 16 August 1966). Historians claim that some 300 MU cadres were killed by the MNF during the uprising.

[19] These included clamping dusk-to-dawn curfews and other restrictions on movements of the civilian population all over the district. But perhaps the most burdensome was the 'Village Grouping' exercise involving the wholesale relocation of populations from their original habitations to camps along the main highways (See Nunthara [1981] and 'Counter Insurgency at its Best', *The Hindustan Times*, New Delhi, 27 June 1978).

with the hardships associated with army operations, led to the MNF violence being seen by people as self-defeating. Over subsequent years, politics in Mizoram was driven by people's desire for an early end to violence. While this demand for peace could be common to most situations of conflict, the reason it worked so successfully in the case of Mizoram must be explained by the existence of a cohesive Mizo society demanding, and exerting pressure for restoration of, peace. That the state in Mizoram is embedded in such a cohesive society and state leaders enjoy widespread social control has enabled state leaders to work in tandem with social organizations to prioritize and pursue their peacemaking goals. Much of the peace moves during the final years of the Mizo insurgency involved negotiations between the MNF leadership and central actors. However, it was the incessant pressure from the Mizo state and certain social actors—leaders of the PC and the Congress and those of the Church and youth organizations—which induced the MNF and central leaders to arrive at a negotiated settlement. The Congress' electoral campaign claiming to be the only party that had the wherewithal to facilitate the return of peace in Mizoram and channel resources for post-conflict reconstruction—being the ruling party in the centre—helped it gain a majority in the 1984 state assembly elections. This formed the backdrop to the signing of the Mizo Peace Accord on 30 June 1986 that ended the two decades of violence in the State. Significantly, the agreement was based on, and led to, the dissolution of the elected Congress ministry, then ruling the State, and to the setting up of a coalition ministry with the top executive position going to Laldenga and several other ministerial ranks going to senior leaders of the MNF. In return, the MNF abjured violence and demilitarized. The Mizo Accord, and the incorporation of rebel cadres in the ruling coalition in Mizoram, is a unique instance of the state co-opting into its structures non-state actors who had challenged its authority.

What were the implications of the MNF movement for state power in Mizoram? The MNF movement led to a readjustment of state power, with those so far excluded from it being brought in and incorporated into the state structure. This may have led to consolidation of the state's authority and to its better grounding in Mizo society, thereby contributing to its present stability. The MU's anti-chiefs mobilization and policies had brought the Commoners, particularly the Hmars and Raltes, centre stage to dominate political power, while excluding the Lushais and their followers. The MNF movement, led and manned in the beginning by the Lushais, and increasingly supported by other Mizos such as Raltes (Goswami 1979: 79), reversed that trend. And changes within Mizo society itself, during the conflict years, particularly the breaking down of social divisions on account of the large-scale relocation of population, contributed to ending the exclusion of the Lushais and their returning to participate actively in politics in the State.[20] Alongside, a fundamental change had taken place in Mizo society that could have contributed to its stability.

In the pre-1966 phase, society in the Lushai Hills had been divided along the chiefs–commoners line, a divide that had helped create the Lushai-non-Lushai fissure. Abolition of chieftainship had removed the economic basis of the divide. Structural changes brought in by the MU itself consolidated these gains in such a way as to have the effect of promoting an ethnic but inclusive basis of participation in the Mizo state. Soon, however, mobilization around Mizo identity took a very different turn. From being inward-looking and trying to define its internal values and symbols, Mizo mobilization in the post-MU phase centred on defining the outer boundaries of the identity and arranging its relationships with those it considered non-Mizos. Together, the two phases—one including and the other excluding—helped state leaders, of different hues and with different interests, to define Mizo society and secure their own legitimacy. The change in the focus of mobilization had been determined as much by changed (external) circumstances and opportunities as by changed interests of state-making leaders. While the MU had sought to change the existing social order dominated by the chiefs, the MNF stood for finding a secure place for the section it represented in the democratic order. Both manners of mobilization were instrumental in political power. The gains for the MNF, of riding the Mizo bandwagon, were as fruitful as they had been for the MU. In the early 1960s, with an increasing sense of their alienation and heightened mobilization by Laldenga, the leaders of the MNF won the party significant victories and established it as a force that could successfully challenge the hold of the MU. As the party that stood for and sacrificed much to defend Mizo interests through armed rebellion the MNF was in a position to take power after signing the 1986 Peace Accord. Its ability to monopolize the claim to uphold and defend pan-Mizo interests while being successful in providing a stable basis

[20] For a discussion of this social base of the state structure in Mizoram see Nunthara (1996: 175–6).

for state power is also contributing to the MNF's dominating politics in the State since (Table 10.5). It is in these integrative aspects of the Mizo Accord that we must see the seeds of the sustenance of peace in Mizoram.

Table 10.5: Party-wise Position, Mizoram Assembly Elections (1987–2003)

Party/Year	1987	1989	1993	1998	2003
MNF	–	14	14	21	21
Congress	13	23	16	6	12
PC	3	1	–	–	–
Others	–	–	–	12	7
Independents	24	2	10	1	–
Total	40	40	40	40	40

Source: Government of Mizoram (2004a, 2004b)

Greater participation of Lushais in the power structure and the cementing of a pan-Mizo identity as the basis of authority have the effect of making state power better grounded in a broader Mizo identity that had elements of both the Lushais and the non-Lushais. This grounding may have provided state agencies in Mizoram with cohesive power. Today, state and civil society's persistent efforts in Mizoram to maintain this pan-Mizo edifice, sometimes at the cost of excluding non-Mizos, may be seen as anxiety of state elites to sustain that social base of power and maintain order.

THE INSTITUTIONAL STRENGTHS OF THE MIZO STATE

How have these strengths played out in cushioning Mizoram against crises and breakdown? Contrary to the general scene of breakdown and collapse so typical of Northeast India, Mizoram seems to have managed to recover from crisis, having regained peace in 1986. Notably, despite the odds common to the whole region—the challenges of economic management and poor growth—and which may have worsened over the past decade, the state in Mizoram seems to have avoided slipping back into crisis (and collapse). This says a lot about the legitimacy of the state institutions and the basis of power in Mizoram.

The state in Mizoram seems to have maintained its centrality in the lives of the people. What is remarkable is that this centrality exists despite the usual challenges to the state system in the Northeast, particularly among its tribal communities. A hilly terrain is not especially conducive to control by the state's security agencies. Furthermore, special concessions for tribal communities have a tendency to erode the 'sovereignty' of the rule system of the state (on account of the multiplicity of legal codes and a largely informal and hence unregulated economy). First, the state in Mizoram has performed a greater range of functions, what is called the 'scope' of state functions. Security, enforcement, and control of laws regulating economic and social interactions rest with the state and its agencies. The state has thus been successful in penetrating society and extending its statewide presence. This limits non-state actors, representing competing social forces, in implanting themselves as rival providers of political goods. As we saw in the previous discussions, these forces that could have posed threats to the state system have either been marginalized or have been co-opted into the state structure thus enabling the cooperative working of state elites with those in society rather than any competition between them.

This state–society dynamic is demonstrated in the close links that exist between state agencies and principal social organizations—the dominant Presbyterian Church and the Young Mizo Association (YMA) with senior functionaries of state departments being active members of the YMA and the churches. This cross-membership across the state–society divide provides for commonality of goals and agendas. The two sections then, representing the same social base, seek to uphold the dominant social and political order, providing for wide-ranging cooperation and consultation.[21] The fact of the reach of the YMA and the churches—based on their wide-ranging membership, their organizational strengths, and their large resources—means that this state–society link goes a long way in preventing social conflicts. An absence of rival claimants to authority and the cooperative working of elites has had positive spin-offs for the strength of the state. State leaders, on account of their embeddedness in what is a cohesive (Mizo) society, are able to plug into the latter for better institutional performance.[22] They are also less hemmed in by (rival) social groups

---

[21] Such as to work for restoration of peace resulting in the 1986 Peace Accord.

[22] Of course there are costs involved in this state–society linkage, especially in terms of its impact on democratic governance. See Sharma and Baruah (2004) for a discussion. I argue in the following pages that it is precisely their thick bonds

and therefore enjoy more autonomy of action. These strengths have enabled state agencies in Mizoram to organize entitlements—such as social services, food security, and livelihoods—and provide justice, enforce laws, maintain tolerable levels of order, and manage inter-group contestations.

An example of the state's better ability to provide entitlements is in the implementation of the Public Distribution System (PDS), a national food security programme, for which Mizoram has received wide acclaim.[23] Crucial to the effectiveness of the PDS in Mizoram is the extensive involvement of elected local bodies and public organization in the management and monitoring of the programme. Similar institutional capacities along with their ability to forge partnerships and co-opt non-state actors and leverage the latter's strengths has enabled Mizoram to stake a claim to being the first e-governance state in Northeast India and the first to introduce the Right to Information Act, an instrument likely to further improve the quality of governance.[24] But it is probably in the field of education that Mizoram has been a trailblazer, becoming the State with the second-highest literacy figures in the country. In the literature, much of Mizoram's success in education has been attributed to the role played by its principal non-state agency, the Presbyterian Church. This account, however, misses the point that behind much of the Christian missionaries' success in promoting education has been the hand of the state as facilitator (McCall 1949: 199–200). It was the colonial state's active involvement in the form of grants and scholarships and other liberal doses of incentives to get people to take to education, combined with the partnership that colonial administrators established with church organizations, which at that time had a better territorial presence in the district, that helped Mizoram achieve such remarkable success with literacy levels. The effects of such state–society partnerships along with the ability of state leaders to commit to and pursue development goals are also evident in Mizoram's success in the wider entitlements arena (Table 10.6). In addition, Mizo leaders have shown some, although tentative, successes

---

with social actors that has allowed state elites, at least until now, the autonomy to moderate exclusivist Mizo mobilization and pursue policies providing access to minorities.

[23] See 'BPL (Below Poverty Line) Scheme Successful', *North East Tribune*, Guwahati, 19 June 2005.

[24] *North East Tribune*, Guwahati, 11 and 28 September 2005.

with better management of finances and better ability to extract revenue, vis-à-vis other States in the region.[25]

TABLE 10.6: Some Key Social Indicators for the Northeast

	Literacy (2001)	Infant Mortality Rate (1991)	Sex ratio (2001)	% of Poor (1999–2000)	Per capita Income Rs/year (2001–2)	HDI Ranking (1991)
Arunachal Pradesh	54.74	91	901	33.47	17,978	29
Assam	64.28	92	932	36.09	10,951	26
Manipur	68.87	28	978	28.54	13,213	9
Meghalaya	63.31	80	975	33.87	14,510	24
Mizoram	88.49	53	938	19.47	–	7
Nagaland	67.11	51	909	32.67	11,119	11
Tripura	73.66	82	950	34.44	–	22
All India	65.20	77	933	26.10	17,978	

Source: GoI (2001, 2006a: 4–5)

In this task of providing public services, state leaders have managed to remain largely autonomous from the limiting social forces. Mizoram's success with land reforms, when similar attempts by state elites in the rest of the Northeast region and much of India proved less tractable, was itself an outcome of this autonomy. The abolition of chieftainship and introduction of land reforms fundamentally changed the basis of property rights in Mizoram—it did away with the rights of the chiefs, brought the tenants in direct contact with the state, and ushered in equity in the management of land.[26] These moves have helped enhance the legitimacy of the state, thereby strengthening its authority. Similarly, reforms of the justice system have meant that the various systems— modern laws and customary codes[27]—exist within the formal legal framework of the state, with the Guwahati High Court at the top. Thus rather than contest the state's claim to determine and adjudicate on rules of behaviour—a sure recipe for crisis—the traditional system of justice has been co-opted by the state and it in turn upholds the authority of

[25] Between 1993–6 and 2000–03, the buoyancy in average Own Tax Revenue (OTR to GSDP) for Mizoram was to a factor of 1.60 (compared to 0.98 for Nagaland and 0.84 for Manipur); see GoI (2005a: 44).

[26] For a discussion on the land system of Mizoram, see Das (1990: 30).

[27] Indian Penal Code (IPC), Criminal Procedure Code (CrPC), Civil Procedure Code (CPC). Mizo Hnam Dham is the Mizo customary code.

state laws. This may be contributing to the better performance of both law courts in Mizoram—those using customary codes and those using the formal state laws—in a much better way than those of other states in the region (GoI 2000: 307; Thanhranga 1994: 9). The authority of the state is also reflected in the ability of its law-enforcing agencies to provide security. A measure is the high chargesheet[28] rate of crimes, which translates into high success with convictions by the law courts (National Crime Records Bureau 2005: 216–17). These capabilities contribute to the low crime rate and lesser violence in Mizoram today, definitively an anomaly in the Northeast.

But it is probably in providing access to minority groups and in managing inter-group contestations that this autonomy of state actors from constraining social pressures is most evident. The state's elite have managed to work out deals with those espousing minority demands despite a noticeable rise in exclusivist mobilization by Mizo public organizations (mostly against the Chakmas and Brus but also against non-Mizo immigrants).[29] This is another aspect of the state leaders' strength that contributes to the capability of the state in Mizoram. The Congress party in power in the 1990s, the ruling MNF today, and other parties at different points in time, have frequently forged political alliances with elites within minority communities and have maintained statewide reach including in areas outside of the 'Mizo' domain. This reflects their desire to represent the entire population of the state, rather than claiming to speak for a section. These inclusionary moves have benefited both sides. Political alliances have played a big part in taking minority demands on board, giving them the much-needed political voice and legitimacy. And political parties have benefited by acquiring statewide legitimacy and a support base among minority constituents which has also helped them acquire the capability to channel and process popular participation. This has resulted in a situation where, at a general level, there is a realization among minorities that the state

[28] Cases where the police were able to press for charges against those accused, reflecting the ability of law and order agencies to perform their investigating and enforcement functions.

[29] In 1997, a large number of Brus fled the state for neighbouring Tripura, alleging violence by Mizo social organizations such as the YMA and Mizo Zirlai Pawl. These organizations have also been known to target other non-Mizo communities, particularly immigrants from Myanmar (in 2003) and from Assam (in 2004).

belongs, not only to the core Mizos, but also to all and that they have a stake in its continuance.

A feature of this inclusive politics is the presence of the Autonomous District Councils (ADCs), one each for the Pawi, Lakher, and Chakma communities. Among other things, elected ADCs have the authority to determine how resources such as land and forests are utilized, what cultural policies are followed, and what personal and customary laws should apply. With assured developmental investments, ADCs also have control over much of the developmental interventions of the national and sub-national state in these pockets. ADCs also employ a large number of the local youth, helping bind local elite into patterns of mutual relationships with the state. On the whole, ADCs have been successful in facilitating the administrative and political representation of the peripheral communities in the power structure.[30] It could be argued that Mizo leaders did not have any direct role in the setting up of the three ADCs. More to the point is the response of the state elites to demands made by the other minorities, for self-governing arrangements for themselves, such as that by the separatist sections of the Hmars and by the Brus. The Singlung Hills Development Council (SHDC), an outcome of negotiations between the rebel Hmar People's Convention (HPC) and the state government, tries to replicate the ADC example for the Hmar community, albeit on a less grand scale.[31] Despite its weaknesses, the fact that state leaders agreed to set up a special developmental mechanism for the Hmars is a demonstration of their readiness to negotiate autonomy for out-groups. This may have helped moderate Hmar grievances. The Mizoram government's agreeing to a similar arrangement for Brus recently was the basis for the Bru National Liberation Front (BNLF) readiness to give up their violent activities (Routray 2005). These demonstrations of the capability of the state help cushion Mizoram from crisis.

CONCLUSION

Clearly, the state in Mizoram enjoys widespread capability allowing it to act as the central force in society, determining citizen's lives. As has

[30] Mizoram's record in empowering local bodies has been equally impressive. The VCs, since their inception in 1956, have worked as effective institutions of local governance. Elections have been held to them regularly. They have also channelled large doses of development resources.

[31] Refer 'Memorandum of Settlement' between Government of Mizoram and HPC (Aizawl, 27 July 1994).

been demonstrated, this has been the result of the unique history of the State and one which has involved internal contests and accommodations among different social forces over authority and social control. The key dynamic here, and one that seems to have had the greatest impact, is Mizoram's unique colonial state-making experience. Unlike the general pattern of 'indirect rule' common to the rest of the region and indeed to much of the developing world, colonial administrators in Mizoram forged something like a 'direct rule' with agents of the state positioned at the apex of the administrative structure that contained local strongmen—the chiefs—as its integral parts. Colonial state presence was also established deep inside the Lushai territory from early on, helping supplant the authority of traditional authorities.[32] The evidently activist role of the colonial state in the Lushai Hills allowed the state to penetrate society, which has resulted, in the final analysis, in state leaders being able to acquire a statewide basis of authority.

But colonial rule in Mizoram went beyond just establishing statewide administrative structures. There was a deliberate attempt, by some administrators at least, to bring about socio-economic changes including popularizing education and ushering in modernity. Quite unwittingly, these interventions together led to the birth of a new social class that found itself in contest with the past rulers over authority and social control. The ability of this section to build and invest in centralized political organizations and undertake institutional reforms while constructing and mobilizing an inclusive Mizo identity helped them acquire legitimacy. The attempt by traditional interests to reclaim authority and the dislocation that their twenty-year-long rebellion caused helped further transform society by concretizing Mizo cohesiveness. The resultant cohesive state is at once embedded in society while it is autonomous from social pressures. Thus contributing to the unique Mizo state formation experience has been the creation of a grand narrative around the Mizo identity that helped state elites

---

[32] In this the colonial state may have been serving its strategic interests. Annexation of the Lushai tract was motivated by the need to prevent the frequent raids by Lushai chiefs on the tea gardens that were cropping up in Cachar and Sylhet plains adjoining Lushai lands (Reid 1978: 9). That these raids and their cost to colonial interests were taken seriously can be gauged by the number and scale of military expeditions undertaken by the government to subdue the chiefs. The Chin Lushai expedition of 1889–90 was the last of these attempts (Nag 2002: 45–9). 'Direct rule' and the many interventions it entailed was perhaps an attempt to break up Lushai society and further concretize Sailo subjugation.

acquire legitimacy and enhance their social control, allowing them to act decisively to govern society and manage conflicts. In sum, state-making in Mizoram was accompanied by internal contests and accommodations that resulted, on the one hand, in a legitimate basis of authority, and on the other, in a cohesive social structure. It is this two-way process of construction of a cohesive state and the mobilization of an integrated society, one enabling the other, that underpins Mizoram's success with political order. That this process was exceptional not only in relation to other states in Northeast India but also to most cases of postcolonial state formation, is what is at the heart of the Mizo exception.

The key question, then, is what are the prospects for the sustenance of this success? Socio-economic challenges in Mizoram, as in the rest of the Northeast, have intensified over the years, due mostly to the rise in aspirations that are not matched by any real growth in opportunities. Unmet aspirations are fuelling frustrations as demonstrated by the rise in exclusivist politics by Mizo (and non-Mizo) groups. Even though it may not have taken the form of armed violence yet, group contestations in Mizoram are on the rise, leading in some cases to violence. The real test of the resilience of the Mizo state then, in the face of these challenges, will depend in part on the endurance of the hitherto inclusive institutions in Mizoram as well as on the ability of state leaders to create opportunities equally for all. There are many constraints here and ample opportunities too. All these require state leaders to priortize and pursue growth policies. Will they be able to show similar levels of commitment to growth for all that they did to building an inclusive identity, undertaking programmatic reforms, and to restoring peace? And crucially, are Mizo leaders able to create arrangements that not only tolerate minorities and enable formation of elite alliances with them, but actually engender a democratic space where all sections of the populace find an equal space within Mizo citizenship? The answers to these questions will determine whether the Mizo story continues to remain a 'success story' that it clearly is today.

CHAPTER 11

Peace sans Democracy?
A Study of Ethnic Peace Accords in Northeast India[1]

SAMIR KUMAR DAS

'Let us excavate in a constitutional site.'

—Bartolome Clavero (2004)

This chapter reviews the changing nature of peace *policy* pursued since Independence by the Indian state towards armed opposition groups and insurgent movements in the Northeast. The policy, we assume, is reflected in the array of peace accords signed by it with many of the insurgent groups in the region since Independence. It also proposes to provide a critique of this policy in terms of its implications for the functioning of a democratic polity in India, particularly in the region under review. Viewed in this light, our review of peace accords and peace policy is likely to reflect on the democratic career of our body politic.

In the existing literature on accords in general and those of the region in particular, there is hardly any reference to the connection or maybe a lack of it, between accords on one hand and the functioning of a democratic polity on the other. In most of these writings, accords are seen as part of realpolitik—a means of crafting and building the state—particularly on its margins that are beset with intense and intractable ethnic and nationality conflicts. Accords are viewed primarily as instruments of managing these conflicts, a technology

---

[1] This article was submitted in February 2007 by the author. The author thanks Sanjib Baruah, Indrani Chatterjee, and Muthiah Alagappa for their comments on an earlier draft (the same presented in a seminar). The standard disclaimers however apply.

of government and an exercise in state's governmentality (Samaddar 2004:168). Accords, therefore, are not to be regarded as a solution to the conflicts. This argument coincides with the commonplace distinction made especially in policy circles between management and resolution of conflicts. When democracy comes to be defined merely as the art of managing and governing conflicts, it hangs on thin air. Clearly, a case is made here for defining democracy as the *excess* of governmentality—consisting not in perpetually deferring conflicts through accords and thereby making the 'disorder durable' without ever trying to break the impasse, but rather in making the state address and resolve them. Thus, the life forces of democracy are sought to be located beyond the realm of accords and governmentality and in the domain of popular politics and resistance. Accords and democracy, according to this framework of analysis, are at odds with each other.

Few scholars have, however, focused on the role of accords in gradually resolving the conflicts and sought to assess their bearing on the democratic character of our polity. Democracy for them is not located beyond the instituted domain of accords. Dasgupta (1995), for example, describes accords as democratic insofar as the very act of signing them underlines 'greater willingness on the part of the political leadership to compromise', and the essence of democracy, according to him, lies in making these compromises and thereby making state policies less rigid and more amenable and responsive to the demands of the disaffected groups and communities. While, for Dasgupta, the very act of signing accords per se is a mark of democracy, his paper does not offer any key to reading them as texts by way of reflecting either on whether signing of these accords becomes synonymous with making compromises at all or the nature of these compromises being made in state policies and their changing nature. Instead, the very act of signing accords is seen only as a culmination of the changes, particularly in leadership, that take place presumably at the level of national politics. Given the kind of union of states we have with all its attendant centralizing trends, effective change in leadership at the national level will be able to bring about the compromises necessary for any functioning democracy. Dasgupta views accords as part of the transition marked by the succession of Rajiv Gandhi as prime minister in 1984 and his preference—unlike that of his mother—for settling ethnic discords by way of signing accords and making compromises in state policies without however changing, in any way, the rules of the democratic game.

If for Dasgupta, signing of the accords reflects a change in political leadership at the national level, de Varennes and others interpret them—albeit in the different contexts of Europe and Africa—as more or less successful responses to the general crisis that democracies have been facing all over the world. Most of the democracies functioning in today's world are 'ethnodemocracies' rather than 'civic democracies' insofar as they encourage popular mobilizations along pre-existing ethnic and communal lines (Snyder 2000: 352–3). Thus, ethnic majorities easily double up as electoral majorities and minority alienation too takes on an ethnic and communal character.[2] Peace accords for de Varennes are mainly concluded in situations where ethnic minorities are involved in some form of discord with the respective majorities and cannot hope to beat them in elections because of their inherent numerical weakness. Accords serve as an instrument whereby the interests and concerns of the minorities are sought to be addressed and taken care of in a *majoritarian* democracy. The very act of signing these accords, in other words, shows a remarkable change in the rules of democratic game in the present-day world:

… [E]thnic groups are protected from the excesses of democracy qua majoritarian rule. It is for this reason also that many peace accords refer to the need for stronger legislative and constitutional guarantees for the protection of the human rights of the minorities, including such a fundamental right as non-discrimination (de Varennes 2003: 158).

It seems that accords are only critical to our understanding of the state's responses to ethnic problems and its democratic character. While it is no longer possible for any democracy—let alone Indian democracy—to simply ignore the crisis mentioned above, what de Varennes sees as a universal change in the rules of the game has been neither already accomplished nor free from its complexities. The incorporation of the so-called minorities[3] into the democratic body calls for certain

[2] The classical liberal theory makes the distinction between an 'ethnic majority' and an 'electoral majority' and this of course presupposes the formation of a 'civic democracy' in which an individual's electoral preferences cut across her ethnic and communal identities. 'Ethnodemocracies' are bound to emerge in societies wherever this line is blurred.

[3] We propose to use the term 'minority' in a very open and contested sense, for, it is only within any *given* national configuration that one becomes a minority or for that matter a majority. One's status as majority or minority changes with any change in the so-called given configuration.

changes in the nature of the body itself. While the nation has always been conceived as the democratic body comprising the nationals or citizens as its sovereign subjects in the sense of having access to the sovereign power of the state and the power of making it accountable to them, the incorporation of ethnic groups and minorities implies a certain disarticulation of the nation as a democratic body. Since the republican doctrine of nationhood continues to dominate the discourse of state sovereignty in India, and sovereignty according to this doctrine always pertains to the nation as a single and indivisible body, it becomes difficult—if not impossible—to gain access to sovereignty without identifying at the same time with the national body. One's membership of the nation or citizenship is what entitles one to the exercise of the sovereign power of the state. Democracy makes it imperative to hold on to a theory of 'shared sovereignty' by way of entitling people of whatever hues—irrespective of their ethnic and communal identities—to it; the state being ensconced in the nation and continuing to subscribe to the doctrine of national sovereignty has refused to adapt itself to the changing circumstances. This doctrine does not always suit the requirements of democracy and we have reached a stage when we cannot think of democracy and democratization without simultaneously bringing in substantial changes in the prevailing notions of nation and national sovereignty.

The problem with Dasgupta's or for that matter de Varennes' analyses is that they seem to describe accords in binary terms—either as democracy-enhancing mechanisms or democracy-debilitating ones and view them essentially as state responses to ethnic and minority problems. We argue that accords cannot be characterized in such simple and binary terms. For, they serve as sites where the forces of state and government(ality) are called upon to negotiate and reckon with the disaffected groups and communities and the texts of accords themselves bear the imprints of such reckoning and negotiation. Accords, therefore, are always complex combinations of moments pointing to their inchoate and amorphous nature and it will be interesting to see how different political practices are read into them. As a result, accords also reflect the stalemate that is sometimes reached by groups in course of their hostility. Viewed in this light, peace policy reflected through hitherto concluded ethnic accords is neither linear nor irreversible.

We also argue that the texts of accords bear the imprints of these complexities. If the constitution is where—as Hannah Arendt puts it—politics is 'housed', then its 'excavation' a la Clavero, requires an appropriate strategy that seeks to read it against its grain and shows how accords mark a *difference* from it, if at all. This article proposes to make a strategic reading of some of the representative texts of accords and seeks to show how accords over the years are seen to embody three relatively distinguishable moments (of beginning, contention, and recognition) in the evolution of our body politic. The three moments should not be seen as chronologically sequenced stages; rather, they should be regarded as specific configurations of forces and any particular accord concluded at any given point of time should be seen as a unique combination of these moments. Moreover, in most cases, politics is seen as external to the texts of accords in the sense that their non-implementation is always held responsible for their 'failures'. We, on the contrary, argue that politics is implicated in and secretes from the accords. Hence, we see texts of the accords as being couched in a language that makes something happen. As Robin Tolmach Lakoff explains: '… Language (is) the maker of a mood, and thereby a force for efficacy. In fairy tales we encounter magic words, say, "abracadabra" or "shazam!" and *something happens*, by the utterance of words alone' (Lakoff 1990:13).

DEMOCRACY'S WAR ON ITS OUTSIDE

How to respond to the insurgencies in the Northeast without reneging on its commitment to democratic norms and principles is the paradox that India as a democracy faces today. The debate on whether democratic norms can be followed while tackling threats to democracy is too serious an issue to be settled here. But there is reason to believe that the tradition of democratic theory spanning from Kant to say, Rawls, does not make it imperative on the part of democracies to observe democratic norms and principles while dealing with those who *themselves* do not observe them. Democracy in simple terms does not have a theory of its outside, that is to say, the forces that remain outside its ambit and pose a threat to its survival. Democratic norms and principles, in simple terms, need to be observed only vis-à-vis those who care to subscribe to them. Those who remain outside the democratic ambit and do not care for its norms and principles, and flout and violate them do not deserve to be democratically treated. While Kant seems to have set forth the norms and principles in maximal terms—the violation of which warrants what he calls a 'just war'—Rawls' contribution lies in formulating them in minimal terms, as mere 'rules of the people' that anyone who deserves to be democratically treated is required to observe and follow. A good number of policy makers and analysts, for example, make an advocacy for firmly dealing with insurgents and insurgencies in India.

There are very few amongst us who continue to recommend a *pure* 'law and order' solution to ethnic and minority problems. The measures suggested in this connection range from overhauling the security structures in order to secure and protect the citizens' interests and greater deployment of security forces to the legislation and implementation of 'emergency' laws (like the controversial Armed Forces Special Powers Act of 1958 presently in force in some parts of the region) often involving temporary suspension and abrogation of rights and liberties that are otherwise enshrined in, and guaranteed by, the constitution and laws of the land. All this is justified as the 'necessary cost' of fighting ethnic insurgencies resulting in serious deterioration of law and order. The emphasis has been to continuously refine and upgrade security structures and technologies to 'suitably deal with' and 'tackle' the insurgency phenomenon (Pachnanda 2002; Singh 2001). This group of policy analysts believes that there should not be any letup in counter-insurgency operations, militant organizations should be 'dealt with, with continued firmness', and that sovereignty of India is uncompromisable (Narahari 2002: 227). The doctrine of national and indivisible sovereignty, as suggested by the republicans, resonates strongly in most of these advocacies. The efficacy of 'multi-force operations' (popularly known as 'unified command') in Assam (Hussain 2001) has already become a frequently referred topic of discussion. General V.N. Sharma makes an advocacy for the deployment of 'armed police units under the operational control of the army' (for, placing them under the home ministry will pave the way to 'party interference') rather than the army per se as the army is not professionally trained to handle 'civic action' (Sharma 2002: 8).

While a law and order solution may be both desperately necessary and effective in the short run, it cannot be an answer to the region's complex ethnic and minority conflicts: 'We need to remind ourselves that the "gun" can never solve the problem; it is necessary to win the "hearts and minds" of the people for which we will have to effect genuine socio-economic changes in their living conditions if we are to retrogress insurgency' (Brar 2002: 203; Nayar 2005: 139). Moreover, even a cursory reading of the personal memoirs and tracts of retired army generals and police officers suggests that a sense of fatigue seems to have imperceptibly set in, in their minds (Nandy 1992). Those amongst us, who take our democratic convictions too seriously and regard democracy and human rights as an absolute value, strongly criticize such a view (Fernandes 2004). The paradox that democracies all over the world face today is how to respond to minority problems and insurgencies without reneging on its commitment to rights and liberties of citizens including those of minorities. As Dasgupta writes: 'Largely dominated by a body of experts, who are mostly former bureaucrats or senior military or police officials, the discourse on security in India has remained heavily pro-state and insensitive to the vulnerabilities of the common man and dismissive of frequent transgression of rights of its own citizens by the state' (Dasgupta 2004: 4469).

THE POST-HISTORY OF BEGINNING

Democracy in the ultimate analysis is predicated on a theory of contract. The 'original contract' embodied in the Constitution of India is never original in the sense of having a determinate point of beginning in any historical sequence. It provides the beginning only when certain 'events' that are subsequent to it are sought to be understood and made sense of, by way of referring them back to an imagined point of beginning (Said 1975). The beginning is imagined to have released and lent legitimacy to the events subsequent to it and excises as it were, certain other events by denying any point of beginning to them. These latter events do not have any pre- or post-history so to say, precisely because they are not imagined to have any beginning. These events fly with time in bits and pieces insofar as they are never 'arrested' by our imagination.

The constitution as an original contract made the beginning only in this sense. Indeed, it was an ensemble of contracts—a grand contract of contracts and the contracts, as I argued elsewhere, were taken to be so obvious that they did not have to be explicitly concluded in the first place (Das 2005: 70–92). The beginning is to be understood precisely with reference to the post-history of the beginning: what happened after the constitution was adopted, was 'given to ourselves', and came into force. This had two major consequences: one, the imaginary beginning made the original contract final and non-negotiable. The presumed finality of the original contract and what it had begun and precipitated subsequently relegate the more widely known accords into 'special provisions'—whether they are made an integral part of the constitution (as in cases of Articles 370 and 371) or not. Political discourse in the immediate aftermath of Independence brings into existence a hierarchy between the constitution as the original document—indeed the founding event—and the accords signed with the relevant parties who supposedly remain outside the original contract and hence are deprived of any beginning. They are destined to be *late* beginners *always* required to catch up with others. It is the imagined beginning of the constitution that marks the difference between the original contract and the accords that followed it. The beginning of the original contract accordingly precedes and prevails over the accords. Unlike the constitution, accords are not privileged with a beginning.

The period that elapses between the coming into being of the constitution and its subsequent ratification by the so-called late beginners through the instrumentality of signing accords is also considered as the time necessary for training them—the hitherto uninitiated—in the intricacies of observing the rules and protocols of the democratic polity and inculcating in them the democratic spirit that was customarily lacking in them. At one level, the late entrants look upon themselves as the outsiders who have been held 'captive' to a political dispensation without being offered the freedom to choose (and equally not to choose) it. Many of the insurgent groups operating in the region trace the basis of their existence to the very mode of their incorporation into the Indian body politic. They view it as a process that made them its constituent parts without conferring on them the requisite freedom of negotiating it. Both the ULFA and United National Liberation Front of Manipur (UNLF) draw our attention to this 'original sin' of the founding moment. An oft-quoted handout prepared by the Naga National Council (NNC) that does not bear the date of its publication but must have been published during the tumultuous days of Indian independence, for example, observes: 'In history, no enemy ever conquered the Nagas except the British who conquered and occupied portions of Naga territory from 1872 to 1947, August 14th. The Nagas have not made any progress during the last seven decades. This is the truth and source of all troubles' (quoted in Kumar 1995: 94). At another level, the non-negotiated nature of their incorporation was viewed by the nationalist political elite in India as the essential first step towards investing the people 'without history'[4] with history and, most importantly, a convenient take-off point from which history makes its beginning—that would gradually regularize them as full contractual partners to the undertaking that was put in place in the wake of India's independence (Das 2001: 31–52).

[4] They are taken as objects of anthropological investigation and not as historical subjects.

Conversely, the accords that ever made any attempt at negotiating the original contract and modifying the already established rules of the democratic game simply became non-starters and were allowed to gather dust. Both Articles 370 and 371 included in the Constitution of India as 'special provisions' with respect to the problems of Jammu and Kashmir and the states of the Northeast, along with some other states, were by all accounts non-starters. Article 371 that applies primarily to the states of the Northeast including several other states enumerates the 'temporary, transitional and special provisions' relating to the states of Maharashtra and Gujarat, Nagaland (Sub-clause A), Assam (Sub-clause B), Manipur (Sub-clause C), Andhra Pradesh (Sub-clauses D & E), Sikkim (Sub-clause F), Mizoram (Sub-clause G), and Goa (Clause 1). The description provided by the article is self-explanatory for its presence indicates that the above-mentioned territories require some 'special' constitutional provisions, which do not apply to the rest of India and which are basically meant for facilitating and supervising their 'transition' to a more general mode of administration prescribed by the constitution and therefore are neither permanent nor a regular feature of it. These provisions address a whole host of issues ranging from the institution of separate development boards, administrative tribunals, central universities, and committees of the legislative assemblies consisting of MLAs elected from some particularly backward areas to ensuring 'equitable opportunities and facilities for the people belonging to different parts of the state in the matter of public employment, education and different provisions' and 'protection of rights and interests of different sections of population'. In cases of Nagaland and Mizoram, the article points out that no act of parliament in respect of 'social practices, customary law and procedure, administration of civil and criminal justice and ownership and transfer of land and its resources' shall apply to these states unless the legislative assemblies of these states by a resolution so decide. The main thrust of the article is to keep these provisions beyond the jurisdiction of legislative bodies including, of course, parliament, presumably on the ground that being under-represented and backward, these areas are likely to be the victims of 'majority rule' and vest them with some form of executive control under the discretion or, as in some cases, 'individual judgement' of the president of India or the governor of the respective state. The executive discretion or 'individual judgement' specified by this article is also kept beyond the purview of judicial review. All this seeks to alleviate the anxiety expressed by de Verennes and his associates of protecting the smaller communities and numerical minorities from 'the tyranny of majority'. Although these accords are built in the constitution, they stand in an uneasy relation to its tenor as much as these 'special provisions' from the very beginning were honoured by their breach.

The Naga–Hydari Accord (1947) provides a paradigmatic illustration of non-accords overshadowed by the moment of beginning marked by the adoption, enactment, and undertaking of the Constitution of India. A reference to the dual nature of this nine-point accord may not be out of place in this context. The accord signed between NNC and Sir Akbar Hydari—the then Governor of Assam—in June 1947 interestingly prescribes for certain institutional mechanisms aimed primarily, though not exclusively, at securing and guaranteeing the autonomy of the Nagas including the Naga traditional institutions, their customary laws, and interestingly the NNC itself in judicial, executive, and legislative matters, and also in matters relating to land, taxation, territorial boundaries, and arms. These institutional mechanisms—as Article 9 of the accord points out—would be in place under the supreme responsibility of the governor for a period of ten years and 'at the end of this period the Naga National Council will be asked whether they require the above agreement to be extended for a further period, or a new agreement regarding the future of the Naga people arrived at'. Even a cursory reading of the accord points to its simultaneously open and closed nature and is sensitive to only two possibilities: either a straightforward renewal for a further period or a 'new agreement' that might be arrived at in future. While the NNC is free to exercise its option, the provision implicitly rules out the exit option, that is to say, the possibility of NNC retaining its freedom of refusing to enter 'a new agreement' and as a result, walking away from the union. Most importantly, it also makes it mandatory on the NNC's part to negotiate a 'new agreement', which in order to be an agreement would obviously have to be agreed upon by both parties. It seems that an agreement would have to be reached in some way or the other and both parties, according to this agreement, are *forced* to agree—for the NNC could not do without 'arriving at an agreement'—that an agreement, in order to be recognized as such, would also have to be agreed upon by the government.

The Government of India by all accounts did not want to allow the NNC to exercise either of the two possible options mentioned above. The stage of non-accords springs from the assumption that it is impossible to negotiate with and compromise in any manner once the constitution comes into existence and a political framework is put in place. Thus, the Naga–Hydari Accord of 1947 that laid down the basis of integration of the Nagas into the new political dispensation was, for all practical purposes, a non-starter on the ground that the Government of India did not consider it as an accord to be honoured by it, on the ground that it was not a party to it,[5] and if it were to be operative, it had to be within the 'four corners' of the Constitution of India. The constitution, according to the government, is fait accompli and irrevocable. As Nari Rustomji, one of the principal architects of the Naga–Hydari accord, observed:

After holding protracted and heated discussions with the Naga leaders, he (Sir Akbar Hydari) entered into an agreement with them (the Nagas) whereunder the existing administrative arrangements would be continued for a period of ten years, after which the Nagas would be asked whether they wished the agreement to be extended for a further period or a new agreement drawn up regarding their future. The Nagas interpreted this agreement to concede that, if they so wished, they were free to opt out of the Indian Union after ten years, whereas the government took the stand that, whatever might be the revised arrangements agreed upon after ten years, they would have to fall within the four corners of the Indian Constitution (Rustomji 1983: 30).

On 9 November 1948, Gopinath Bordoloi, for the first time, admitted that the Government of India did not consider the agreement as valid. Thus, many of the accord-makers like the NNC in this instance became part of the body politic without even actually entering into it and correspondingly without enjoying whatsoever the right to stage an exit from it. The NNC took little time to discover that they were increasingly pushed into a box that had no exit point. The agreement was reached at the instance of A.Z. Phizo, who as the NNC supremo sent a memorandum to the British government on 20 February 1947 for establishing an interim government for a period of ten years, 'at the end of which the Naga people could be left to choose to form a government under which to live'. The Council in the same memorandum explicitly stated that a constitution drawn up by 'the people having no knowledge of the Naga Hills and its people' would be quite 'unsuitable and

---

[5] Nunthara describes it as an 'unwanted child': 'The British who signed the accord were not responsible for honouring it for it had no authority over its implementation. The Government of India who signed the accord and were responsible for honouring it had no authority over its implementation' (Nunthara 2002).

unacceptable' (Kumar 1995:102). Identification with the nation, or more precisely with the groups and communities tacitly accepted as hallowed parts of the 'original contract', was considered as a prerequisite for entering the democratic body of rights-bearing citizens. Citing the case of American Indians in the USA, Clavero—with whose epigraph we began this essay—advises us to read the accords against their grain by way of bringing the 'indigenous narratives' in order to 'excavate' in the constitutional site: 'Indigenous narrative is an account you need in order to understand the constitutions, past or present, which resolutely ignore an entire and fundamental side of the history or even succeed in becoming blind and unaware nowadays' (Clavero 2004).

Two, whenever the state perceives any challenge coming from the smaller communities or minorities believed to have hitherto remained outside the pale of democratic body politic, it treats this as a law and order problem and brings along the entire repertoire of force and coercion lying at its disposal in order to tame and curb them. The state lays down the rules of the game in clearer terms and anyone violating them is brought promptly to book. This was precisely the reason why the army was called in the early 1950s in the then Naga Hills, a district of undivided Assam, to tackle the situation. The discursive resemblance between the Indian state and the insurgents and armed opposition groups remaining outside the democratic ambit brought them face to face in a prolonged state of warfare. The hierarchy between an original contract with a beginning that unleashes history and accords without it is more often than not expressed through the spate of wars that occur between them. The Naga rebels found themselves being involved in a war that too, according to them, is guided by certain rules and protocols. The Nagas, for example, extended 'prisoners of war' (POW) status to the aircrew held hostage by them in the late-1960s when they shot down an IAF airplane by their very conventional weaponry. On being asked why the Nagas missed the bus when in 'the late sixties and early seventies' India was engaged in war with Pakistan and was prepared to extend 'a Bhutan-type status' to them, a Naga leader replied: '...we thought that we should not attack the enemy when he is in danger. This is the Naga sense of honor' (Perera 1999: 19). It seems that war was omnipresent with all its associated imageries of the Geneva Convention and conferral of POW status, Naga national pride, and their sense of honour. Similarly, it may not be out of place to remember that one of the reasons why Paresh Barua, the ULFA supremo and 'the head of the Government of Assam', reportedly refuses to take part in peace talks with the Government of India is that he can sit on the negotiating table only with another head of state as per the diplomatic protocols that govern the summit-level talks between two states. He wants such protocols to be meticulously observed, if talks are to be initiated between them. Their observance may sound ritualistic; but was considered as the first step towards their recognition as 'sovereign' and 'independent' entities.

THE CONTENTION

The state is seen to respond to only those demands in which the forces remaining outside the contract represent themselves as *state*, when it realizes that the outside also acts as another state questioning its very authority and with this, its monopoly over the legitimate instruments of violence and coercion. The state-building agenda is thus sought to be hijacked from the established state in course of violent conflicts but not of course with the same degree of success.

What we call the outside, elicits responses from the state by seemingly questioning its monopoly over violence and thereby inviting counter-violence. The path to mark a new beginning as visibly distinct and distinguishable from the one made by the founding moment of the constitution is to engage the existing state in violence and thus challenge its authority. The violence that seems to accompany these conflicts is mainly of two types: on the one hand, we can think of such institutionalized forms of violence which are employed and mobilized routinely more as a means of making an otherwise 'deaf' state listen to its demands and move accordingly. While the demand for forming a separate state within the Indian union is by no means un-constitutional (the Constitution of India stipulates the modalities of formation of new states by an act of parliament),[6] the Bodo Liberation Tigers' Force (BLTF), one of the militant Bodo outfits, had to resort to violence for a considerable length of time in order to eventually settle for a Bodoland Territorial Council (BTC) only recently in 2005 as per the Constitution of India. In this instance, the outside does not constitute itself as yet another state while confronting the Indian state and the violence that ensues between them cannot be construed as one between

---

[6] Articles 2 and 3 of the Constitution of India, for example, deal with the admission or establishment of new states and alteration of areas, boundaries, or names of the existing states.

two 'sovereign' and 'independent' states. The outside continues to look upon the Indian state as the potential provider of its demands.

Here we propose to concentrate on another type of violence, which is carried out more in consonance with the imperative of state building, while enabling the groups and communities to create a sovereign political unit of and on their own—that is to say, independently of what the prevailing state thinks and feels about their demands. The violence unleashed in this instance is not intended to make the state respond to the insurgent demands. Rather, it is perpetrated with the specific purpose of attaining a certain degree of coincidence between an ethnic community and the territorial space that it claims as its 'homeland'.

In their coincidence, they produce an 'ethnic space'. How does this coincidence come about? Even a cursory glance at political trends in contemporary India points to at least three modalities of such coincidence: One, coincidence may be effected through the consolidation of a particular ethnic community by way of bringing together its fragments strewn over a host of states and administrative units of our union under one political dispensation. The newly resurgent demand for the formation of a greater 'Nagalim' comprising the present state of Nagaland and the Naga-inhabited areas of the neighbouring states of Manipur, Assam, and Arunachal Pradesh—although vociferously resented by the communities that are going to be affected by the decision—will have to be understood in this light. Two, coincidence is often achieved by getting rid of those areas where members of another community are concentrated in numbers, thereby making the political unit smaller, culturally compact, and ethnically homogeneous. The Sylhet referendum of 1947 may be cited as an illustration. The then leadership of the Assam Pradesh Congress Committee (APCC), dominated mostly by the Assamese-speaking Varna-Hindus, is said to have virtually conceded the district to East Pakistan supposedly on the ground that its inclusion as a Bengali-majority area in Assam would have meant a percentage decline of the Assamese-speaking populace in the state and thus put them to a disadvantage (Chakrabarty 2002: 346–7; Guha 1977: 320). Last but not the least, coincidence is also sought to be achieved through ethnic cleansing. The strategy of 'ethnic cleansing' resorted to by a section of militant Bodo leadership was initially characterized by their potent desire of *creating* a majority of their own for laying hold of the villages under the jurisdiction of the Bodoland Autonomous Council (BAC) that were denied to them on the ground that they had not formed a numerical majority (50 per cent or more) in them. Similarly, the Hmar–Dimasa clashes that have been intermittently taking place in North Cachar (NC) Hills since March 2002 also exemplify the point. Besides, in Karbi Anglong, the Karbi National Volunteers (KNV) was formed in March 1995 with the specific objective of combating the Citizens' Rights Preservation Committee (CRPC) whom it considers as the umbrella organization representing the non-Karbi groups in the district. It accuses the latter of spreading communal feelings among the people 'with active help from the centre' and vowed to oppose the 'imposition' of Hindi as the official language in its memorandum.

The policy followed by the Indian state is basically that of keeping the conflicts from exploding into serious and violent outbursts. However, if violence does break out, the state intends to subject violence to certain rules of the game so that it does not go completely out of its control. The state's attempts at transforming violence into a game by subjecting it to the rules and protocols legitimizing and privileging the exercise of state violence is itself a violent game and is implicated in violence. The rules and protocols by no means rule out violence, but seek only to restore the reins of violence to the state. The game of violence itself is a violent game, for it involves beating violence through the application of superior (counter-)violence by way of setting forth certain rules. It is important to remember that whenever a conflict passes beyond a threshold and takes a violent turn questioning the state's monopoly over it, it elicits strong state responses. Accord-making at the moment of contention is, therefore, marked by a certain gaming of violence. For, it is by way of setting forth the rules and exercising greater counter-violence through the observance of those rules that the state can prove its superiority, its invincibility to those whom it claims to represent as part of the nation, in this regard. The rules are set in a manner that the state finds it easier to establish the superiority of violence at its command. Violence, in short, triggers off a game that the state cannot afford to lose. We argue that the state often engages the insurgent outfit in the so-called peace dialogues, not so much to find out solutions but to gauge and fathom their 'climb-down positions'[7] and the state enters into peace dialogues only when it has reason to believe that the outfits are considerably weakened—if not decimated—and it

---

[7] 'A climb-down position' accounts for the extent to which the armed group is prepared for compromise and accepting a solution. I thank Subir Bhaumik for having coined this phrase for me.

can easily 'force' an accord on them (Rupesinghe 2001 [1996]: 180). It breaks off the dialogues when the 'climb-down position' is not sufficiently 'low' to allow an agreement that at the same time ensures its invincibility and triumph over them. The break-up of peace talks with the People's Consultative Group (PCG), nominated by the ULFA, and the recent resurgence of violence have, for example, been interpreted by a section of the press as the state's exercise in ascertaining the 'climb-down position' of the ULFA. The state restarted military operations ('Operation Rhino II' over and above 'Operation Rhino I' that was still going on) with renewed vigour on 9 January 2007 precisely because it found the 'climb-down position' too high to be negotiated upon, let alone accepted. Interestingly, the army, unlike on previous occasions, had been advised to 'bring ULFA to the negotiating table' instead of finishing them off. It is important to remind us that a full-scale military operation is launched in order to initiate discussions and peace talks! Although army operations are supposed to be spread all across Assam, the three Upper Assam districts of Sivasagar, Dibrugarh, and Tinsukia happen to be the epicentre. Peace dialogues at this moment are an extension of war—a war 'continued through other means'. Thus, it is no longer possible to make any distinction between war and peace. Even at the height of military operations, the prime minister of India extends an offer of 'safe passage' to the ULFA leaders who might come to take part in talks, should the ULFA agree to the government's peace proposal. It is reflective of the mutually embedded nature of war and peace. By 'absorbing violence within the larger discourse of warfare', the state, Barbora argues, contributes to the complete 'depoliticization' of the political agenda that informs the practices of the armed groups and a distance is created between the warring parties (Barbora 2006: 3807). The dialogical space supposedly between them in effect gets completely eroded. This compels the armed groups to commit themselves to an open war from their hitherto followed strategy of 'armed engagement'. 'Armed engagement', unlike war, is not meant to defeat the Indian state in any direct war. It is more of a symbolic gesture of defiance and resistance that seeks to mobilize ever-larger bodies of people against the state. The ULFA too once argued that the primary objective of their armed engagements was to gradually train the people in the art of surviving state repression and not relenting under pressure as it might be unleashed in extreme situations of crisis.

Peace has been defined by the state primarily as a game in which it wins whether by setting forth the rules of the game or by beating its adversary in it or both. The transformation of limited 'armed engagement' into open and full-scale 'war' is only an example of how the rules of the game, if not the game itself, are changed by the state. Both these exercises are expressed through the signing of accords. Accords announce albeit a momentary outcome of the game. For, as we will see, they also make way for further conflagration and violence. Each accord almost by definition is prefaced by a disarmament clause that is intended to disarm the adversary and make it submit to the authority of the constitution and the state's superior power of violence almost as part of a ritual. The state actions in this regard are meant for making its adversaries realize that it continues to hold un-contestably the *superior* power of violence and it is in no hurry till it is able to get across the message. Thus force ratio becomes an important determinant of peace. Peace construed under these circumstances is predicated on a politics of contention and is determined by its outcome.

Viewed in this light, the reference to the constitution in almost every ethnic accord may sound ritualistic. The Shillong Accord (1975) may be regarded as the classical paradigm of peace established through war, and of war continued through the act of peace-making. In spite of being excruciatingly brief, two of the three clauses that make up Article 3—the only substantive article in this three-article accord—provide for the 'acceptance of the Constitution of India, without condition and of their own volition' and the instrumentalities of 'depositing' arms by the underground. While Article 1 names the parties signing the accord, Article 2 briefly lays down the historical background of 'the series of discussions' that led to the act of signing the accord. Article 3 clause (iii) holds out the promise of arriving at what it describes as the 'final settlement' in the following terms: 'It was agreed that the representatives of the underground organizations should have reasonable time to formulate other issues for discussions for final solution.'

One wonders why the signatories were in such tearing hurry to work out the modalities of 'depositing' of arms and 'the reasonable time' was not allowed to pass for finalizing the terms of a political solution. While the details of 'depositing' of arms were further worked out as per clause (ii) in the Supplementary Agreement to the Shillong Accord signed on 5 January 1976, the rather dismissive phrase of 'other issues' never came up for discussion in the first place, let alone reaching a solution. It is not clear whether the representatives of the 'underground' had ever thought of reclaiming their arms that they had deposited—but not surrendered—from the Peace Council that was ultimately responsible for the 'safety' of these arms, if there is any procrastination on the government's part in the process of arriving at the final settlement promised in the accord. In the absence of any such discussion promised in the accord and the reclaiming of arms deposited in accordance with its terms, the accord turned into a non-starter and was soon interpreted as a 'surrender pact' by the National Socialist Council of Nagaland or NSCN (now Nagalim) IM. NSCN was born the day the Shillong Accord proclaimed the victory of the government. No war is violent enough to force a victory on the vanquished. It is always a continuing war, a war of attrition that continues till the problem is politically solved.

Likewise, the Preamble to the Memorandum of Settlement that was signed between the All-Tripura Tribal Force (ATTF) and the Government of Tripura on 23 August 1993, for example, points out: '... All-Tripura Tribal Force have given a clear indication that they would like to give up the path of violence and would like to resume a normal life and they have decided to abandon the path of violence and seek solutions to their problems within the framework of the Constitution of India ...'

Every accord of this genre proudly announces the state's victory in re-establishing its command over the legitimate instruments of violence once challenged by the insurgent outfits. The ATTF had also to give 'the undertaking' that it would not 'extend any support in any manner whatever to any other underground or extremist group by way of training, supply of arms, providing protection, providing shelter or in any other manner'. Article 18 of the Bodo Accord (1993) similarly points out that the

ABSU (All-Bodo Students'Union)-BPAC (Bodo Peoples'Action Committee) will take immediate steps to bring overground and deposit with the District authorities all arms, ammunition and explosives in the possession of their own supporters and will cooperate with the administration in bringing overground all Bodo militants along with their own arms and ammunition etc. within one month of the formation of the interim BEC (Bodoland Executive Council).

Article 4 Clause 1 of the accord signed with the Hmar Peoples' Convention (HPC) on 27 July 1994 duly puts on record the latter's 'agreement to undertake' the responsibilities of disarmament within 'an agreed time-frame'. The script is exactly the same. By contrast, the NSCN (IM)—although it has entered into a ceasefire agreement with the Government of India in 1997—refuses to surrender its arms and ammunition till the 'final settlement' is reached. It continues to look upon the instruments of violence as a necessary means of leveraging the outcome of peace talks. Whether it will be able to remobilize its army and cadres after a prolonged spell of ceasefire is an altogether different question.

It is important to make a distinction between warfare at the moment of beginning and that at the moment of contention. The moment of beginning turns the parties away from the language of accords, resulting in open war or unmitigated hostility between them till the insurgents are tamed and they submit to the constitution. When the Indian army was pressed into action in the then Naga Hills in the early 1950s, the idea was to establish the state's command over the area and bring them under the newly established constitutional framework. The army action was inspired by the simple imperative of establishing law and order in the area. There was hardly any question of signing any accord, for it was never treated as a political problem that called for political solution. Contention on the other hand is expressed and enacted through the instrumentality of signing accords. Indeed, we can say that the accords can make *their* beginning only by way of contending with the state. Besides, as one contends with the state, one is dragged into the game of violence. While the NNC maintained that it was involved in a war much in the same way as wars are fought between sovereign and independent states with due observance of the rules and protocols meant for defining the relations between mutually hostile parties, the state simply looked upon it as a game—the rules of which are or will be unilaterally set by it. The observance of war rules as per international law would have implicitly given recognition to the adversary.

THE RECOGNITION

The Naga peace process initiated after the present ceasefire agreement was signed with the NSCN-IM in 1997 makes it imperative on our part to appreciate the role recognition plays in making peace accords democratic. It was aptly prefaced by the setting forth of the rites of negotiation between the parties. In 2004, by the admission of the Naga rebel leaders, 'substantive talks' began and the political question was addressed. It is perhaps the first time in history when the constitution as an original document was no longer considered the beginning with a view to make a new beginning. A realization dawned on the political elite that the constitution is more an open document that can be discussed and negotiated upon as and when necessary. Time does not change with the constitution; the constitution changes with time.

The process promises autonomy and we have elsewhere defined it as the 'difference' accords seek to make from and to the country's constitution or the established law of the land (Das 2005). The difference made is not necessarily to be interpreted as being reflective of what Misra calls, 'the resilience and accommodative power of the country's Constitution' (Misra 2002a). It may be the strength of the negotiating parties that makes the difference—a difference that more often than not remains unacknowledged by the state.[8] Autonomy, as Dent too defines it, is located in a 'plateau of institutions' that lies between complete separatism and full membership to 'a coercive single state'. This is based on the principle of divisibility of sovereignty and the Naga issue can, according to him, be resolved by the 'granting of a sovereign land status within the independent state of India' (Dent 2004: 65). This evidently calls for a redefinition of state sovereignty and a certain redesigning of institutions that can accommodate it.

Recognition first of all implies the making of a subject or what Foucault would have termed, subjectification. We understand it predominantly as a process whereby conditions are created for the articulation of an otherwise war-torn and visibly divided community into *a* collective subject with whom a credible accord may be signed. The subject does not remain *out there* and with whom negotiations can subsequently be conducted. In most cases, the organizations involved in peace negotiations turn out to be the spokesmen of an otherwise fractured voice of their community. The Nagas, for example, remain in a highly fragmented social state strewn across a number of administrative units—either as a minority as in Assam, Arunachal Pradesh, Manipur, and bordering Myanmar or as a majority as in Nagaland yet continuously facing the threat of becoming a minority in no time. Recognition means that the negotiating groups and communities exist as a single collective self, cutting across the strong administrative and demographic boundaries that otherwise set them apart and are represented by organizations whose representative character is not in doubt. It is only through the opposition to the given administrative and state-enforced categories of self-formation that a subject comes into being and can

---

[8] I have discussed this in greater detail in Das (2005). I refrain from elaborating on it here.

articulate itself. The fight of the Palestinians, as Edward Said tells us, is not for a piece of territory, but against the 'territorial fetish' that has been imposed on them (Said 1996a: XXXV). The fight for justice is therefore central to the process of subjectification of the party that gets involved in the peace process. This also implies subjection for it means that the collective imaginary that emerges from these processes is considered as the only one, ruling out alternative possibilities of collective self-formation. The representativeness of the body claiming to represent a group or a community is often a matter of dispute as there remains invariably more than one claimant and none of them may represent the community in question. It is therefore important that those who sign an accord on behalf of a community are also representative of the community and are considered as such by it. The community does not exist before the accords. It gets formed precisely through the accords. This is contrary to the claim commonly made by the parties involved in the peace process. Yet, in a situation of political turmoil when the established representative institutions evidently do not function or may even have collapsed, it is very difficult to ascertain the degree of representativeness that the political leadership and the organizations claiming to represent their communities actually enjoy.[9] On being repeatedly asked to prove their representative character, the All-Party Hurriyat Conference (APHC), operating mostly in the Kashmir valley, instituted an 'Election Commission' of its own a few years ago in order to fathom and assess their popularity in the area. The Indian government immediately shot it down as 'ridiculous' because according to them, only the Indian constitution provides for the institution of such a body. It is on such occasions that civil society plays an important role in restoring democratic institutions within the community and making the circulation of opinions possible within it.

The Naga reconciliation process as we know was initially considered as only complementary to the Naga peace process. The leaders of the Naga civil society seemed to have veered to the realization that while setting the peace initiative with the Indian state in motion, it was also necessary to reconcile the differences that separate the Nagas and generate hostility between them—thanks to the 'territorial fetish' that characterizes their existence. As the declaration for the reconciliation made on 20 December 2001 at Kohima points out: 'Nagas targeting

[9] Abdul Ghani Lone, the slain leader of the APHC, pointed this to me in an interview.

the Nagas cannot solve the Naga political issue.' The Concept Note prepared by the Naga Hoho (parliament) Coordination Committee defines the 'rebuilding of the Naga family' as the principal objective of the reconciliation process (Lasuh 2002: 605). Both processes of peace and reconciliation were considered as mutually complementary, for peace without reconciliation, as history teaches us, is not durable as much as reconciliation without peace is partial and incomplete. As the Workshop on Reconciliation and Unity that adopted the declaration, puts it: '[The] Reconciliation process should continue for the growth and well being of the Naga society. The political negotiations should be the priority concern of all Nagas while at the same time pursuing the reconciliation process with vigour' (Bangkok Consultation Meet 2002: 9).

The Naga reconciliation process meant to bridge the inter-tribal differences amongst the Nagas received a jolt when a section of Naga rebels publicly expressed their reservations about a couple of members of the Naga Reconciliation Commission. The enthusiasm of an otherwise strong Naga civil society comprising such organizations as Naga Mothers' Association (NMA), Naga Students' Federation (NSF), and Naga Peoples' Movement for Human Rights (NPMHR) was considerably diminished by the impasse. Much of the space for civil society today depends on the *contingencies* of recognition extended to them by the rebel groups.

The Shillong Accord (1975), referred to earlier, should be cited as an obvious counter-text in the absence of a text that may un-problematically be cited as recognition. The signing of the accord was followed immediately by some of the worst ever crackdowns and repressive measures taken by the Indian state. This also throttled the Naga civil society and either ripped it apart or sent it underground. For one thing, a national emergency was declared immediately after the accord was signed. It was immediately followed by fierce military action. The very act of signing the accord itself was reflective of a deeper wedge that the state was successful in driving within the rebel ranks. The excruciatingly brief text of the accord did not even make any mention of the NNC spearheading the movement—at that time under the leadership of Angami Zapu Phizo—widely regarded as the father of the Naga insurgent movement. Interestingly, it was signed by six 'representatives of the underground organization' who always remained anonymous in the text. The anonymity of authorship was also a means of escaping the burden that came with it. The NNC neither accepted nor dissociated from the accord; but it never claimed its authorship or ownership. Phizo was 'silent' on the issue (Aosenba 2001: 78). In the words of Luingam Luithui and Meredith Preston: '... there was no political space to function under such circumstances' (1999: 4). For another, there were reported attempts at rallying the Naga civil society behind the signatories in order to get it to 'rubberstamp' the accord. According to Luithui and Preston, the government was wrong in taking the accord leaders as representing either the Naga civil society or the NNC. As they were neither, their representative character was once again under a cloud.

Nowhere in the Northeast is civil society considered to be as vigilant as it is in present-day Nagaland. And it will not be an exaggeration to say that civil society vigilantism is part and parcel of the Naga peace process. As Misra (2002a) observes:

Civil society intervention has reached such a stage in Nagaland today that no insurgent organization, however strong it might be, can afford to bypass it .... Since the overwhelming response of Naga society has been for a peaceful settlement of the issue, the NSCN (IM) cannot afford to swim against this current. This, therefore, has been one of the positive developments in favour of a peaceful settlement.

It is interesting to see that the Naga peace process looks like an unusually long haul. It means that there is an eagerness on the part of both parties to let the region's civil society grow and develop thereby contributing to the formation of collective selves to be involved in the peace process. Misra advocates a greater and freer role for civil society in the current Naga peace talks. In his words: 'Efforts must be made to replace state activism with people's activism and in this, the traditional structures of power and civil society organizations can be made to play a meaningful role' (Misra n.d.). On the one hand, civil society, according to him, has a crucial role to play in 'working out a formula to resolve the points of difference that exist between the major underground and overground political groups' and this has acquired enormous significance in view of the fact that 'no single group can really claim any hegemonic status' (Misra 2002a). On the other hand, the sensitive nature of the territoriality issue (concerning the NSCN-IM demand for integration of Naga areas of Manipur, Assam, and Arunachal Pradesh) also makes it imperative for the civil society to act as a cementing force against 'intercommunity clashes' (Misra 2002b). The most difficult hurdle to any solution to the tangled 'Indo-Naga' question comes both from inside as well as from outside the Nagas themselves. The 'quit notice' issued in 2006 by the NSCN (Khaplang) to the Tangkhuls (a tribal group predominantly living in Manipur that Mr Muivah hails from) living in the Indian state of Nagaland is a case in point. This further widened the rift between the two factions of the NSCN.

It is to be noted, however, that a civil society driven by a community's concern for autonomy can seldom create a civil space. While civil societies amongst both the Nagas—whether of Nagaland or of Manipur—and the Meiteis of Manipur are unusually strong and vibrant, there is little or hardly any interaction between them. In the turbulent days of June 2001 when the ceasefire with the NSCN (IM) was initially 'extended without territorial limits' beyond Nagaland, very strongly worded statements were exchanged between both sides, which almost resulted in the burning of bridges between them. While all this embittered their interrelations, there is no denying that hardly any direct clash was reported between them. A convention represented by the United Naga Council, Manipur; Naga People's Movement for Human Rights (Manipur Sector); Naga Women's Union, Manipur; All-Naga Students' Union, Manipur; and Naga People's Convention held in Senapati on 28 June 2001, for example, noted with concern 'the belligerent and confrontationist approach of the Meitei (sic) community towards the extension of ceasefire in the Naga areas outside the present Nagaland state including Manipur' and 'concluded that the well articulated agenda for the territorial integrity of Manipur by the Meitei community is a move to deny the rights of the Naga people'. It seems that neither of them is in a mood to engage in any civic interaction in order to reconcile the conflicting rights claims. It has to be noted that recently some initiatives have been adopted, particularly by some women's organizations to build bridges between the two communities. It is ironic for the civil societies in the Northeast that wherever they have refused to 'rubberstamp' the state-crafted (non-)accords[10] and act as stooges of the state, they have turned into one of its parties.

The Mizo Accord (1986) is often celebrated as the culmination of a process that contributed to the process of collective self-formation of the Mizo society in general and the Mizos in particular. It is argued,

[10] Subir Bhaumik, for example, describes the Shillong Accord (1975) as 'the accord that never was' (Bhaumik 2005).

for example, that it could successfully weld diverse sections of the Mizo society together by reconciling their differences, while many other accords in the region could not. As Nunthara argues:

In case of the Mizo movement, the charismatic quality of Laldenga, the president of MNF, was able to channelize any factional rivalry and prevented organizational division. The MNF thus remained the representative authority of both underground organization and the overground politics in the peace process. This is not the case with Assam and Bodo movements (Nunthara 2002).

However, it will be useful to keep in mind that the much-touted subjectification process implicit in the Mizo Accord is facing newer sources of crisis today. Peace accords, according to Nunthara, become successful wherever the parties signing them act as homogeneous subjects and the schisms internal to each of them are substantially reduced, if not completely eliminated. Each party speaking in many voices only complicates the conflict instead of resolving it. He defines 'entrenchment' as a process whereby such constitutive ambiguities, associated with the formation of an ethnic subject considered eligible for signing an accord with the state, are reduced and avoided. His analysis of the Mizo Accord (1986) leads him to arrive at such a conclusion. Mizoram is usually showcased as a success story. The entrenchment clause, according to him, is the key to the obvious success of the Mizo Accord. Since factionalism within the MNF—that spearheaded the Mizo insurgency in the pre-accord era—was reportedly nominal and because by all accounts, Laldenga, its chief, took his comrades into account almost at every step, it was possible for him to get his organization to accept it although by the time the accord was signed, the MNF had already earned 'notoriety' for having repeatedly backed out from many a verbal commitment to ceasefire and peace.

What Nunthara calls 'entrenchment' and we call 'subjectification' is believed to have slowly produced an 'illiberal' society in which individual dissent is more or less throttled and dissenters are forced to give way to the commands of the established civil society organizations. The so-called success story of the accord will have to be read together with many other stories that compel us to read it against its grain. The Hmars fell apart from the Mizos the moment the separate state of Mizoram came into existence in 1986. The HPC demand for 'Hmar Ram', to be carved out from the newly formed state of Mizoram, symbolizes a deep ethnic divide between the two hitherto friendly communities of the Mizos and the Hmars. Interestingly, the Hmars joined the Mizos in their struggle for the statehood of Mizoram.

Reangs constitute the second largest population group in Tripura and are spread across several northern and southern subdivisions of Dharmanagar, Kailasahar, Kamalpur, Udaipur, Amarpur, Belonia, and the bordering states of Assam and Mizoram, and of course, Bangladesh. Insofar as they are scattered over a number of territorial and administrative units, they face the problem of being reduced to a minority everywhere. The general perception of the Reangs—from interviews with their political leaders—is that their culture cannot flourish 'because of the dominance of other majority groups within the recognized territorial spaces in Mizoram, Tripura or in Assam' (Chakraborty 2004: 426). Sawibunga (the first Reang graduate from North Eastern Hill University, Shillong) formed Reang Peoples' Union, the first modern socio-cultural organization amongst the Reangs. In December 1989, it changed its name to Bru Socio-Cultural Association (BSCA) with a vision to unify the diverse segments of Reangs scattered in different parts of the region, including Bangladesh. Sawibunga was also instrumental in floating the political organization the Reang Democratic Convention that further changed its name to Reang Democratic Party. The party started interacting with the Reangs of different parts and strove hard for pan-Reang (Bru) solidarity. The Reangs in Mizoram are encouraged by the Mizos to embrace Christianity (Saha 2004:167). Being non-Christians, their difference from the Mizos is only too visible, and after the formation of Mizoram as a separate state, the Reangs are supposed to be part of the Mizo mainstream. Many of their names have allegedly been struck off from the electoral rolls and in the Mizo assembly polls held in November 2003, only 637 voters—a dismal 14.93 per cent—cast their votes 'because of the failure of the Mizoram government to provide adequate security' (Chakma 2004). The Reangs of Mizoram are involved in building alliances with other minorities of the state too, like the Chakmas. The Mizo Zirlai Pawl has already branded them as 'the outsiders'. For the last few years, these organizations have intensified their campaign against the Reangs and according to an unofficial estimate, over 50,000 of them have been forced to leave the state and take shelter in Assam and Tripura.

Mizo society's intolerance to dissent was illustrated very clearly when Vanramchhaunvy, a leading Mizo woman activist, was threatened in May 2005 by the Young Mizo Association (YMA) while protesting against the deaths of four persons and cruelty towards many others for their alleged involvement in peddling drugs and liquor. The YMA had launched a programme to curb drugs and liquor and the victims who had died or had to suffer other forms of cruelty were 'punished' by the organization as part of its campaign for meting out instant justice to deviants and offenders in society. When Vanramchhaunvy saw two women, apparently accused of some offence, on the roadside with large placards around their necks, she pleaded with the YMA for turning them over to the appropriate authorities and trying them according to the constitution and the law of the land. She was summoned the next day by the YMA and nine local YMA leaders descended on her place as per the orders of the central committee and threatened her. In an open letter she pointed out that she was under pressure from the YMA and made a reflection on Mizo society: 'These faith-based and community-based organizations dictate our lives since they are so powerful and there is no scope for the development and flowering of individuality and individual freedom. We have seen so much of unique talents and personalities being suppressed because of fear of these organizations.'

Recognition should not be regarded as a simple bilateral act depending on the goodwill and trust between two signing parties interested in making peace—a process whereby 'we' confer(s) recognition on 'them' and vice versa and remain exactly what the two categories were: 'we' and 'them'—even after the act of conferring recognition on each other. It has its deeper implications in that a common institutional framework that makes us its parts and labels us 'we' and 'them' will have to be self-critical for generating categories such as 'we' and 'them' in the first place. The common framework will have to be so designed that it does not produce or reproduce such stereotypes and profiles of the communities.[11] This cannot be ensured either by force or by the simple act of charity and goodwill. It requires some sort of institutional intervention and redesigning of institutions with the effect that we arrive at a self-being 'enlarged through the mediation of the other' (Williams 1997: 54). The accords as per this formulation are expected to give us clues to the redesigning of our institutions. The Hegelian traces

---

[11] This requires more than the mere 'erasure of demeaning images' as Neera Chandhoke (1999: 9) would have us believe. Our 'intentionality' of erasing these images will not be enough to erase them. It needs to be institutionally effected and guaranteed.

of the theory of recognition are clearly discernible when Elizabeth Kiss proposes to further consolidate and institutionalize it: 'Mere tolerance of difference is not enough, nor is it sufficient for democratic societies to allow citizens to express different identities ... Equal moral and political status, and hence democracy cannot be achieved unless social institutions and sensibilities become more attentive to, and reflective of, cultural differences' (Kiss 1999: 193).

We need institutions that produce a self-consciousness that is not pure, for, it is not predicated on 'exclusion of every other from itself' (Hegel 1910: 231). Recognition, therefore, calls for an alternative agenda for institutionalization that holds out the promise of exceeding the grids of governmentality. States all over the world have learnt—and sometimes at great cost—that they cannot always operate with the constitutional fundamentals that they have promised to adhere to and be guided by in course of their day-to-day operations. There is reason to believe that the state often finds it difficult to continue to uphold and abide by the early doctrine of indivisible sovereignty and seems to have imperceptibly modified it in recent years. While all this goes on quietly, the state by definition cannot concede in *public*, for example, to the ULFA's demand for including the right to national self-determination by making a suitable constitutional amendment. The ULFA, it may be noted, set this as a precondition for holding talks with the Government of India. While the ULFA has consistently shunned the idea of holding talks with the government on this ground (along with a few others), the Nagas, since 1997, engaged themselves in a series of talks with the government notwithstanding their assertion of the 'right to self-determination irrespective of what the Constitution said' (Perera 1999: 16). Unlike the NSCN-IM, the ULFA has so far taken a very legal stand in this regard and wants this right to be included in the constitution by a suitable amendment. One has to understand that the peace process is more than, if at all, a legal and constitutional process. Peace in other words is premised on a certain flexibilization of the constitution and the established law of the land.

As a result, the notion of 'indivisible sovereignty' has undergone a significant transformation in recent years: First, the state today has no difficulties in conducting negotiations with rebel leaders in foreign countries. Bangkok, Chiang Mai, Geneva, and Amsterdam have already become favourite destinations for talks between rebel leaders and the Government of India. In most cases, these talks are held in complete confidence and with very little media coverage, if at all.

If the state's notion of sovereignty is in the throes of a profound change, so too is the sovereignty of the armed groups and organizations. Insofar as the NSCN is concerned, the integration of all contiguous Naga areas spread over three Indian states and part of Myanmar is one of its top priorities and as one NSCN leader recently said, sovereignty is *negotiable* on a 'phase-wise formula'. To the NSCN, there can never be a solution without the Naga areas being put under one administrative roof. As Lotha (2004) interprets it: 'It is also important to note that the Naga Movement is not a demand for sovereignty but a struggle to resist colonization of its area and a struggle for identity against the colossal advancement of occupational force and race for assimilation of unique culture and tradition of the Naga race.'

Similarly, Mamoni Raisom Goswami[12] and Manoranjan Mohanty have reportedly prepared a draft framework on the issue of 'Assam's sovereignty' on the basis of which the Government of India might be involved in some form of dialogue with the ULFA. The draft is still kept unknown and, as Goswami informed us, would be released at an opportune moment. This is expected to set new terms of reference on the issue of sovereignty in contemporary India. Now that the ongoing talks have hit a dead end, it is unlikely that the draft will have any serious taker.

Second, the state too feels that the government depends on the success of accords and not their failures. The success of accords in turn depends not so much on handling the demands of autonomy from within the given federal structure but on some adventurous experimentation with our institutions. The debate over institutions has already begun. In other words, efforts are being made to break free from the institutional paradox in which consolidation of a particular ethnic community within a geopolitical space necessarily creates its minorities. The vicious circle in which a minority becomes a majority by way of getting the borders redrawn and thereby creates its own minority and the circle continues to roll with nauseating regularity is inherent to our established federal set-up. Attempts are now being made to explore newer institutional alternatives.

[12] Goswami's two-year initiative to bring back the ULFA and the Government of India to the negotiating table after the Bhutan operations of December 2003 led to the formation of the People's Consultative Group and very recently ended in a fiasco.

We may refer to at least three interesting strands, not necessarily mutually exclusive, of this debate: First, reform-minded scholars and activists like B.K. Roy Burman (referred in Routray 2001) recommend a Scandinavian SAMI-like multilayered parliamentary system in which ethnic communities will have the right to represent themselves instead of being bound by the majoritarian commands of our existing parliamentary system. Second, some have argued that the 'first-come-first-serve' electoral system in which the minorities dispersed over a large space are constantly under the subjection of the numerical, and therefore political, majority is incompatible with the pluralistic nature of our society (Narayan 2003: 38). Even reservation of seats will not help the situation. Narayan advocates introducing proportional representation as a means of protecting these groups from majority rule and retaining their autonomy. Third, a case has been made for widening the consociational (power sharing) base of our democratic system. Arend Lijphart (1996), for example, shows how the basic preconditions of a consociational democracy were met during the first few decades of our independence and how that base has been weakened as a combined result of the 'centralization of the Congress Party and the federal system' in the 1980s and the growing 'attack on minority rights' in different parts of India. He, in fact, pleads for resuscitating the institutions and practices of consociational democracy that protected India reasonably well in the first few decades of independence against inter-group violence and communal riots.

Yet it seems that these changes do not easily translate into the texts of the accords signed in recent years. There is no linear or irreversible path to peace. Everyone is looking expectantly to the end result of the Naga peace talks and, most importantly, to the kind of fresh institutional arrangements that the long haul might bring into existence. The Naga peace talks, too, have occasionally reached a stalemate and both Muivah and Swu have threatened more than once to break away from them. What Edward Said pointed out about the Palestinian peace process in 1990 is also true of today's Naga peace talks: 'I think this is perhaps the most difficult period because it is very easy to get discouraged. The important thing is to engage in a detailed way with this very complex moment ...' (Said 2004: 356). The prolonged ceasefire with no mutually acceptable political solution in sight and fratricidal warfare between the two factions of the NSCN becoming more and more intense seem to have taken a toll on the Naga negotiators. Yet peace, as Said informs us, is always perched on hope than despair. It is always easy to plunge into despair than to keep hope. The peace process in the Northeast is now clearly at a crossroad.

CHAPTER 12

Hills–Valley Divide as a Site of Conflict

Emerging Dialogic Space in Manipur[1]

H. KHAM KHAN SUAN

BACKGROUND AND CONTEXT

Since colonial times, the hills–valley divide has been a major theme in understanding ethnic relations in the eastern parts of South Asia and in Southeast Asia. India's northeastern state of Manipur is no exception. The hills nestle numerous historical communities, also known in India's constitutional discourse as 'tribe(s)',[2] and embody disparate self-governing autonomous structures largely under hereditary chiefs. They are, to borrow from James C. Scott,[3] considered to occupy a 'non-state space', an 'illegible space'. State building impels a certain measure of political engineering, which in turn entails an imposition of

---

[1] Modified version of a paper presented at an international conference on 'State and Democracy in India: Critical Reflections', organized by the Centre for Political Studies, Jawaharlal Nehru University, and University Grants Commission–Special Assistance Programme, New Delhi (23–24 March 2006). I thank Balveer Arora, Asha Sarangi, the convenor of the seminar and her team for their kind invitation. An earlier draft of the paper was presented at a seminar on 'Problems and Prospects of Marginalized Hill People of Manipur', organized by the Zomi Human Rights Foundation, Delhi Cell at Deputy Speaker Hall, Constitution Club, New Delhi, 16–17 December 2005. Thanks are due to the organizers and participants of both the seminars. The paper also benefited from comments of colleagues, among others, Rajani Ranjan Jha and Amarnath Mohanty at Banaras Hindu University, Varanasi; and Bimol Akoijam, Gurpreet Mahajan, Sajal Nag, and David Vumlallian Zou.

[2] Hereafter I will use the two terms 'historical communities' and 'tribe(s)/tribal groups' interchangeably in the same sense.

[3] Scott cited in Baruah (2005c: 8).

its institutions and structures. State manoeuvring of this kind, however, is stoutly resisted by the hill people as 'alien' and antithetical to their cherished traditional institutions and world view. The colonial British state's encounter with these communities in Northeast India since the late nineteenth century bears out this antipathy.[4] Hence, patronizing the friendly tribal chiefs by envisaging special protective administrative regimes and using them as a via media to extend the paraphernalia of the state became the modus vivendi of colonial British state policy in India. This implies that the state has not been able to exercise direct and effective societal control on the hill tribes; and the latter continue to confront and contest the authority of the former to do so. The postcolonial state in India is an inheritor to this state–society rupture which in a way exemplifies the hills–valley divide.[5] Not surprisingly all socio-economic, cultural, and political development or non-development trajectories are seen through the prism of this divide.

This essay seeks to explore the hills–valley divide as a site of conflict which spills over to confront the Indian state[6] and democracy at two levels. The first level of conflict emanates from what I call *perceived non-democratic space* and the second level is located within a *purportedly democratic space*. Both the levels engender totalizing projects (in the form of autonomy movements)[7] which run parallel to and are counter-posited against India's state–nation-building project; the second level with a more pronounced propensity to challenge the efficacy of the component unit of the Indian union. The corollary of this is that every claim of stateness[8] and democracy by the Indian state is contested and

---

[4] For a first-hand account on this see, *inter alia*, Mackenzie (2001). The original title is *History of the Relations of the Government with the Hill Tribes of the North-East Frontier of Bengal*, 1884. Also see Reid (1997). This work was originally published in 1942 by the Assam Government Press, Shillong.

[5] On this count, see Hassan (2006); available online at http://www.crisisstates. com/download/wp/wp79.pdf, accessed on 29 September 2006.

[6] By Indian state I imply the union, state, and local government(s).

[7] Most nation building is engaged in a totalizing project, which is a performative aspect of the ultimate end, that is, a totality. Hence, most nation building is exclusivist and is conducted in the language of monistic authenticity. This being the case especially in a diverse country like India, the totalizing project of the state spawned parallel totalizing projects from disparate ethnic communities which consider the former project as insensitive to, and non-accommodating vis-à-vis, their particularities.

[8] 'Stateness' as an explanatory variable depends, in J.P. Nettl's formulation, on

its legitimacy questioned as if it were 'implanted' and 'transported' to alien conditions with altogether different contexts, which are considered to be no less democratic.[9]

These projects by their very nature tend to collide against each other and provide ample space for the efficacy of the stateness–democracy continuum to be tested. Once this takes place we have interesting counter-positions of the 'self' and the 'other'.[10] Since the credence of each project depends heavily upon monistic authenticity which is at once imperial, hegemonic, and homogenizing in its orientation, the sustenance of each impels the emergence of a dialogic space. Here the ways/modes of representation and the concomitant dissensual politics, which each totalizing project engenders, would determine the efficacy of institutions, norms, and principles of the state. These would in turn determine the durability of the state and would also attest to the level of democratization which it envisaged for the governed. A word of caution, however, is in order here, as Francis Fukuyama (2005) reminds us:

Before you can have a democracy, you must have a state, but to have a legitimate and therefore durable state you eventually must have democracy. The two are intertwined, but the precise sequencing of how and when to build the distinct but interlocking institutions needs very careful thought (p. 88).

Coming back, the first space is perceived to be non-democratic precisely because of the contestable nature of India's state–formation which had been enacted out of 'conciliation and pressure' vis-à-vis the state of Manipur, and for that matter all of India's Northeast. The failure of the Naga representatives to finally endorse the Bordoloi Committee Report, 1947,[11] which literally left the Indian state bereft

---

the extent 'individuals have generalised the concept and cognition of state in their perception and actions'. While the Weberian idea of state as envisioning a 'coercive monopoly of power' is widely considered a 'given', stateness is considered largely to be a 'sociocultural phenomenon' marked by distinct historical development across societies. See Nettl (1968).

[9] For a related discussion see Krasner (2005); Linz and Stepan (1996); Stepan (1999).

[10] Interestingly, once totalizing projects are at odds against each other they tend to take the position of the 'self' against the differentiated totalizing 'other'.

[11] The Bordoloi Committee also known as the Sub-committee on the North-East Frontier (Assam) Tribal and Excluded Areas was set up by the Constituent Assembly of India's Advisory Committee on the Rights of Citizens, Minorities and Tribal and Excluded Areas on 27 February 1947 to suggest a mode of tribal self-governance. It finally suggested the setting up of a separate constitutional

of legitimate structures to incorporate the Naga Hills, and the highly charged atmosphere under which the regent of Manipur, Bodhi Chandra, was 'coerced' to sign the merger agreement with the Indian state in October 1949 are two illuminating cases that still continue to inform the contours of the parallel totalizing projects in Manipur and elsewhere in the Northeast. Later incorporations and consequent Indian state–nation building in this part of the country was contested for not being sensitive to their 'unique history and political situation'. Once this contestation took a separatist/independentist turn, it generated a psychosis of fear of uncertainty and disorder. The outcome of this is, as Javeed Alam has pointed out, the exclusive reliance of the Indian state 'on the inherited bureaucracy and police and armed forces to contain upheavals and beat back popular movements/agitations' (Alam 2002: 98). Alam painstakingly elaborated upon the long-term consequences both on the immediate exercise of power as well as on the nature of state in India:

It allowed these structures of power so constructed to *insulate themselves from popular pressure* or accountability, to acquire a certain degree of permanence *by making the state dependent on them in maintaining societal control*. This had one immediate repercussion for state power in India. The state in India was *unable to become the vehicle/inheritor* of the values and aspirations of the national movement (ibid., emphasis mine).

The second space operates within the component unit (that is, the state of Manipur) of the Indian union. Though purportedly democratic, it failed to address and accommodate the legitimate democratic aspirations of the hill people for substantial devolution of powers to their hitherto extant local institutions. As a corollary it spawned autonomy movements directed against the component unit. In effect, protagonists of these movements considered them as minimum and necessary, and yet insufficient in maintaining the distinct and separate administrative dispensation in place since 1835.[12] Consequently, the

---

arrangement for the tribals under the Sixth Schedule of the Indian Constitution. See Suan (2002: 71); Rao (1967: 684–5).

[12] From 1835, when a Political Agency was set up by the British to govern the princely state, the hill tribes were placed under different British officers and political agents. The British sustained this separate politico-administrative treatment till 1947 when they left India. Thereafter, the July 1947 Manipur State Constitution, which envisaged the Manipur State (Hill Administration) Regulations, 1947; the Manipur (Village Authorities in Hill Areas) Act, 1956;

space gets transformed into a site of contestation wherein *civilizational uniformity* and shared *cultural unity*[13] become at once the point of reference and departure. I will discuss this in the section 'Emerging Dialogic Space'. Perched on this point of reference, the Indian state and for that matter the state of Manipur tend to locate this fissure within the political economy—like uneven economic growth and regional imbalances. Hence they consider them to be the product of an antecedent administrative anomaly which can be rectified using the structural–functional approach.

Given the interspersed nature in which these two levels play themselves out this essay is structured in a way which would help in engaging the problems in their own right. The next section contextualizes the enigma of ethnoscape[14] by exploring sites of narrative conflicts. This is done by positing autonomy as a political resource which engenders parallel totalizing projects in the hills and the valley of Manipur. 'Emerging Dialogic Space' deals with the emerging contours of dialogic space facilitated by *transvaluation*[15] which could transform violent-prone situations by perching the space upon a pluralistic understanding of societies. Next, I analyse the intersection of the two levels by invoking an institutional pendulum and democracy deficit as two striking variables which underpin the hills–valley divide and its implications for stateness–democracy continuum in the hill areas of Manipur. The final section contains a few concluding remarks.

and the Manipur Hill Areas District Council Act, 1971, *inter alia,* continued this tradition. See Neihsial (1996: 5) and Bose (1979). Also see Suan (2002).

[13] Javeed Alam contends that India's *civilizational uniformity* and *cultural unity* predate colonialism and help in easing undue reliance upon a coercive-centralized state in carving out the unity and integrity of the nation. He considers *co-governance*—of sharing of powers between national parties (representing the nation-state) and regional parties (representing subnational identities)—as the key to strengthen this. See Alam (2002).

[14] Following Sanjib Baruah who borrowed the term 'ethnoscape' from Arjun Appadurai to imply that ethnic identities in Northeast India are not objectively given but are 'deeply perspectival construct', I will employ it in the same sense. For details see Baruah (2005a: 7–8) and Appadurai (1990).

[15] I will use the term 'transvaluation' in the same sense as Northrop Frye who used it to imply 'looking back on oneself with a glance informed by contact with others'. See Northrop Frye cited in Karmis and Maclure (2001); cf. Todorov (1995: 79).

AUTONOMY AND TOTALIZING PROJECTS AT ODDS: SITES OF NARRATIVE CONFLICT

Manipur is home to thirty-three recognized Scheduled Tribes (STs), which broadly belong to the ethnic Naga and Zo (Chin/Kuki/Lusei) groups (Gangte 2005: 2). According to the 2001 Census, the Meiteis, constituting the majority group and inhabiting 10.02 per cent of the total geographical area of the state, account for about 65.8 per cent of the total population of the state. Conversely, the Naga and Zo people combined occupy 89.98 per cent of the total geographical area and account for 34.2 per cent of the total population of the state.[16] They are represented by twenty (out of sixty) and one (out of three) elected members in the state legislative assembly and the Indian parliament, respectively.[17] Most strikingly, the Meiteis are concentrated in the four plains districts, namely, Bishnupur, Imphal East, Imphal West, and Thoubal and are surrounded by the Naga and the Zo people who are scattered in the remaining five hill districts. It is a classic case where ethnocultural boundaries broadly coincide with territorial space.

It is little wonder then that the demands of the Naga and the Zo peoples for carving out separate autonomous homelands for themselves have posited uneasy questions and challenges to the Meiteis' totalizing project. The problem is aggravated not only by the parallel ethnoscape engendered by such demands but more importantly by the fact that the term 'autonomy' itself is couched in the quagmire of international legal complexities. It would be helpful to understand how the concept of autonomy evolves over time before we delve into the discursive practice of totalizing projects undertaken by the different ethnic communities in Manipur and address the attendant politics of territoriality integral to this debate.

Charles Taylor, intervening in this debate, convincingly shows how the politics of recognition (read here as autonomy) and the contingent positions of the 'self' and the 'other' undergo transformation. This, he contends, takes place at two levels: (*i*) at the intimate (or personal/private) sphere, and (*ii*) at the public sphere (Taylor 1994). He argues that the question of recognition becomes more pronounced and problematic in the public sphere as it is always conducted in a dialogical

---

[16] GoI (2004). It excludes Mao-Maram, Paomata, and Purul sub-divisions of Senapati district. Available at: http://www.censusindia.net/t_00_005.html; accessed on 12 May 2006 (released in April 2004).

[17] See http://manipurassembly.gov.in/memlistcon.htm; accessed on 12 May 2006.

relationship with the 'significant others'. In other words, this being conducted in the dominant majoritarian language (with its thrust on monistic authenticity[18]) it is ill-prepared to give 'meaningful contexts' of choice for other peripheral/marginal communities to enable them to participate in the public sphere.[19] This is crucial as the failure or unwillingness to give recognition to each other can inflict or cause harm to the image of the 'self' which can have widespread ramifications for the 'significant others' as well. It is precisely here that the Westminster model of majoritarian rule founders if it doesn't envisage an expansive framework of power sharing (Bogdanor 1997). I will discuss this in the section titled 'Institutional Pendulum and Democracy Deficit'.

Stretching out Charles Taylor's theoretical premise to a broader empirical frame, it may be pointed out here that the ongoing autonomy demands of indigenous peoples (around the world under the banner of the United Nations Working Group on Indigenous Populations [UNWGIP] to which the Nagas and the Zo people are partner members) have reached a crucial point where the right to self-determination would not be limited to the passive right to land, culture, and identity. A case has now been made to encompass the active participation of the indigenous peoples in the protection and management of their resources and endowment which would help maintain, preserve, and protect their distinct and separate culture and identity.[20] This however has come about after crossing innumerable international legal hurdles.

To be sure, much of the problematic of the debate on autonomy stems from the fact that autonomy as a right is often conflated with the right to self-determination accruable to people of colonized and non-independent states but untenable for, and being denied to, 'people' within 'independent state (s)' (Hannum 1992). The Treaty of Versailles, 1919, in its attempt to explicate the meaning rather confounded the problem by positing that autonomy engenders self-government, not self-determination (Gilbert 2002). The intricate mess of complexity that this concept is premised upon is further compounded by the

[18] Dimitrios Karmis and Jocelyn Maclure argued that modern nation building (read here as totalizing project) smacks of the imperial thrusts on a hegemonic, universal, and 'monistic authenticity' which privileges the state and its majoritarian instrumentalities. See Karmis and Maclure (2001).

[19] See Kymlicka (2001) and his other works, inter alia: Kymlicka (1992, 1995); Kymlicka and Norman (2000).

[20] See http://www.ohchr.org/english/issues/indigenous/decade.htm.

United Nations Charter (1945) which considers 'self-determination' in contrast to 'sovereignty' simply as one of the *desiderata* of the Charter and never considered it as its operational principle. Hence, it was never accorded the status of a legal right. Later international treaties and agreements persevere with the prevailing predilection to accord formal and explicit recognition—as the Helsinki Final Act of 1975 which recognized 'internal self-determination'(ibid.: 336) and the Organisation for Security and Cooperation in Europe's (OSCE) *Copenhagen Document* (29 June 1990), inter alia, convincingly showed. The latter slightly amplifies the concept by affirming: 'Participating states will respect...national minorities' right to effective participation in public affairs including the protection and promotion of the identity of such minorities' (ibid.: 320).

With the dawn of the 1980s, however, this debate entered into an altogether critical trajectory in which hitherto suppressed indigenous peoples' voices began to be taken seriously and heard at various international fora. This may be attributed to the incremental yet crucial role played by the UNWIGP set up in 1985 as a separate Agency of the Sub Commission on the Promotion and Protection of Human Rights under the UN Human Rights Commission (UNHCR), which again came under the overall supervision of the Economic and Social Council of the United Nations.[21] One positive outcome of this is the adoption of the UN Draft Declaration on the Rights of Indigenous Peoples on 16 August 1994. Article 3 of the Draft unequivocally states: 'Indigenous peoples have the right to self-determination. By virtue of that right they freely determine their political status and freely pursue their economic, social and cultural development.'[22]

To be precise, it has now been accepted that there are at least two instruments of autonomy rights guaranteed by international law. These are: (*i*) the right to self-determination, and (*ii*) the right of members of ethnic, linguistic, and religious groups to enjoy their own culture (Gilbert 2002: 340). The implications of self-determination vis-à-vis autonomy, however, are still befuddled by the intricate maze of international legal complexities.

This explains why demands for autonomy which often take the shape of what Charles Taylor calls 'authenticity' movements have been variedly

---

[21] For details, see http://www.undp.org/cso/ip.html.

[22] See http://www.unhchr.ch/huridocda/huridoca.nsf/(Symbol)/E.CN.4. SUB.2.RES.1994.45.En?OpenDocument.

interpreted. Participating in the debate, Eric Nordlinger, one of the first American political scientists to take an interest in ethnic conflict regulation, rejected the use of federalism (of sharing of power) as an instrument for accommodating minorities as he feared it would lead to the break up of the state and to the abuse of power by ethnocentric minorities.[23] Another leading American specialist on nationalism argues that giving federal autonomy to minorities promotes divisive identities and implies that (at least some of) these identities would not exist in the absence of such autonomy.[24] At the heart of this debate lies the assumption that minority nationalism is what Seymour Martin Lipset calls 'backward and ethno-centric' which is nothing but a 'revolt against modernity';[25] hence a passé and a transient phenomenon which can be resolved by affirmative action. I will show in the Section 'Institutional Pendulum and Democracy Deficit' how, at least in the hill areas of Manipur, this fails to address the particularities of their demands.

Recent studies on federalism and conflict resolution by John McGarry (2002) and Nancy Burmeo (2002),[26] among others, however, have convincingly shown that it is not autonomy concessions per se which cause conflicts and breakdown of nation-states but rather the failure/unwillingness to grant autonomy which lies at the heart of the breakdown of (or perceived threat to) the nation-state. These findings seem to hold true in the present study as the section 'Institutional Pendulum and Democracy Deficit' will show.

At this juncture, it must be qualified that the underpinnings of such totalizing projects undertaken by the three major ethnic groups in Manipur, namely, Meiteis, Nagas, and Zo people as counter-positions to the Indian state are embedded in the 'thesis of separateness' espoused by two British officials in the first quarter of the twentieth century: John H. Hutton, the then deputy commissioner of the Naga Hills District and N.E. Parry, the former deputy commissioner of the Garo Hills. Later, Sir Robert Neil Reid, drawing from this thesis of separateness—racial, historical, cultural, and linguistic—suggested to the Government of India (GoI) the separation of the Northeast tribal hill areas 'perhaps under some appropriate department at Whitehall' in his confidential

[23] Eric Nordlinger cited in John McGarry (2002: 429); cf. Nordlinger (1972: 31–2). I have discussed this elsewhere, see Suan (2006).

[24] Rogers Brubaker cited in McGarry (2002: 429); cf. Brubaker (1996).

[25] Seymour Martin Lipset cited in McGarry (2002: 431).

[26] Also see Hale (2004) and Cornell (2002). For related studies on Northeast India, see Bhattacharjee (1996); Prasad (1994); Samaddar (2005); Singh (2002).

twenty-two page pamphlet: *A Note on the Future of Present Excluded, Partially Excluded and Tribal Areas of Assam* (Syiemlieh 1996: 24). It is not surprising, therefore, that when India's independence drew near and serious debate on the future of these areas began to take shape, the thesis got incorporated into various memoranda and representations of Naga and Zo people (Mizo/Zomi) to the colonial and postcolonial Indian government, forming the basis of their totalizing projects till today.[27]

As mentioned before, for the Nagas the issue of 'unique history and political situation' untrammelled by colonial political vicissitudes is inseparably linked with their totalizing project. The Nagas have buttressed this ever since they submitted a memorandum to the Indian Statutory Commission way back in 1929 (Longkumar 1996; Shimray 2004). They repeated their case in the Nine Point Agreement, infamously called the Akbar Hydari Agreement, 1947, and thereafter forcefully in the sixteen Point Agreement, 1960, which laid down the foundation of the present state of Nagaland. However, the demand for the 'integration of Naga territory', an integral part of the latter agreement, was not fructified as far as the Naga inhabited areas of Manipur are concerned (Fernandes 2005: 7; Horam 1975; Prabhakara 2005: 10). The Zo people have also painstakingly put forward their totalizing project since 1947 when they (under the banner of the Mizo Union) submitted a memorandum which, inter alia, demanded 'territorial integrity and solidarity and self-determination'. Their totalization project is an attempt to retrieve the spirit which informed the Chin-Lushai Conference of St Fort William 1896 (in Calcutta). Convened by the British, the conference is credited as the first serious attempt of the Zo people to find ways to bring about administrative and political unification to territories occupied by them and which are by now apportioned between the independent states of Bangladesh, India, and Myanmar (Go 1996; Khai 1995; Vumson n.d.). The common seam which weaves together these two totalizing projects is that they are steeped in a relatively modern historical exigency wherein they had been, via colonial politico-administrative fiat, dismembered into disparate and distant borderlands. The 'unity and integrity' of such peoples are therefore central to and lie at the very heart of these projects.

[27] See details of various memoranda posted by the Zo people on http://www.zogam.org.

At the other end, the Meiteis' totalizing project draws largely from the state royal chronicle and other official historiographical attempts to reinforce a larger image of Meitei nationhood which had, for a considerable period of time, a clearly marked territorial space spanning over areas occupied by the hill people. More importantly, it has been argued that the state has been successful in subsuming disparate identities within such a construct. The image of the 'hill people' as a distinct and separate category of discourse vis-à-vis the construct of pan-Meitei identity crept in via an historical accident. To strengthen the veracity of such a claim, this historical accident was traced to the eighteenth century, when Vaishnavite Hinduism began to have sweeping influences upon the Meiteis under the patronage of the kings of Manipur (Baruah 2003; Chaube 1999; Nag 2002; Oinam 2005; Ray 1999). Religion as a distinct social identity marker and as a narrative of constructing the 'self' and the 'other' assumed greater saliency towards the close of the nineteenth century when the hill areas came under the influence of Christian missionaries mostly belonging to the American Baptists and the Welsh Presbyterians (Go 1996; Dena 1988).

The nascent ethnoscape is now readily politicized with the patronage of the colonial British administrators who, it was contended, deliberately imposed this 'separate' construct in a phased manner since the Treaty of Yandaboo, 1826. Consequently, the administration of the hill areas was formally separated from the administration of the plains by the British (Srivastava 1997). However, this nagging politico-legal question was considered to have been resolved even prior to India's independence by incorporating a representative institution in the form of the Manipur State (Hill Administration) Regulation, 1947, via the Manipur State Constitution Act, 1947. The latter was alleged to have the consent and endorsement of prominent persons from the hill areas including T.C. Tiankham and Athiko Daiho.[28] It is pertinent to note here that they (the hills representatives) tried to incorporate a rider to the act which specifically made clear 'the right of any section of the hill people to secede at the end of the five year period, should the conditions within the Constitution not be satisfactory'.[29] F.F. Pearson, the chairman of

[28] See Singh (1991), especially chapter 28, pp. 413–22. Also see U.A. Shimray, 'Naga Integration Movement: A Historical Perspective', available at http://kanglaonline.com/index.php?template=kshow&kid=585&Idoc_Session=ed4710 a3eedcffa2170f008c68645eab, accessed on 9 December 2005.

[29] Ibid.

the Constitution Making Committee, drew the personal attention of the Manipuri Maharaja to the dissension of the hill people. However, the latter failed to take this into account by making it applicable to the hill areas of Manipur, albeit with a provision that 'it shall not apply in any matter where a specific reservation of powers is made to any Authority in the hills under the provisions of the Manipur State (Hill Administration) Regulation, 1947'.[30]

In post-Independence India, the legacy of this act was carried forward in providing six Autonomous District Councils (ADCs) for the hill areas—under the Manipur (Hill Areas) Act, 1971—since 1973 when the first elections were held. Subsequent working of the constitutional provisions impressed upon the hill people that it might engender nothing but what Vernon Bogdanor aptly calls 'reconcentration at the centre' (Bogdanor 1997; Suan 2003) as it provided an administrative mechanism without contingent legislative and judicial powers. Elections to the ADCs have been held in abeyance owing to the boycott launched by the Sixth Schedule Demand Committee, Manipur, since 1984 on these very grounds.

It is this historical baggage, these dissenting voices that echo in the wilderness of the hills and the valley of Manipur. They now seem to have indelible bearings on all developmental or non-developmental trajectories of the state encompassing socio-economic, cultural, and political spheres.

EMERGING DIALOGIC SPACE

Of late, these echoes of totalizing projects have become more vocal and are increasingly at sharp variance from one another, leading to a series of contestations and debate. Through the din of this debate emerge possible contours of transvaluation which would determine prospective dialogic space. It is also increasingly realized that if the dialogic space is to be sustained, the narrative of the dialogue has to transcend the language of rights to encompass the language of 'minimal justice' (Samaddar 2005: 9–31). I will come to this point later.

To be sure, the present predicament may be traced back to August 1997 when the Government of India started enforcing a ceasefire agreement with the National Socialist Council of Nagalim–Isaac Chisi Swu and Thuingaleng Muivah (hereafter simply as NSCN–IM). The crucial point however came on 18 June 2001 when the former sought

---

[30] Ibid.

to extend the agreement 'without territorial limits'. The overture of the GoI was considered likely to disturb the 'territorial integrity' of, and entail profound political implications for, the states of Manipur, Assam, and Arunachal Pradesh where the Nagas are scattered. As a result, the agreement was received with hostility by the state governments on the one hand, and by several civil society organizations of the state of Manipur in particular on the other.

The first set of institutional responses engendered by this is the passage of a series of resolutions to uphold, protect, and defend the integrity of the state(s) concerned at any cost. The gravity of the situation can be gauged from the fact that the Manipur Legislative Assembly, for instance, within a limited span of five years (1997–2002)[31] passed five resolutions which unflinchingly 'resolved unanimously to protect the Territorial Integrity of Manipur that existed at the time of merger of the State of Manipur with the Union of India, while urging upon the Union of India to take all necessary actions for protecting the Territorial Integrity of Manipur'.[32] It further:

resolves to urge upon the Government of India to make suitable amendments of Article 3 of the Constitution of India or to insert appropriate provisions in the constitution of India for protecting the Territorial Integrity of the State of Manipur and pending the aforesaid amendments and incorporation, the Government of India be urged upon to assure the People of Manipur on the floor of the Parliament that the Territorial Integrity of Manipur will not be disturbed at any cost.[33]

One interesting aspect of this institutional response is that it reinforces the need to introspect and rethink the edifice of its (the state of Manipur/Meiteis) totalizing project which seems to have failed to incorporate the hill people into its fold. The Manipur Culture Policy 2002 (hereafter MCP 2002) must be considered as a response to this

[31] These resolutions are apart from the one passed earlier on 24 March 1995. Internet editions are available at http://manipurassembly.nic.in/rm240395a.htm. The other resolutions can respectively be accessed at: http://manipurassembly.nic.in/rm170798.htm for 17 July 1998, http://manipurassembly.nic.in/rm171298.htm for 17 December 1998, http://manipurassembly.nic.in/rm220301.htm for 22 March 2002.

[32] The Manipur Legislative Assembly resolution dated 12 June 2002 is available at its official website: http://manipurassembly.nic.in/r120602.htm.

[33] Ibid.

need.[34] Widely circulated in the mainstream newspapers of the state, MCP 2002 attempts what it calls, 'an arm's length intervention' into the cultural realm of the state. It clearly reflects the present mood of anxiety and insecurity of the majority Meitei community and affirms its commitment which is explicitly mentioned in Part II of the draft under the title 'Objective', inter alia, as: 'The preservation and promotion of our culture should be made in such a manner and spirit that the *unity and integrity of the state of the country*, the ethos of secularism, socialism, democracy, social justice and peaceful co-existence are maintained and strengthened.'[35]

The feasibility of a common cultural policy is suspect in the first place as it will amount to homogenizing the diverse and sharply divided heterogeneous ethnic communities. It is appreciable, however, to note the pain taken by MCP 2002 in reiterating its holistic approach and avowed commitment to preserving the multicultural and plural ethos of diverse communities of the state. Despite its good intentions, the act unwittingly gets bogged down to the majoritarian language in delineating the possible contours on which the future totalization project of the state (of Meitei nation-state) could be best realized. This would be evident after careful and critical appraisal of the language of the draft. However, it enlivens and extends the debate on this totalizing project and opens avenues for other voices to be heard.

The second set of responses comes from civil societies of the state of Manipur. It is best encapsulated in a booklet, *Ceasefire or Setting the North East on Fire? Peace in Jeopardy*, distributed by the People's Solidarity for Peace and Democracy (PSPD). The PSPD booklet lambasted the ceasefire agreement as 'an historical' appropriation which is 'ignorant or dismissive' of 'peoples' historical moorings' (PSPD 2004: 1). It adumbrated upon 'shared legacies of the people in the hills and valleys'. To quote:

The affinity between the people in the hills and valley of Manipur runs much deeper than these historical and political facts. Racially, linguistically and culturally, the people in the hills and valley of Manipur can never be called 'two different peoples'. Folklores and myths talk about the common origin, and shared mythical and ritual spaces between the people in the hills and valley of

---

[34] Manipur Culture Policy posted by the director, Art and Culture, Government of Manipur at Imphal Free Press, Imphal (20 December 2002), p. 3.

[35] Ibid. The emphasis is mine.

Manipur. For example, Meetei/Meitei rituals and myths during the Laiharaoba festivals, Mera Haochongba, marriage ceremony, and for that matter, the coronation ceremony of the king of Manipur (during the monarchy) attest to their affinity with the people in the hills. To deny these deeper linkages, over and above the shared historical and political heritage, can only be either due to ignorance or a malicious intention or both (ibid.: 14).

Furthermore, the PSPD booklet painstakingly tried to substantiate the 'shared legacies' by pointing out how the hill people have been given a fair measure of opportunity in the democratic governance of the state.[36] A critical analysis of the text shows how hard it tries to retrospectively appropriate a genre of colonial writings in the nineteenth century to back up its case for *civilizational uniformity* and *cultural unity*[37] which permeates both the valley and hills of Manipur.[38] Implicit in the core idea of the PSPD booklet is the assumption of *monistic authenticity*; of how successful the Meiteis have been in accommodating and subsuming disparate tribal identities within their fold. While appreciating the veracity of claims posited by retrospective appropriation of history in support of Meiteis' *civilizational uniformity and cultural unity*, problems inherent in such claims cannot be overlooked.

While the historical veracity of this claim is beyond conjectural

---

[36] The PSPD booklet shows how the hill peoples were accommodated in the *co-governance* of the state by making them members of the state's Constitution Drafting Committee (1947) and Council of Ministers (1948) even prior to the merger of the state of Manipur with India in October 1949. It also tries to show the accommodative nature of the state by pointing out how, till date, two tribals have become chief ministers of the state, that too with one holding the longest term in office. See PSPD (2004: 15, 18, 20).

[37] Grierson (1904) is a classic thesis on the linguistic and cultural unity of the hills and valley communities of Manipur whom Grierson calls 'The Kuki-Chin and Burma Group'. Interestingly, Grierson included the Meiteis within the former group. Historical contingency and differing 'perspectival constructs', however, both within the hills and the valley, increasingly tend to disown this thesis.

[38] This type of genre is exemplified in the writing of James Johnstone, a colonial officer, who alluded to this dimension when he mentioned that, 'the investiture ceremony of the Manipuri Kings required the queen to appear in Naga costume; the royal palace always had a house built in Naga style; and when the King traveled he was attended on by two or three Manipuris with Naga arms, dress and ornaments'. See James Johnstone, quoted in Baruah (2005a: 79), cf. Johnstone (1971: 83). The original title of Johnstone's book was *My Experiences in Manipur and the Naga Hills*.

doubt, as convincingly shown in G.A. Grierson's *Linguistic Survey* (1904), the problem may be considered both in terms of the *symbolic* and *discursive* significance or non-significance of a custom of the Meitei kings during specific epochs. If, for example, the royal wearing of a costume (during coronation) and arms (during itinerary) is considered to be of symbolic significance to accommodate and represent diverse cultural practices of the purported subjects, it must also be admitted that it provides inadequate ground to legitimize the rightful claim of the Meiteis that their kingdom and 'civilization' encompassed the hill tribal people—the Naga and the Zo. Careful reading of the Naga and Zo historiographies convincingly show that they were largely 'self-contained' people ruled by disparate chiefs in several 'village republics' in the mould of ancient Greek city states. In fact, the hill tribal people whom the Meiteis referred to as *hao*—now a pejorative term implying 'menial/subjugated'[39]—never lacked strong and stable political organization and illustrious rulers/chiefs. This is corroborated by, inter alia, one of the triumphal songs that the Sukte (a Zo clan) chief, Za Pau, composed in the middle of the nineteenth century:

Siahtaang kaihna Teimei dong e,
Ka hialna Lamtui hi;
Sakciang Teimei Khang ciang Lamtui,
A lai-ah Kamkei hing e.[40]

[Free translation]

What I rule extends to Manipur in the north,
And ends at Falam in the south;
Manipur to the north and Falam to the south,
I am the tiger in the middle.

Discursive practices of the Naga and Zo people, drawing largely from such symbolic superstructure audaciously confront the oft-repeated narrative of the Meitei totalizing project which employs the solitary image of the 'other' hill tribes as haos—largely consisting of disparate warring tribes—who are incapable of putting up a stable

[39] For a helpful discussion on the evolution of 'hao' as a stigmatizing discursive practice see K.I. Singh (1998: 110–20). Also see Yonuo (1974: 44–5).

[40] Khai (1995: 26). Za Pau was the youngest son of the illustrious Sukte chief, Khan Thuam. Khan Thuam brought peace and solidarity to hitherto nine warring Zo chiefs under his chiefship, which made the task of governance easier for his succeeding generations.

political organization meriting a nation-state. The projection of an image of this kind fails to recognize the innumerable 'equal' ways in which inter-cultural and inter-political exchanges took place.[41] It may be asserted here that 'identity creates itself homogeneously by inventing a heterogeneous outside' (Karmis and Maclure 2001: 364). For transvaluation to take ground, however, it is imperative to accept that 'a community is a site of deliberation and articulation, not of subsumption' (ibid.: 367). In a way this would imply the realization, to quote Karmis and Maclure, that:

...communities do not hold together because of their foundation in a set of shared values about the good or the right, but rather because they constitute agonic sites of narration, disclosure, deliberation and often disagreement. In other words, cultural communities are dissensual 'communities of conversation' (ibid.).

Given that the ongoing Naga 'integration' movement springs from a dialogic space not only *outside of*, but also *despite*, the domain of *civilizational uniformity and cultural unity*, it necessitates flexibility to emerging contours of transvaluation. Possible contours of this kind need not essentially be perched solely on an ossified understanding of 'historic rights' which by now are deadly 'confrontational'—with its concomitant position of 'self-contained' ethnic communities. There is an urgent imperative to cultivate a sense of 'minimal justice' so that ethnic communities in Manipur may get their due 'recognition' and have 'meaningful contexts' of/for choice.

Minimally put, this implies that the state government must immediately fulfil the autonomy demands of the hill tribal people and upgrade the existing ADCs to those of their counterparts in the Sixth Schedule. This is considered to be the minimum prerequisite for maintaining their identity and restoring their 'self-respect' (ATSUM 2005). Innovative ways of incorporating traditional local tribal institutions must be evolved towards this end. Second, the state government must fructify section 4(2)(a) of the Manipur Reservation of Vacancies in Posts and Services (For Scheduled Castes & Scheduled Tribes) Act, 1976, which clearly states that the percentages so calculated for reservation would 'in no case be less than the percentage of the persons belonging' to the said categories 'as recorded in 1971 Census'

---

[41] For an illuminating discussion on the danger of violence engendered by a solitarist approach of putting 'civilization into different boxes', see Sen (2006).

(GoM 1977). Notwithstanding the fact that Scheduled Tribes (STs) constituted 31 per cent of the population of the state according to the 1971 Census, it is despairing to note the dismal implementation of the Act as a memorandum submitted to the National Commission for Scheduled Castes and Scheduled Tribes, New Delhi in April 2006 showed.[42]

The memorandum, drawing from 1994 statistics, showed that in fourteen departments of the state under scanner, only 404 STs out of the total 2,927 were appointed in gazetted posts. This accounted for a measly 13.8 per cent which was 17.2 per cent short of the quota allocated by the act according to 1971 census. It is further appalling to note that ST representation in the Veterinary and Animal Husbandry Department was just 4.7 per cent followed closely by the Irrigation and Flood Control Department (IFCD) with 7.5 per cent, Education Department (8 per cent), and Power Department (10 per cent). Surprisingly, representation of STs was the highest in Industries (26 per cent), which still, however, was 5 per cent below the stipulated quota. It further pointed out that out of the 80,000-odd employees of the state government of Manipur in 1994, members of STs accounted for 13,900 (17.4 per cent), which again was 13.6 per cent short of the allocated quotas. The figure would be worse if we factored in 1991 census data wherein the proportion of STs to the total population of the state was 34.4 per cent.

The third way to foster 'minimal justice' is to facilitate adequate representations of the hill people in diverse sports and cultural disciplines, which in turn demands the laying out of essential infrastructure. In the fifth National Games held in the state in 1999 (22 February–6 March), for instance, not a single stadium was constructed nor a sporting event (including outdoor events) held in the hill areas. The hill people also took umbrage at the way in which the marathon race was conducted. The race rallied from the state capital, Imphal, and made a U-turn at Kangvai, the point where the hill district of Churachandpur starts. This was interpreted by a prominent educationist based in the hills as typical Meitei psyche to indicate 'as if Manipur is Imphal and valley environs only', which he considers is one 'among other inconsistencies that make

---

[42] Scheduled Tribes Welfare Association of Manipur, *Memorandum to National Commission for Scheduled Castes & Scheduled Tribes, New Delhi* (Churachandpur, 25 April 2006).

one doubt the Meitei claims of great antiquity, civilisation ... as well as closeness to the tribal "brethren"!'.[43] The 'arm's length intervention' that the Manipur Culture Policy envisaged needs to seriously think of ways to avoid such omissions. Concerted and serious efforts must be made to incorporate the folklore, dances, and legends of the hill people in the state's education curricula and policies. Moreover, state cultural troupes, deputed by the state government to perform both at the national and international levels, must also showcase the diverse cultures of the hill people. This is imperative as the 'unity and integrity' of the state can be sustained only through building a pluralistic ethos which permeates both state institutions and ethnonationalist aspirations.

INSTITUTIONAL PENDULUM AND DEMOCRACY DEFICIT

The burden of this lies on the state and the institutional paraphernalia it entails. At the outset, the state is not able to sustain, as it were, its transformative and liberating role by giving in to the compulsions of *societal control*. The reliance of the state on a centralized bureaucracy and the armed police, military, and accompanying coercive machineries of law has long shaken the faith of the people on the viability of state security, and its schemata of 'law and order'.[44] It is precisely here, in the *purportedly democratic space*, that ethnonationalist manoeuvres in Manipur and India's Northeast have to be located.

Not surprisingly, the anxieties and insecurities apparent in the face of all ethnic communities in the state of Manipur are accentuated in a situation of state failure. The concomitant aura of 'security dilemma', wherein no security guarantees (of law and order) from the state ensue, aggravates this. Apparently, the near anarchic situation and a situation of state breakdown, if not collapse, can be best explained by the multiplicities of armed militias propped up by almost every conceivable ethnic community. The South Asia Terrorism Portal, run by the Institute of Conflict Management, New Delhi, in its weekly assessments and briefings titled 'South Asia Intelligence Review', in 2006, ranked Manipur as the state with the highest concentration of armed militias numbering 39, followed closely by Assam (36), Tripura

[43] See Vunglallian (2006).

[44] Rajni Kothari has convincingly analysed how the state began to lose its transformative and liberating role. See Kothari (2005). Also see Jayal (2001). For a radical interpretation, see Jessop (2001).

(30), Meghalaya (4), Nagaland (3), Mizoram (2), and Arunachal Pradesh (1).[45]

The proliferation of armed militias and the political economy in which they thrive have disturbing implications for sustaining democratic institutions and contingent efficacy of 'law and order' especially in a state like Manipur, notorious for its stifling institutional pendulum and democracy deficit. Plainly speaking, this implies parallel and shadow governments, which run more often than not at gunpoint. Sanjoy Hazarika, in a recent article, convincingly shows the nefarious ways in which such militias coerced 'without fuss or tumult, government employees, from the junior to the senior levels (to) pay not less than 24% annual "tax" (calculated at two percent per month)'.[46] Given the fact that payment of tax in most parts of the world is seen as recognition of the government's authority, contended Hazarika, 'it could be viewed as a measure of the state government's abdication of responsibility as well as the power of the insurgent groups' (Hazarika 2004). He further adumbrated upon what he calls 'a classic copout' wherein the chief minister of Nagaland even defended the insurgents with this refrain: 'The people pay them with trust. When the people want to pay, how can the state government stop them?' (ibid.)

This psychology of state amnesia in dealing with the problem of 'militancy'/'insurgency' can have disastrous consequences. Between 1 January 1992 and 15 October 2006, for example, 4,185 people lost their lives in insurgency-related killings in Manipur.[47] Strikingly, and as is always the case, the civilians bore the brunt of such killings, accounting for 41.8 per cent (1,751) followed by the 'terrorists' who shared 37.6 per cent (1,571) and the security force personnel contributing 20.6 per cent (863). These are rough figures and the actual numbers could be much higher.

It is pertinent here to examine the long-term effect of 'counter-insurgency' operations undertaken by the armed forces to supplement the role of the state civil police force on democratic governance. For one thing, it is interesting to note that India's northeastern states

[45] For details, see assessments made by the Institute of Conflict Management, New Delhi, from time to time at http://www.satp.org/satporgtp/countries/india/terroristoutfits/index.html, accessed on 22 May 2006.

[46] See Hazarika (2004: 773).

[47] See online edition available at http://www.satp.org/satporgtp/countries/india/states/manipur/data_sheets/insurgency_related_killings.htm; last accessed on 16 October 2006.

have an overwhelming deployment of police (per million population) as Table 12.1 clearly shows. It is strange, however, to note that this does not positively translate into the easing of insurgency or help in maintaining 'law and order' in this part of the country. The record of these states, especially Manipur, in the dispensation of criminal justice is nerve-racking as it disposes a minuscule 0.6 per cent of cases (see Table 12.1).

TABLE 12.1: Deployment of Police and Disposal of Criminal Cases by Courts, 1998

	Number of police person (per million population), 1998	Disposal of IPC criminal case by court (per cent), 1998
Arunachal Pradesh	4,540	19.3
Assam	2,000	19.0
Manipur	5,930	0.6
Meghalaya	3,720	8.7
Mizoram	7,520	12.4
Nagaland	9,500	7.1
Tripura	3,410	39.9
Sikkim	6,230	49.7
Jammu and Kashmir	4,380	16.2
Punjab	2,940	22.5
All India	1,360	19.0

Source: GoI (2002a: 279)

The inability of the state to restore 'law and order' is justified in the use of such draconian laws as the Armed Forces (Special Powers) Act, 1958, in these states which opens avenues for 'disguised wars'—to borrow from A. Bimol Akoijam and Th. Tarunkumar.[48] Given the fact that such armed interventions, carried out in the guise of 'counter-insurgency operations', derived their success from the number of 'insurgents/terrorists' killed (which of course is recently recast in terms of the number of insurgents/terrorist surrender), they carry the inherent danger of transforming citizens into 'enemies' of the state (Navlakha 2005). It is not uncommon in such a 'militarized zone' for supposedly clear-headed administrative officers to resort to armed

[48] Akoijam and Tarunkumar (2005). For a related discussion see Suan (2005: 7) and Haokip (2001).

violence, including shooting, which involves serious human rights violations.[49]

One of the fundamental problems engendered by the increasing militarization of the state is deinstitutionalization. This is further accentuated by the absence of legitimate local democracy, at least in the hill areas, which in turn generates an unseemly pendulum of such institutions paving the way for collusion with certain vested interests. For instance, in the aftermath of an Army operation called 'Operation All Clear' carried out on 19 April 2004 at Sajik Tampak, a remote and difficult terrain in the Chandel District of Manipur, to flush out about 3,000 odd members of the Manipur People's Liberation Front (MPLF),[50] innovative counter-state armed incursions were started (Hussain 2005). Now landmines have entrapped most of the remote areas of Churachandpur District of Manipur. A recent Zomi Human Rights Foundation (ZHRF), Delhi Cell, release counted the number of landmines casualties at thirteen.[51]

The physical toll apart, these episodes, allegedly unleashed by underground militants from the plains (read here as Meitei underground elements), ushered a veritable 'reign of terror' which forced the villagers out of their lands leaving them open to easy incursions and takeover by the former. In a way these 'militants' become the veritable de facto *owners* of a major chunk of the district, converting the locals into pliant de jure owners. This is a subversion of democracy. The failure of the state to prevent this is a manifestation of the deinstitutionalization and erosion of the Manipur Land Revenue and Land Reforms Act, 1960, which gives exclusive right of ownership to the hill people and purportedly kept the hill areas out of the purview of state legislation pertaining to land (GoM 1960).

A case has now been made that this insidious 'population transfer' of Meitei militias to the hill areas with alleged state connivance amounts to the perversion and subversion of the cherished hill peoples' right

---

[49] The 19 August 2005 case, wherein Ibocha Singh, the deputy commissioner of Churachandpur, Manipur, resorted to indiscriminate shooting on unarmed Zomi Students Federation agitators is a case in point. See Ngaihte (2005).

[50] MPLF is a conglomerate of three Meitei underground elements, namely, the United National Liberation Front (UNLF), the People's Liberation Army (PLA), and the People's Revolutionary Party of Kangleipak (PREPAK).

[51] *ZHRF Newsletter*, 1(1), 2005, p. 3.

to their land, culture, and identity.[52] On 12 December 2005 several tribal chiefs in three subdivisions of Churachandpur district, namely, Churachandpur, Henglep, and Thanlon made a representation to the chief minister of Mizoram to extend the presence of security forces and maintain 'law and order'.[53] Their frantic plea stems from the futility of persistent pleas made to the GoM to restore 'law and order' and rule over the militias flooding their lands. It is striking that since July 1998 all the subdivisional administrative offices of Churachandpur district have been concentrated at the district headquarters. They are yet to be restored to their respective subdivisional headquarters pending the construction of 'good roads' for communication. The absence of a rudimentary state administrative mechanism gives leeway to indeterminate players/stakeholders to apportion powers under duress. The unsavoury mass rape allegedly committed by UNLF and Kangleipak Communist Party cadres on innocent Hmars girls and women at Parbung and Lungthulien villages in Tipaimukh district on 6 and 16 January 2006 respectively was an outcome of this. The National Commission for Women and other non-governmental organizations (NGOs) which visited the villages were struck by the grave 'violence and violation' of human rights.[54]

The ramification of such subversions is appalling in a situation where local democratic institutional arrangements have been kept in suspended animation since 1984 with the boycott of elections to the ADCs. For one thing, even when such institutional arrangements are functional, they follow the single line of administration by privileging the role of the district commissioner(s) (Suan 2002). Such an institutional bedrock can easily 'reconcentrate at the centre' in the absence of simultaneous

---

[52] See ATSUM (2005). Also see the text of the Memorandum of Understanding signed between the Zomi Students' Federation, Churachandpur, and the Government of Manipur (25 August 2005), Churachandpur.

[53] See the text of joint representations made to the chief minister of Mizoram, Aizawl, dated 12 December 2005. Also see *The Imphal Free Press*, Imphal, 13 January 2006.

[54] The Rajkhowa Commission appointed by the state government, Human Rights Alert, and other independent NGOs, after conducting extensive ground appraisal, were unequivocal in indicting the two outlawed militant outfits despite their persistent and unceremonious denial. It is disquieting to note however that there is no mechanism in place to book the 'invisible' eighteen-odd cadres who committed the crime thus adding salt to the wounds of the victims. See Bhattacharya (2006).

devolution of legislative and financial powers. It is precisely on this ground that the Sixth Schedule Demand Committee, Manipur (SSDCM), boycotted the elections to the ADCs. The Manipur Hill Areas Autonomous District Council Act, 2000, is an attempt to address these misgivings. The SSDCM, however, considered it a 'second bluff' and rejected it by contending that it fails to address the legitimate demands of the hill people to devolve substantial legislative, financial, and judicial powers.[55] It has now demanded the implementation of the Sixth Schedule provisions.

Of late, the imperative of recasting—remodelling, if you like—local democratic institutions to protect, preserve, and maintain the unique identity and political situations of the hill people has assumed greater saliency. This is more impelling as this demand is not just procedural but a substantive redress. The National Commission to Review the Working of the Constitution, realizing the import of this in its report (2002), strongly recommended the extension of the Sixth Schedule provisions to the hill areas 'with certain local adjustments' (GoI 2002b). This is yet to be implemented by the Government of Manipur.

In the absence of this and the boycott of the ADC Act 2000 by the SSDCM in the hill areas of Manipur, there is an insignificant element of local democracy in this part of the state. This implies at least two things: one, there is no plausible democratic institution sans Village Authorities[56] to address the local needs, rights, and demands (Suan 2006). Two, it shows the non-seriousness of the state about decentralization and empowering the hill people; hence the near, and in some case total abdication, of state responsibilities. The first one explains why legitimate ethnic demands are often met with ad hoc measures without the necessary structural devolution of powers to accommodate and process such demands into supporting linkages of the state (Dasgupta 1998). The second leads to legalism and a mechanistic interpretation of the 'rule of law'. It is in this space that popular and legitimate democratic upsurges are put down on the grounds that they

---

[55] See GoM (2000). Also see Dewan (2003).

[56] The Village Authority system was put in place by the Manipur State (Hill Administration) Regulations, 1947, and was sustained and given recognition in the mould of a single line administration under the overall supervision and control of the district commissioner since the Manipur (Village Authorities in Hill Areas) Act, 1956. The system is headed by a village chief locally known as *Hausa, Khulakpa*, etc., and can be either hereditary or elective. See Suan (2002).

are nothing but instances of 'insurgency/militancy' which disrupt the edifice of 'law and order'.

CONCLUDING REMARKS

It is apparent from this essay that the hills–valley divide in Manipur is embedded in a socio-cultural and historical contingency which informs the trajectory of the stateness–democracy continuum. It is implausible to have democracy without having a minimum threshold of stateness—of law and order (via a centralized state), independent judiciary, and legitimacy. Given the nature of state–nation building, which is often conducted in the majoritarian language and which tends to bundle congeries of ethnic communities within its totalizing projects, there are always spaces where its efficacy will be questioned. The unprecedented fifty-two days' economic blockade imposed by the All Naga Students Association, Manipur (ANSAM), following a Government of Manipur resolution to observe 18 June 2005 as a public holiday to mark 'state integrity' day, was a pointer to this. Consequently, ANSAM threatened to sever all socio-economic and political ties with Manipur. To fructify this it contended that all future taxes collected from the Naga inhabited areas of Manipur be entirely credited to the state of Nagaland.[57] The recent manoeuvre to register schools in these areas under the Nagaland Board of Secondary Education is another calculated move to foster Nagalim (Greater Nagaland).

Similarly, the Zo people in Churachandpur strongly protested what they considered 'selective ethnic cleansing' undertaken by the majority Meitei community in the wake of a chain of assassinations of 'high ranking tribal officers' which culminated in the killing of T. Thangthuam, the inspector general of police (Intelligence Bureau) on 31 December 2005 by the People's Liberation Army (Phanjoubam 2006: 7). The protest vigorously renewed the solidarity and the resolve of the seemingly fragmented Zo people as the agreement signed by the representatives of the Mizo, Hmars, Kuki, and Zomi on 7 January

---

[57] The blockade caused severe hardship and misery to the already impoverished people of Manipur. The situation was so bad that the Indian Air Force had to airlift forty tonnes of essential food supplies. See *The Imphal Free Press*, Imphal, 6 August 2005, at http://kanglaonline.com/index.php?template=headline&newsid =25193&typeid=1&Idoc_Session=eb5aad1c9caa7eea5551d80e159683cd.

2006 at Lamka/Churachandpur public ground convincingly showed.[58] The episode also provided a welcome opportunity for the Zo people to ignite the flames of Zo nationalism and demand a separate politico-administrative arrangement under the central government which would help preserve, protect, and maintain their identity.[59]

Instances of this kind give necessary latitude to militant ethno-nationalist upsurges. Disparate echoes of such upsurges are then woven together into a seam of totalizing narratives which are often at odds against one another. They in turn question the efficacy of 'stateness' and democracy. The propensity of the state to rely on 'counter-insurgency' strategies in a situation already marked by ascendant ethnonationalist upsurges is likely to leverage a militarist regime in the long run. A regime of this kind is more often than not countered by militant ethnonationalism(s) with their attendant ethnic 'armed militias'. Hence the two seem to sustain one another in a protracted battle. If not properly managed, it could lead to deinstitutionalization and eventual collapse of the state.

It is imperative for an emerging dialogic space to transcend normative understanding of stateness which puts a premium on the institutional efficacy of 'law and order.' There is an increasing urgency to look beyond the Westminster model of democracy and a willingness to craft institutions outside the existing constitutional framework which will envision expansive sharing of powers. One way of doing this would be to incorporate an indigenous constitutional framework like the Yehzabo alongside the state's democratic institutions. The Yehzabo provides an innovative Naga supra-traditional institution in the mould of a modern parliament that draws disparate Naga tribes' representatives from the village, regional, and 'national' level. A classic bottom-up democratic model, the Yehzabo has a parallel model in the form of the Zomi Council among the Zo people as well. This bottom-up model may be legitimized and given a larger quasi-political role in deciding matters

[58] The agreement, signed at Lamka Public Ground on 7 January 2006, cited the killings of 'high ranking tribal police officers' like Tualkhanpau and R. Parte, both belonging to MPS (Manipur Police Service). The ceremony was attended by overwhelming numbers of the public representing cross-sections of ethnic communities in the state. See the text of the Agreement available at: http//www. zogam.org. Also see *The Imphal Free Press*, Imphal, 2 January 2006 at http:// kanglaonline.com/index.php?template=headline&newsid= 28735&typeid=1&I doc_Session=b596d385c0a5268089003a4996e9bd43.

[59] See text of the agreement (7 January 2006, Churachandpur).

pertaining to Naga and Zo culture, identity, and land. Needless to say, institutional crafting in a conflict-prone state like Manipur should be sensitive to the immanent hills–valley divide and be prepared to process and accommodate conflicting demands/totalizing projects of ethnic communities into supporting network of state actions.

PART V

Breaking the Impasse

CHAPTER 13

Just Development
A Strategy for Ethnic Reconciliation in Tripura

SUBIR BHAUMIK

At a 2006 conference of the Northeast Peoples Initiative in Guwahati, I had argued that one of the major challenges confronting civil society in India's Northeast is to draw up a roadmap for ethnic reconciliation.[1] Confronting Delhi to secure people's rights was all very fine but I argued that the movements of self-determination in the region would serve no purpose if they ran into each other and exacerbated the ethnic conflicts afflicting the region. Within a month, my concerns were vindicated. The Karbi–Dimasa massacres in Assam's Karbi Anglong, almost on the eve of the first talks between the federal government and Peoples Consultative Group set up by the ULFA, emphasized the need to reconcile the aspirations of the battling ethnicities.

Barely a month later, I was in Bangkok interviewing the National Socialist Council of Nagaland (NSCN) general secretary, Thuingaleng Muivah. Muivah insisted there could be no solution to the Naga problem unless Delhi agreed to the 'reunification of all Naga territories'. When asked how he would react to opposition in Manipur and Assam for any such proposal, Muivah thundered: 'If Delhi thinks it can deprive the Nagas to please the Meiteis and Assamese, there can be no settlement.'[2] The two instances only serve to emphasize the fact that without ethnic reconciliation, there can be no solution to the ongoing

---

[1] North-east Peoples Initiative Conference held in Guwahati, 9–10 October 2005 at Vivekananda Kendra.

[2] Muivah, interview with BBC correspondent Subir Bhaumik at Bangkok airport on 3 November 2005 (broadcast on BBC World Service on 4 November 2005).

imbroglios in India's Northeast. Negotiating with Delhi and getting something out of the centre is one side of the picture; the other side involves the more difficult problem of reconciling apparently conflicting demands for ethnic homelands.

In Tripura, my home state, ethnic conflicts between Bengali settlers and indigenous tribespeople have scarred the state's once peaceful landscape since the first ethnic riots in 1980. With the experience of Tripura in mind, I will argue that (*a*) land is the key to any durable political settlement in such agrarian or pre-agrarian societies where it is the major resource and also the major source of conflict; (*b*) only an equitable control over resources can bring down ethnic temperatures and lead to conflict resolution; (*c*) accords and highly publicized surrender of militants are only cosmetic manifestations of state-sponsored conflict management strategies which actually achieve very little other than coming up with a power-sharing arrangement that placates the elites or neo-elites of a particular community unhappy with the existing order. So let's now look at Tripura and see how the conflict there can be resolved.

At 10,039 square kilometres, Tripura is Northeast India's smallest state. But this was not always so. Maharaja Bijoy Manikya is said to have bathed in seven large rivers of East Bengal, which means he controlled a large swathe of land between hill Tipperah and Bangladesh's present capital Dhaka. The Manikyas controlled much of East Bengal's Comilla region during medieval times—a region my ancestors hailed from. Their governance was marked by fairness and balance in the handling of ethnic aspirations. With royal patronage, tolerance and multiculturalism flourished in an area divided by ethnicity and religion and torn by conflicts born out of it. Not surprisingly therefore, readers of *Tripura Observer* (an Agartala-based English daily), in 2000, voted Maharaja Bir Bikram as the 'Tripura's Man of the Millenium' in preference to those who have led the state since the end of the royal order.

Even after the advent of the British, when the Tripura kingdom was restricted to its present hill confines, Bengalis and indigenous tribespeople lived in peace. No riot, not even sporadic ethnic clashes were ever reported between Bengali settlers and indigenous tribespeople from princely Tripura. If the Manikyas welcomed Bengali professionals or peasants to modernize their administration or increase their land revenue through the spread of settled wet rice agriculture, they also created the tribal reserve that, in many ways, is the precursor of the Tripura Tribal Areas Autonomous District Council.

The Partition unleashed a wave of migration from East Pakistan to Tripura and other states on its borders. Though the indigenous tribespeople in the state never enjoyed a decisive majority like in neighbouring Chittagong hill tracts or the Mizo hills, they accounted for anything between 50 to 60 per cent of the total population. In the three decades after Partition, the indigenous tribespeople were reduced to below 30 per cent of the state's population, a situation which left them completely marginalized in both self-perception and reality.

The influx intensified the land alienation of the tribespeople and added to their collective sense of loss and marginalization. Almost all writers on Tripura insurgency have identified land alienation amongst the tribespeople as the major cause that has fuelled the violent insurgency that has eaten into the vitals of the once vibrant state.

As long as the tribals had enough land and the Bengali population was limited to certain urban or semi-urban pockets or rural areas around the capital, land alienation of tribals did not emerge as a major problem. That began to change with Independence and the merger of princely Tripura in the Indian Union. Between 1947 and 1971, 609,998 Bengalis displaced from East Pakistan came to Tripura for rehabilitation and resettlement. Since the total population of the state in 1951 was 645,707, it is not difficult to gauge the enormous population pressure created on tiny Tripura by Partition. During this period, the state government primarily resettled the refugees on land under different schemes, some enabling the refugees to settle down with financial assistance and some just helping them buy land.[3]

The operation of these schemes accelerated the process of large-scale loss of tribal lands. The pauperization of the tribals can also be discerned from the growing number of tribal agricultural labourers in the three decades since Partition. In 1951, cultivators constituted 62.94 per cent of the total tribal workforce in the state while only 8.93 per cent were in the category of agricultural labourers. But in 1981, only 43.57 per cent of the tribal workforce was cultivators and the number of agricultural labourers had risen to 23.91 per cent (Ganguly 1987). But it would be wrong to assume that tribals alone became landless paupers and their lands taken over by Bengali settlers who grew at their

[3] In Tripura, the tribals were never a decisive majority, but they were always in majority prior to the Partition, constituting just over 50 per cent of the population. By 1981, however, they were accounting for barely 30 per cent of the population. See Tripura Census Reports, 1951, 1961, 1971, and 1981.

expense—a stereotype that tribal extremist groups seek to create.[4]

It is true that tribals account for 41 per cent of the agricultural landless labourers in Tripura, but the rest are non-tribals, almost wholly Bengalis (Bhattacharya 1999). It is true that the percentage of tribals amongst the landless agricultural labourers in Tripura's rural workforce has sharply risen from 4 per cent to 20 per cent in 1971, to 29 per cent in 1981, but it is also true the rest are Bengalis and that's almost in keeping with the population ratio of the two communities in the state. Of the nearly half a million agrarian population in 1951, 2.5 per cent were rent receivers, 97.5 per cent owner cultivators, 11.6 per cent tenant cultivators, and 6.4 per cent were labourers. In 1981, agricultural labourers had become 29 per cent of the total rural workforce. In 1961, 16.9 per cent of the tribals and 29.9 per cent of the Bengali settlers controlled much of Tripura's land. The World Agriculture Census (1970–71) shows that, in Tripura, 11 per cent of the total population controlled 46 per cent of the total land, while 70 per cent of the population controlled 28 per cent of the operational holdings (Law Research Institute 1990).

But while the Bengalis who came were used to sharp class differences in the erstwhile homeland—East Bengal—the tribespeople were not. At an individual level, they lost lands mostly to Bengalis, rich or poor. Studies conducted by the Law Research Institute in Guwahati, show the huge land loss suffered by the tribespeople at the hands of the Bengali settlers in certain areas of Tripura.

The study analysed the land transfer pattern in seven scheduled and seven non-scheduled villages in south and west Tripura. In the seven non-scheduled villages, out of the total 240 plots transferred, 145 plots were transferred by tribals to non-tribals (read Bengalis), 76 by tribals to tribals, and 19 by non-tribals to non-tribals.

So 60 per cent of the land transfers were from tribals to non-tribals. In the seven scheduled villages, the position was worse. Out of 282 plots transferred, 191 were transferred from tribals to non-tribals (68 per cent of the total land transfers). Of the villages under study, the heaviest tribal to non-tribal transfer took place at Hawaibari on the Assam–Agartala road.

One has to go to Teliamura, once a small village but now a vital road junction connecting west, north, and south Tripura to see the scale of

---

[4] Website of the Tripura People's Democratic Front (TPDF) in www. geocities.com.

land transfer. Gunomoni Sardar, the grandfather of the Indigenous National Party of Tripura (INPT) leader, Debabrata Koloi, and former Tribal National Volunteers (TNV) military wing chief, Chuni Koloi, owned almost 70 per cent of the lands in Teliamura. He was a great friend of my grandfather, Kashinath Bhowmik, who established the police station in Khowai town, from where Teliamura was covered those days. In thirty years, Gunomoni Sardar's descendants have hardly got a few hectares left for themselves by the side of the Tripura Road Transport Corporation (TRTC) bus stand on the Assam–Agartala road.

Under the Congress administration, some Bengali refugee leaders even set up 'land cooperatives' like the Swasti Samity in north Tripura. These cooperatives violated the Tribal Reserves regulations and began to take over large swathes of tribal land, a process that was legitimized by conniving bureaucrats. The Communist Party mobilized the tribesmen and even took the matter to court to secure a favourable verdict that was not honoured by the bureaucracy. Angry at such rampant loss of their traditional lands, a large number of tribal youths took to the jungles and the first significant underground group in post-merger Tripura, the Sengkrak or the 'Clenched Fist', was born.[5]

The Sengkrak movement, Tripura's first manifestation of overt ethnic militancy, started in 1967 as a direct fallout of the large-scale alienation of tribal lands, accentuated through state patronage. The ruling Congress government backed the forcible occupation of tribal lands in the Deo valley by Bengali settlers grouped into an organization called the Swasti Samity while the Reang tribesmen organized themselves into a militant group to hit back at the new Bengali settlers. This writer conducted a correlation analysis between land alienation and tribal insurgency in August 1984 by choosing to interview the family members of eighty-four extremists of the TNV.

These family members had been gathered at a government hostel as part of Chief Minister Nripen Chakrabarty's 'Motivation Drive' to facilitate the return of the guerrillas to normal life. It was found that 64 per cent of the families had suffered loss of land to Bengalis while 32 per cent of them were from families of *jhumia*s or shifting cultivators who were under increasing pressure to find fresh lands for cultivation due to the growing occupation of hill stretches by Bengali refugees.

[5] For a detailed account of the Sengkrak movement, see Bhaumik, 1996.

Only 4 per cent were from families with enough land that had not been lost to the settlers.[6]

In settled agricultural areas like Khowai and Sadar, all within 100 kilometres of the state's capital Agartala, between 20 to 40 per cent of the tribal lands had been alienated by the end of the 1970s, when tribal insurgency gathered momentum. In some parts of south Tripura district, as much as 60 per cent of the tribal lands were alienated, sold in distress conditions as a sequel to an unequal economic competition with the Bengali settlers.[7]

The land loss at the level of the individual was further compounded by large-scale loss of tribal lands to huge government projects like the Dumbur hydroelectric project, where an estimated 5,000 to 8,000 tribal families lost their lands and only a small percentage of them possessing title deeds to prove ownership managed to secure rehabilitation. The pauperization of Dumbur's once prosperous tribal peasantry and the huge benefits that Bengali urban dwellers gained by electricity and Bengali fishermen gained by being able to fish in the large reservoir were not lost on a generation of angry tribal youths who took up arms and left for the jungles to fight an administration they felt was only working in the interests of the Bengali refugees. Insurgent leader Bijoy Kumar Hrangkhawl, now back to mainstream politics after his TNVs returned to normal life following an accord in 1988, used to refer to Nripen Chakrabarty as the 'refugee chief minister' of Tripura.[8]

The heartburn over steady land loss on a one-to-one basis was further exacerbated by the submergence of a huge swathe of arable land owned by the tribals in the Raima valley as a result of the commissioning of the Gumti hydel project in south Tripura. This project not only disturbed the fragile ecology of the Raima valley in the south district of Tripura, but also left a permanent sense of loss in the tribal psyche. All tribal organizations including the Communist-backed Gana Mukti Parishad, fiercely protested the commissioning of the Gumti

---

[6] Findings of the study were used for a Press Trust of India (PTI) special report, 18 August 1984.

[7] The writer has collated the statistics available with the Tripura Land Revenue Department and the Agriculture Census Reports. The Land Revenue department had entertained applications from tribals for restoration of their alienated landholdings. The percentage figures given are a result of this collated exercise.

[8] B.K. Hrangkhawl's letters to Chief Minister Nripen Chakrabarty, 1983–7, available with the writer.

hydroelectric project in 1976. But the Congress government crushed the protests. It was determined to augment Tripura's deficit power supply, but it ended up augmenting the catchment area of tribal unrest by dispossessing thousands of them of their only economic resource and collective symbol, their land.

A thirty-metre-high gravity dam was constructed across the river Gumti about 3.5 kilometres upstream of Tirthamukh in south Tripura district for generating 8.60 megawatts of power from an installed capacity of 10 megawatts. The dam submerged a valley area of 46.34 square kilometres. This was one of the most fertile valley regions in an otherwise hilly state, where arable flatlands suitable for wet rice agriculture account for a mere 28 per cent of its total land area. Official records suggest that 2,558 tribal families were ousted from the Gumti project area, but these were families who could produce land deeds and were officially owners of the land they possessed.[9]

Unofficial estimates varied between 8,000 to 10,000 families or about 50,000 to 60,000 tribespeople displaced by the project. In the tribal societies of the Northeast, ownership of land is rarely personal and the system of recording land deeds against individual names is a recent phenomenon. So, most of those ousted by the hydroelectric project failed to get any rehabilitation grant and were forced to settle in the hills around the project, returning to slash and burn agriculture called *jhum*.

The Left government has recently announced that all Dumbur oustees, wherever they are, will be covered under the Kutir Jyoti programme. A list of 500 Dumbur oustee families has been supplied to the power department. The department has given electricity connections to 114 families who do not have power connections under the Kutir Jyoti programme. But what these families need more than free electricity is arable land and resources to earn their livelihoods from (Dasgupta 1989).

The dam destroyed the once surplus tribal peasant economy of the state. Tripura's leading economist Malabika Dasgupta has shown in her study on the Gumti hydel project that 'attempts either to protect the environment to the exclusion of considerations for the well being of the people or to improve their level of well being without consideration for the environmental impact of such policies can neither protect

[9] Progress Report on 25 point Tribal Development Package (1999 to 2002).

the environment nor improve the standard of living of the people'
(Dasgupta 1989).

The Gumti, Tripura's principal river, is formed by the confluence
of two small rivers, Raima and Sarma, the former flowing out of the
Longtharai range and the latter originating from the Atharamura range.
Before the construction of the dam, the river Gumti flowed southwards
through a gorge in the Atharamura range beyond the confluence
point of Raima and Sarma. It spilled over a series of rapids which
were locally known as the Dumbur falls at the point of Tirthamukh
(literally, 'Pilgrim's Point'), a place considered holy by the tribals and
also the Bengali settlers who would bathe in the river during the Pous
Sankranti every winter.

Beyond Tirthamukh, the Gumti flows westwards up to Malbassa
village and then changes direction again, cutting through the Deotamura
range. After crossing the Deotamura, it flows for another 60 kilometres
before it enters Bangladesh. After flowing about 80 kilometres through
eastern Bangladesh, it joins the Meghna river which flows into the
Bay of Bengal. The upper catchment of the Gumti comprises eleven
Gaon Sabhas—nearly sixty villages in all—in the Gandacherra block
of Tripura's newly formed Dhalai district.

The upper reaches of the catchment area are steep and hilly, located
on the east of the river, but as the river flows towards, Tirthamukh, it is
flanked by small flat-topped hills locally called *tilla*s with many *lunga*s
or lowlands between them. And as it comes down to Tirthamukh, the
Gumti valley waters huge flatlands all along its course into Bangladesh.
Before the commissioning of the hydel project, the upper catchment
supported a small population of tribals.

The small Bengali population practised wet rice cultivation around
Boloungbassa and Raima and some were into trading, while the tribals,
originally almost all slash-and-burn agriculturists called jhumias, had
began to settle down to wet rice cultivation, having learnt it from
the Bengali farmers. The kings of Tripura had settled some Bengali
farmers even in such remote areas to encourage tribals to pick up wet
rice cultivation and abandon jhum, which is ecologically damaging.
Before the dam, the hills around the present project area were sparsely
populated and the area was almost wholly under dense forest cover
supporting wildlife.

The Tripura Gazetteer of 1975 talked of sighting 'large herds of
Indian elephants in the Raima-Sarma region alongwith some tigers
and bears in the dense forests'. Dasgupta (1989) says the area 'was an

abode of deers, bears, wild boars, tigers, elephants and a wide variety jungle cats'. The vegetation was rich, and so was the flora and fauna. But after the hydel project was commissioned, not only did almost half of the tribal families displaced by the dam move into the hills in the river's upper catchment area, but the roads built to first transport construction material and then to support the hydel project opened up the rich forests of the area to the illegal loggers. The surplus-producing tribal peasantry were not only angry for having lost their rich flatlands and lungas, they were forced to revert back to slash-and-burn jhum cultivation that has, in Dasgupta's opinion, 'caused irreparable damage to the ecology of the upper catchment of the Gumti' (ibid.).

Illegal logging by businessmen, backed by politicians, has further damaged the ecology. During two extensive trips into the Gumti valley in 1985 and 1998, this writer found extensive felling of trees and no presence of forest guards to check it. The tribal insurgents of the National Liberation Front of Tripura or the NLFT have not banned tree felling, as some rebel groups in the Northeast like the National Democratic Front of Bodoland (NDFB) has done. They have encouraged it. In large parts of the Gumti valley upstream of Tirthamukh, tribal villagers told this writer that the NLFT had allowed loggers to operate freely so long as they paid them off.

Relatives of some insurgent leaders were in the business, entering partnership deals with the Bengali-owned saw mills of Amarpur, Udaipur, and Sonamura. So the tribal insurgents who had capitalized on the community's anger at the large-scale displacement at Gumti were now collaborating with the most exploitative segments of settler society to raise funds. It is my contention that (*a*) the present ethnic conflict that pits the Bengali settlers against the indigenous tribespeople in Tripura has much to do with the large-scale land alienation of tribals because land is seen not only as the prime economic resource in a rather backward pre-capitalist agrarian society like Tripura but also as the symbol of the ethnic preponderance; (*b*) the psychological alienation of the tribespeople was further aggravated by the Dumbur hydel project which, in one stroke, contributed the most to the ongoing process of land alienation; (*c*) the Dumbur hydel project has caused huge damage not only to the ecology of the Raima–Sarma valley but also to ethnic relations in the state; (*d*) the project is now a white elephant and can be decommissioned to make way for large-scale land reclamation that can be used to resettle landless tribespeople in a major gesture of undoing injustice.

WHY MUST THE DAM GO?

The Gumti hydel project must be decommissioned. It is now not producing more than 7 megawatts of power even in the peak season when the reservoir is full during monsoon. The state government says that by investing Rs 11.80 million, it has been able to restore the output to the original installed capacity of 10 megawatts. It also says that while the running cost of the project is around Rs 30 million per annum, it rakes in nearly Rs 210 million through sale of electricity. Officials in the Tripura power department describe the project as 'very profitable'. But experts say the siltation levels will continue to increase and unless the reservoir can be dredged, there will be no rise in output. The power output from this project will progressively diminish.

With huge natural gas reserves now discovered in Tripura and major gas thermal power projects in the pipeline (including one with the capacity to generate 740 megawatts against the state's current peak demand of 125 megawatts), it is wastage of funds to invest in the Gumti hydel project. If the state can produce three to four times more electricity than it now uses, there is a strong case for decommissioning the dam that will free a huge area for other pressing causes. An ideal power strategy for Tripura would be to produce around 1,000 megawatts of electricity, feed half of that into the Northeastern Grid, use 150 to 200 megawatts within the state keeping in mind the rising demand, and sell the balance to Bangladesh as the former chairman of the North Eastern Electric Power Corporation (NEEPCO) P.K. Chatterji, had suggested.[10]

In the long run, as Bangladesh augments its own power capacity, the surplus Tripura power could be used locally in the event of major industrialization or fed into the regional grid for neighbouring, perpetually power deficit states like Mizoram which lack the gas reserves of Tripura. Since at least 64.6 square kilometres can be reclaimed from under water if the Gumti hydel project is decommissioned, a huge fertile tract of flatland would be opened up for farming and for the resettlement of the landless tribal peasantry of the state. The fertility of this land is likely to increase after so many years under water.

At least 30,000 tribal families of Tripura, perhaps the whole of its landless population, can be gainfully resettled in this fertile tract. Before the dam, this area's fertility was a talking point in the state. Tripura is

---

[10] www.petrowatch.com, 27 July 2001.

a food deficit state and turning this area into a modern agrarian zone will solve the state's food problem forever. Needless to say, the entire tribal landless population of the state, estimated at between 25,000 to 27,000 families, can be gainfully resettled in the Gumti area, once the entire land in and around the reservoir area is reclaimed.

Each family can be given at least one hectare of prime agricultural land—thrice the average landholding size in Tripura. The problem of tribal land alienation can be tackled in one go. Solutions to conflicts need both symbols and substance—this gesture could provide both. Never before has a development project been dismantled to preserve the interests of the indigenous peoples. Since this project is proving to be a bit of a white elephant, it is not very difficult to justify its decommissioning in view of its potential to solve the problem of tribal landlessness in one stroke.

If the entire or almost the entire tribal landless population can be gainfully resettled in the Gumti project area, it will free the hilly forest regions from human pressure. Since most of these landless tribals practice jhum cultivation which is dangerous for the ecology of the hills and the forests, it is essential to settle this entire population in wet plains like those of the Gumti area. The hills cannot take the high pressure of human settlements, but the plains can. So, from an ecological viewpoint, the resettlement of the landless tribals of Tripura in the Gumti project area will be welcome. The state's forest cover, now receding, will improve and degraded forests may be turned into gainful plantations by large-scale private investments. The area likely to be reclaimed in the Gumti project area should be used only for resettling the tribal landless—a compact area in keeping with Maharaja Bir Bikram's tribal reserve concept.

This decommissioning proposal should be implemented before ethnic polarization between Bengali settlers and indigenous tribespeople snowballs beyond control. The state is still ruled by the CPI(M)-led Left Front, a left-of-centre coalition which has support both amongst Bengalis and the tribespeople. Tribal parties and militant groups will support the dam's decommissioning and Bengali extremist groups are not yet around to resist it.

A political dialogue can be initiated to create the proper climate for decommissioning and the creation of an alternative economy for the tribals. Even security agencies benefit from this settlement as a happily settled tribal population, easily monitored, is less of a headache for the keepers of law and order than a disgruntled tribal population spread out over a vast hill region in small hilltop hamlets with little food and livelihood. Otherwise the graph of insurgent violence in Tripura, very considerable for a small state, cannot be controlled.

Since 2004, tribal insurgency in Tripura has weakened, rebel groups have been split and they have wilted under some determined counter-insurgency action. The numbers alone tell an extraordinary—though necessarily incomplete—story. The number of extremist incidents fell from 380 in 2003 to 210 in 2004. Civilian fatalities were down from 302 to 81 and among security forces fatalities from 216 to 105. Terrorist fatalities rose marginally from 61 in 2003 to 63 in 2004. But the subsequent years have witnessed a further consolidation of downward trends in violence. Only 30 civilian fatalities were reported in 2005 and 14 in 2006. Fatalities of security personnel have also fallen sharply. More crucially, as many as 573 militants surrendered to the authorities in 2003–04 (2003: 251; 2004: 322). The year 2004 saw the surrender of 72 cadres of the Montu Koloi and Kamini Debbarma faction of the NLFT, on 6 May. As many as 138 cadres of the NLFT's Nayanbashi subsequently surrendered on 25 December 2004. The combined result of the loses weakened the NLFT and though it is too early to write it off, neither the NLFT nor the All Tripura Tiger Force (ATTF) is now capable of launching the kind of serial kidnappings and killings they had been able to until 2003.

In the early 2000s, Tripura had emerged as the 'abduction centre' of the Northeast, accounting for nearly half of all abductions for ransom in the region. A dramatic decline, from 445 abductions in 2000 and 311 in 2003, has been reported. In 2004, 200 persons were abducted in Tripura, 115 in 2005, and 73 in 2006, signalling the diminishing sway of the insurgent groups, and their inability to exploit what constituted the major source of revenues in the past. Police sources indicate that militant capacities to secure revenues by extortion have also declined radically, and the NLFT's collection in 2004 is estimated to have fallen short of targets by about 50 per cent, while the ATTF collections were even lower, at 60 per cent of targeted revenues.

The most dramatic impact of the weakening of the insurgent forces was seen in the elections for the Tripura Tribal Area Autonomous District Council (TTAADC) held on 5 March 2005. Traditionally, the TTAADC elections have been the playground of the rebel groups that have terrorized tribal voters, kidnapped and killed candidates, political workers and their relatives, and undermined the polling process. During the three months preceding the last TTAADC elections in 2000, there were 176 extremist incidents, with 100 persons killed, another 86 injured and 172 persons abducted—including 12 relatives of candidates abducted in the month prior to the elections.

This time around, however, TTAADC elections were nearly completely peaceful, with just one significant incident: an ambush on the troops of the Central Reserve Police Force (CRPF) who were escorting ballot papers after the polls, on 6 March 2005 in Dhalai District, in which one policeman was killed (Sahni and Routray 2005).

The return of relative normalcy can provide a good launching pad for initiating a process of ethnic reconciliation. Many rebel groups have come and gone in Tripura—the Sengkrak, the TNV, the ATTF, and the NLTF may all fade into the pages of history but that will not mean that tribal insurgency will not return to the hills of Tripura. A strategy to assuage the community's sense of marginalization is a must if Tripura has to get durable peace.

But the success of the Tripura police and intelligence in its counter-insurgency drive can never be translated into long-term political gain and tribal militancy in Tripura can never be rooted out unless the state's Left government finds a way to ensure just development—not promote development for the sake of it, something that can only benefit the advantaged sections. It is important to break the back of the insurgent groups in the tribal areas because they have done nothing for the community and only engaged in self-perpetuation. Tripura's Marxist-led Left Front government would do well to realize that the roots of tribal insurgency in Tripura can never be eliminated unless the tribal peasantry's angst over marginalization is addressed and they are empowered with fertile lands capable of providing a stable livelihood.

In Tripura, restoration of lands to the tribal peasantry rather than persisting with a small and inefficient hydel power project would mean just development. If all landless tribals in Tripura get back their fertile lands, which is surely possible if the Gumti hydel project is decommissioned and the lands under the reservoir reclaimed, it will not merely mean financial empowerment for them, it would also go a long way to psychologically assuage the entire tribal community. Rarely in modern times has a development project been pulled down to benefit the disadvantaged.

The latest Comptroller and Auditor General of India (CAG) report (2005–06) on Tripura blames the state government for 'idle expenditure' on the Gumti hydel project. It says the government's failure to 'properly plan and execute the renovation/modernization of the Gumti hydel Power station led to an idle expenditure of Rs 55.54 lakhs beside loss of benefits of modernization'.[11]

Considering the increasing lack of water in the reservoir of the project that has led to complete production stoppage since March 2007, it will be a waste to invest any more funds into the Gumti hydel project. In April 2007, this writer visited Dumbur and found that thousands of tribals had converged on the Gumti hydel project to reclaim their lands that had emerged out of the reservoir due to subsiding water levels. Most of those were Reangs, the tribe that suffered the most after the commissioning of the project. Local lawmaker, Rabindra Debbarma, suggested that the government decommission the project, systematically reclaim the lands, and redistribute them amongst the tribal landless, giving first priority to those who had been ousted from the area in 1974 after the commissioning of the project.[12]

Actually, it is not merely the Gumti hydel project that is suffering from lack of water in the reservoir. Due to climatic changes, caused by less and less rain in Northeast India, all the seven existing hydel power plants in the area are under-performing (current production is 319 megawatts against an installed capacity of 875 megawatts). So, when Tripura is on the threshold of producing more than 1,000 megawatts of power from gas-based thermal plants—what with the Oil and Natural Gas Corporation (ONGC) alone coming up with a 740-megawatt gas-fired plant—it sounds ridiculous to persist with a white elephant like the Gumti hydel project. The fertile lands under the project's reservoir are more useful than the water in it that produces power (and that too perhaps may not any more).

In one bold stroke, it is possible for the Bengalis to buy peace through the process of ethnic reconciliation that the decommissioning of the Dumbur hydel project and redistribution of the lands reclaimed from the project can kickstart. That is how the root cause of the tribal insurgency can be addressed. The tribal peasantry can be substantially empowered through this relocation of priorities. If the dam goes, some Bengali fishermen in the area may feel upset at the loss of the Dumbur lake (as the Gumti reservoir is popularly known).

---

[11] See http://www.cag.nic.in/html/cag_reports/tripura/rep_2006/chap_7.pdf

[12] See http://news.bbc.co.uk/2/hi/south_asia/6509771.stm (Land reclaim dispute over drying dam).

In the larger interest of ethnic reconciliation, the dam must go. Tribal insurgency in Tripura, now largely criminalized, must be fought relentlessly. So far, the government has rewarded insurgents for challenging the state by offering them rehabilitation packages and funding them for covert operations against their former colleagues. That must stop. The insurgents must be given the opportunity to return to normal life if they so wish, but the real thrust of government policy should be to empower and benefit the tribal peasantry. The tribals must be reminded that these insurgents never addressed grassroot development issues like land. They have focused only on power-sharing concerns or resorted to mafia-style extortions rather than look at strategies for the empowerment of the tribal peasantry.

Only such empowerment can lead to percolation of the fruits of development and make it an equitable process. I am not suggesting that the decommissioning of the Gumti hydel project and large-scale land reclamation there will calm ethnic temperatures and bring about a durable solution in Tripura. But it will surely kickstart a process of ethnic reconciliation that can be carried forward. The next logical step would be to provide the tribespeople with 50 per cent reservation for the seats in the state legislative assembly, so half the state's lawmakers are tribals.

CHAPTER 14

Grounds for Democratic Hope in Arunachal Pradesh

Emerging Civic Geographies and the Reinvention of Gender and Tribal Identities[1]

BETSY TAYLOR

Democratic prospects for Arunachal Pradesh are perilous but not fragile. Potential perils are real, if too often exaggerated in outsider's views of the Northeast. Intractable identity politics could emerge from Arunachal Pradesh's astonishing cultural diversity—among the several dozen tribal groups, or between immigrants and indigenous populations. Rich natural resources of forest and hydropower could create the usual moral and political traps of extractive industry—steep inequalities, cultural marginalization, and disempowerment of many sectors; political corruption, lack of economic diversity, and entrepreneurial creativity; environmental devastation, structural regional underdevelopment, outflow of capital and profits, and demographic displacements.

However, contrary to these stereotypes, there are creative reinventions of tribal and gender identities in Arunachal Pradesh, which open spaces of hope for an alternative path to development. This hope, while hedged by dangers, has solid grounds—able to build from self-sufficient local economies, new freedoms for women, new spaces of imagination rooted

[1] I wish to acknowledge the insights and inspiration I have received from the hundreds of activists, scholars, and leaders with whom I have worked in Arunachal Pradesh. Much of the focus of this paper is on the NGO Future Generations (Arunachal). For more information on their excellent programmes, readers can contact: Dr Tage Kanno (Executive Director), Future Generations Arunachal, Vivek Vihar, H-Sector, Itanagar, Arunachal Pradesh, e-mail: kanno@future.org and at www.future.org.

in reappropriated cultural pasts and new civic networks. Emerging forms of grass-roots civil society can gain strength from factors that early 'developmentalist' models would portray as weakening. This essay suggests that subsistence tribal economies provide resilience, safety nets, and psycho-cultural security that strengthen social bases for economic and civic experimentation. Some would see only infrastructure problems in the fiercely precipitous terrain of the eastern Himalayas. But, this terrain harbours ecological mega-diversity which could provide a uniquely intact material basis for decentralized, post-industrial 'green' economies based on small-scale industries which create high value products with sustainable use of forests and forest products (Agarwal 1999). Ecologically embedded and resilient economies, under the right political conditions, have the capacity to diffuse economic prosperity through dispersed rural populations in ways that nurture cultural and political security, creativity, and equity. Scaled up, democratic political will could structure the emerging, possibly vast hydropower industries in ways that do not lock the region into the political instability, capital flight, and economic inequality often associated with extractive or energy industries.

CIVIC SPACE, CIVIL SOCIETY, PUBLIC SPACE, AND THE GROUNDS OF DEMOCRACY

This article attempts to understand the possibilities for democratization, sustainable prosperity, equity, and multiculturalism in Arunachal Pradesh. It grapples with these wider questions through an analysis of ten years (from 1997 to 2006) of community mobilization in three tribal areas of the state. The goal is to understand how democratic public space can be nurtured, expanded, and deepened. I get at this question by asking about what *surrounds, enables, and buffers public space*. I am interested in the social spaces and pathways through which individuals and groups get access to public legitimacy and public action (or do not). These intermediate spaces are crucial to a vibrant democracy because these are the arenas in which people groom themselves for public action, build self-confidence, clarify thinking and strategies, reflect on individual and collective needs and values, build alliances and political will, help each other heal from collective tragedies, and nourish their capacity for hope. A diversity of such sub-public spaces is essential to inclusive and pluralistic democratic public space, and, is particularly important for those who have been excluded from public life. Almost by definition, the powerful have garnered such resources already—like movie stars with the best coaches, dressing rooms, and retinues of backstage support crews.

This article attempts to look at the micro politics *behind* democratizing public spaces in Arunachal Pradesh, in order to understand those social and psychological forces which might provide durable foundations for democratic public life at the local level and beyond. If public space is looked upon as the social arena in which the common good is defined or celebrated, and in which collective actions are debated, legitimated, and authorized, this eassy, then, is concerned with those spaces through which people travel in order to get to a public space. I call these spaces 'civic spaces'. By 'civic' I mean that which is transitional between social life and public life—those webs of cultural meanings, social skills, identities, discourses, practices, and labours which can translate the social into the public, and the public into the social. 'Civic space' is different from 'civil society'. Baruah, drawing on Bayart and others, defines 'civil society' as those forms of civic life which are sufficiently well organized to be able to confront, critique, and engage the state (Baruah 2005a : 134–5; Bayart 1993). This is an important distinction, and, crucial to my analysis.[2]

KEY QUESTIONS

This article grapples with these questions primarily through an in-depth case study of the work of an Indian non-governmental organization (NGO), Future Generations (Arunachal) or FGA.[3] It

[2] For an extended discussion of this definition of 'public' and 'civic', see Reid and Taylor (2009). My usage is similar to what Baruah (2005a: 135) calls 'social space' except that he contrasts society to the state. The contrast I would draw is between society and a notion of 'public space' which includes both official government structure and the extra-governmental spaces of collective citizen action, debate, and celebration which is the shadowy but vital co-presence of the 'people' as the ultimate source, guarantor, and protector of a legitimate democratic republic. I also include *pre-state public authorities*, as is importantly the case in Arunachal Pradesh where there are complex and shifting interactions between the unfortunately labelled 'traditional tribal' political structures, established state, and the emerging Panchayati structures.

[3] This article is written from a philosophy of engaged and participatory scholarship. I first went to Arunachal Pradesh in 1995, as senior social scientist with a small NGO, Future Generations (International) based in USA. From this process, the Indian NGO FGA emerged in 1997. From 1997 through 1998, I was a liaison between the two organizations, spending three to four months in Arunachali villages over the course of a year. In addition to this grass-roots

attempts to answer three questions. First, it asks how new civic spaces are emerging from the diversity of prior public spaces in different tribal groups—forms of polities which have historical contexts that are both unique and interrelated. Second, it examines how FGA grass-roots activists are creating new webs of mutual empowerment by working hard to open new civic spaces. It suggests that there are different 'trajectories of empowerment' within different groups but that these intra-tribal dynamics would not be possible without the inter-tribal civic infrastructure that the FGA has built up. Third, I ask what lessons can be learned from this experience that can contribute to global efforts to create new forms of democracy—forms more appropriate to twenty-first-century problems and global cultural diversity than those that came from the eighteenth-century West. Many are struggling to find models for democratic participation that strike a healthy balance between local and trans-local—between citizen-driven local action and trans-local support systems (technical expertise, government, etc.) that create the necessary enabling conditions for long-term local democracy (Bell et al. 1990; Cavanagh 2002; Fischer 2000; Korten 1995; Shutkin 2000; Taylor-Ide and Taylor 2002). At their best, emerging Arunachali civic life is articulating civic practices that *arise from, and are embedded in,* tribal identities, with pan-tribal, national, and transnational forms of imagination and action. Herbert Reid and I describe this as a process of *tranversalizing* of particular into collective identity rather than the *universalizing* of collective identities that are so basic to liberal Western political traditions (Reid and Taylor 2009).

---

fieldwork, I spent many weeks with Arunachali academics and social activists at the state level—including extensive collegial interactions at Rajiv Gandhi University (formerly Arunachal University), in regular visits and several workshops and seminars. In February 2006, I spent two weeks revisiting the three programme sites that I had earlier visited, and did a ten-year evaluation report at the request of the FGA. For this we visited twenty villages and had long meetings with members of thirty-six Mahila Mandals and four Farmer's Clubs, as well as many other civic leaders, officials, and interested citizens. These community meetings lasted from one to four hours, giving us the opportunity for in-depth conversations with well over 700 villagers by the end of the trip. I draw my reflections from field journals kept over this eleven-year period, in addition to the available scholarly literature.

CASE STUDY IN EMPOWERMENT: FUTURE GENERATIONS (ARUNACHAL)

The FGA was formally incorporated as an Arunachali voluntary society in March 1997. This followed two months of community meetings in many villages in the Adi, Apatani, and Tangsa tribal areas, to identify felt needs and interested communities. Due to security concerns in eastern Arunachal Pradesh, it was not possible to implement projects in the Tangsa area. Within a few months, however, work did begin in the Nyishi tribal area in western Arunachal Pradesh. The FGA is based on three action principles:

1. Base action on locally specific data
2. Build three-way partnerships between community, officials, experts
3. Develop a community work plan to change collective behaviour

There were six criteria for evaluating outcomes: equity, sustainability, interdependence (building healthy linkages between partners), holism, collaboration, and iteration (circular movement between action and reflection).[4] The FGA model nurtures and supports volunteer community action groups for holistic community change. As these groups identify needs, the FGA helps to facilitate training and partnerships with appropriate experts and government agencies. Highly motivated volunteers can become Village Welfare Workers (VWW) trained in public health, infant and maternal health, and leadership and organization development, by the FGA in collaboration with the Comprehensive Rural Health Project (CRHP) in Jamkhed, Mahrarashtra (Arole and Arole 2002). Each VWW has a certain number of households to care for and monitor and plays a key leadership role. Support for grass-roots voluntary work is provided by Learning and Doing Centres, which are accessibly situated in the web of villages they support. Each site is managed by a voluntary Local Coordinating Committee (LCC) which sends representatives to a statewide Master Coordinating Committee which meets regularly to set policy guidelines for the NGO. The centres and the community groups are supported

---

[4] This model for community-based empowerment and sustainable development is described in detail in Taylor-Ide and Taylor (2002).

by one or more paid staff who live on site and report to the executive director of the FGA. The executive director is a professional staff person responsible for statewide administration of the FGA within the policy guidelines formulated by the voluntary members of the Master Coordinating Committee.

The FGA's first goal was to cultivate community action groups in each of the three sites. Although more men than women attended the initial community meetings, almost all the men dropped out after several sessions. The result was the development of about a half-dozen Mahila Mandals (women's organizations) in each of the three sites by the end of 1997. By 2006, the number grew to 72 Mahila Mandals (and 57 Self-Help Groups), 16 Farmers' Clubs (men's voluntary organizations) spread across six sites. The outpouring of creative voluntary action from these Mahila Mandals has galvanized FGA projects ever since, following a pattern found elsewhere in India of strong grass-roots leadership by women in social movements (Ray 1999). Health has been the primary focus of FGA activities and in responding to the grass-roots initiative, many issues have been tackled. These include sanitation, microcredit, agricultural improvement and experimentation, income generation (especially weaving and other cottage industries), problems of alcohol and addiction, violence against women, child marriage and non-consensual marriage, forestry, environmental awareness, Panchayati raj training, and civic leadership training. Although geographically uneven the outcomes have been excellent and have included plummeting rates of infant and maternal mortality and violence against women, increased literacy, thriving microcredit schemes, transformation of village landscapes, and diverse programmes of local economic development. But, on my recent trip to visit FGA work, it is the empowerment of women and cultivation of grass-roots civic leadership that community volunteers spoke most about, repeatedly, with passion and thoughtfulness.

THE QUESTION OF 'TRIBAL' IDENTITY: ARUNACHAL PRADESH IN (SUB)NATIONAL CULTURAL POLITICS

Years spent in India had habituated me to the cultural diversity that often astonishes Americans. However, just as I have watched Americans in India rethink their understanding of, and pride in, the different multiculturalism of the USA, I watched myself on my first trip to the Northeast in 1995 reweaving my understanding of India's multicultural nationalism. It was only after I had been in the Northeast that I understood how invisible it is in the Indian mainstream. And, Arunachal Pradesh has been an occlusion within an occlusion—because of its internal complexity, its lack of salience in mainstream national and sub-national popular awareness, and the paucity of scholarly research. The staggering density of ethnic diversity of the Northeast, rises, as it were, exponentially in Arunachal Pradesh. With just over one million people spread over the precipitous easternmost Himalayas at the lowest population density in India, the state currently recognizes twenty major tribal groups, with eighty sub-tribal groupings (Census of India 2001).

The term 'tribe' is always problematic as it carries many stereotypes. Recent scholarship in India notes the ambiguities and contradictions of 'tribal' or 'adivasi' identities, including the tendency to romanticize tribal communities as pure cultures, living in harmony close to nature, but disjunct from surrounding society (Baviskar 1996; Sivaramakrishnan 2000). Sophisticated recent scholarship deconstructs tribal identities showing that tribal economies and identities are less isolated than often portrayed, and are profoundly shaped by, and embedded in, the complex histories of wider interaction. The distinctive cultural and political economic features of Arunachal's many tribes arose not simply from isolation, but *from the kinds of interrelationships* they had with the plains. Baruah is right to describe a kind of articulation as well as a historic two-way continuum between the hills and the plains, driven by raids to capture slaves, shifting trade and labour markets, and environmental changes (Baruah 2005a 102–6). Sikdar provides detailed historical evidence of the strong impacts on hill tribal economies and societies of British imperial attempts to establish and control trade routes between the Indian plains and China in the nineteenth century (Sikdar 1982). Borooah provides a fascinating and in-depth ethnographic picture of the impact of regional trade on Wancho society (in eastern Arunachal Pradesh) from the 1960s to the present, as *internal* gender and class power structures were structured and restructured in response to waves of *external* restructuring in regional and transnational flows of consumer goods, non-timber forest products, and opium (Borooah 2000). Analysing the relationship of Sulung foragers and Nyishi horticulturalists, Taylor-Ide argues that the flow of trade and warfare among hill tribes creates their differences as well as their interdependencies as different tribes specialize in different ecological niches (Taylor-Ide 2006).

GENDER IN 'TRADITIONAL' ARUNACHAL PRADESH POLITIES AND ECONOMIES

Many traditional tribal societies in the Northeast accord women considerable authority and power. This is most notable among the Khasis. All Arunachali tribes, however, show a distinctive combination of male political authority and female economic power, which a senior IAS officer aptly described to me as 'woman-centred but male dominant'. There is a glaring lack of comparative scholarship on gender in Arunachal Pradesh, but it seems evident to me that endemic warfare is the primary structural cause of male dominance in traditional tribal societies. This is a typical gender pattern in horticultural societies with chronic warfare such as New Guinea and the Amazon (Sanday 1981). Male dominance is predominant in traditional Arunachali kinship and marriage systems, but with much inter-tribal variation.

Traditionally, women were the primary farmers and foragers in all Arunachali subsistence economies. Men clear the land, help maintain

Photograph 14.1: Apatani girls at work, repairing rice paddies
Source: Betsy Taylor

fields, manage forests, hunt, help with fieldwork, and do much of the construction of buildings. The great bulk of the labour—feeding and maintaining the family—is done by the women. Women are also active traders.

'TRADITIONAL' TRIBAL PUBLIC SPACES AS GROUNDS FOR TWENTY-FIRST-CENTURY CIVIC EXPERIMENTATION

There are fascinating differences between tribal groups in the kinds of public and civic spaces that have been created by community groups active in the FGA. One of the necessary paradoxes of public space is that it must create the appearance of both certainty and openness (Lefort 1998). This sense of public authority comes from the ability of a public space to represent collective social order and common good as self-evident. However, to make a compelling demonstration that this collective order is legitimate, it must create at least the appearance of freedom by including dramas in which individuals and groups appear to voluntarily assent to, and participate in, this order (Rappaport 1999). On the one hand, the social geography of initial community meetings exemplified constitutive local power structures. On the other, all of them had structured spaces of openness, *built into their 'traditional' form*, which created room to manoeuvre, re-invent, and transform received forms of power and prestige. It is my argument that different forms of local tribal publics have distinctive modalities for their self-undoing and self-transformation. The conclusion of this article is that this leads to different 'trajectories' of empowerment, for example, forms of emergent civic space that were distinctively 'Nyishi', 'Apatani', or 'Adi'.

ETHNOSCAPES OF DEVELOPMENT

It is striking to compare the actual trajectories of empowerment, with what was predicted by senior officials and state-level leaders at the beginning of the project. These were knowledgeable and concerned leaders, so I consider this unpredictability to be not a sign of their ignorance, but of the necessarily emergent and open-ended nature of empowerment. From the beginning, I and other FGA team members had extensive conversations with high-level administrative, legislative, and scholarly leaders.[5] Uniformly, they counselled that we could expect

---

[5] The fact that it was extremely difficult for foreigners to get government permits to work in Arunachal Pradesh necessitated that we have strong support

the greatest successes among the Apatani because they were renowned for their hard work, civic solidarity, and follow through. The Adi, they predicted, would be the second most successful. Closest to the plains and enjoying the earliest political contacts with the outside world during the colonial and post-Independence period, the Adi dominated much of politics, with (I was told) a gift for rhetoric, a progressive 'can-do' attitude as well as education and wealth from early modernization. The Nyishi were described as needing the programmes the most, but, it was with them that the programmes of self-help and empowerment would be the most difficult to implement. They were described as most 'backwards', isolated, warlike, intensely individualistic, and less oriented towards collective goals.[6]

What actually happened was the opposite. By 2006, everyone agreed that the programmes were more creative and dynamic in Nyishi areas. Apatani work had grown in fits and starts but seemed solid. Grass-roots, holistic empowerment in Adi areas was not as vibrant, although there were successful and interesting issue-targeted programmes. To understand these outcomes, this article argues that one needs to analyse the differing 'trajectories of empowerment' discussed earlier. My central argument is that the 'top down' predictions made sense if you analysed the differences between tribal groups in the forms of collective action and the public spaces available at the grass-roots level. As I argue in the following sections, there were dramatic differences in levels and kinds of democratic access, and the forms of public deliberation. However, at the end of the article, I argue that, contrary to appearances, these *public spaces* contained surprising potentials for new *civic spaces*. What

---

from the state government. In the past, my approach has been more 'bottom up', but the necessity in Arunachal Pradesh to also work from the 'top down' taught me valuable lessons. It led me to more nuanced and actor-centred understandings of how bureaucracies and governments work. It also led me into warm personal friendships with members of the new elite of the state which helped me understand the perspectives of emerging, highly educated youth trying to build a pan-Arunachali, pan-tribal identity in the context of sophisticated experience and understanding of global cosmopolitan culture. This cosmopolitanism includes what Tsing (2005) describes as the travelling 'packages' of ideas in transnational discourses of global civil society such as 'environmentalism' and 'sustainability'.

[6] Such state-level construction of typologies of 'tribal personalities' is an interesting part of what Baruah (2005a: 6) calls ethnoscapes of development in which different groups essentialize each other in ways that are complexly over-determined, but which help establish the horizons of expectation for different groups in competition with each other sub-nationally.

I describe earlier as 'structured spaces of openness' within 'traditional' tribal publics could be opened to transformation by new civic networks. *The un-structuring of public structures, follows the immanent logics of its structures.* Most dramatically, the Nyishi women surged into these gaps, widened them, transformed them, and, working with various partners, did difficult civic labour to create new forms and spaces of imagination and action, thus winning over many of the initially fiercely antagonistic men, after years of hard work. The FGA created an *inter-tribal civic infrastructure* that was a crucial force in enabling the transformative work *within* the different tribal communities.

TANGSA PUBLIC SPACE

More than any other area, the first Tangsa community meeting was explicitly hierarchical in its social microgeographies. It was hosted by a prominent chief in the open air of his large compound. His three wives were busy orchestrating preparations for a large feast, overseeing many people behind the scenes in his large home of many rooms and outbuildings. The seating was oval in shape with large, store-bought chairs and couches for special guests at one end, facing two circular rows of seats, which graduated from smaller chairs to backless benches. The chief managed the event most hospitably, welcoming people graciously into their seats. It seemed to me that this garnered him cultural capital in two ways—winning credit for generosity and managing events through poetics of tact, without incurring the costs of overt dominance. He initiated the topics and no one spoke out of turn.

Like other societies in eastern Arunachal Pradesh, traditional Tangsa society was stratified within structured villages with the chiefs holding formal political power and exercising considerable economic control over land and trade. This was true even though the Tangsa seem to have migrated to the eastern lower lands from the related cluster of more egalitarian tribes in the central and western parts of the state, which practised semi-nomadic swidden horticulture—for example, the Adis, Akas, Apatanis, Bangnis, Nyishis, Mishmis, and Mijis.

Despite the clarity in the overt choreographies of power, I was struck by the way in which the unfolding of this event over many hours opened up more covert, alternative geographies. For one thing, periodically, a visible absence of enthusiasm from the crowd to certain ideas seemed to speak volumes. Also, at different points, the chief's oldest and youngest wife drew me aside, down hallways, and into more private rooms, to give me gifts and to talk about issues. The emotional and cultural texture of this happening felt similar to my childhood experiences in the rambling, extended family compounds of Punjab's villages. Despite official acquiescence to male control over space and speech, and the burden of overwork, women and girls were able to open alternative, subaltern theatres of action and communication. In fact, some would argue that some of the remarkable vibrancy of grass-roots women's organizations in India springs from the social microgeographies of oppression. Exclusion from authoritative public space, paradoxically, constitutes homosocial social spaces for women that can be protected and invisible to power because of men's lack of interest, until the women have been able to use these women's spaces as a springboard for new collective action.

ADI PUBLIC SPACE

Traditionally, the Adis were renowned for having what Elwin describes as the 'most highly developed tribal councils' in Arunachal Pradesh (Elwin 1988: 157). He says, each village had a chief and a council, called the *kebang*, which was held in the village hall, traditionally called a *morung*.[7] These councils were large affairs with elaborate debates in which all the villagers could participate. They controlled such decisions as when and where to clear the forest, to sow, hunt, and fish, as well as when and how to celebrate festivals and sacrifices. Our first meetings were held in the village of Sille, in the village hall, which is a public space in the middle of the village and is a collectively owned and managed structure. Like Adi homes, the building itself was oblong in shape and raised on stilts. At one end was a raised platform where I and other people who were being treated as 'VIP' guests were seated (these included government officials and wealthy or influential notables). In the usual 'durbar' mode, featured speakers were given a chance to speak in what seemed some sort of order of rank precedence. But, the event quickly opened up into a mode of rapid-fire give and take, with questions and comments coming from all sides. The discussion seemed to epitomize 'democratic deliberation' in the sense of open-ended give and take, in which people pose arguments, express interests, state their demands, and make counter claims—some critical, much humorous. No women originally sat at the central floor. They were vocally clustered on the periphery along with many children. The press of people, their

[7] However, in my experience, village people also called the building the kebang.

Photograph 14.2: An Adi home
Source: Betsy Taylor

mobility, their glances at each other, the sub-conversations, and the unpredictability as to who was to speak next—all this as a performance of collective public voice(s) conveyed a different tone of collective will formation from our experiences in Tangsa villages.

After this, the FGA team was lead on a sort of yatra around neighbouring houses and villages. Periodically, we were stopped at homes where meetings or hospitality had been planned for us. Held on large porches or around hearths, these civic spaces mirrored the social geography of the morung because of the socio-spatial layout and the architecture and how people used it. The host and special guests were at one end, on the most substantial seating, with mostly men in the centre, shading into a periphery that was more (but not exclusively) female and younger. While initial presentations and prestations were structured, formalized and conducted among those who seemed highest in status (*goanbura*, male home owner, professionals, and officials), and spatially central, the peripheries were lively, vocal, and often pressing close. Most notably, the 'centre stage' seemed to be mobile; when someone on the peripheries made a statement, it was as if the funnel of attentiveness realigned itself, allowing them the time and the social space to speak their mind. Once, when I asked a question about the health of young children, a young woman, with a child on her back, began to talk from the far periphery. She said the men did not know enough to answer the question. One of the centrally placed men called her to stand in the middle where she spoke with confidence and at length.

APATANI PUBLIC SPACE

Flowing from common cultural roots, the Adi, Tangsa, Nyishi, and Apatani have created very different social geographies as they migrated into distinct ecological–economic niches. For some hundreds of years, the Apatani have been settled in the deeply rumpled western mountains, in a valley that is uniquely flat and circular for Arunachal Pradesh. In Ziro Valley, the Apatani have created one of the most intensively cultivated and ecologically sustainable economies ever achieved anywhere in the world. From the lush soils they have built a densely variegated, highly structured, and mutually interdependent web of economic activities: laboriously hand-crafted terraces with a unique system for integrating wet rice and fish cultivation; cleverly constructed and collectively managed irrigation systems; gardens and orchards; and a patchwork of forestry plantations (including bamboo, firewood, hardwood). In the last four decades, the Apatani have been at the forefront in seizing the possibilities of modernization—attaining high levels of education, professional achievement, government employment, and linkages with external markets. About half of all Apatanis are employed elsewhere, but most return regularly to Ziro Valley for annual religious festivals and other collective cultural events. The small valley had a population of about 30,000 (12, 289 in the town of Ziro) in 2001. Agriculture thrives and diversifies, but the towns resemble any Indian town in dense and busy clusters of businesses, vehicles, shops, and government offices.

The 2001 Census of India shows the following literacy rates as percentage of population:

TABLE 14.1: Literacy Rates, Arunachal Pradesh

	Total %	Male %	Female %
India	65	76	54
Arunachal Pradesh	55	64	44
Ziro Valley	66	72	60

Over the centuries, Apatani socio-cultural forms have grown in intricacy, structure, and mutual interdependence, as population density, prosperity, and intensity of land utilization has grown (Fürer-Haimendorf 1980). The clan is the unit of government which seems to be the primary site, traditionally, for democratic deliberation. Each village can have several clans and clans work collectively to manage common village issues. The clans were run by all-male councils called *bulyang*s. There are three kinds of bulyangs—these are graded by age, with the most powerful being the one for men who are past active economic roles. These councils regulate the elaborate ritual cycle and

Photograph 14.3: Apatani clan platform with a young boy playing
Source: Betsy Taylor

resolve disputes. There were three types of land ownership: individual ownership of land, groves of bamboo, pines, fruit trees, and of homes and granaries; clan ownership of assembly platforms, pasturage, burial grounds, and hunting grounds; and common village ownership of pasturage and forests. Other social groups which fostered a sense of collectivism were the important work groups called *patang*.

Like the Adi, traditional Apatani society had clearly demarcated and formal public spaces, highly visible in the social geography of every village. But, Apatani public space was adapted to their far more corporately bounded, structured, and self-consciously codified lifeways. Each clan has a platform on which the clan council meets. These platforms are the most formal, sacred, and official public spaces in traditional Apatani society. They represent the essence of the democratic deliberation at the heart of the polity. But, women and girls were prohibited from these platforms by strong religious taboos. Unlike the Adi morung, the peripheries of these deliberative spaces are not constructed as socially fluid, expandable, or permeable.

Our initial community meetings were held in a public school on the edge of a large village. Organized by local schoolteachers, they were primarily for exchanging information about possible programmes, and ceremonial gifts, leading to long, in-depth discussions with interested individuals afterwards. It was my impression that the real decisions as to whether anybody wanted to become involved with the FGA would be made elsewhere. This was followed by walks to show our team the large village during which we gathered amused and friendly crowds. Land scarcity creates an extraordinarily closely packed landscape with strongly marked social demarcations and meanings. Walking along the densely packed and twisting lanes, I quickly realized from the commentary that the social landscape of the village was an intricate jigsaw of clans, working closely, cooperatively, and competitively together.

NYISHI PUBLIC SPACE

Traditionally, shifting horticulturalists such as the Nyishi, the Adi, and the Miri, tended to have the least corporate notions of political structure. Being semi-nomadic and needing to keep reapportioning access to land as they move their holdings, they had flexible decision-making networks. Ultimately, all land was understood to be communally held by clans which apportion specific plots at specific times according to informal decision-making within clans and lineages. The boundaries to these holdings were loosely defined.

The Nyishi had no stable socio-political units larger than the lineages which traditionally live together in longhouses with as many as sixty to seventy people. Viewed as warlike and unruly by their neighbours, there are some signs that they did have some traditional bodies for dispute resolution. Robinson, in 1851, describes them as ordered by

Photograph 14.4: The first class of Village Welfare Workers in Nyishi area
(with Betsy Taylor)
Source: Betsy Taylor

a 'sort of tacit commonsense law' and Elwin describes intermediaries called *gingdung*s, who arranged for ransom and could call councils called *nele* to which all concerned people could come for debate (Elwin 1988: 154).

The combination of mobility, warfare, and male control of marriage systems led to some of the strongest gender inequality in Arunachal Pradesh. Bride prices required many *mithun*s (a unique Arunachali type of forest-living cattle) and other expensive wealth, and were a major factor in cementing what structured social relations there were in this mobile, highly dispersed population. Child marriage and forced marriage were common, and isolated polygynous households encouraged strong concentration of power in older men. Wealth exchanges in marriage negotiations were central to the prestige system. In these circumstances, women and girls traditionally lacked countervailing sources of power such as publicly authoritative inter-household or women-controlled social webs. But, if they lacked authority, they had the informal power that could come from their crucially important labour power.

We selected Palin, one of the largest Nyishi towns, to begin meetings. The six hours plus on a very jolting, bad road to Palin highlighted the relative isolation. On the way, traditional Nyishi longhouses could be seen widely scattered over distant mountains. But many little settlements strung along the road evinced the demographic trends towards smaller houses, as people move to get access to schools and markets, and away from large, polygamous householding patterns and self-subsistent *jhumming* ('slash and burn' shifting cultivation). Unlike the other sites, the social geography of Palin did not provide any obvious or easy place for public meetings. There was no established, traditional architecture for public meetings and objections were raised to the few existing government buildings. After some negotiation, a largish room was rather grudgingly found in the government Inspection Bungalow. The lack of facilities in Palin meant that this bungalow was frequently the only option to lodge travelling government officials, but our use of it as a place for a public gathering seemed unusual. Our first meeting, like the Apatani, seemed more informational and ceremonial. Virtually all were men; the meeting seemed to attract established older leaders, such as many gaonbura and lower-level officials, and focused on questions as to what the FGA had to offer. The atmosphere felt subdued and perfunctory, and I expected a future of much difficulty in grass-roots empowerment and self-activity.

All this changed as soon as we set up the first workshops (on community-based health care). The first day almost no men appeared but about thirty women did. After the first day, word spread like wildfire and each day more and more women came crowding in—most of them young and with young children. In the first several years, attendance seemed constantly changing, as we heard reports about women walking for many hours from surrounding mountains and experiencing much suspicion and hostility from men. The half dozen, earliest and very dynamic Mahila Mandals rapidly replicated themselves into far-flung communities. They enthusiastically sent out their own representatives, over often arduous footpaths, to found new groups as requests flowed in through women's informal, inter-village networks.

From 1997–8, I vividly remember the distinctive tone of these first meetings. While extremely attentive, the women in Palin, unlike the Apatani and Adi women, were reticent. They were often tongue-tied or collapsed in giggles, and required a lot of encouragement. On my return in 2006, I found a remarkable transformation. In many vibrant meetings across the Nyishi area, women I knew as afraid even to look up, now stood to speak with great eloquence, clarity, and self-confidence about their own empowerment.

CIVIC SPACE, PUBLIC SPACE, AND THE POETICS OF SUB-NATIONALISM

Baruah makes the following very important point:

Actual civil society, it is now widely recognized, does not just include associations that might conform to a liberal democratic vision of the world. But many liberal analysts seem reluctant to separate their vision of a good society from their definitions of civil society... actually existing civil society includes organizations that liberal democrats might despise, e.g. illiberal cultural and social organizations and closely knit ethnic solidarity network (Baruah 2005a: 9).

As Reid and I argue elsewhere (Reid and Taylor 2009) this is partly because of the provincialism (Chatterjee 1993) of Western traditions of democracy which overemphasize voluntarism, reason, disembodied and universalized identities, and individualism, for reasons having to do with its unique historical origins. Civil society, in this tradition, is in those zones of freedom in which individuals can act, associate, and deliberate on collective issues, disembedded (by reason and

Photograph 14.5: Mahila Mandal singing welcome song in Adi area
Source: Betsy Taylor

dispassionateness) from material necessity, state coercion, and private responsibilities. In a fascinating discussion of the permeability of the public and the private in Indian lifeways, Baruah (2005a: Chapter 6) points out that the sharpness of the public/private distinction in Western democracies (such as USA) is historically specific, carries its own threats to democracy, and hinders an understanding of the contradictions and trajectories of actual political imaginations and civic labours in Northeast India.

To help develop analytic categories that allow us to both compare democratic struggles globally and be less ethnocentric, I propose sharper analytic distinctions between civic space, civil society, and public space. Civic spaces are *those spaces that are emergent from people's everyday life practices in which they reflect with each other on how everyday lifeways translate into collective questions, and how collective and public issues translate into everyday life.* This is the basis for what Dallmayr calls 'transformative democracy' which is rooted in concrete experiences of suffering, exploitation, and domination. It takes hard labour (of thought, social caring, often political or economic courage, and shrewdness) to open up these spaces in the thick of ordinary, highly sedimented, contentious, and contradictory everyday lives—hence Dallmayr speaks of 'achieving our world' in common (Dallmayr 2001). These civic spaces, by definition, have to emerge from the particularities of local places and local social geographies. Therefore, one cannot predict exactly when and how empowerment will happen. As Arendt repeatedly emphasized, this movement towards a world in common depends on the unimaginable natality of unique human creativity—which generates new forms which cannot be predicted. As Tinker says, empowerment when it happens, is often something that 'just happens', despite or outside of what 'development programmes' intended or planned (Tinker 2006).

In the context of Arunachal Pradesh, the FGA has been able to support grass-roots women (and increasingly, men) in building remarkable new civic spaces that are responsive to local realities, but link local groups pan-tribally. These civic spaces have been primarily within and between their households. The emotional engine of the work is the regularity of meetings of the Mahila Mandals and Farmer's Clubs which are often hosted by members within their homes. The heart of these meetings are the sharing of personal experiences and mutual support and analysis. When these spaces—intermediate between private and public life—have been vital and creative, they have worked with FGA staff to open up new forms of public space, or reclaim and transform old ones. Each site has built, and helped maintain, various buildings for the Learning and Doing Centres where they conduct workshops, host guests, and stage public events. In each site, but particularly in the Palin area, FGA women took pride in describing to me their collective performances in big political and religious gatherings—singing and dancing, wearing their FGA regalia, winning prizes. Celebratory civic culture—in song, dance, and storytelling—has been pervasive in meetings and public events. This cultivation of expressive arts and the ability to listen to and to tell their unique stories has been crucial to developing what Boyte would call 'civic skills' for 'public work', demonstrating, as Young says, that the fabric of public space is storytelling (Young 1996).

Increasingly, this decade of building up civic capacity, rooted in highly local civic spaces, is leading to public action. In February 2006, I was astonished to be excitedly told by the Palin women that they (and the male supporters who are growing in number and status) were going to lead a march through Palin on International Women's Day, in March, carrying signs saying 'No Child Marriage!', 'No Forced Marriage!', 'Give Education for Your Girl Child!', etc. This would have been unthinkable and physically dangerous for them in 1997. I do not yet have quantitative data, but in all three sites in my 2006 fieldwork, I was repeatedly told that many FGA VWWs were running for Panchayati Raj office, with unusual success because they were known across many households. The FGA is one of two NGOs in Arunachal Pradesh conducting training for Panchayat representatives, concentrating on the lowest levels who have received no training from governmental or non-governmental agencies.

ANALYTIC DISTINCTIONS BETWEEN CIVIL SOCIETY AND CIVIC SPACE

The definition of civil society as 'voluntary association' has tended to confuse two types of questions, which are analytically very different. One cluster has to do with questions of how *civic life emerges from everyday local practices* that I have addressed earlier. The second cluster has to do with daunting *organizational questions* about how one keeps durable, effective organizations alive and able to express and defend that civic life, and to engage authoritative structures of public power. If I had addressed the second cluster of questions in this article, I would have focused on the organization of the FGA; how it manages to keep itself alive and how it relates to other civic organizations (statewide, nationally, internationally), and to the state and to the remnants of pre-state public authority (which are unhelpfully called 'traditional' and 'tribal'). These are important questions. In the context of Arunachal Pradesh, challenges have been faced and defeats and successes experienced. It is not easy to build statewide civic organization in an intensely multicultural context. Civic organizations are essential to provide what I call *multiscalar civic infrastructure* (Reid and Taylor 2009) that facilitates extra-local resources for grass-roots actors, and assists local groups in the *processes* of mutual empowerment, without managing the *content* of the programmes that emerge. For this, the FGA model is a particularly good one.

However, to nurture democratic hope and the forms of civic life that create the basis for it, the primary focus should be on what Sivaramakrishnan aptly calls the 'craft' of creating, sustaining, and transforming the public sphere (Sivaramakrishnan 2000). This can only be done from the self-activity of grass-roots actors, working creatively within the constraining and enabling structures of local publics. If we go looking for 'civil society' with the idea that we are going out to find worthy and efficacious *voluntary organizations,* we will go with preset (and deeply Western biased) understandings of what civic life is. If we go out looking for openings for civic space within existing local publics as they actually are, we might find fascinating new experiments in, and possibilities for, democracy.

CHAPTER 15

Rethinking Delhi's Northeast India Policy

Why neither Counter-insurgency nor Winning Hearts and Minds is the Way Forward

BETHANY LACINA

Analysis of the security situation in Northeast India is characterized by all-round frustration. Inhabitants of the region have endured decades of conflict—at times smouldering, often quite active—that have kept much of the region militarized, subject to restrictions on civil rights and political activity, and economically depressed (for history of the Northeast and its conflicts see Hazarika 1994; Nag 2002; C. Singh 2004). Opinion polls suggest most people of the area are disillusioned with Delhi's interventions in the region and are distressed by the conditions that they continue to endure (Cline 2006: 135; Goswami 2004; S. Singh 2004). At the same time, from Delhi's perspective, counter-insurgency in the region is doctrinally sound[1] and the area has been given repeated political concessions and a stream of development aid intended to address the conflicts' presumed root causes (Shani 2005; Singh 1987). Yet, violence persists. Thus the frustration: the centre argues it is 'doing all the right things', while human rights groups, academics, and, most importantly, civilians in the Northeast rightly complain that people in the region remain severely impoverished and insecure and that there is limited understanding at the centre of the Northeast and its grievances (Baruah 1999; Mukhim 2002; Narahari 2002).

---

[1] Based on the author's interviews of retired government personnel conducted in 2005. See also *Indian Army Doctrine* available at http://indianarmy.nic.in/indianarmydoctrine.htm.

This essay argues that both sympathetic and critical discussions of Delhi's approach to the Northeast tend to downplay a key intervening variable between social grievance and violence: local northeastern politics. Delhi's counter-insurgency policy has not come to terms with how well embedded insurgent groups are in the region's political process. Meanwhile, critics of Delhi legitimately point out unaddressed grievances in the region and the often patronizing, misguided, or even overtly hostile approach of policy makers to the Northeast, while glossing over the fact that public discontent does not translate directly into violence without the intermediate step of the strategic decisions taken by political elites (Fearon and Laitin 2003).

This essay proceeds as follows: in the section which follows, I highlight some features that distinguish the insurgencies in the Northeast from other countries' experiences and from archetypal conceptions of guerrilla war. Next, I explain the roles insurgents have come to play in local politics and present data on violent events in the region. Much of the violence in the Northeast can only be understood as a component of a system of politics in which rule of law is nearly absent. I then go on to discuss the implications of the intimate connection between violence and politics in the region for standard models of counter-insurgency and India's policies in the Northeast to date. I argue that *neither* military interventions in the region nor emphasis on development is the most important priority for the region because both can be thwarted by an environment of corruption and coercion and both fail to address civilians' lack of confidence in the Northeast's formal institutions. In the final section of the chapter, I argue that rule of law—rather than military counter-insurgency or development—should move to the top of the list of political priorities for the region. Visible and even-handed prosecution of abuse is the best way to restore public confidence in elected government.

I am not the first commentator on the situation in the Northeast to argue for reform of the police and judiciary. But what seems to be missing from existing analysis is stress on the primary importance of rule of law for the efficacy of any other attempts to stabilize the region. That analytical point implies that much of the commentary on the Northeast is a false debate over the right mix of military might and winning hearts and minds through aid and political concessions.

INSURGENCY IN THE NORTHEAST

This essay cannot present anything like a full history of the conflicts in

Northeast India, but only draw the reader's attention to a few salient features of insurgent activity in the area. Northeastern insurgent groups are numerous, fissiparous, and frequently engaged in violence against targets other than the state. These conflicts have been long lasting and have resulted in repeated rounds of negotiations with, and political concessions from, the centre.[2]

The northeastern states of India are geographically and culturally distant from the rest of India. They are home to a number of ethnically and linguistically distinct groups and 'tribes'. The area was never fully colonized by the British. At the time of Indian independence there was an attempt to institutionalize some local autonomy for the region's peoples, most notably through the creation of autonomous district councils under the Sixth Schedule of the Constitution. Since that time numerous ethnic groups in the area have called for greater autonomy or independence and 'sons of the soil' movements have developed in response to migration within the region and, especially, from West Bengal and Bangladesh (Weiner 1978).

A major feature of rebellion in the Northeast is the sheer duration of these conflicts, which are punctuated by amnesties or political solutions acceptable to some part of the insurgent leadership but objectionable to a sub-group that continues to fight. If Naga violence is dated from its first upsurge in 1954, the region bears the dubious distinction of being home to the longest-lived insurgency in the world today (Fearon 2004). In Tripura, Manipur, and Assam, conflict has likewise stretched for decades, although political and military interventions have quelled violence for periods. This duration is exceptional even by the standards of rural insurgency (ibid.).

Second, almost all currently active insurgent groups have a history of splits along clan and ideological lines or according to personal rivalries. As a result, the area faces an extraordinary number of self-proclaimed insurgencies—one observer estimates more than fifty as active (Shani

---

[2] At present, the most important rebel groups in the Northeast are the ULFA, two factions of the National Socialist Council of Nagaland (NSCN-IM and NSCN-K), the National Liberation Front of Tripura (NLFT), the All Tripura Tiger Force, and the United Liberation National Front (UNLF) and People's Liberation Army, which espouse the cause of Manipur's Meitei population. The Kuki National Front (KNF) is also based in Manipur. For information on these conflicts and other groups active in the Northeast see http://www.c-nes.org, www.neportal.org, www.satp.org, and http://www.pcr.uu.se/database/.

2005). Although rebel groups in many parts of the world have shown themselves to be quite vulnerable to fracture, the Northeast is an outlier by world standards (Uppsala University 2006). Proliferation occurs, in part, because of conflicting claims between ethnic groups. For example, the Bodo call for a homeland runs afoul of the fact that the Bodos are not actually in the majority in the area they claim as the historical Bodoland. The Naga insurgency calls for a 'greater Nagaland', several districts of which are claimed by the Kuki tribe and currently within Meitei-dominated Manipur. The zero-sum nature of different groups' demands leads to competitive mobilization and violence between insurgent groups as well as against the state. But proliferation also occurs, as we shall see, because of the symbiosis between insurgent groups and local politics.

Finally, war in the Northeast has persisted in spite of the fact that most observers agree that secession, either through military victory or a collapse of the centre's resolve, is probably impossible (Hardgrave and Kochanek 2000: 155; Subba 2002) and that even overthrowing a state government would be almost unthinkably difficult for one of these groups. Presently, even the largest insurgent groups have only a few thousand members; none has ever grown large enough to drag the region into a war on the scale of the violence that prevailed in Jammu and Kashmir in the 1990s or in Punjab in the 1980s (Lacina and Gleditsch 2005; Uppsala University 2006). Much of the fighting in the region is inter-communal, aimed at running a rival militant group off certain pieces of territory, ethnic cleansing or pogroms against civilians, or dispensing vigilante justice. And commentators point out that many insurgent groups in the area are difficult to distinguish from criminal organizations because they are heavily involved in extortion, kidnapping, and the cross-border drug trade (Deka 2006).

THE POLITICAL ROLE OF INSURGENTS IN THE NORTHEAST

From the point of view of traditional theories of guerrilla war, the persistence of insurgencies in the Northeast seems puzzling. As fighting forces the groups in the area are badly organized, not particularly ideologically disciplined (Cline 2006), and have lost much of their popular support (Hazarika 1994). These tiny insurgencies are unlikely to succeed according to the classic blueprint of guerrilla war: building military strength by organizing peasants so as to either forcibly eject the government or compel it to abandon the region (Johnson 1968).

The influence and the endurance of insurgency in the Northeast are due to the fact that armed groups are embedded in the workings of northeastern civilian politics. Acting like the combination of a racketeer and a policy lobby, an insurgent group can cut political deals and influence elections, and become enmeshed in a network of extortion and corruption that makes it difficult for politicians or bureaucrats to act independently of the rebels.

Using Data on Violence to Demonstrate the Relationship between Politics and Insurgent Activity

The degree to which violent activity is embedded within the political system rather than being determined by military considerations can be seen by looking at patterns in rebel attacks. Using news reports collected from the conflict monitoring project at the Uppsala University's Department of Peace and Conflict Research (Uppsala University 2006), which searches for accounts of internal conflicts from a variety of global wire services, I compiled a list of violent episodes in Northeast India during 2003 and 2004.[3] Much of the violence was inter-communal or aimed at intimidating or extorting money from civilians: among militant-initiated attacks, there were seventy attacks against civilian targets and just sixteen against government targets; for comparison's sake, there were more occasions—eighteen—on which rebel groups were reported to have made a formal statement to the press.

The timing of events is also tellingly correlated to the political calendar. To demonstrate this pattern, Table 15.1 uses statistics to investigate temporal patterns in militant-initiated attacks in four states: Assam, Nagaland, Manipur, and Tripura. A logistic regression was used to estimate the probability of a militant-initiated event in one of these four states, conditional on information contained in the following variables. The first variable considers whether the day in question is a *national holiday*[4]—Republic Day (26 January), Babasaheb Ambedkar's birthday (14 April), Independence Day (15 August), or Mahatma Gandhi's birthday (2 October). One of the patterns commentators have noted is that militant-initiated attacks are frequently staged on

[3] Episodes are tracked in state–day format. Violent events often lead to further violence. In this case, the day a sequence of attacks began is noted and the remaining days are considered part of the same event.

[4] For both national and non-national holidays I consider the day before and the day of the holiday to be the potentially significant moments for rebel attacks.

dates of political significance, such as the visits of federal officials or federal holidays. For example, 'It has become a tendency for the ULFA to engage in ... violence on important national days, such as Republic Day and Independence Day' (Deka 2006: 4). To further improve confidence in the strength of association between political holidays and rebel attacks, I also look at whether apolitical, *non-national holidays* are associated with a higher probability of violence as well. I defined these dates as federal holidays that do not have nationalist themes: New Year's Day, Labour Day (1 May), Children's Day (14 November), and Christmas Day (25 December).

TABLE 15.1: Logistic Regression for Probability of a Militant Attack in Northeast India, 2003–4

Unit of Analysis: State–Day Dependent Variable: Rebel-initiated Attack Model 1				
Indep. Variable	*Coefficient*	*Standard Error*	*z*	*P>z*
Rain (mm)	−0.00171	0.00097	−1.76	0.078
National Holiday	1.57	0.35	4.43	0.000
Other National Holiday	0.618	0.47	1.31	0.191
Lok Sabha Opening	1.13	0.58	1.96	0.050
Rajya Sabha Opening	−1.49	0.82	−1.83	0.068
Day of Election	2.32	1.1	2.03	0.043
Manipur	−1.51	0.43	−3.53	0.000
Nagaland	−3.46	1.0	−3.4	0.001
Tripura	−0.945	0.35	−2.71	0.007
Intercept	−3.17	0.28	−11.23	0.000

Notes: n = 2920
Pseudo R-Squared = 0.1310

Another set of events of significance in the political calendar is the *Lok Sabha openings* and *Rajya Sabha openings*. Statistical analysis, therefore, was used to ask whether the week leading up to the opening of a new session of either house of Parliament tended to be a time of heightened insurgent activity.[5] Finally, the *day of an election* is probably the most important event of the entire political calendar, so I also test whether there is an elevated probability of an insurgent attack on days

---

[5] The legislative schedule of both houses of India's parliament is available at www.parliamentofindia.nic.in.

when there was polling taking place in the state. Finally, the probability estimates here also take into account differences in the probability of violence among the four states[6] and average rainfall[7] in the area because insurgency theory suggests that monsoon conditions interfere with the ability of insurgents to launch attacks.

The results of this exercise demonstrate how closely linked insurgent activities are to the political calendar.

Rainfall, which military theory says should be related to how likely insurgents are to carry out an attack, does have a negative relationship with the probability of rebel-initiated violence, as predicted. But both the substantive and statistical strengths of that result are weak. Political events, however, are powerful predictors of insurgent activity. National holidays are strongly associated with an increased probability of attack. This result cannot be explained by arguing that holidays simply create attractive civilian targets, as holidays without nationalist themes have no statistical relationship to the probability of rebel violence. The incipient opening of the Lok Sabha increases the probability of violence, while the calendar of the largely ceremonial Rajya Sabha does not predict insurgent activity, again suggesting the fine-grained sensitivity of insurgent activity to the political cycle. And the largest increase in the probability of an attack comes on election days, the most important part of the calendar for any politician.

The substantive significance of politics for the timing of rebel attacks is quite dramatic. The statistical estimate above is that the probability of a militant-initiated violent event in Assam on a day with average rainfall is 3 per cent. Those odds increase to 8 per cent if the Lok Sabha will be opening within a week and to 12 per cent if it is the day before or of a national holiday. The probability of attack climbs to 23 per cent on the day of an election.

Describing the Link between Politics and Insurgent Activity

Many commentators have the noted rebels have close ties to politics in the Northeast (Cline 2006; Haokip 2003; Kumar 2003; Routray 2003b). The ties between insurgents and the political process also

[6] I include dummy variables for Manipur, Nagaland, and Tripura. Assam is the reference category. The data used for this exercise and more details on the statistical estimations used are available with the author.

[7] Rainfall is based on the monthly average rainfall in Assam from data collected in 2001–2 (GoA 2002).

sometimes take the form of semi-cooperative linkages between active rebels, bureaucrats, and politicians. These linkages are not the same as the incorporation of insurgents into the normal political process. The incorporation of rebels into the lawful political process is not a bad thing; what is detrimental is when active insurgents can distort political life through illegal means, most notably extortion and corruption.

The political dynamic in local northeastern politics to which I allude is quite similar to the interaction between organized crime and weakly institutionalized democracy in other parts of India and, indeed, the world over. To speak generically: insurgents can manipulate electoral and other politically salient outcomes (such as forcing a general strike or blocking commerce) and, in exchange for using that power to support a certain politician, party, or other political organization, they may be rewarded with monetary kickbacks or immunity for acts of racketeering and violence. Politicians and bureaucrats depend to some extent on insurgents for their career advancement, and for building their fortunes. They may also get a share of the money the rebels bring in through the black market, kidnapping, and other crimes. At each stage in these transactions there is the potential for coercion as well as cooperation. For example, a rebel group might keep people away from a polling place in exchange for a bribe, but may also demand a bribe in exchange for refraining from using violence against polling places.

More specifically, in the Northeast—with the partial exceptions of Arunachal Pradesh, Meghalaya, and Mizoram[8]—there frequently is a tacit association between political organizations and insurgent groups. In some cases, there are historical origins in common between the organization and the rebel group. In other cases, as in the alleged alliance between the Congress (I) and the National Liberation Front of Tripura (Kumar 2003), the connections seem more arbitrary. Insurgents' known ties to some politicians are an implied threat that law and order could deteriorate should the results of the normal political process be 'incorrect'. In some cases, rebels and politicians cooperate in outright fraud or insurgents vet political decisions, such

[8] Part of the reason for Mizoram's current stability is that the peace process brought insurgent leaders into government and the Mizo National Front has proven to be a disciplined political party, able to discredit the few rump groups that have tried to continue the insurgency and, based on data from opinion polls, are apparently able to win credit from the public for improving the quality of public services (Satapathy 2004).

as nomination of candidates. In still another scenario, parties or other political organizations, such as unions, join the rebels to obstruct normal political proceedings, a boycott that may be enforced with violence.

The involvement of insurgents in politics is a self-reinforcing situation and any one actor who tries to challenge the system will suffer. Local politicians receive sufficient benefits from conditions of ongoing insurgency and are hence unlikely to attempt to disrupt the equilibrium in the short term. (Of course, they would probably benefit from being able to cut insurgents out of the loop and act as sole power brokers in the region.) Low levels of insurgency keep development money from Delhi flowing and local politicians often administer this money in an astonishingly corrupt fashion (Hazarika 1994: 137–66). Contraband flows through the Northeast, especially along the border with Myanmar (Shani 2005), and the rebel groups in the area practise extortion and racketeering. These profits not only end up in the coffers of politicians who are willing to coordinate with violent organizations but they also allow insurgents and criminals to manipulate the local police and judiciary: 'An arrested insurgent can become a petty thief in the police records if the inspector in charge receives sufficient *Cha thaknaba* [a bribe]' (Haokip 2003).

The persistence of nationalism as a salient issue, which rebel groups help to ensure, also benefits politicians in less tangible ways. Politicians who represent a group that is a minority within a state can call for greater recognition and autonomy, while majority ethnic elites can blame other ethnic groups for economic grievances or lack of loyalty and champion the causes of their co-ethnics in other states. The centre can be blamed for failure to support any of these positions, in addition to its general neglect of the region and the transgressions of the security forces. So long as ethnic nationalism remains central to local politics, political accountability on issues like development is checked.[9]

On the flip side, there are also strong disincentives for any bureaucrat, politician, or private individual to resist violence. Given the importance of cooperating with rebels in order to survive in so much of local political and economic life, it is a trivial matter for the rebels to use intimidation as well as bribes to attain desired outcomes. In the absence

---

[9] See, for example, coverage of elections in Assam, Manipur, and Arunachal Pradesh that makes clear the salience of nationalist issue and the relatively limited differentiation parties display on most questions of substance (Bath 2004; Goswami 2004; S. Singh 2004).

of the rule of law, an individual can resist the nexus between violence and politics only at great personal peril.

One might wonder why the democratic political process does not cure persistent violence and corruption. Why are politicians not disciplined into ending ties with illegal actors by elections? Sympathy for nationalist claims, coercion of civilians, and pure electoral fraud no doubt play some role; there is also a demand for insurgent groups insofar as they provide security against other ethnic groups and crime in general. The strength of the present equilibrium is also due to the perception that the centre cannot or will not establish rule of law. Persistent violence and corruption erode the credibility of the central authorities who nominally have the power to put a stop to these abuses; comparative experience shows, repeatedly, that disgust with local elites and rebel groups destroys confidence and trust in the national government rather than inspiring a move towards the centre's position (Joes 2000; Johnson 1962; Shaw 2001). Residents of the Northeast know that Delhi's spending on officials that it cannot hold accountable enables much of the rotten politics in the region (Cline 2006). And the state's credibility as a provider of rule of law is gravely damaged by instances of human rights abuses by security forces in the area (for recent coverage see: Sengupta and Kumar 2005) and the use of legal measures that, in essence, suspend the rule of law for the sake of security, such as the Prevention of Terrorism Act (POTA), the Armed Forces Special Powers Act, and the Disturbed Areas Act. Again, comparative experience tells us that even in cases of extensive abuses by insurgents, civilians rarely risk cooperating with a national government they do not trust and whose credibility as a provider of swift and fair justice is low (cf. Sanchez 2003; Vinci 2005).

Implications of the Links between Violence and Politics for Counter-insurgency

Delhi's response to the uprisings in the Northeast has been a two-pronged strategy of tough counter-insurgency combined with development aid aimed at ending popular grievance. The argument over which of these two strategies is more important is misguided. Neither confronts the local political role of violence in the Northeast: both security and development programmes are inefficacious in the face of a system of violent politics, corruption, and immunity for the powerful. When outside security forces stay in the region for too long they create resentment among civilians, but violence breaks out when the local security forces are in control because they do not have the ability and/or incentives to resist the ties between insurgents and politics. Underdevelopment persists because aid ends up being used for private gain, and lawlessness destroys the investment climate and limits entrepreneurialism.

But what is the alternative to Delhi's security plus development strategy? There are several outstanding points of consensus in the literature on counter-insurgency that point in a new direction. First, the solution to an insurgency is always primarily political rather than military—militaries can enable political change, but destroying a rural insurgency to its last man is not just costly in human terms, it is nearly impossible (see Joes 2000; O'Brien 2001 for case evidence). This is one reason governments agree to negotiations with rebels and encourage desertion. Yet, for the most part, negotiations have not been able to halt the proliferation of armed groups in the Northeast. Given the opportunities created by the difficult border, confusing demography, and trends in politics in the rest of India, it seems safe to predict that small groups of individuals will continue to see a potential pay-off to violence so long as the environment of lawlessness persists. The zero-sum nature of rebel demands and rebels' waning bases of civilian support also bode ill for the efficacy of negotiations. This does not necessarily mean negotiation should not be pursued or that Delhi should abandon its policy of encouraging surrender but only that rebel groups will probably continue to emerge so long as the political system is extremely vulnerable to corruption and coercion.

Thus, it is worthwhile to take into account a second point of consensus in the comparative literature on counter-insurgency, which is that political solutions to guerrilla conflict are often based on separating insurgents, both physically and morally, from their sources of support. In classic treatments of guerrilla war this base is presumed to be the peasantry; in the Northeast, as we have seen, support comes through a web of political elites. Yet the point still holds that without the provision of security sufficient to ensure that guerrillas cannot coerce civilians, the centre can hardly wonder when local politicians, bureaucrats, and private citizens toe the insurgent line (Shaw 2001). The degree of interconnectedness between the rebels and the political system means that the security that must be provided should be against not just rebel military or terrorist attacks but against crime, extortion, assassination, and attacks on the normal political process. Finally, the moral separation of civilians from guerrillas depends on making sure that government forces act with rectitude that compares very favourably to the ways of the insurgents (cf. Kilcullen 2006). The centre must demonstrate first and foremost that it is committed to promoting a system of governance and security that is based on rule of law and that, therefore, will provide lasting protection against violence from any source.

Restoring Rule of Law and Confidence in Government

Civilians in the Northeast, as well as insurgents and local politicians, have little faith that the formal political process can be purged of violence. The means to do so are reform of and support for local police and judicial institutions. Violence, electoral manipulation, corruption, black market transactions, extortion, and inter-communal violence are only rarely effectively prosecuted in the Northeast. Illegal acts by security forces and agents of the centre are not always dealt with quickly and decisively. Only in an environment where civilians feel safe and would-be rebels or collaborators are deterred by a belief that there may be real penalties for their actions, does the equilibrium described above dissolve.

Aggressive prosecution of crimes committed by insurgents, local politicians, and agents of the centre is an important goal. Careful, transparent, and fair criminal proceedings aimed at demonstrating the centre's commitment to supporting rule of law in the Northeast are more likely to win public support than frantic claims about the security threats looming in the region. In fact, one of the insights of the study of counter-insurgency is that engaging rebels as a military force ratifies their claim to being a legitimate political actor:

…armies tended, by their very nature, to lend a certain amount of political legitimacy to their opponents. On the other hand, proper police forces maintained an air of law and order and, accordingly, by their nature, cast a mantle of criminality upon their opponents. After all, policemen arrest and jail criminals—they do not necessarily want to slay them as enemies on a battlefield or put them in prisoner of war camps (Shaw 2001: 56).

In the Northeast, the political coherence of insurgencies is currently at a low point and their blatantly criminal activity is on the rise. As we saw above, attacking military targets is a relatively rare activity for most insurgent groups in the Northeast. They are thus particularly vulnerable to being marginalized as antithetical to a political system based on rule of law.

In addition to high profile and heavily scrutinized prosecutions, the centre has on hand a fast and rhetorically powerful means of signalling that rule of law is its most important goal in the Northeast. This is to overcome the mindset that prosecution of malfeasance by agents of the centre is an unthinkable luxury. In the past, policy makers have too often brushed aside recommendations coming out of the judiciary for investigations into charges against security forces. Many commentators point out that human rights abuse in the region erodes goodwill towards Delhi. But what is under-appreciated is that the failure to aggressively prosecute such actions signals that, in the Northeast, the writ of formal institutions will never be as powerful as the law of violence. This is precisely the belief that allows insurgency to persist.

Human rights groups are a tremendous asset in the struggle to re-establish the credibility of rule of law. Sympathizers of the centre often adopt a persecuted attitude towards human rights activism in the Northeast (Deka 2006; Routray 2003a). To be sure, any verifiable instances of fraud or complicity with insurgency by non-governmental organizations (NGOs) should be dealt with by the police and the courts. But sceptical advocacy groups are generally assets to Delhi. Human rights advocates not only provide monitoring of the centre's agents at no cost, they compile and publicize alleged infractions and the centre's attempts to deal with them. This creates a well-publicized forum for Delhi to demonstrate its commitment to restoring rule of law. Thus, the general scepticism of the NGOs and even their hostility towards the centre can actually be useful for establishing the credibility of the government's efforts.

Finally, much of the discussion of policy elites over POTA, the Armed Forces Special Powers Act, and the Disturbed Areas Act, weighs the (empirically unverified) benefits of these acts against the public dissent they encourage. But an equally important cost generated by these measures is that they are a signal that insurgent groups in the Northeast are a uniquely severe and fundamentally political threat to the Indian state—a rather mighty image, which many of these groups would be hard-pressed to sustain on their own given their military weakness, criminality, and inchoate ideology. The centre will continue to find it very hard to simultaneously extend these measures under the rationale that rebels are powerful threats to the state and convince civilians that insurgency has no future in the Northeast.

Conclusions

Delhi has gone a long way down the path of treating violence in the Northeast as a dire military threat and putting itself in a situation where it is forced to either extinguish or negotiate with fractious, ill-disciplined, and numerous violent actors. And debate over policy in the Northeast is stuck in a false conversation over the relative importance of tough military measures and development aid. But neither can restore civilian confidence that elected, formal government structures can establish rule of law in the region. It should be the centre's paramount goal to engage with the Northeast not as a persistent security problem but as a region where it is determined to ensure that the elected government can and will enforce the rectitude of politicians, bureaucrats, security forces, and private actors. Only that shift can convince politicians, guerrillas, and civilians alike that the region is on a new and positive course.

References

Agamben, Giorgio, *Means without End: Notes on Politics*, translated by Vincenzo Binetti and Cesare Casarino, Minneapolis, MN: University of Minnesota Press, 2000 [1996].

——, *Remnants of Auschwitz: The Witness and the Archive*, translated by Daniel Heller-Roazen, Palo Alto, CA, New York: Zone Books, 1999.

——, *Homo Sacer: Sovereign Power and Bare Life*, translated by Daniel Heller-Roazen, Stanford University Press, 1998 [1995].

Agarwal, Arun, 'Mayhem in Arunachal', *Down to Earth*, 7 (11), 31 October 1999.

Aitchinson, C.U. (ed.), *A Collection of Treaties, Engagements and Sanads relating to India and Neighbouring Countries*, Volume II: 'The Treaties &c. relating to Burma, Nepal, Eastern Bengal and Assam, Bhutan, Sikkim, Tibet, Siam and the Eastern Archipelago', Calcutta: Superintendent Government Printing, India, 1909.

Akoijam, A. Bimol, and Th. Tarunkumar, 'Armed Forces (Special Powers) Act, 1958: Disguised War & its Subversions', *Eastern Quarterly*, 3 (1), April–June, pp. 5–19, 2005.

Akoijam, A. Bimol, 'Another 9/11, Another Act of Terror: The Embedded Disorder of the AFSPA', *Sarai Reader 2005: Bare Acts*, Delhi: Centre for the Study of Developing Societies, pp. 481–91, 2005.

Alam, Javeed, 'The Nation and the State in India: A Difficult Bond', in Zoya Hasan, E. Sreedharan, and R. Sudarshan (eds), *India's Living Constitution: Ideas, Practices and Controversies*, New Delhi: Permanent Black/Orient Longman, 2002.

Allen, B.C., *Assam District Gazetteer: Naga Hills and Manipur*, Vol. IX, Part 2, Calcutta: Baptist Mission Press, 1905.

Améry, Jean, *At the Mind's Limits: Contemplations by a Survivor on Auschwitz and its Realities*, translated by Sidney and Stella P. Rosenfeld, Indiana University Press, 1980 [1966].

——, *On Suicide: A Discourse on Voluntary Death*, translated by John D. Barlow, Bloomington, IN: Indiana University Press, 1999 [1976].

Amnesty International, 'India: Briefing on the Armed Forces (Special Powers) Act, 1958', November, Available at: http://web.amnesty.org/library/Index/ENGASA200312006?open&of=ENG-2S4, 2006.

Ananthamurthy, U.R., 'Why not Worship in the Nude?' in *Bahuvachan: An Occasional of the Arts and Ideas*, Bhopal: Bharat Bhavan, February, pp. 95–117, 1988.

Anderson, Benedict, *Imagined Communities: Reflections on the Origin and Spread of Nationalism*, London: Verso, 1991.

Aosenba, *The Naga Resistance Movement: Prospects of Peace and Armed Conflict*, New Delhi: Regency, 2001.

Appadurai, Arjun, 'Disjuncture and Difference in the Global Cultural Economy', *Public Culture*, 2 (2), Spring, pp. 1–23, 1990.

Arole, Mabelle and Raj Arole, 'Jamkhed, India: the Evolution of a World Training Center', in D. Taylor-Ide and C.E. Taylor (eds), *Just and Lasting Change: When Communities Own their Futures*, Baltimore: The Johns Hopkins Press in association with Future Generations, 2002.

Asian Development Bank, *Technical Assistance to India for Preparing the Northeastern States Trade and Investment Creation Initiative*, October, Available at: http://www.adb.org/Documents/TARs/IND/tar-ind-37407.pdf, 2004.

Assam Tourism: Its Potential for Investment, Department of Tourism, Government of Assam, 2004.

ATSUM (All Tribal Students' Union, Manipur), *Caucus: Reasoning our Rights Together*, Churachandpur: All Tribal Students' Union, Manipur, 2005.

Baden-Powell, B.H., 'Forest Settlements in India', *The Indian Forester*, 18, pp. 1–2, 1892.

Bajpai, Kanti P., *Roots of Terrorism*, New Delhi: Penguin Books India, 2002.

Balwally, D., *Growth of Totalitarianism in Arunachal Pradesh, Mizoram, and Nagaland*, New Delhi: Spectrum Publications, 2003.

Bangkok Consultation Meet, *North East Sun*, New Delhi, 1–14 June 2002.

Barbora, Sanjay, 'Rethinking India's Counter-insurgency Campaign in North-East', *Economic and Political Weekly*, 41 (35), 2 September 2006.

Barpujari, H.K. (ed.), *The Comprehensive History of Assam*, Volume IV: Modern Period: Yandabo to Diarchy, 1826–1919 AD, Guwahati, Assam: Publication Board, 1992.

Baruah, Sanjib, *Postfrontier Blues: Toward a New Policy Framework for Northeast India*, Washington D.C.: East-West Center (Policy Studies Series No. 33), 2007.

———, *Durable Disorder: Understanding the Politics of Northeast India*, New Delhi: Oxford University Press, 2005a.

———, 'The Problem', *Seminar* (Special issue on 'Gateway to the East: A Symposium on Northeast India and the Look East Policy'), 550, June, pp. 12–16, 2005b.

———, 'Take the Jungle to the Law', *The Indian Express*, 9 March 2005c.

———, 'Confronting Constructionism: Ending India's Naga War', *Journal of Peace Research*, 40 (3), pp. 321–38, 2003.

——, *India Against Itself: Assam and Politics of Nationality*, Philadelphia University of Pennsylvania Press and New Delhi: Oxford University Press, 1999.

——, 'Ethnic' Conflict as State-Society Struggle: The Poetics and Politics of Assamese Micro-Nationalism', *Modern Asian Studies*, 28 (3), pp. 649–71, 1994.

Basu, Amrita, and Atul Kohli (eds), *Community Conflicts and the State in India*, New Delhi: Oxford University Press, 1998.

Bath, N., 'Arunachal Pradesh: Victory for the BJP', *Economic and Political Weekly*, 39 (51), pp. 5531–2, 2004.

Baviskar, Amita, 'Reverence is not Enough: Ecological Marxism and Indian Adivasis', in E.M. DuPuis and P. Vandergeest (eds), *Creating the Countryside: the Politics of Rural and Environmental Discourse*, Philadelphia: Temple University Press, pp. 205–24, 1996.

Bayart, Jean-Francois, *The State in Africa: The Politics of the Belly*, translated by M. Harper, C. Harrison, and E. Harrison, London: Longman, 1993.

Bayly, C.A., *Origins of Nationality in South Asia: Patriotism and Ethical Government in the Making of Modern India*, New Delhi: Oxford University Press, 2001 [1998].

Bell, Brenda, John Gaventa, and John Peters (eds), *We Make the Road by Walking: Conversations on Education and Social Change (between Myles Horton and Paulo Freire)*, Philadelphia: Temple Press, 1990.

Belting, Hans, *Likeness and Presence: The Image before the Era of Art*, Chicago: University of Chicago Press, 1994.

Benhabib, Seyla, 'Unholy Politics', *Constellations: An International Journal of Critical and Democratic Theory*, 9 (1), pp. 34–45, 2002.

Bettelheim, Bruno, *Surviving and Other Essays*, New York: Alfred A. Knopf, 1979.

——, *The Informed Heart: Autonomy in a Mass Age*, New York: The Free Press, 1960.

Bhabha, Homi, *The Location of Culture*, London and New York: Routledge, 1994.

Bhattacharjee, Chandana, *Ethnicity and Autonomy Movement: Case of Bodo-Kacharis of Assam*, New Delhi: Vikas, 1996.

Bhattacharjee, S., 'Dilemma of Culture: A Polycontextual Discourse', in M.M. Agrawal (ed.), *Ethnicity, Culture and Nationalism in North-East India*, New Delhi: Indus Publishing Company, 2002.

Bhattacharya, Harihar, *Communism in Tripura*, Delhi: Ajanta Publishers, 1999.

Bhattacharya, Malini, 'Violence and Violation', *Frontline*, 23 (11), pp. 40–42, 3–16 June 2006.

Bhattacharya, Milly, 'Emergence of Mizo Union Party', Proceedings of the 18th Annual Session of the North East India History Association, Shillong: North East India History Association, 1998.

Bhattacharyya, Hiranya Kumar, *The Silent Invasion: Assam versus Infiltration*, Guwahati & Delhi: Spectrum Publications, 2001.

Bhaumik, Subir, 'The Accord that Never was', in Samir Kumar Das (ed.), *Peace Accords and Peace Processes: South Asian Peace Studies II*, New Delhi: Sage, pp. 200–21, 2005.

——, *Insurgent Crossfire: Northeast India*, Delhi: Lancers, 1996.

Bhuyan, B.C., *Political Development of the North East*, Vol. II, New Delhi: Omsons Publications, 1992.

Biswas, P., 'Ethnophilosophy: Politics of Culture in North-East India', in M.M. Agrawal (ed.), *Ethnicity, Culture and Nationalism in North-East India*, New Delhi: Indus Publishing Company, 2002.

Bogdanor, Vernon, 'Forms of Autonomy and the Protection of Minorities', *Daedalus*, 126 (2), pp. 65–87, 1997.

Bordoloi, B.N., *Report on the Survey of Alienation of Tribal Land in Assam*, Guwahati: Assam Institute of Research for Tribals and Scheduled Castes, 1999.

Borooah, Romy, 'Transformations in Trade and the Constitution of Gender and Rank in Northeast India', *American Ethnologist*, 27(2), pp. 371–99, 2000.

Bose, Manilal (ed.), *Historical and Constitutional Documents of North-Eastern India (1824–1973)*, Delhi: Concept, 1979.

Bourdieu, Pierre, *Outline of a Theory of Practice*, Cambridge: Cambridge University Press, 1977.

Bower, Ursula Graham, *Naga Path*, Guwahati: Spectrum Publications, 2002.

Brar, K.S., 'India's Turbulent Northeast: Over Five Decades of Isolation, Neglect and Alienation', in Shekhar Basu Ray (ed.), *New Approach*, Issue on 'Our East and North East', XI (I & II), 2002.

Brass, Paul R., *The Production of Hindu-Muslim Violence in Contemporary India*, New Delhi: Oxford University Press, 2003.

Brettell, Caroline B, 'Theorizing Migration in Anthropology', in Caroline B. Brettell and James F. Hollifield (eds), *Migration Theory: Talking Across Disciplines*, New York and London: Routledge, 2000.

Brubaker, Rogers, *Nationalism Reframed*, Cambridge: Cambridge University Press, 1996.

Bruner, Edward H., *Culture on Tour: Ethnographies of Travel*, Chicago & London: University of Chicago Press, 2005.

Burmeo, Nancy, 'The Import of Institutions', *Journal of Democracy*, 13 (2), pp. 96–110, 2002.

Butalia, Urvashi, 'The Body as Weapon', *New Internationalist*, No. 371, Available at: http://www.newint.org/columns/viewfrom/2004/09/01/body-as-weapon, September 2004.

Calhoun, Craig, *Nationalism*, Minneapolis: University of Minnesota Press, 1997.

Carter, Paul, *The Road to Botany Bay: An Essay in Spatial History*, London: Faber, 1987.

Caruth, Cathy, *Unclaimed Experience: Trauma, Narrative and History*, Baltimore and London: The John Hopkins University Press, 1996.

Cavanagh, John, *Alternatives to Economic Globalization: A Better World is Possible*, San Francisco: Berrett-Koehler Publishers, 2002.

Chakma, Bidyut, 'Déjà vu for the Brus', *The Statesman* (Kolkata), 3 April 2004.

Chakrabarty, Bidyut, 'The "Hut" and the "Axe": The 1947 Sylhet Referendum', *The Indian Economic and Social History Review*, 39 (4), October 2002.

Chakraborty, Amalendu Kishore, *The Quest for Identity: The Tribal Solidarity Movement in North-East India, 1947–69*, Kolkata, Asiatic Society, 2004.

Chandhoke, Neera, 'A State of One's Own: Secessionism and Federalism in India', Working Paper No. 80 (series 1), London: Crisis States Research Centre, London School of Economics, 2006.

——, 'The Logic of Recognition', *Seminar*, No. 484, 1999.

Chandra, Sudhir, 'Understanding the Problem of Northeast India' (A review of Sanjib Baruah, *Durable Disorder: Understanding the Politics of Northeast India*), *India Review*, 6(1), pp. 46–56, 2007.

Chatterjee, Partha, 'Community in the East', *Economic and Political Weekly*, 33(6), 7 February 1998.

——, *The Nation and Its Fragments*, Princeton, N.J.: Princeton University Press, and New Delhi: Oxford University Press, 1993.

Chaube, S.K., *Hill Politics in Northeast India* (reprint), Delhi: Orient Longman, 1999 [1973].

Chaudhuri, Kalyan, 'A Rich Heritage', *Frontline*, 20 (1), 18 January 2003.

Cixous, Helene, 'We Who Are Free, Are We Free?' in Barbara Johnson (ed.), *Freedom and Interpretation: The Oxford Amnesty Lectures 1992*, New York: Basic Books, 1993.

Clavero, Bartolome, 'Claiming for History: An American Herd Case', mimeo, 2004

Clifford, James, *The Predicament of Culture*, Cambridge: Harvard University Press, 1988.

——, *Routes: Travel and Translation in the Late Twentieth Century*, Cambridge, Mass. & London: Harvard University Press, 1997.

Cline, L.E., 'The Insurgency Environment in Northeast India', *Small Wars and Insurgencies*, 17 (2), pp. 126–47, 2006.

Collier, Paul, 'Rebellion as a Quasi-Criminal Activity,' *The Journal of Conflict Resolution*, 44 (6), pp. 839–53, 2000.

Collingwood, R.G., *An Essay on Metaphysics*, Oxford: The Clarendon Press, 1962.

Cooper, T.T., 'Expedition of Mr. T. T. Cooper from the Yang-tze-Kiang to Thibet and India', *Proceedings of the Royal Geographical Society of London*, 12 (5), pp. 336–9, 1867–8.

——, *The Mishmee Hills: An Account of a Journey Made in an Attempt to Penetrate Thibet from Assam to Open New Routes for Commerce*, London: Henry S. King & Co, 1873.

Cornell, Svante E., 'Autonomy as a Source of Conflict: Caucasian Conflicts in Theoretical Perspective', *World Politics*, 54 (1), pp. 245–76, 2002.

Cornford, Jonathan, and Michael Simon, *Breaking the Banks: The Impact of the Asian Development Bank and Australia's Role in the Mekong Region*, CAA-Oxfam Australia, 2001.

Dallmayr, Fred, *Achieving our World: Toward a Global and Plural Democracy*, Lanham: Rowman and Littlefield Publishers, 2001.

Das, J.N., 'Genesis of Tribal Belts and Blocks of Assam', in B.N. Bordoloi (ed.), *Alienation of Tribal Land and Indebtedness*, Guwahati: Tribal Research Institute, 1986.

——, *A Study of Land System of Mizoram*, Guwahati: Law Research Institute, 1990.

Das, Parag Kumar, *Changlot Fenla* (Revolutionary Soldier), Guwahati: Udangshri Prakashan, 1997 [1993].

Das, Samir Kumar, 'Where do the Autonomous Institutions Come from?', in Ranabir Samaddar (ed.), *Politics of Autonomy: Indian Experiences*, New Delhi: Sage Publications, pp. 79–85, 2005.

————, 'Nobody's Communique: Ethnic Accords in Northeastern India', in Ranabir Samaddar and Helmut Reifeld (eds), *Peace as Process: Reconciliation and Conflict Resolution in South Asia*, New Delhi: Manohar, New Delhi: Konrad Adenauer Foundation, 2001.

——, *ULFA: A Political Analysis*, New Delhi: Ajanta Books International, 1994.

Dasgupta, Anindita, 'Civilians and Localisation of Conflict in Assam', *Economic and Political Weekly*, vol. 39 (40), pp. 4461–70, 2 October 2004.

Dasgupta, Jyotirindra, 'Community, Authenticity and Autonomy: Insurgence and Institutional Development in India's North-East', in Amrita Basu and Atul Kohli (eds), *Community Conflicts and the State in India*, Delhi: Oxford University Press, 1998.

——, 'Developmental Federalism: India's Evolving Institutional Enterprise', mimeo, 1995.

Dasgupta, Malabika, 'The Gumti Hydel Project of Tripura', *Economic and Political Weekly*, 7 October 1989.

Davis, A.W., *Gazetteer of North Lushai Hills*, Shillong: Assam Secretariat Printing Office, 1894.

de Varennes, Fernand, 'Peace Accords and Ethnic Conflicts: A Comparative Analysis of Content and Approaches', in John Darby and Roger MacGinty (eds), *Contemporary Peacemaking: Conflict, Violence and Peace Processes*, Houndmills: Palgrave Macmillan, 2003.

Deane, Seamus, 'Introduction', *Nationalism, Colonialism, and Literature*, Minneapolis: University of Minnesota Press, 1990.

Deka, A.K., 'ULFA & the Peace Process in Assam', *IPCS Special Report 21*, New Delhi: Institute of Peace and Conflict Studies, 2006.

Deka, Harekrishna, 'The Assamese Mind: Contours of a Landscape', *IIC Quarterly* (New Delhi: India International Centre Quarterly), 32 (2&3), pp. 189–202, 2005.

——, *Bandiyar* (The Captor), Guwahati: Lawyer's Book Stall, 1996.

Deka, Kanak Sen, *Ulfar Swadhin Asom* (Ulfa's Independent Assam), Guwahati: Dispur Print House, 1994.

Dena, Lal, 'The Kuki-Naga Conflict: Juxtaposed in the Colonial Context', in Kailash A. Aggarwal (ed.), *Dynamics of Identity and Intergroup Relations in North East India*, Shimla: Indian Institute of Advanced Studies, 1999.

——, *Christian Missions and Colonialism: A Study of Missionary Movements in North East India with Particular Reference to Manipur and Lushai Hills, 1894–1947*, Shillong: Vendrame Institute, 1988.

Dent, Martin J., *Identity Politics: Filling the Gap between Federalism and Independence*, Aldershot: Ashgate, 2004.

Dev, Rajesh, 'Institutional Design and Ethnopolitical Conflict Transformation: Assessing Peace-building Initiatives in North East India', in Prasenjit Biswas and C.J. Thomas (eds), *Peace in India's Northeast*, New Delhi: Regency Publications, 2006.

Dewan, Deepak, 'Manipur Tribals Seek 6th Schedule', *North-East Sun*, 9 (5), pp. 1–14, 9 October 2003.

Elwin, Verrier, *A Philosophy for NEFA*, Itanagar, Arunachal Pradesh: Directorate of Research, Government of Arunachal Pradesh, 1988 [1957].

—— (ed.), *The Nagas in the Nineteenth Century*, Bombay: Oxford University Press, 1969.

Endle, S., *The Kacharis (Bodo)*, New Delhi: Low Price Publications, 1997 [1911].

Escobar, Arturo, *Encountering Development: The Making and Unmaking of the Third World*, Princeton: Princeton University Press, 1995.

Fearon, J.D., 'Why do Some Civil Wars Last so Much Longer than Others?', *Journal of Peace Research*, 41 (3), pp. 275–301, 2004.

Fearon, J.D., and D.D. Laitin, 'Ethnicity, Insurgency, and Civil War', *American Political Science Review*, 97 (1), pp. 75–90, 2003.

Fernandes, Walter, 'Naga Imbroglio', *The Statesman* (New Delhi), 30 July 2005.

——, 'Limits of Law and Order Approach to the North-East', *Economic and Political Weekly*, 39 (42), pp. 4609–11, 16 October 2004.

Fischer, Frank, *Citizens, Experts, and the Environment: The Politics of Local Knowledge*, Durham: Duke University Press, 2000.

Fukuyama, Francis, '"Stateness" First', *Journal of Democracy*, 16 (1), pp. 84–8, 2005.

Fürer-Haimendorf, Christoph von, *The Naked Nagas: Headhunters of Assam in Peace and War*, Guwahati: Spectrum Publishers, 2004.

——, *A Himalayan Tribe: From Cattle to Cash*, Berkeley: University of California Press, 1980.

Galanter, M., *Competing Equalities*, Berkeley, CA: University of California Press, 1984.

Gangte, T.S., 'Ethnicity and Identity Management in Manipur', *Imphal Free Press*, 22–25 June 2005.

Ganguly, J.B., 'Problem of Tribal Landlessness in Tripura', in B.B. Dutta and M.N. Karna (eds), *Land Relations in Northeast India*, Delhi: People's Publishing House, 1987.

Ghosh, Amitav, *Countdown*, New Delhi: Ravi Dayal, 2003 [1999].

Giddens, Anthony, *Modernity and Self-Identity: Self and Society in the Late Modern Age*, Stanford, CA: Stanford University Press, 1991.

Gilbert, Geoff, 'Autonomy and Minority Groups: A Right in International Law?', *Cornell International Law Journal*, 35 (2), pp. 307–54, 2002.

Gilroy, P., *There ain't no Black in the Union Jack: The Cultural Politics of Race and Nation*, London: Hutchinson, 1987.

Go, Khup Za, *A Critical Historical Study of Bible Translations among the Zo People in North East India*, Churachandpur: Chin Baptist Literature Board, 1996.

Gogoi, Manorom, *Parag Dasor Xannidhyot* (In Proximity with Parag Das), Guwahati: Prapti Prakash, 2005.

Gohain, Hiren, 'Chronicles of Violence and Terror: Rise of the United Liberation Front of Assam', *Economic and Political Weekly*, 42 (12), pp. 1012–18, 24 March 2007.

GoA (Government of Assam), *District-wise Monthly Normal Rainfall in Assam*, New Delhi: Indiastat.com, 2002.

GoI (Government of India), *Annual Report of the Ministry of Development of North Eastern Region, 2005–2006*, New Delhi: Ministry of Development of North Eastern Region, 2006a.

——, *Annual Report of the Ministry of Home Affairs, 2005–2006*, New Delhi: Ministry of Home Affairs, 2006b.

——, *Report of the Twelfth Finance Commission, 2005–2010*, New Delhi: Ministry of Finance, 2005a.

———, *Report of the Committee to Review the Armed Forces (Special Powers) Act, 1958*, Government of India: Ministry of Home Affairs, Available at: http://www.hindu.com/nic/afa/, 2005b.

———, *Primary Census Abstracts: Census of India 2001*, Office of the Registrar General and Census Commissioner, Government of India, 2004.

———, *National Human Development Report 2001*, New Delhi: Planning Commission, Government of India, 2002a.

———, *Report of the National Commission to Review the Working of the Constitution*, New Delhi: Government of India, Ministry of Law, 2 vols, Available at: http://lawmin.nic.in/ncrwc/finalreport.htm, 2002b.

———, *National Human Development Report*, New Delhi: Planning Commission, 2001.

———, *Report of Eleventh Finance Commission*, New Delhi: Ministry of Finance, 2000.

———, *Census of India*, New Delhi: Office of the Registrar General and Census Commissioner, Government of India, various years.

GoM [Government of Manipur], 'The Manipur Hill Areas Autonomous District Council Act, 2000', in *Manipur Gazette Extraordinary*, No. 291, Imphal: Government of Manipur, 6 September 2000.

———, *The Manipur Reservation of Vacancies in Posts and Services (For Scheduled Castes and Scheduled Tribes) Act, 1976 (Manipur Act No.1 of 1977)*, Imphal: Law Department, Government of Manipur, 24 February 1977.

———, *The Manipur Land Revenue and Land Reforms Act, 1960*, Imphal: Government of Manipur, 1960.

Goswami, B.B., *The Mizo Revolt: Politicisation of Culture*, Jaipur: Alakh, 1979.

Goswami, Manoj Kumar, *Samiran Borua Aahi Aase* (Samiran Borua is on His Way), Guwahati: Navajeevan Prakash, 1993.

Goswami, Manu, *Producing India: From Colonial Economy to National Space*, Chicago and London: University of Chicago Press, 2004.

Goswami, Praphulladatta, *Essays on the Folklore and Culture of North-Eastern India*, Guwahati: Spectrum, 1983.

Goswami, S., 'Assam: Mixed Verdict', *Economic and Political Weekly*, 39 (51), pp. 5523–6, 2004.

Government of Mizoram, 'Brief Report on Elections to Mizoram Legislative Assembly and Lok Sabha (Parliament) 1972–1999', Aizawl: Directorate of Elections, 2004a.

———, *Report of the Fifth General Elections to Mizoram Legislative Assembly*, Aizawl: Directorate of Elections, 2004b.

Grass, Günter, *My Century*, Faber and Faber, 1999.

Grierson, G.A., *Linguistic Survey of India*, Vol. 3, Part 3, Calcutta: Government Printing Press, 1904.

————, Amalendu, *Medieval and Early Colonial Assam: Society, Polity, Economy*, Calcutta: Centre for Studies in Social Science, 1991.

Guha, Amalendu, *Planter Raj to Swaraj: Freedom Struggle and Electoral Politics in Assam, 1826–1947*, New Delhi: People's Publishing House, 1977.

Guha, Ramachandra, *India after Gandhi: The History of the World's Largest Democracy*, New Delhi: Pan Macmillan, Picador India, 2007.

Gupta, Akhil, 'Song of the Nonaligned World', in James Ferguson and Akhil Gupta (eds), *Culture Power, Place*, Duke University Press, 1997.

Gupta, Akhil and James Ferguson, 'Beyond "Culture": Space, Identity, and the Politics of Difference', *Cultural Anthropology*, 7 (1), pp. 6—23, 1992.

Gupta, Shekhar, *Assam: A Valley Divided*, New Delhi, Vikas, 1984.

Gurdon, P.R., *The Khasis*, New Delhi: Low Price Publications, 2002 [1906].

Guttal, Shalmali, 'Marketing the Mekong: The Asian Development Bank and the Greater Mekong Sub-region Economic Cooperation Program', Available at: http://www.jubileesouth.org/news/EpZyVyEAZFESZsvoiN.shtml, 12 December 2003.

Hale, Henry E., 'Divided We Stand: Institutional Sources of Ethnofederal State Survival and Collapse', *World Politics*, 56 (1), pp. 165–93, 2004.

Hames-Garcia, Michael R., 'Who are Our Own People: Challenges for a Theory of Social Identity', in Paula Moya and Michael R. Hames-Garcia (eds), *Reclaiming Identity*, Hyderabad: Orient Longman, 2001.

Hannum, Hurst, *Autonomy, Sovereignty and Self-determination: The Accommodation of Conflicting Rights*, Philadelphia: University of Pennsylvania Press, 1992.

Haokip, P., 'Counter-insurgency in the North-East: A Counter-perspective', *Manipur Online*, 5 January 2003.

Haokip, P.S., *Zale'n-gam the Kuki Nation*, KNO Publication, 1998.

Haokip, Paolienlal, 'Counter-insurgency in the North-East: A Counter-perspective', Available at: http://www.ipcs.org, 2001.

Haraway, Donna Jeanne, *Simians, Cyborgs, and Women: The Reinvention of Nature*, New York: Routledge, 1991.

Hardgrave, Robert L., and S. A. Kochanek, *India: Government and Politics in a Developing Nation*, New York: Harcourt College Publishers, 2000.

Harpham, Geoffrey Galt, 'Symbolic Terror', *Critical Inquiry*, 28 (2), pp. 573–9, 2002.

Harriss, John, 'The State, Tradition and Conflict in the North Eastern States of India', Working Paper No. 13, London: London School of Economics, Crisis States Research Centre, 2002.

Harvey, David, *The Limits to Capital*, London: Verso, 1999.

Hassan, M. Sajjad, 'Explaining Manipur's Breakdown and Mizoram's Peace: The State and Identities in North East India', Working Paper No. 79,

London: London School of Economics, Crisis States Research Centre, 2006.

Havel, Vaclav, 'Letter to Gustav Husak, General Secretary of the Czechoslovak Communist Party', in Vaclav Havel and Jan Vladislav (eds), *Living in Truth*, London: Faber and Faber, 1989.

Hazarika, Sanjoy, 'Land, Conflict, Identity in India's North-East: Negotiating the Future', *Futures*, 36 (6–7), pp. 771–80, August–September 2004.

——, *Rites of Passage: Border Crossings, Imagined Homelands, India's East and Bangladesh*, New Delhi: Penguin Books India, 2000.

——, *Strangers of the Mist: Tales of War and Peace from India's Northeast*, New Delhi: Viking, 1994.

Hegel, G.W.F., *The Phenomenology of Mind*, translated with an introduction and notes by J.B. Baillie, London: George Allen & Unwin, 1910.

Hesselbein, Gabi, Frederick Golooba-Mutebi, and James Putzel, 'Four Nation Study of State Collapse and Reconstruction', London: London School of Economics, Crisis States Research Centre, 2006.

Hibou, Beatrice, 'Conclusion', in J. Migdal (ed.), *Boundaries and Belongings: States and Societies in the Struggle to Shape Identities and Local Practices*, Cambridge: Cambridge University Press, 2004.

Hitson Jusho, P.T., *Politics of Ethnicity in North East India (With special reference to Manipur)*, New Delhi: Regency Publications, 2004.

Hodson, T.C., *The Meitheis*, New Delhi: Low Price Publications, 2003 [1908].

——, *The Naga Tribes of Manipur*, New Delhi: Low Price Publications, 1996 [1911].

Horam, M., *Naga Polity*, Delhi: B.R. Publishing Corporation, 1975.

Horowitz, Donald L., *The Deadly Ethnic Riot*, New Delhi: Oxford University Press, 2001.

Hrishikeshan, K., 'Assam's Agony: The ULFA and Obstacles to Conflict Resolution', in K.P.S. Gill and Ajai Sahni (eds), *Faultlines. Writings on Conflict and Resolution*, 12, New Delhi: Bulwark and Institute for Conflict Management, 2002.

Hudson, Alan, 'Offshoreness, Globalization and Sovereignty: A Postmodern Geo-Political Economy?', *Transactions of the Institute of British Geographers*, New Series, 25 (3), pp. 269–83, 2000.

Hussain, Monirul (ed.), *Coming Out of Violence*, New Delhi: Regency Publications, 2005.

——, *The Assam Movement: Class, Ideology and Identity*, Delhi: Manak Publications, 1993.

Hussain, Wasbir, *Homemakers without the Men: Assam's Widows of Violence*, New Delhi: Indialog Publications, 2006.

——, 'Manipur: Impending Collapse of Governance', Website of the Institute for Conflict Management, South Asia Terrorism Portal, Available at: http://

www.satp.org/satporgtp/sair/Archives/3_4.htm#ASSESSMENT3, Accessed on 9 December 2005.

——, 'Multi-force Operations in Counter Terrorism: A View from the Assam Theater', mimeo, 2001.

Hutton, J.H., *Dairies of Two Tours in the Unadministered Areas of Nagaland*, New Delhi: Mittal Publication, 2002.

——, *Report on Naga Hills*, New Delhi: Mittal Publication, 1986.

Institute of Conflict Management, 'State-level Data Sheet', Available at: www.satp.org, Accessed on 5 April 2006.

Jackson, Richard, 'The Social Construction of Internal War', in Richard Jackson (ed.), *(Re)Constructing Cultures of Violence and Peace*, Amsterdam and New York: Rodopi, 2004.

Jacobs, Julian, Alan MacFarlane, Sarah Harrison, and Anita Herle, *The Nagas: The Hill People of Northeast India: Society, Culture and the Colonial Encounter*, London: Thames and Hudson, 1990.

Jafa, V.S., 'Mizoram: Contours of Non-military Intervention', in K.P.S. Gill and Ajai Sahni (eds), *Faultlines. Writings on Conflict and Resolution*, 4, New Delhi: Bulwark and Institute for Conflict Management, 2000.

Jayal, Niraja Gopal, 'Reinventing the State: The Emergence of Alternative Models of Governance in India in the 1990s', in Niraja Gopal Jayal and Sudha Pai (eds), *Democratic Governance in India: Challenges of Poverty, Development and Identity*, New Delhi: Sage, 2001.

Jenkins, Brian N., *Will Terrorists Go Nuclear?* Rand Report P5541, Santa Monica, CA: Rand Corporation, 1975.

Jenkins, Henry Lionel, 'Notes on the Burmese Route from Assam to the Hookoong Valley', *Proceedings of the Royal Geographical Society of London*, 13 (3), pp. 244–8, 1868–9.

Jessop, Bob, 'Bringing the State Back In (Yet Again): Reviews, Revisions, Rejections, and Redirections', *International Review of Sociology*, 11 (2), pp. 149–73, 2001.

Jin, Liqun, 'Regional Cooperation and Integration: Keys to Unlocking Asia's Economic Potential', Address at the Mekong Development Forum: Promoting India-Mekong Cooperation, New Delhi, Available at: http://www.adb.org/Documents/Speeches/2005/ms2005077.asp, 10 November 2005.

Joes, A.J., 'Isolating the Belligerents: A Key to Success in the Post-counterinsurgency Era', in M.G. Manwaring (ed.), *Beyond Declaring Victory and Coming Home: The Challenges of Peace and Stability Operations*, Westport, CT: Greenwood Publishing Group, 2000.

Johnson, C, 'The Third Generation of Guerrilla Warfare', *Asian Survey*, 8 (6), pp. 435–47, 1968.

Johnson, Chalmers S., 'Civilian Loyalties and Guerrilla Conflict', *World Politics*, 14 (4), pp. 646–61, 1962.

Johnstone, James, *Manipur and the Naga Hills*, Delhi: Vivek, 1971[1896].

Kabui, Gangmumei, *History of Manipur*, New Delhi: National Publishing House, 1991.

Kaplan, Caren, *Questions of Travel: Postmodern Discourses of Displacement*, Durham and London: Duke University Press, 1996.

Kar, Bodhisattva, 'Framing Assam: Plantation Capital, Metropolitan Knowledge and a Regime of Identities, 1790s–1930s', unpublished PhD dissertation, Centre for Historical Studies, Jawaharlal Nehru University, New Delhi, 2007.

Karmis, Dimitrios and Jocelyn Maclure, 'Two Escape Routes from the Paradigm of Monistic Authenticity: Post-imperialist and Federal Perspectives on Plural and Complex Identities', *Ethnic and Racial Studies*, 24 (3), pp. 361–85, 2001.

Khai, Sing Khaw, *Zo People and Their Culture: A Historical, Cultural Study and Critical Analysis of Zo and its Ethnic Tribes*, Churachandpur: Khampu Hatzaw, 1995.

Khan, Adeel, *Politics of Identity: Ethnic Nationalism and the State of Pakistan*, New Delhi and London: Sage Publications, 2005.

Khanna, Sushil, 'Look East, Look South: Backward Border Regions in India and China', Paper presented at the Conference on Northeast India and Its Transnational Neighbourhood, Guwahati: Indian Institute of Technology, 17 and 18 January 2008.

Kikon, Dolly, 'Operation Hornbill Festival', *Seminar*, 550, pp. 36–9, June 2005.

———, 'Destroying Difference, Schooling Consent: A Critical Analysis of Educational Policy in Indian Administered-Nagaland', *Inter-Asia Cultural Studies*, 4 (2), pp. 232–48, 2003.

Kilcullen, D., 'Globalisation and the Development of Indonesian Counter-insurgency Tactics', *Small Wars and Insurgencies*, 17 (1), pp. 44–64, 2006.

Kimura, Makiko, 'Memories of the Massacre: Violence and Collective Identity in the Narratives on the Nellie Incident', *Asian Ethnicity*, 4(2), pp. 225–9, 2003.

Kiss, Elizabeth, 'Democracy and the Politics of Recognition', in Ian Shapiro and Casiano Hacker-Gordon (eds), *Democracy's Edges*, Cambridge: Cambridge University Press, 1999.

Korten, David, *When Corporations Rule the World*, West Hartford, Conn.: Kumarian Press, 1995.

Kothari, Rajni, *Rethinking Democracy*, New Delhi: Orient Longman, 2005.

Krasner, Stephen D., 'The Case for Shared Sovereignty', *Journal of Democracy*, 16 (1), pp. 69–83, 2005.

Kumar, B.B., *Tension and Conflict in North-east India*, New Delhi: Cosmo, 1995.

Kumar, Praveen, 'Tripura: Beyond the Insurgency-Politics Nexus', in K.P.S. Gill and Ajai Sahni (eds), *Faultlines. Writings on Conflict and Resolution*, 14, New Delhi: Bulwark and Institute for Conflict Management, 2003.

Kydd, Andrew and Barbara F. Walter, 'The Strategies of Terrorism', *International Security*, 31 (1), pp. 49–80, 2006.

Kymlicka, Will, *Politics in the Vernacular: Nationalism, Multiculturalism, and Citizenship*, Oxford: Oxford University Press, 2001.

——, *Multicultural Citizenship*, Oxford: Clarendon Press, 1995.

——, 'The Rights of Minority Cultures', *Political Theory*, 20 (1), pp. 140–46, 1992.

Kymlicka, Will and Wayne Norman (eds), *Citizenship in Diverse Societies*, Oxford: Oxford University Press, 2000.

Lacina, B. and N.P. Gleditsch, 'Monitoring Trends in Global Combat: A New Dataset of Battle Deaths', *European Journal of Population*, 21(2–3), pp. 145–66, 2005.

Lakoff, Robin Tolmach, *Talking Power: The Politics of Language in Our Times*, New York: Basic Books, 1990.

Lalthangliana, B., *Ram Leh Hnam Humhalh*, Aizawl: Central Young Mizo Association, 1998.

Lasuh, Wetshokhrolo, *The Naga Chronicle* (Compiled by V.K. Nuh), Shillong: Indian Council of Social Science Research and New Delhi: Regency, 2002.

Law Research Institute, *A Study of the Land System of Tripura*, Guwahati: Law Research Institute, Gauhati High Court, 1990.

Lefort, Claude, *Democracy and Political Theory*, translated by D. Macey, Minneapolis: University of Minnesota Press, 1998.

Levi, Primo, *The Drowned and the Saved*, translated by Raymond Rosenthal, New York: Vintage International, 1989 [1988].

——, *'Survival in Auschwitz' and 'The Reawakening': Two Memoirs*, translated by Stuart Woolf, New York: Summit Books, 1983.

Lijphart, Arend, 'The Puzzle of Indian Democracy: A Consociational Interpretation', *American Political Science Review*, 90 (2), pp. 258–68, 1996.

Lindgren, James, 'Unravelling the Paradox of Blackmail', *Columbia Law Review*, 84 (3), pp. 670–717, 1984.

Linz, Juan J. and Alfred Stepan, 'Toward Consolidated Democracies', *Journal of Democracy*, 7 (2), pp. 14–33, 1996.

Longkumar, Lanusashi, 'Core-periphery Relationship in North-East India with a Focus on Nagaland', Unpublished PhD thesis, Jawaharlal Nehru University, New Delhi, 1996.

Lotha, Senchumo N., 'Critical Analysis on the History/Courses of Indo-Naga Political Negotiation in Terms of Autonomy', Paper to the Second International Conference on Regional Autonomy of Ethnic Minorities at Uppsala, Sweden, 11–14 June 2004.

Ludden, David, 'Where is Assam? Using Geographical History to Locate Current Social Realities' (CENISEAS Papers 1), Guwahati: Centre for Northeast India South and Southeast Asia Studies, Omeo Kumar Das Institute of Social Change and Development, 2003.

Luithui, Luingam and Meredith Preston, 'The Politics of Peace in Nagaland Today', mimeo, 1999.

M'Cosh, John, 'On the Various Lines of Overland Communication between India and China', *Proceedings of the Royal Geographical Society of London*, 5 (2), pp. 47–55, 1860–61.

MacGregor, C.R., 'Journey of the Expedition under Colonel Woodthorpe, R.E., from Upper Assam to the Irawadi, and Return over the Patkoi Range', *Proceedings of the Royal Geographical Society and Monthly Record of Geography*, 9 (1), pp. 19–42, 1887.

Mackenzie, Alexander, *History of the Relations of the Government with the Hill Tribes of the North-East Frontier of Bengal*, Calcutta: Superintendent of Government Printing, 1884.

———, *The North East Frontier of India*, New Delhi: Mittal Publications, 2001[1884].

Malkki, Liisa, 'National Geographic: The Rooting of Peoples and the Territorialization of National Identity among Scholar and Refugees', *Cultural Anthropology*, 7 (1), pp. 24–44, 1992.

Mamdani, Mahmood, *When Victims Become Killers: Colonialism, Nativism, and the Genocide in Rwanda*, Princeton, N.J.: Princeton University Press, 2001.

Marchal, Roland, 'The Economic Analysis of Civil War According to Paul Collier: A Sociologist's View', Available at the website of the Social Science Research Council, New York: http://programs.ssrc.org/gsc/publications/gsc _activities/globalization_conflict/marchal.doc, 2001.

Mauza Note: Laharighat, Settlement Report, Nowgong District: Government of Assam, Nowgong District Record Room, 1931.

Mawrie, H.O., *The Khasi Milieu*.New Delhi: Concept Publishing Company, 1981.

Mbembe, Achille, 'Necropolitics', translated by Libby Meintjes, *Public Culture*, 15(1), pp. 11–40, 2003.

——, *On the Postcolony*, Berkeley, CA and London: University of California Press, 2001.

McCall, A.G., *Lushai Chrysalis*, London: Luzac & Co. Limited, 1949.

McClintock, Anne, *Imperial Leather: Race, Gender and Sexuality in the Colonial Contest*, New York: Routledge, 1995.

McGarry, John, 'Federal Political Systems and the Accommodation of National Minorities', in Ann L. Griffiths (ed.), *Handbook of Federal Countries*, Montreal and Kingston: McGill-Queen's University Press, 2002.

Migdal, Joel S., *Strong Societies and Weak States: State-Society Relations and State Capabilities in the Third World*, Princeton, New Jersey: Princeton University Press, 1988.

——, *Through the Lens of Israel: Explorations in State and Society*, Albany: State University of New York Press, 2001.

Mills, A. J. Moffatt, *Report on the Province of Assam*, Guwahati: Publication Board, Assam, 1984 [1864].

Mills, J.P.S., *The Lhota Nagas*, Guwahati: Spectrum Publishers, 2003 [1922].

Miri, Mrinal, 'Community, Culture, Nation', *Seminar*, 550, June 2005.

Misra, Udayon, 'The Margins Strike Back: Echoes of Sovereignty and the Indian State', *IIC Quarterly* [New Delhi: India International Centre Quarterly], 32 (2&3), pp. 265–74, 2005.

——, 'Centre's Dialogue with the Naga Rebels: Problems and Prospects', mimeo, 2002a.

——, 'Towards a Resolution of the Naga Issue', mimeo, 2002b.

——, *The Transformation of Assamese Identity: A Historical Survey*, Shillong: The North East History Association, 2001.

——, *The Periphery Strikes Back*, Shimla: Indian Institute of Advanced Study, 2000.

——, 'Ethnicity, Territoriality & Autonomy in India's North East: From Fragmentary Politics to an Inclusive Space', mimeo, n.d.

Mitchell, John F., *Report (Topographical, Political and Military) on the North-East Frontier of India*, Calcutta: Superintendent of Government Printing, 1883.

Mitchell, Timothy, *Rule of Experts: Egypt, Techno-Politics, Modernity*, Berkeley LA and London: University of California Press, 2002.

Mitchell, W.J. T., '911: Criticism and Crisis', *Critical Inquiry*, 28 (2), pp. 567–72, 2002.

——, *Iconology: Image/Text/Ideology*, Chicago: University of Chicago Press, 1987.

Mukhim, Patricia, 'Intellectualising Crime', *The Telegraph* [Guwahati], 24 October 2006.

——, 'Where is this North-east?' *IIC Quarterly* [New Delhi: India International Centre Quarterly], 32 (2&3), pp. 177–88, 2005.

——, 'Conflict and Its Resolution: A Case Study of a Modern Tribal Situation', in M.M. Agrawal (ed.), *Ethnicity, Culture and Nationalism in North-East India*, New Delhi: Indus Publishing Company, 2002.

Nag, Sajal, *Contesting Marginality: Ethnicity, Insurgency and Subnationalism in North-East India*, New Delhi: Manohar, 2002.

Nagaraj, D.R., *The Flaming Feet: A Study of the Dalit Movement in India*, Bangalore: South Forum Press, 1993.

Nandy, Ashis, 'The Discreet Charms of Indian Terrorism', in Nilanjana Gupta (ed.), *Cultural Studies*, New Delhi: Worldview Publications, pp. 153–84, 2004a.

——, 'Final Encounter: The Politics of the Assassination of Gandhi', in *Bonfire of Creeds: The Essential Ashis Nandy*, New Delhi: Oxford University Press, 2004b.

——, *The Intimate Enemy*, New Delhi: Oxford University Press, 2002 [1983].

——, 'Terrorism-Indian Style: The Birth of a Political Issue in a Populist Democracy', in Subrata Kumar Mitra and James Chiriyakandath (eds), *Electoral Politics in India: A Changing Landscape*, New Delhi: Segment Books, 1992.

Naorem, Sanajaoba (ed.), *Manipur: Past and Present*, Vol. 3, New Delhi: Mittal Publications, 1995.

——, *Manipur: Past and Present*, Vol. 1, New Delhi: Mittal Publications, 1988.

Narahari, N.S., *Security Threats to North-East India: The Socio-ethnic Tensions*, New Delhi: Manas Publications, 2002.

Narayan, Jayaprakash, 'Early Barriers in Politics: Time for Change', *Liberal Times*, 11 (4), 2003.

Nasar, Sylvia, *A Beautiful Mind: A Biography of John Forbes Nash. Jr.*, New York: Simon and Schuster, 1998.

National Crime Records Bureau, *Crime in India 2004*, New Delhi: National Crime Records Bureau, 2005.

National Tourism Policy, Department of Tourism, Government of India, 2002.

Navlakha, Gautam, 'Understanding the Army Doctrine', *Economic and Political Weekly*, 40 (13), pp. 1315–17, 26 March 2005.

Nayar, V.K., *Crossing the Frontiers of Conflict in the North East and Jammu and Kashmir: From Real Politik to Ideal Politik*, New Delhi: Shipra/Centre for Policy Research, 2005.

Neihsial, Tualchin, *This is Lamka: A Historical Account of the Fastest Growing Town of Manipur Hills*, Lamka, Manipur: Zougam Book Centre and Library, 1996.

Nettl, J.P., 'State as a Conceptual Variable', *World Politics*, 20 (4), pp. 559–92, 1968.

Nevill, G.A., *Report on the Aka Promenade submitted to the Chief Secretary to the Hon'ble the Chief Commissioner of Assam on 2nd July 1914*, Guwahati: Assam State Archives, 1914.

Ngaihte, Thangkhanlal, 'Playing with Lives', *North East Sun*, 11 (8), 16 November 2005.

Nongbri, Tiplut, 'Culture and Biodiversity: Myths, Legends, and the Conservation of Nature in the Hills of North-East India', *Indian Anthropologist*, 36 (1&2), 2006.

Nordlinger, Eric, *Conflict Regulation in Divided Societies*, Cambridge, MA: Harvard Centre for International Affairs, 1972.

Nunthara, C., 'Peace Accords as Instruments of Conflict Transformation: Arrangements that Work and Arrangements that Don't (Mizo Accord, 1986, Assam Accord, 1985, Bodo Accord, 1993)', mimeo, 2002.

——, *Mizoram: Society and Polity*, New Delhi: Indus Publishing Company, 1996.

——, 'Grouping of Villages in Mizoram: Its Social and Economic Impact', *Economic and Political Weekly*, pp. 1237–40, 25 July 1981.

O'Brien, K.A., 'Special Forces for Counter-revolutionary Warfare: The South African Case', *Small Wars and Insurgencies*, 12 (2), pp. 79–109, 2001.

Oinam, Bhagat and Homen Thangjam, 'Indian Nation State and Crises of the Periphery', in Prasenjit Biswas and C.J. Thomas (eds), *Peace in India's Northeast*, New Delhi: Regency Publications, 2006.

——, 'Receiving Communities: The Encounter with Modernity', *Eastern Quarterly*, 3 (2), July–September 2005.

——, 'Patterns of Ethnic Conflict in North-East: A Study on Manipur', *Economic and Political Weekly*, 38(21), 24 May 2003.

Pachnanda, Ranjit, *Terrorism and the Response to Terrorist Threat*, New Delhi: UBSPD, 2002.

Pande, G.C., *The Dawn of Indian Civilization*, New Delhi: PHISPC & Munshiram Manoharlal, 1999.

Pandey, Gyanendra, *Remembering Partition: Violence, Nationalism and History in India*, Cambridge: Cambridge University Press, 2001.

Pandey, N.N., *India's North-Eastern Region*, New Delhi: Manohar & ISAS, 2008.

Parry, N.E., *A Monograph on Lushai Customs and Ceremonies*, Shillong: Assam Government Press, 1928.

Perera, Jehan, *Peace Process in Nagaland and Chittagong Hill Tracts: An Audit Report*, Kathmandu: South Asia Forum for Human Rights, 1999.

Phadnis, Urmila, and Rajat Ganguly, *Ethnicity and Nation-Building in South Asia*, New Delhi: Sage, 2001[1989].

Phanjoubam, Pradip, 'Ambush Implications', *The Statesman* [New Delhi], 7 January 2006.

Prabhakara, M.S., 'Naga Talks: Territory First, Sovereignty Later', *The Hindu* [Chennai], 10 May 2005.

——, 'The Furies Come to Life', *Hindu* (Chennai), 30 July 2004.

Prasad, R.N. (ed.), *Autonomy Movements in Mizoram*, New Delhi: Vikas, 1994.

Przeworski, Adam, *Democracy and the Market: Political and Economic Reforms in Eastern Europe and Latin America*, Cambridge: Cambridge University Press, 1991.

PSPD [People's Solidarity for Peace and Democracy], *Ceasefire or Setting the North East on Fire? Peace in Jeopardy*, Imphal: People's Solidarity for Peace and Democracy, 2004.

Ramesh, Jairam, 'Northeast India in a New Asia', *Seminar*, 550, pp. 17–21, June 2005.

Rammohan, E.N., 'Blue Print for Counterinsurgency in Manipur', *Faultline*, 12, 2002.

Rao, B. Shiva, *Framing of India's Constitution*, Vol. 3, New Delhi: Indian Institute of Public Administration, 1967.

Rappaport, Roy A., *Ritual and Religion in the Making of Humanity*, Cambridge: Cambridge University Press, 1999.

Rawls, John, *A Theory of Justice*, Oxford: Oxford University Press, 1971.

Ray, Raka, *Fields of Protest: Women's Movements in India*, Minneapolis: University of Minnesota Press, 1999.

Roychowdhuri, Ambikagiri, *Racanavali* (Collected Works), Satyendranath Sarma (ed.), Guwahati: Asom Prakashan Parishad, 1986.

Read, Arthur Cotton, 'On a Communication between India and China by the Line of the Burhampooter and Yang-tsze', *The Journal of the Royal Geographical Society of London*, 37, 1867.

Reid, Herbert G. and Betsy Taylor, *Democracy's Portals: Ecology, Justice and Democratic Space*. Champaign: University of Illinois Press, 2009.

Reid, Robert, *History of the Frontier Areas Bordering on Assam, 1883–1941*, Guwahati: Spectrum, 1997 [1942].

——, *The Lushai Hills, culled from the History of the Frontier Areas Bordering on Assam from 1883–1941*, Aizawl: Tribal Research Institute, 1978 [1942].

Report of the Line System Committee, Shillong: Assam Government Press, 1938.

Report of the Special Officer Appointed for the Examination of the Professional Grazing Reserves in the Assam Valley, Shillong: Assam Government Press, 1944.

Ricoeur, Paul, 'Imagination in Discourse and in Action', in Gillian Robinson and John Rundell (eds), *Rethinking Imagination: Culture and Creativity*, London & New York: Routledge, 1994.

Robb, Peter, 'The Colonial State and Constructions of Indian Identity: An Example on the Northeast Frontier in the 1880s', *Modern Asian Studies*, 31 (2), 1997.

Robinson, W., 'The Origin of the Nagas', in Verrier Elwin (ed.), *India's North-East Frontier*, London: Oxford University Press, 1959.

Rosaldo, Renato, *Culture and Truth: The Remaking of Social Analysis*, Boston: Beacon, 1989.

Routray, Bibhu P., 'Mizoram: An Accord for Peace', *South Asia Intelligence Review*, 3(42), 2005.

——, 'Fuelling Dissent: Anti-terror Laws in India's Northeast', *Peace and Conflict*, 6 (5), 2003a.

——, 'Politics and Insurgency: Not so Strange Bed-fellows', *Peace and Conflict*, 6 (5), 2003b.

——, 'Analysing an Insurgency: On the Trail of Negation', in *Bharat Rakshak Monitor*, 49 (2), September–October 2001.

Roy, Arundhati, 'The Greater Common Good', *Frontline*, 16(11), 22 May 1999.

Roy, Beth, *Some Trouble with Cows: Making Sense of Social Conflict*, New Delhi: Sage, 1994.

Roy, Jyotirmoy, *History of Manipur*, Calcutta: Eastlight, 1973.

Roy Burman, B.K., *Tribes in Perspective*, New Delhi: Mittal Publications, 1995.

Ruggie, J.G., 'Territoriality and Beyond: Problematizing Modernity in International Relations', *International Organization*, 47, pp. 139–74, 1993.

Rupesinghe, Kumar, 'Strategies for Conflict Resolution: The Case of South Asia', in Kumar Rupesinghe and Khawar Mumtaz (eds), *Internal Conflicts in South Asia*, London: Sage Publications, 2001 [1996].

Rustomji, Nari, *Imperilled Frontiers: India's North-Eastern Borderlands*, New Delhi: Oxford University Press, 1983.

Saha, Anindya, and Siddharth Mallavarapu, 'State Weakness and State Failure', *Economic and Political Weekly*, 41 (39), pp. 4257–60, 2006.

Saha, Dinesh Chandra, *Bingsha Satabdir Tripura* [Tripura in the Twentieth Century], II, Agartala: Writer's Publication, 2004.

Sahni, Ajai, 'Survey of Conflicts and Resolution in India's North East', in K.P.S. Gill and Ajai Sahni (eds), *Faultlines: Writings on Conflict and Resolution*, 12, New Delhi: Bulwark and Institute for Conflict Management, 2002.

——, 'The Terrorist Economy of India's Northeast: Preliminary Explorations', in K.P.S. Gill and Ajai Sahni (eds), *Faultlines: Writings on Conflict and Resolution*, 12, New Delhi: Bulwark and Institute for Conflict Management, 2001.

Sahni, Ajai and Bibhu Prasad Routray, 'Tripura: Counter-insurgency Success', *South Asia Intelligence Review*, 4 (7), Available at: http://www.satp. org/satporgtp/sair/Archives/4_7.htm, 2005.

Said, Edward W., *Power Politics and Culture: Interviews with Edward W. Said*, Edited and with an introduction by Gauri Viswanathan, London: Bloomsbury, 2004.

——, *Reflections on Exile*, New Delhi: Penguin Books India, 2001.

——, *Peace and Its Discontents: Essays on Palestine in the Middle East Peace Process*, New York: Vintage, 1996a.

——, *Representations of the Intellectual*, New York: Vintage, 1996b.

——, *Orientalism*, New York: Vintage Books, 1979.

——, *Beginnings: Intention and Method*, New York: Columbia University Press, 1975.

Saikia, Jaideep, 'Template for Anti Terror Doctrine', *Aakrosh*, 29 (8), 2006.

Saikia, Yasmin, *Assam and India: Fragmented Memories, Cultural Identity, and the Tai-Ahom Struggle*, Delhi: Permanent Black, 2005.

——, *Fragmented Memories: Struggling to be Tai-Ahom in India*, Durham: Duke University Press, 2004.

——, 'A Name without a People: Searching Tai-Ahom in Modern India', unpublished PhD dissertation, University of Wisconsin-Madison, 1999.

Samaddar, Ranabir (ed.), *The Politics of Autonomy: Indian Experiences*, New Delhi: Sage, 2005.

——, *The Politics of Dialogue: Living under the Geopolitical Histories of War and Peace*, Aldershot: Ashgate, 2004.

——, *Biography of the Indian Nation 1947-1997*, New Delhi: Sage Publications, 2001.

Sanchez, W.A., 'The Rebirth of Insurgency in Peru', *Small Wars and Insurgencies*, 14, pp. 185–98, 2003.

Sanday, Peggy Reeves, *Female Power and Male Dominance: On the Origins of Sexual Inequality*, Cambridge; New York: Cambridge University Press, 1981.

Sangma, Milton (eds), *Essays on North-East India*, New Delhi, 1994.

Sartre, J.P., *Being and Nothingness*, rev. ed., New York: Washington Square Press, 1993.

——, *Critique of Dialectical Reason*, translated by Alan Sheridan-Smith, Jonathan Rée (ed.), London: Verso/NLB, 1982 [1960].

Sassen, Saskia, *Losing Control?: Sovereignty in an Age of Globalization*, New York: Columbia University Press, 1996.

Satapathy, R.K., 'Mizoram: Positive Vote for the State Government', *Economic and Political Weekly*, 39 (51), pp. 5527–8, 2004.

Schendel, Willem van, 'A Politics of Nudity: Photographs of the 'Naked Mru' of Bangladesh', *Modern Asian Studies*, 32 (2), pp. 341–74, 2002a.

———, 'Geographies of Knowing, Geographies of Ignorance: Jumping Scale in Southeast Asia', in *Environment and Planning D: Society and Space*, No. 20, pp. 647–68, 2002b.

Schmid, Alex P. and Albert J. Jongman, *Political Terrorism: A New Guide to Actors, Authors, Concepts, Databases, Theories and Literature*, New Brunswick, NJ: Transaction, 1988.

Scott, James C., 'Southeast Asian Appalachia', Tentatively titled chapter 1 of unpublished and untitled book manuscript, Yale University, Department of Political Science & Department of Anthropology, 2006.

———, 'Hill and Valley in Southeast Asia ... or ... Why the State is the Enemy of the People who Move Around ... or ... Why Civilizations Can't Climb Hills', Unpublished Paper, Yale University, Department of Political Science & Department of Anthropology, 2000.

Sebald, W.G., *On the Natural History of Destruction*, translated by Anthea Bell, New York: Random House, 2003 [1999].

Seminar, 512, 'States of Insecurity: Symposium on Emergency Laws, Human Rights and Democracy', April 2002.

Sen, Amartya, *Identity and Violence: The Illusion of Destiny*, London: Allen Lane, 2006.

———, *The Argumentative Indian: Writings on Indian History, Culture and Identity*, New Delhi: Penguin Books India, 2005.

———, *Development as Freedom*, New Delhi: Oxford University Press, 2001.

Senapati, Bolairam, *Atitar Sandhanat* (In Search of the Past), Jagiroad: Tiwa Mathonlai Takhre, 2000.

Sengupta, S. and H. Kumar, 'A Forgotten Civil War in Northeastern India', *New York Times*, 3 September 2005.

Shakespear, L.W., *History of the Assam Rifles*, reprint, Delhi: Cultural Publishing House, 1983[1929].

Shakespeare, John, *Lushai Kuki Clans*, London: Macmillan and Co, 1912.

Shani, A., *Survey of Conflicts & Resolution in India's Northeast*, South Asia Terrorism Portal, New Delhi: Institute for Conflict Management, 2005.

Sharma, Chandan, 'The Indian State and Ethnic Activism in North East India', *North East India Studies*, 1 (1), June 2005.

Sharma, Mahesh, *The Realm of Faith: Subversion, Appropriation and Dominance in the Western Himalaya*, Shimla: IIAS, 2001.

Sharma, Manorama and Apurba K. Baruah, 'Mizoram at Crossroads: Democracy vs. Traditional Values', London: Crisis States Programme, 2004.

Sharma, V.N., 'Northeast Imbroglio', in Shekhar Basu Ray (ed.), *New Approach: Our East and North East*, XI (I&II), 2002.

Sharma-Thakur, S.G., 'Land Alienation and Indebtedness in the I.T.D.P. Areas of Assam—A Case Study of Marigaon I.T.D.P.', in B.N. Bordoloi (ed.),

Alienation of Tribal Land and Indebtedness, Guwahati: Tribal Research Institute, 1986.

Shaw, G.D.T., 'Policemen versus Soldiers, The Debate Leading to MAAG Objections and Washington Rejections of the Core of the British Counter-insurgency Advice', *Small Wars and Insurgencies,* 12 (2), pp. 51–78, 2001.

Shimray, U.A., 'Socio-political Unrest in the Region Called North-East India', *Economic and Political Weekly,* 39 (42), pp. 4637–43, 16 October 2004.

Shourie, Arun, 'Come What May', *India Today* [New Delhi], pp. 28–37, 15 May 1983.

Shutkin, William A., *The Land that Could Be: Environmentalism and Democracy in the Twenty-first Century,* Cambridge: The MIT Press, 2000.

Sikdar, Sudatta, 'Tribalism vs. Colonialism: British Capitalistic Intervention and Transformation of Primitive Economy of Arunachal Pradesh in the Nineteenth Century', *Social Scientist,* 10 (12), pp. 15–31, 1982.

Sikri, Rajiv, 'Northeast India and India's Look East Policy', Lecture at Forum on 'Towards a New Asia: Transnationalism and Northeast India', Centre for Northeast India, South and Southeast Asia Studies (CENISEAS), Omeo Kumar Institute of Social Change and Development, Guwahati, 11 September 2004.

Silke, Andrew, 'Terrorism', *The Psychologist,* Vol. 14, 2001.

Simeon, Dilip, 'OK Tata, Mobil Oil Change, and World Revolution', in *Civil Lines 3: New Writing from India,* New Delhi: Ravi Dayal, 1997.

Singh, B.P., *The Problem of Change: A Study of North-East India,* New Delhi: Oxford University Press, 1987.

Singh, Bhupinder, *Autonomy Movements and Federal India,* Jaipur and New Delhi: Rawat, 2002.

Singh, C., *North-east India: Politics and Insurgency,* New Delhi: Manas Publications, 2004.

Singh, K.M., *History of the Christian Missions in Manipur and Neighbouring States,* New Delhi: Mittal, 1991.

Singh, Karam Manimohan, *Hijam Irabot Singh and Political Movements in Manipur,* New Delhi: R.B. Publishing Corporation, 1989.

Singh, Ksh. Imokanta, 'Stigmatisation through Language: The Case of "Hao" in Manipur', *Social Sciences Research Journal,* 6 (1), pp. 110–20, 1998.

Singh, L. Ibungohal and N. Khelchandra Singh, *Cheitharol Kumbaba* (in Manipuri), Imphal: Manipur Sahitya Parishad, 1989 [1967].

Singh, M. Amarjeet, 'Challenges before Tribal Autonomy in Assam', *Eastern Quarterly,* 4 (1), April–June 2006.

Singh, N. Joykumar, *Social Movements in Manipur,* New Delhi: Mittal Publications, 1992.

Singh, N. Lokendra, *Unquiet Valley,* New Delhi: Mittal Publications, 1998.

Singh, Prakash, *Kohima to Kashmir: On the Terrorist Trail*, New Delhi: Rupa, 2001.

Singh, S.M., 'Manipur: Elections in the Context of Social Conflict', *Economic and Political Weekly*, 39 (51), pp. 5528–30, 2004.

Sivaramakrishnan, Kalyanakrishnan, 'Crafting the Public Sphere in the Forests of West Bengal: Democracy, Development, and Political Action', *American Ethnologist*, 27 (2), pp. 431–61, 2000.

Snyder, Jack, *From Voting to Violence: Democratization and Nationalist Conflict*, New York: W.W. Norton & Company, 2000.

Spencer, Jonathan, 'Collective Violence', in Veena Das (ed.), *The Oxford India Companion to Sociology and Social Anthropology*, New Delhi: Oxford University Press, pp. 1564–80, 2003.

Srikanth, H. and C.J. Thomas, 'Challenges and Predicaments of Naga Nationalism', *Eastern Quarterly*, 3 (4), January–March 2006.

Srivastava, S.C., 'Local Self-government Institutions in Manipur', in B.P. Maithani (ed.), *Local Self-government System in North-East India*, Hyderabad: National Institute of Rural Development, pp. 139–204, 1997.

Stepan, Alfred, *Arguing Comparative Politics*, New York: Oxford University Press, 2001.

———, 'Federalism and Democracy: Beyond the U.S. Model', *Journal of Democracy*, 10 (4), pp. 19–34, 1999.

Suan, H. Kham Khan, 'State Versus People: Understanding Minority Nationalism in North-East India', Unpublished paper presented at an international conference on 'Wounded History and Social Healing: South Asian Experience', organized jointly by the Developing Countries Research Centre, University of Delhi and the Vidyajyoti College of Theology, Delhi, on 23–25 February 2006.

———, 'State vs People', *The Statesman* [New Delhi], 19 February 2005.

———, 'Asymmetry in Local Democracy: An Overview of North-East India's Experience', *Indian Journal of Federal Studies*, No. 2: 103–28, 2003.

———, 'Special Status of the North-East in Indian Federalism', Unpublished M.Phil dissertation, Jawaharlal Nehru University, New Delhi, 2002.

Subba, T.A., 'Ethnicity, Culture and Nationalism in North-East India: A Conspectus', in M.M. Agrawal (ed.), *Ethnicity, Culture and Nationalism in North-East India*, New Delhi: Indus Publishing Company, 2002.

Syiemlieh, David R., 'The Future of the Hills of North-East India, 1928–1947: Some British Views', in B. Datta Ray and S.P. Agrawal (eds), *Reorganisation of North-East India since 1947*, New Delhi: Concept, 1996.

Taylor, Charles, 'Different Kind of Courage', *The New York Review of Books*, 54 (7), 26 April 2007.

——, 'The Politics of Recognition', in Amy Gutmann (ed.), *Multiculturalism and the Politics of Recognition*, Princeton, NJ: Princeton University Press, pp. 25–73, 1994.

Taylor-Ide, Daniel and Carl E. Taylor, *Just and Lasting Change: When Communities Own Their Futures*, Baltimore: The Johns Hopkins University Press, 2002.

Taylor-Ide, Luke, 'Reestablishing Identity and Social Advancement in a Bonded People: The Sulung Tribe of Arunachal Pradesh', unpublished manuscript, 2006.

Thanhranga, H.C., *Administration of Justice in Mizoram*, Aizawl: PC Chuauhrangi, 1994.

Thapar, Romila, 'Decolonizing the Past: Historical Writing in the Time of Sachin and Beyond', *Economic and Political Weekly*, XL (14), p. 1448, April 2005.

Thaung, Ma, 'British Interest in Trans-Burma Trade Routes to China, 1826–1876', Unpublished PhD Dissertation in History, University of London, 1954.

Thomas, C.J. (ed.), *Dimensions of Displaced People in the Northeast India*, Shillong: NERC and ICSSR, 2001.

Tinker, Irene, 'Empowerment just Happened: The Unexpected Expansion of Women's Organizations', in J.S. Jaquette and G. Summerfield (eds), *Women and Gender Equity in Development Theory and Practice: Institutions, Resources, and Mobilization*, Durham and London: Duke University Press, 2006.

Todorov, Tzvetan, *The Morals of History*, Minneapolis: University of Minnesota Press, 1995.

Tourism Policy 2001, Department of Tourism, Government of Meghalaya.

Tsing, Anna, *Friction: An Ethnography of Global Connection*, Princeton: Princeton University Press, 2005.

Tully, James, *Strange Multiplicity: Constitutionalism in an Age of Diversity*. Cambridge: Cambridge University Press, 1995.

Turner, Victor Witter, *The Forest of Symbols; Aspects of Ndembu Ritual*, Ithaca, N.Y.: Cornell University Press, 1967.

Upadhyay, R., 'Mizoram—From Insurgence to Resurgence', Paper No. 1665, South Asia Analysis Group, 2006.

Uppsala University, Uppsala Department of Peace and Conflict Research, *Armed Conflict Database*, 2006.

Vajpeyi, Ananya, *Prolegomena to the Study of People and Places in Violent India*, Preface by Pratap Bhanu Mehta, New Delhi: Women in Security Conflict Management and Peace, Perspectives #26, October 2007.

——, 'From Nation to Camps: Two Alternative Views of Migration', in *Biblio*, 9 (11 & 12), pp. 13–14, November–December 2004.

Vinci, A., 'The Strategic Use of Fear by the Lord's Resistance Army', *Small Wars and Insurgencies*, 16 (3), pp. 360–81, 2005.

Vumson, *Zo History*, Aizawl, n.d.

Vunglallian, T., 'Manipur Situation: A Draft', Unpublished paper presented at a seminar, 'Problems and Prospects of Marginalised Hill People of Manipur', organized by Zomi Human Rights Foundation, Delhi Cell, New Delhi, 16–17 December 2006.

Wee, Vivienne and Kanishka Jayasuriya, 'New Geographies and Temporalities of Power: Exploring the New Fault Lines of Southeast Asia', Working Paper No. 30, City University of Hong Kong, Southeast Asia Research Center, 2002.

Weiner, Myron, 'The Political Consequences of Preferential Policies: A Comparative Perspective', *Comparative Politics*, 16 (1), pp. 35–52, 1983.

———, *Sons of the Soil: Migration and Ethnic Conflict in India*, Princeton, NJ: Princeton University Press, 1978.

White, Hayden, 'The Value of Narrativity', in W.J.T. Mitchell (ed.), *On Narrative*, Chicago: University of Chicago Press, 1981.

Wilcox, R., 'Memoir of A Survey of Asam and the Neighbouring Countries, Executed in 1825–6–7–8', *Asiatick Researches*, 17, 1832.

Williams, Robert R., *Hegel's Ethics of Recognition*, Berkeley, CA.: University of California Press, 1997.

Williamson, Noel., 'The Lohit-Brahmaputra between Assam and South-Eastern Tibet, November 1907, to January 1908', *The Geographical Journal*, 34 (4), pp. 363–83, 1909.

Winder, W.H.D., 'The Development of Blackmail', *The Modern Law Review*, 5 (1), pp. 21–50, 1941.

Winichakul, Thongchai, *Siam Mapped: A History of the Geo-body of a Nation*, Chiang Mai: Silkworm Books, 1998.

Withanage, Hemantha, Ronald Masayda, Romil Harnandez, and Arturo Nuera, *Development Debacles: A Look into ADB's Involvement in Environmental Degradation, Involuntary Resettlement and Violation of Indigenous People's Rights*, NGO Forum on ADB [Asian Development Bank], Quezon City, Philippines, 2006.

Wohlforth, William and Tyler Felgenhauer, 'Self-Determination and the Stability of the Russian Federation', in Wolfgang Danspeckgruber (ed.), *The Self-Determination of Peoples: Community, Nation, and State in an Interdependent World*, Boulder: Lynne Rienner Publishers, 2002.

Wood, Elisabeth Jean, *Insurgent Collective Action and Civil War in El Salvador*, New York: Cambridge University Press, 2003.

Woodthorpe, R.G., 'A Topographer on Tour', in Verrier Elwin (ed.), *India's North-East Frontier*, London: Oxford University Press, 1959.

World Bank, *Natural Resources, Water and the Environment Nexus for Development and Growth in Northeast India*, Strategy Report, Washington D.C., 28 June 2006.

Yambem Sanamani, 'Nupi Lan: Women's Agitation, 1939', *Economic and Political Weekly*, 11 (8), pp. 325–31, 21 February 1976.

Yonuo, Asoso, *Rising Nagas: A Historical and Political Study*, Delhi: Vivek, 1974.

Young, E.C., 'A Journey from Yün-nan to Assam', *The Geographical Journal*, 30 (2), pp. 152–80, 1907.

Young, Iris Marion, 'Communication and the Other: Beyond Deliberative Democracy', in S. Benhabib (ed.), *Democracy and Difference: Contesting the Boundaries of the Political*, Princeton: Princeton University Press, pp. 120–36, 1996.

Contributors

SANJIB BARUAH is professor of Political Studies at Bard College, Annandale-on-Hudson, New York.

SUBIR BHAUMIK, a former BBC correspondent, has been named the editor of a new Guwahati-based daily newspaper.

SAMIR KUMAR DAS is professor of Political Science, University of Calcutta.

NANDANA DUTTA is professor of English, Gauhati University.

M. SAJJAD HASSAN is an Indian Administrative Service (IAS) officer working for the Government of Manipur.

RAKHEE KALITA is senior lecturer, Department of English, Cotton College, Guwahati.

BODHISATTVA KAR is fellow in History, Centre for Studies in Social Sciences, Calcutta.

DOLLY KIKON is a doctoral student at the Department of Anthropology, Stanford University, Stanford, California.

MAKIKO KIMURA is researcher, International Peace Research Institute, Meiji Gakuin University, Tokyo.

BETHANY LACINA is assistant professor, Department of Political Science, University of Rochester, Rochester, New York.

BHAGAT OINAM is associate professor of Philosophy, School of Social Sciences, Jawaharlal Nehru University, New Delhi.

PRADIP PHANJOUBAM is the editor of *Imphal Free Press*, an English daily published from Imphal, Manipur.

H. KHAM KHAN SUAN is assistant professor, Department of Political Science, Banaras Hindu University, Varanasi.

BETSY TAYLOR is senior research scholar, Alliance for Social, Political, Ethical and Cultural Theory, Virginia Tech, Blacksburg, Virginia.

ANANYA VAJPEYI is assistant professor, Department of History, University of Massachusetts at Boston.

Index